THE EIGHTY-THIRD ANNUAL MEETING OF THE AMERICAN ACADEMY OF POLITICAL AND SOCIAL SCIENCE

APRIL 6 AND 7, 1979
THE BENJAMIN FRANKLIN HOTEL
PHILADELPHIA, PENNSYLVANIA

The Annual Meeting will be addressed at each session by prominent scholars and officials and will be devoted to

THE ENVIRONMENT AND THE QUALITY OF LIFE: A WORLD VIEW

Approximately 800 persons will be in attendance sometime during the two days of sessions, representing a wide variety of cultural, civic and scientific organizations.

Members are cordially invited to attend and will automatically receive full information.

● Proceedings of this 83rd Annual Meeting will be published as the July issue of THE ANNALS

● FOR DETAILS WRITE TO: THE AMERICAN ACADEMY OF POLITICAL AND SOCIAL SCIENCE ● BUSINESS OFFICE ● 3937 CHESTNUT STREET. PHILADELPHIA, PENNSYLVANIA 19104

VOLUME 441

JANUARY 1979

THE ANNALS

of The American Academy *of* Political
and Social Science

(ISSN-0002-7162)

RICHARD D. LAMBERT, *Editor*

RALPH B. GINSBERG, *Acting Editor*

ALAN W. HESTON, *Assistant Editor*

RACE AND RESIDENCE IN AMERICAN CITIES

Special Editor of This Volume

WADE CLARK ROOF

*Associate Professor of
Sociology*

*University of Massachusetts
Amherst*

PHILADELPHIA

Library of Congress Card Number 78-72993

79- 367

Copy Editor

KIM HOLMES, PH.D.

International Standard Book Numbers (ISBN)

ISBN 0-87761-237-4, vol. 441, 1979; paper—$4.50
ISBN 0-87761-236-6, vol. 441, 1979; cloth—$5.50

Issued bimonthly by The American Academy of Political and Social Science at 3937 Chestnut St., Philadelphia, Pennsylvania 19104. Cost per year: $18.00 paperbound; $23.00 clothbound. Add $2.00 to above rates for membership outside U.S.A. Second-class postage paid at Philadephia and at additional mailing offices.

Claims for undelivered copies must be made within the month following the regular month of publication. The publisher will supply missing copies when losses have been sustained in transit and when the reserve stock will permit.

Editorial and Business Offices, 3937 Chestnut Street, Philadelphia, Pennsylvania 19104.

CONTENTS

BOOK DEPARTMENT   PAGE

INTERNATIONAL RELATIONS AND POLITICS

AFRICA, ASIA AND LATIN AMERICA

EUROPE

CONTENTS

UNITED STATES

SOCIOLOGY

ECONOMICS

PREFACE

Few conditions of American cities today represent so blatant a departure from democratic ideals as does racial residential segregation. Americans believe strongly in the rights of citizens to decent housing and, for most families, living in the community of their choice is valued as an integral part of our way of life. Yet, for countless numbers of blacks in American society this remains an unfulfilled aspiration. Poor housing and segregated residence stand in the way, blocking their fuller participation in the society.

The papers assembled in this collection view the problems of race and residence from various vantage points: sociologically, demographically, historically, economically, and psychologically. These diverse approaches make for a rich and enlightened understanding of racial residential segregation, its patterns and consequences. Generally the papers are organized into three sections. The first offers broad perspectives on residential segregation, covering topics on its changing significance in American race relations, assimilation, and attitudes toward integration. The second section presents case studies of four major cities—Boston, Detroit, New Orleans, and Philadelphia. The third and final section examines a number of specific issues and policy considerations, including housing discrimination, homeownership, school desegregation, private schools, and governmental intervention.

Thanks are due to each of the authors, and to *The Annals* for the opportunity of presenting this collection of papers. Hopefully the papers will shed new insight as well as generate concern about race and residence in contemporary America.

WADE CLARK ROOF

Annals, AAPSS, 441, Jan. 1979

Race and Residence: The Shifting Basis of American Race Relations

By Wade Clark Roof

ABSTRACT: Racially-segregated ghettos evolved in the early decades of this century, first in northern cities and later throughout the nation. Levels of urban residential segregation for blacks have remained high over the years and—unlike the earlier pattern for European immigrants—have not declined as blacks have made economic progress. Despite modest declines in segregation in the sixties, metropolitan decline in the seventies and structural shifts in employment conditions for blacks have resulted in growing concern for problems of de facto segregation. Mounting attention to housing discrimination and the residential basis of current black-white tensions are discussed.

Wade Clark Roof is Associate Professor of Sociology at the University of Massachusetts, Amherst. Educated at Wofford College, Yale University, and the University of North Carolina, he is the author of numerous publications on race relations, sociology of religion, and contemporary American society.

1

"SEPARATION by residence of the Negro from the white," Ernest Burgess wrote in *The Annals* in 1928, "exists in some form in all American cities."[1] Burgess described the extent of separation between the races and suggested that racial segregation in residence—not unlike that for ethnic immigrant groups—was a result of ecological patterning inherent in the growth of the city. Now, fifty years later, what is most striking about Burgess' analysis, and also quite distressing, is how little the parameters of racial segregation have changed in American cities, and how little progress has been made in coming to grips with this very serious urban problem. Separation of blacks from whites in residential neighborhoods persists in even more staggering proportions today, as evidenced by the presence of massive black ghettos at the center of virtually all the nation's metropolitan areas. And as far as urban remedies go, few problems of American cities are as baffling to try to deal with, or as difficult to exercise some control over, as the "web of discrimination" surrounding housing opportunities for blacks.

Doubtlessly, however, there have been changes in the last half-century in racial residential segregation, and especially in the role it plays in American race relations. So encompassing are the changes, in fact, particularly in recent years, that we can justifiably speak of a new realism today insofar as the problems of race and residence are concerned. The "exposed nerve" of racial tension and turmoil at present is neither jobs nor even school desegregation; rather

1. Ernest W. Burgess, "Residential Segregation in American Cities," *The Annals of The American Academy of Political and Social Science* 140 (November 1928) 105–115.

it is more basic than either of these— de facto segregation and the problems it presents in obtaining equality of opportunity for blacks. Having moved beyond the early phases of the civil rights movement, concerned essentially with social and economic barriers to participation in American society, more and more attention is being given to issues stemming from segregated residence. For many Americans, white and black alike, the ghetto stands as a powerful symbol of the nation's unfinished business in the pursuit of justice and equality; it is a reminder that without some resolution of segregation as a problem itself, chances for further gains for blacks are slim indeed.

This essay focuses on the matter from the perspective of race relations generally, and offers an overview on race and residence currently in American cities. Since other papers included in this collection examine specific topics relating to segregation, the concern here is with a broader set of questions: What are the major trends in racial residential segregation over the past fifty years? How do these trends for blacks compare with those for earlier immigrant groups? What evidence is there to indicate that the character of American race relations is changing, with mounting attention to the underlying structures of residential segregation?

RACIAL RESIDENTIAL SEGREGATION—ITS DEVELOPMENT AND SIGNIFICANCE

Residential segregation as a problem of American race relations, is a peculiarly northern phenomenon of the twentieth century. To be sure, there were concentrated areas of black settlement much earlier in cities throughout the nation; but the number of blacks involved was relatively small and the settlements were typically scattered throughout the cities. Racially mixed residential areas were not uncommon even in the larger northern cities in the 1880s and early 1890s. Soon afterwards, however, the color line in residence began to intensify resulting from the spread of "Jim Crow" sentiment throughout much of the nation. Unlike in the South, where the hardening of racial lines brought about disenfranchisement and the solidification of racial norms governing all forms of social contact, northern segregation took shape largely as residential preference. Less virulent in expressing their racial animosities and less concerned with dominating blacks economically and politically, nonetheless northern whites condoned, and indeed insisted upon, racial separation in patterns of residence. Consequently, well-developed ghettos were evident by the early years of this century in northern and border cities— for example, New York, Chicago, and Washington—laying the foundations for the massive phenomenon of de facto segregation that was later to come.[2]

The large, institutionally self-contained ghettos of the modern era are a product of the mass migrations of blacks out of the rural and small-town South to large, densely settled northern cities. Although the northern-bound black movement had begun to increase by 1915, World War I was really the impetus that led to its acceleration. The war

2. See Gilbert Osofsky, *Harlem: The Making of a Ghetto* (New York: Harper, 1966); Allan Spear, *Black Chicago: The Making of a Negro Ghetto* (Chicago: University of Chicago Press, 1967); and Constance M. Green, *The Secret City* (Princeton, NJ: Princeton University Press, 1967).

effectively curtailed migration from Europe and stimulated industrial production, thus creating job opportunities for blacks and setting into motion the "Great Migration" to the new land of promise. Successive waves of black migrants for a half-century to come—during the twenties, World War II, and into the fifties and sixties—made their way to the cities of the North in search of the American dream. Blacks moved not only to the North but to cities throughout the nation, in hopes of finding a better life.

In sheer demographic terms, this movement of blacks to the cities is staggering. As of 1900, 90 percent of all blacks in the United States lived in the South, but by 1970 just slightly more than half remained in the region. Furthermore, by 1970, 81 percent of all blacks lived in urbanized areas and were more urbanized and metropolitanized than whites. This massive movement was predominately, of course, a migration to the central cities of metropolitan areas. Among the nation's largest metropolitan areas in 1970, roughly 16 percent of the population were black; but in the central cities of these areas 31 percent were black, while outside the cities in the suburban rings the black population was only about 5 percent. Some cities, such as Washington, DC, Atlanta, Newark, and Gary, were more black than white. Not only did blacks migrate to the cities during this period but the size of their population also grew dramatically—from about 8.8 million in 1900 to 20.5 million in 1970. Thus, factors both of growth and central city location are key considerations in the development of a massive, nationwide system of segregated residence along racial lines.

But demography alone hardly

explains why racial ghettos and segregated residences exist. As they have moved to the cities, blacks have encountered strong resistance and pressure from whites to remain in their own enclaves and not to settle in white neighborhoods. "Invasion" into white neighborhoods, resulting often from overcrowding in all-black areas, has at times provoked violence and racial confrontation. Usually, however, less violent and often legal means have made it possible for whites to exercise strong social control over where blacks lived. Discriminatory mechanisms, such as restrictive covenants, neighborhood protection associations, and zoning ordinances, were widely practiced in the past and continue to be so in some places today. Restrictive covenants between individuals preventing homeowners from selling houses to particular groups were especially effective as a discriminatory device and were not ruled unconstitutional until as late as 1948. In the years since, whites have come to rely less on overt sanctions and more upon informal social pressures, real estate practices, and the discriminatory tactics of lending institutions for maintaining residential segregation. Despite efforts to ban discrimination in housing, there is still an extensive and highly institutionalized web of discrimination which serves to perpetuate a dual housing market in American cities.

The combined factors of demographic processes and racial discrimination have resulted in residential segregation playing a prominent role in American race relations. Despite improvements in black socioeconomic conditions over the decades, and improved attitudes on the part of whites toward blacks, racial residential segregation persists on a massive scale, virtually unaffected by racial changes in other realms. And because it persists in this way there are many consequences that follow. The most important of these can be summed up as follows:

Structural—As Charles S. Johnson pointed out long ago, "racial segregation in residential areas provides the basic structure for other forms of institutional segregation."[3] Groups segregated residentially are, unless altered by means of intervention, de facto segregated in schools, hospitals, stores, parks, and in any other facilities organized on an area basis. Institutional and residential forms of segregation are intimately linked, and not easily separated.

Interactional—Separated residences minimize opportunities for interracial contact and thereby diminish the likelihood that members of both races will come to know and interact with one another as individuals. While interaction need not always result in greater respect and acceptance, it is clear that those who have had good contact experiences—especially of an equal-status sort—are far more likely to develop positive racial attitudes and an openness to the possibilities of integration. Ghettos restrict opportunities for such contact at the neighborhood level, which is perhaps the most critical level of all for reinforcing a sense of trust, understanding, and genuine acceptance.

Visibility—Racial concentration increases the possibility that a group's distinctive characteristics will stand out more prominently—a problem blacks' in this country experience to a far greater extent than other minorities. Traditionally in Anglo-Saxon culture blackness has been a mark of inferiority and a stimulant to white prejudice, fear, and perceptions of threat. A crucial ingredient in racial prejudice in a competitive society is what Blumer calls a "sense of group position;"[4] hence

3. Charles S. Johnson, *Patterns of Negro Segregation* (New York: Harper and Brothers, 1943), p. 8.
4. Herbert Blumer, "Race Prejudice as a Sense of Group Position," *Pacific Sociological Review* 1 (1958): 3–7.

a group's visibility bears directly upon the collective processes of creating and perpetuating racial images.

Psychological—Finally there are the psychological costs of segregation for the people involved—the experience of rejection, feelings of defeat and despair, ambivalence toward self and one's group. For those who entertain some hope of escaping the ghetto, segregated existence need not be a debasing experience; but for the masses of blacks unable to leave and who must accommodate to the realities of deprivation and disorganization, the waste of human resources is the most serious consequence of all.

One way or another, the end result is structured inequality. The ghetto serves as the base for an institutionalized system of race relations, the cost of which is borne mostly by blacks but also by the American society at large.

RECENT TRENDS IN SEGREGATION

Segregation levels for blacks are uniformly high in American cities, and vary remarkably little from place to place.[5] Cities in the South are somewhat more highly segregated than those in the Northeast; and those in the Northeast are higher still than those in the West. Larger cities and metropolitan areas are more segregated than smaller ones, and cities with large proportions of blacks are somewhat more segregated than those with small proportions. At most, however, these are rather modest differences, indicative of the fact that cities in the

United States are generally characterized by a high degree of residential segregation between blacks and whites. Though relatively few blacks have made it to the suburbs, here too it is clear that segregation, not integration, is the experience of the vast majority who have taken up residence in these neighborhoods.

Moreover, levels of segregation for blacks have remained high over the past couple of decades and show little promise of substantial decline for the future. No place is this better demonstrated than in the nation's largest cities where, historically and currently, racial segregation has been most acute. Most of these cities have segregation indexes above 80, and some above 90, meaning that 80 percent or more of blacks (or whites) would have to shift residential locations to bring about an even, unsegregated distribution. Scores are slightly lower in 1970 than they were in 1940, in most instances, but this reduction is quite small and considerably less than one might expect, given the extent of racial changes in other realms of American life during this period. Continuity, not change, describes the residential experience of blacks, from the early days of ghetto-creation and expansion up until the present; and one word more than any other characterizes that experience—isolation.

In this respect two further observations are of interest about racial residential patterns. The first is that for the nation's cities as a whole there was some decline in segregation during the sixties, more than in previous decades.[6] Yet, the declines were small and should not be heralded

5. See Annmette Sørensen, Karl E. Taeuber, and Leslie Hollingsworth, Jr., "Indexes of Racial Residential Segregation for 109 Cities in the United States, 1940 to 1970," *Sociological Focus* 8 (1975): 125–42; and Thomas L. Van Valey, Wade Clark Roof, and Jerome W. Wilcox, "Trends in Residential Segregation: 1960–1970," *American Journal of Sociology* 82 (1977): 826–44.

6. Sørensen, Taeuber, and Hollingsworth, "Indexes of Racial Residential Segregation for 109 Cities in the United States."

as anything like a major breakthrough in residential integration. More than anything else, the modest declines probably reflect the movement of considerable numbers of whites to the suburbs during the period and the resulting availability of housing for blacks in transitional inner-city areas previously occupied by whites. The second is that segregation for blacks is more intense than for other nonwhites. In all the large American cities, white-versus-black segregation was more pronounced in 1970 than was white-versus-non-white, and in some cases differences between these two types of segregation is substantial (for example, San Francisco, Los Angeles, Minneapolis). Nonwhites are generally segregated from whites, but blacks in particular experience a high level of residential isolation.

BLACK AMERICANS AND THE IMMIGRANT ANALOGY

Group isolation in American cities is, of course, an experience hardly peculiar to blacks. White immigrant groups settling in the cities in the late nineteenth and early twentieth centuries knew ghetto life, segregated neighborhoods, and separation from the larger society. But most such groups have also managed, with time, to move out voluntarily from the ethnic enclave and to become residentially dispersed in the society as they became more prosperous. Changes in social status were reflected in changes in spatial position—a pattern observed by Burgess and other urban ecologists as fitting especially northern, industrial cities in the early decades of this century. At the time these cities were expanding economically and absorbing new populations, thus making it possible for individuals to

break with their ethnic communities and to move into residential areas organized along social class lines. The fact that as many second- and third-generation immigrants of European origin were as successful as they were in moving out of the ghettos is evidence of how well these cities served as centers of assimilation into the larger society.

Without exaggerating the extent of ethnic residential assimilation, it is clear that blacks have not enjoyed a similar urban experience. The historic immigrant-group pattern of declining segregation as a result of socioeconomic progress does not hold for blacks. Evidence available does not support a view of blacks as the "latest" of immigrants to the city following in the path of the earlier groups. The black experience in the city is simply different, so much so as to render the immigrant analogy superficial and misleading.

Trend data for Chicago help to underscore this point.[7] It is true that segregation levels in the city of Chicago have declined somewhat over the decades. From a high of 95.0 in 1940, Chicago's racial segregation dropped to 88.8 by 1970, a net change of -6.2 index points. During this time there were also marked improvements in the socioeconomic conditions of blacks, in both absolute and relative terms. Hence there might appear to be a relationship, albeit a modest one, between black economic advance and segregation decline for the city. Yet

7. For an expanded version of this interpretation, see Wade Clark Roof, "'The Negro as an Immigrant Group'—An Update on Chicago's Racial Trends," *Ethnic and Racial Studies* 1 (1978): 450–62. Also see Karl E. and Alma F. Taeuber, "The Negro as an Immigrant Group: Recent Trends in Racial and Ethnic Segregation in Chicago," *American Journal of Sociology* 69 (1964): 374–82.

even this most favorable interpretation is misleading and only partially correct. Analysis at the metropolitan-wide level indicates that segregation has if anything *increased*, certainly not decreased, in this period. With the movement of large numbers of affluent whites to the suburbs, racial segregation in residence has become more intensified for the metropolitan area as a whole. Even if there were advances in integration within the city, these get lost when looked at from a broader metropolitan perspective. In Chicago, as in most other large metropolitan areas, the patterns justify Farley et al.'s "Chocolate City, Vanilla Suburb" description.[8]

Data such as these are obviously gross, and thus it might be argued that a better test of black residential assimilation should concern only those blacks most likely to become assimilated—that is, the middle classes. Indeed there is some reliable evidence to suggest that the modest declines in residential segregation in the 1960s may have been due mostly to decreases in segregation between whites and upper-status blacks.[9] Given the fact that more and more middle-class blacks are making their way to the suburbs, perhaps a more detailed examination of suburban blacks would yield a greater promise for residential integration. Even here, however, the Chicago data fail to offer much basis for an optimistic scenerio for the future.

Blacks moving to Chicago's suburbs, as no doubt occurs widely in American metropolitan areas, settle predominantly in the older, highly segregated black communities; only a small proportion of all who moved out of the city have actually purchased homes in racially integrated communities. And while it is true that middle-class blacks in the suburbs are less segregated from whites than working-class blacks, the actual status characteristics of suburban blacks appear not to be as important in affecting residential integration as is often thought to be the case. Segregation scores for twelve of Chicago's suburbs correlate more strongly with percent black than with black family income or black educational attainment, thus implying that segregation in the suburbs—not unlike that in the central cities—is more sensitive to minority numbers than to their socioeconomic characteristics. For whites generally, the presence of large numbers of blacks, regardless of socioeconomic status level, poses a serious challenge to their perceptions of neighborhood status and their own neighborhood identities.[10]

But why are racial segregation patterns so different from those of ethnic groups? Why is the black experience so different, compared with the earlier immigrants to America's cities? Some fundamental considerations that are overlooked in discussions of how groups are assimilated in American cities are worth review.

8. See Reynolds Farley, Howard Schuman, Suzanne Bianchi, Dianne Colasanto, and Shirley Hatchett, "Chocolate City, Vanilla Suburbs: Will the Trend Toward Racially Separate Communities Continue?" *Social Science Research* (December 1978).

9. Albert A. Simkus, "Residential Segregation by Occupation and Race in Ten Urbanized Areas, 1950–1970," *American Sociological Review* 43 (1978): 81–93.

10. A similar interpretation is offered by Brian J. L. Berry, Carole A. Goodwin, Robert W. Lake, and Katherine B. Smith, "Attitudes toward Integration: The Role of Status in Community Response to Racial Change," in *The Changing Face of the Suburbs*, ed. B. Schwartz (Chicago: University of Chicago Press, 1976), pp. 221–64.

It is often assumed that residential assimilation happens pretty much as an individual, "bring-yourself-up-by-your-own-bootstraps" type of activity. Movement out of the ghetto is thought of as something occurring once minority individuals adjust to the larger culture and become integrated into mainstream institutional structures. Both *culturally* and *structurally*, however, assimilation is more than simply a process of individuals finding their way out of one group context into another.[11] Other considerations also affect assimilation as an outcome, a crucial one being the urban setting in which the migrants have settled. "Urban setting" means, of course, a host of variables describing the structural conditions under which assimilation must occur: the type of economy, the availability of jobs, the degree to which there is a need for skilled laborers, transportation facilities, the location of jobs in relation to the minority community, and discrimination in the job market. All these factors, and more, vitally affect not only opportunities for upward mobility, and hence the pace of assimilation, but also the viability and stability of the minority community.

Differences in urban conditions are important for understanding American immigrant group experi-

ences generally. White immigrants arriving in northern industrial cities before the Civil War—for example, the Irish and Germans—entered at a time when employment opportunities were generally dispersed throughout the city. Mainly for this reason, and also because of the limited supply of abandoned housing, these groups were able to find housing in many sections of the city, and often in "shanty-towns" beyond the physical limits of the city. Consequently, they were never as residentially concentrated as groups that migrated to the cities in large numbers in the decades that followed.[12]

Groups arriving toward the end of the century—for example, those from southern and eastern Europe—came to cities at a time when employment opportunities were becoming increasingly concentrated in central locations. Job opportunities in the expanding commercial and manufacturing activities were to be found in the central cities, and groups finding work in these sectors usually settled in areas close to their places of employment. The availability of older, low-cost housing in areas on the fringe of the central business manufacturing districts made it possible to establish strong ethnic communities in the cities, and also meant that levels of segregation for the "new" immigrants would be higher than for the "old."

The crucial difference so far as blacks are concerned is the ab-

11. Milton M. Gordon, in his *Assimilation in American Life* (New York: Oxford University Press, 1964), distinguished between the cultural and structural aspects of assimilation. More recently, Gordon has elaborated further on the types of variables affecting assimilation and other intergroup relations outcomes. He identifies three major types: biosocial development variables, interaction process variables, and societal variables. See his "Toward a General Theory of Racial and Ethnic Group Relations," in *Ethnicity: Theory and Experience*, ed. Nathan Glazer and Daniel P. Moynihan (Cambridge: Harvard University Press), pp. 84–110.

12. See David Ward, *Cities and Immigrants* (New York: Oxford University Press, 1971), especially Chapter Four; Sam Bass Warner and Colin Burke, "Cultural Change and the Ghetto," *Journal of Contemporary History* 4 (1969): 173–188; and William L. Yancey, Eugene P. Ericksen, and Richard N. Juliani, "Emergent Ethnicity: A Review and Reformulation," *American Sociological Review* 41 (1976): 391–403.

sence of a close, functional relation between work and residence. White immigrant groups generally settled near manufacturing industries or other kinds of work opportunities; blacks, on the other hand, have typically found themselves restricted to areas not in close proximity to the more reliable, promising job opportunities. Usually they have been forced to accept the oldest and least expensive housing where they could find it, with little consideration for access to jobs or the relevance of work to their communities. Many consequences have followed from this fundamental situation: lack of stability in jobs, especially better-paying jobs; lack of strong and stable neighborhoods; and a chronic condition of psychological dependency.

Put simply, the avenues of upward mobility and integration open to European immigrants and their children have not been the same for blacks. The structural conditions of black life in the city have encouraged neither assimilation nor a self-sufficient community, with the result that urban blacks have often suffered from loss of pride, apathy, despair, and hopelessness. Whereas other migrants to the city had reason to believe they would with time escape the ghetto, for the most part blacks have not enjoyed the benefits of positive orientations toward "making it" in the larger society. Differences of color, too, have given them an enduring visibility as a racial minority which, unlike ethnic characteristics—language, religion, national origins—time does little to erode. Rather this badge of distinctiveness has served to perpetuate the memories of a distinctive group experience, and to provoke among whites a continuing, and quite distinctive set of racial responses and reactions.

GROWING CONCERNS ABOUT DE FACTO SEGREGATION

In the seventies, new developments, both in American cities and race relations, have brought about a greater awareness of the crucial importance of racial residential segregation. Two developments especially have attracted wide attention in recent years: one, a period of metropolitan decline and crisis, and two, some major shifts in the cutting edge of racial change and confrontation in contemporary American society.

Metropolitan decline

It has become increasingly evident that the era of mass migration to the metropolis could not be sustained indefinitely. The long-established patterns of movement for whites and blacks, especially to large metropolitan areas, has slowed down considerably in the seventies; nonmetropolitan areas actually began to grow more rapidly than did metropolitan, representing a sharp contrast to the trends of previous decades. Black population in cities has continued to grow, largely as a result of net natural increases, but the rate of in-movement into metropolitan areas has dropped substantially and will likely continue to do so in the foreseeable future.

As migration patterns have changed, so have regional growth trends. Major shifts are underway, of people and jobs, away from the Northeast and North Central states toward the South and West. Not just whites but blacks as well, are moving in growing proportions out of the older, high density urban areas to other parts of the country.

The recent fiscal crisis of New York City served to sensitize Americans to a new set of realities for the older, large metropolises: the possibility of near-collapse, or at least serious decline and stagnation. As Brian J. L. Berry observes,

Those areas declining most rapidly have been the central cities of the metropolitan areas that emerged during the 19th century, built on productive power, massed population and industrial technology. By the end of the century, these new cities had been credited with the creation of a system of social life founded on entirely new principles. A short half-century later they have become obsolete. These flowers of industrial urbanization—the great manufacturing-belt metropolitan areas—are lagging.[13]

Unfortunately, blacks in these lagging areas cannot escape a disproportionate share of the ill-effects. Having been kept out of many of the better industrial jobs in earlier times and unable to create stable neighborhoods built around manufacturing centers, they now find themselves facing an even more dismal prospect of losing the jobs they have. Economic stagnation is resulting in further set-backs in related goods and services—in housing quality, neighborhood upkeep, and protection. Fiscal strains on the large cities force reductions in public services, affecting more acutely the poor, the elderly, and the unemployed.

Metropolitan decline, or fear of decline, accentuates other debilitating conditions for blacks. The decentralization of manufacturing, for example, has continued throughout the seventies, as central city locations have become less desirable and suburban locations more attractive. In contrast to the earlier twentieth-century city, as described by Burgess, with its centralized com-

13. This is quoted in *Post-Industrial America: Metropolitan Decline and Inter-Regional Job Shifts*, ed. George Sternlieb and James W. Hughes (New Brunswick, NJ: Center for Urban Policy Research, 1975), p. 5.

mercial activities, blacks today are confronted by a city in which manufacturing and industrial activities have become dispersed, and workers rely much more upon the use of the automobile and mass transportation facilities for getting to work. That jobs are moving out of the cities at just the time when blacks are becoming highly concentrated within them, again points to the persisting problem for blacks of work and residence. Lacking a strong functional relation between these in the past, contemporary forces in the American city work against, not in favor of, a stronger economic and community structure for large numbers of working-class blacks.

Considering that an expanding metropolis has generally been seen as the means whereby migrants to the city become economically, socially, and culturally integrated in modern society, the significance of metropolitan decline for blacks is obvious. Even under the best of conditions they have not made much progress in becoming residentially assimilated. And now, under more stringent circumstances, many feel trapped more than ever in segregated neighborhoods, with fading hope of finding their way into the American mainstream.

Shifts in race relations

Problems of residential segregation are of increasing concern, in part also because of progress made in other realms of American race relations. Major efforts in the civil rights movement were directed at job discrimination, educational opportunities, voting rights, and desegregation of public and commercial facilities. As a result of the passage particularly of the 1964 Civil Rights Act and the 1965 Voting Rights Act, tangible results were achieved in these various realms: blacks registered to vote in record numbers; blacks' children began to enter previously all-white schools; they gained entrance to facilities previously denied to them; and they had new and better-paying jobs opened up for them. In the beginning, the focus of attention for civil rights was primarily the South where de jure segregation was overt, enforced, and an egregious deviation from democratic norms, and hence easy in a sense to grasp and deal with as a target for change.

As attention has shifted from the South to the rest of the nation, so have racial priorities—away from the most fundamental of civil rights to more covert, institutionalized aspects of racial inequality. Equal rights of participation in public institutions has come to be less a goal than equal opportunity in a more general sense. Individual discrimination in public life is viewed as less a barrier than the structural conditions of society that inhibit racial progress. De facto residential segregation surfaces in this context as perhaps the most basic, yet unsolved problem of American race relations. Housing discrimination is of course part of the dilemma, but more fundamentally such segregation serves to institutionalize inequalities and to exacerbate social and psychological ills afflicting the black community. Increasingly the issue of concern is that of achieving equality of social opportunity— including equal results in the system —in the presence of such conditions.

In addition to the changing goals of civil rights, important structural changes in the American economy over the past two decades make for growing concerns with de facto segregation. Many blacks in recent years have benefitted from the growth of better-paying job opportunities in the expanding corporate and government sectors. While this improved job situation has done little to help the large black underclass, we have come to recognize that their current plight is probably a result less of racial discrimination than of the labor market conditions of an advanced industrial society. In effect, as William J. Wilson argues,[14] class considerations are becoming increasingly salient in determining black life chances in the nation's urban areas. Changing structural conditions—including the implementation of affirmative action programs—bear many implications, one of which, as Wilson points out, is the shift of racial antagonisms from the economic sector to social, political and community concerns. The residential community in particular, has emerged as an arena of conflict and confrontation between whites and blacks.

PROJECTIONS FOR THE FUTURE

As concern continues to mount over problems of the black community, several developments can be anticipated. Briefly, two of these call for comment.

One, housing discrimination will undoubtedly receive more direct attention in the future. Some impetus in this direction is already evident as a result of the Housing and Community Development Act of 1974. This legislation breaks some new ground in federal housing policy: (1) for the first time, Congressional findings have been directed to the problem of economic as well as racial segregation; (2) housing needs are dealt with in relation to the location

14. William J. Wilson, *The Declining Significance of Race* (Chicago: University of Chicago Press, 1978).

of employment possibilities; and (3) communities in order to be eligible for a broad range of federal funds, must prepare and implement housing plans for people in low- and moderate-income brackets. To a much greater degree than in the past, this legislation sets out to achieve "the spatial deconcentration of housing opportunities for persons of lower income." It is still too soon to tell, but one would like to think that this legislation musters the sanctioning power needed to deal with housing segregation in American metropolitan areas.

Two, black-white tensions will continue to surface over attempts at overcoming the deleterious effects of *de facto* segregation. Aside from whatever "white flight" may occur, court-ordered desegregation of schools and busing plans create a context for defining interracial attitudes and serve as a basis for collective action. Probably more than any other, these serve as the basis around which prevailing views between the races are shaped and maintained. Most public opinions polls show that whites overwhelmingly oppose busing, and even those who are least prejudiced toward blacks typically view themselves as being forced to give up something they value—the neighborhood school. Blacks are more divided over mandatory desegregation but are nonetheless crucially aware of the significance of control over neighborhood institutions. The social identities of blacks and whites alike are intimately tied up with their community and its institutions, and this fact is probably more relevant in American race relations now than ever before.

ANNALS, AAPSS, 441, Jan. 1979

The Role of Residential Segregation in the Assimilation Process

By WILFRED G. MARSTON and THOMAS L. VAN VALEY

ABSTRACT: The assimilation process and the fact of residential segregation are both major emphases in the literature on race and ethnic relations. For a variety of reasons, however, the tendency has been to neglect their relation to one another. This paper offers an explicit connection between the two. We offer an elaboration of the notion of assimilation and suggest that it can be viewed as a sequential process, beginning with the cultural dimension, proceeding with the socioeconomic, and ending with the structural. Furthermore, we contend that the residential segregation of racial/ethnic groups has important consequences for the assimilation process at every juncture.

Wilfred G. Marston received his Ph.D. from the University of Washington, Seattle and is currently a Professor of Sociology and Chairman of the Urban Studies Program at the University of Michigan-Flint. He has taught at York University, Toronto and California State University, Long Beach. His publications include studies of racial segregation in the United States and ethnic segregation in Canada. He is currently involved in a project dealing with ethnic assimilation and pluralism in cities of varying size.

Thomas L. Van Valey is currently an Associate Professor and Director of the Urban Studies Program in the Department of Sociology at Western Michigan University. He received his B.A. from Hanover College, his M.A. from The University of Washington, and his Ph.D. from The University of North Carolina. In addition to racial residential segregation, his substantive interests include socioeconomic inequality and urban area analysis.

13

RESIDENTIAL segregation has
been a continuing reality in
American racial and ethnic relations.
Understandably, therefore, the description and analysis of existing
patterns has received much attention. Similarly, the volume of international immigration to the United
States has led to considerable inquiry into the nature of the assimilation process.

For the most part, however, these
two emphases in racial and ethnic
relations have been pursued separately. By and large, studies dealing
with the assimilation process have
only given passing attention to the
role of residential segregation. In
fact, residential segregation is more
often viewed merely as one indicator
for the lack of assimilation. Consequently, its importance as a factor in
the process of assimilation itself is
often overlooked. By the same token,
studies of racial and ethnic residential segregation, while usually drawing attention to the link between
residential patterning and the assimilation process, typically suffer
from an inadequate conception of
assimilation. More specifically, assimilation is usually treated as uni-
dimensional, with little consideration given to the possibility that
certain groups may be assimilated
in some ways but not in others,
or that residential segregation may
not be related to all measures of
assimilation in the same way.

The purpose of this paper is to
bridge the gap between these two
emphases in the study of racial and
ethnic relations, first by elaborating
on the concept of assimilation, and
additionally by demonstrating its
relation to the fact of residential
segregation. In particular, we propose that one aspect of assimilation
—socioeconomic assimilation—is
an important intermediary step in

the general assimilation process, and
further, that it helps clarify the
crucial links between residential
segregation and assimilation. We
therefore contend that a complete
understanding of the process of
assimilation, as it relates to an ethnic or racial minority, must simultaneously confront the multidimen-
sionality of assimilation, and deal
with the intermediary effects of residential segregation.

ETHNICITY AND ASSIMILATION: MULTIDIMENSIONAL CONCEPTS

The notion of ethnicity has been
defined in a variety of ways; yet,
controversy continues as to its
proper meaning. Isajiw even argues
that the inconsistency in meaning
has led to a situation where very few
researchers actually attempt its formal definition.[1] In this paper, we
will follow Milton Gordon's usage,
and employ a multidimensional
definition. Thus, ethnicity refers
to any group "set off by race,
religion, or national origin, or some
combination of these categories."[2]
While this conception of ethnicity
has received considerable acceptance in recent years, it is not
difficult to find those who view
race and/or religion as distinct from
ethnicity, with the latter referring
only to national origin. It is particularly common for race to be
considered separate from ethnicity,
with the former referring to in-
herited characteristics, such as
skin color, and the latter referring
to socially acquired characteristics,
such as culture, religion, or language.

Gordon has argued convincingly,
however, that race, religion, and na-

1. Wsevolod Isajiw, "Definitions of Ethnicity," *Ethnicity* 1 (July 1974): 111–24.
2. Milton Gordon, *Assimilation in American Life* (New York: Oxford University
Press, 1964), p. 27.

tional origin all share a common social-psychological referent, such that they serve to create a sense of "peoplehood" for groups.[3] This is further supported by the notion of primordial ties or attachments, which refers to a person's sense of belonging to something that gives him/her a sense of identification and self-worth.[4] Moreover, an important feature of this multidimensional conception of ethnicity is that it views all persons as members of some ethnic group.[5] In this way, ethnic status is not simply equated with minority status. There are both minority and majority ethnic groups, and everyone is ranked according to ethnic status as they are ranked according to socioeconomic status. Treating White-Anglo-Saxon-Protestants as an ethnic category is a case in point.

Assimilation, like ethnicity, is surrounded by controversy. But, in this case, the controversy centers less on the appropriate definition to be employed than on its validity in depicting interethnic relations. For example, there is general agreement

that assimilation refers to the process whereby ethnic group members become increasingly similar to majority group members with respect to basic values, norms, and behavior patterns. In addition, the tendency toward increased social contact among members of ethnic and majority groups (both secondary and primary in character) has become generally recognized to be part of the process.[6] Despite the relative consensus as to its meaning, however, assimilation has been severely criticized with respect to its ideological and conceptual bases.[7] Nevertheless, the position taken in this paper is that a multidimensional conception of assimilation avoids most of the pitfalls suggested by such criticism.

First, assimilation is viewed neither as inevitable nor even necessarily desirable, but rather as a cultural and social possibility in a multiethnic society. Furthermore, a multidimensional approach suggests that an ethnic group may become assimilated in terms of one or more dimensions, but not assimilated in terms of others. Whether, in fact, it does or not is a function of other dynamics within the society.

In his work on assimilation, Milton Gordon makes an important distinction between the *cultural* and *structural* dimensions.[8] On the one hand, cultural assimilation refers to the racial or ethnic group's par-

3. Gordon, *Assimilation*, pp. 27–28.
4. See for example, Clifford Geertz, "The Integrative Revolution: Primordial Sentiments and Civil Politics in the New States" in *Old Societies and New States*, ed. Clifford Geertz (New York: Free Press, 1963) pp. 105–57; Andrew Greeley and William McCready, *Ethnicity in the United States: A Preliminary Reconaissance* (New York: John Wiley, 1974).
5. There are, of course, other characteristics that might be considered additional dimensions of ethnicity. Immigrant status, birthplace, and language may well tap aspects not totally captured by race, religion, or national origin, see Gordon Darroch and Wilfred Marston, "Ethnic Differentiation: Ecological Aspects of a Multidimensional Concept," *International Migration Review* 4 (Fall 1969): 71–95. For the purposes of this paper, however, it is unnecessary to specify all of the facets involved in the notion of ethnicity.

6. See for example, Gordon, *Assimilation*; and Richard Alba, "Social Assimilation Among American Catholic National-Origin Groups," *American Sociological Review* 41 (December, 1976): 1030–46.
7. See for example, L. Paul Metzgar, "American Sociology and Black Assimilation: Conflicting Perspectives," *American Journal of Sociology* 76 (January 1971): 627–647; Robert Blanner, *Racial Oppression in America* (New York: Harper and Row, 1972).
8. Gordon, *Assimilation*.

ticipation in the basic institutional arrangements of society. Even within a pluralistic society, it is usually assumed that most members will conform to the basic values and norms, and will work within the existing institutional structures. Gordon also suggests that cultural assimilation involves the incorporation of certain basic behavior patterns of the host society into the ethnic group's own way of life. On the other hand, structural assimilation refers to the wide-scale involvement of ethnic group members in *primary-type* relationships with members of the host society— entrance into clubs, cliques, and social networks. In Gordon's view, this type of assimilation is both a necessary and sufficient condition for the eventual elimination of racial or ethnic status as an important basis of social differentiation. It, therefore, represents the final barrier for the minority groups and the host society alike. As racial and ethnic groups approach the point of structural assimilation, the ability of and need for them to maintain subcultural distinctiveness is undermined. Moreover, the ability of and need for host society members to continue discriminatory practices is reduced.

RESIDENTIAL SEGREGATION

Residential segregation can be defined simply as the physical separation of population groups in residential space.[9] Studies of residential

segregation have been carried out for subpopulations identified by a broad array of social and demographic characteristics, including race, ethnicity, occupation, age, and family status.[10] In general, it appears that black-white segregation continues to remain at a high level, while segregation among other nonwhite ethnic groups, Orientals, Puerto Ricans, Mexican-Americans, tends to be marginally lower. In contrast, segregation scores for white ethnic groups tend to be at moderate levels; yet even they are generally greater than scores of occupational or class segregation, and definitely greater than segregation by family status and age.

The basis for conceptualizing residential segregation as an integral

9. The concept of residential segregation is, of course, more complex than this definition suggests. Although it is typically used to refer to the overall level of separation between two groups within an urban area, there are other aspects that bear upon the probability of physical and social contact among different population groups. For example, the extent to which ethnic groups are concentrated or clustered in one large area—a "ghetto"—versus several noncontiguous smaller areas, and the extent to which specific location patterns of segregation prevail, both constitute important variations in spatial distribution. These may well have distinct impacts on the several dimensions of the assimilation process.

10. See Karl Taeuber and Alma Taeuber, *Negroes in Cities* (Chicago: Aldine, 1965); Thomas L. Van Valey, Wade Clark Roof, and Jerome Wilcox, "Trends in Residential Segregation: 1960–1970," *American Journal of Sociology* 82 (January 1977): 826–44; Stanley Lieberson, "The Impact of Residential Segregation on Ethnic Assimilation," *Social Forces* 40 (October 1961): 52–57; Stanley Lieberson, *Ethnic Patterns in American Cities* (New York: Free Press, 1963); Nathan Kantrowitz, *Ethnic and Racial Segregation in the New York Metropolis* (New York: Praeger, 1973); Avery Guest and James Weed, "Ethnic Residential Segregation: Patterns of Change," *American Journal of Sociology* 81 (March 1976): 1088–1111; Otis Duncan and Beverly Duncan, "A Methodological Analysis of Segregation Indexes," *American Sociological Review* 20 (April 1955): 210–17; Gordon Bultena, "Structural Effects on the Morale of the Aged: A Comparison of Age-Segregated and Age-Integrated Communities" in J. Gubrium, ed., *Late Life* (Springfield: Charles C. Thomas, 1974), pp. 18–31; Avery Guest, "Families and Housing in Cities" (Ph.D. diss., University of Wisconsin, 1970).

component of the assimilation process is found in the classic ecological statements of Park and Hawley.[11] Both argue that the degree of physical separation between two groups is closely associated with the nature of social relations between them. Hawley further articulated the impact of segregation on the assimilation process of minority groups. He argued first, that segregation is a necessary condition for the maintenance of subordinate status, and second, that desegregation is likely to result in a dissipation of the subordinate status, and, therefore, assimilation of the subjugated group into the social structure.[12]

Thus, the segregation of racial and ethnic groups has clear consequences for social relations, both internal and external. It limits access between members of different groups, thereby discouraging social contact. This results both from physical distance and social isolation. It also enables groups to develop and maintain distinctive subcultures and, at the same time, encourages the institutionalization of inequalities in such crucial areas as education and social services.[13] Finally, it increases the visibility of minority groups which, in turn, gives rise to social psychological reactions on the part of the dominant groups. In fact, Roof argues that the greater the physical concentration of racial groups, the more likely they will be perceived as a threat, especially in a traditional racial order such as the American South.[14]

SOCIOECONOMIC ASSIMILATION

The distinction between the cultural and structural dimensions of assimilation is widely accepted. However, it is clear that this distinction does not deal sufficiently with one aspect of the overall assimilation process that is currently of interest, particularly with regard to black-white comparisons—that is, the distribution of socioeconomic status within a racial or ethnic group and its similarity to that of the host population. More specifically, this aspect of assimilation, which we are labelling *Socioeconomic Assimilation*, refers to the degree to which the distributions of income, occupation, and education in racial or ethnic groups are proportionate to those in the balance of the population. Operationally then, if a group is socioeconomically assimilated, the proportion of its members in each category of income, occupation, and education would be equal to the proportion of the remainder of the population in each category. Thus, if ten percent of the nonblack population in the labor force falls in the "professional, technical, and kindred" category, we would also expect ten percent of the black population in the labor force to be in that same category, or else socioeconomic assimilation is incomplete.

In both of his major works on assimilation, Gordon focuses his

11. Robert Park, *Race and Culture* (Glencoe, IL: Free Press, 1950); Amos Hawley, "Dispersion Versus Segregation: Apropos of a Solution of Race Problems," *Papers of the Michigan Academy of Sciences, Arts, and Letters* 30 (1944): 667–674, and his *Human Ecology* (New York: Ronald, 1950).

12. Hawley, "Dispersion versus Segregation," p. 674.

13. See for example, Davis McEntire, *Residence and Race* (Berkeley: University of California Press, 1960); Robin Williams, *Strangers Next Door* (Englewood Cliffs, N.J.: Prentice-Hall, 1964).

14. Wade Clark Roof, "Residential Segregation of Blacks and Racial Inequality in Southern Cities: Toward a Causal Model," *Social Problems* 19 (Winter, 1972): 393–407.

attention upon the articulation of the cultural and structural dimensions, and their consequences for each other and for the other types of assimilation that follow the structural. He only deals tangentially with the issue of socioeconomic similarity.[15] Gordon even goes so far as to suggest that cultural assimilation refers to the acceptance by immigrant groups of the cultural patterns of white, *middle-class*, Protestant Americans, who constitute "the dominant subsociety which provides the standard to which other groups adjust or measure their relative degree of adjustment.[16] Thus, it would appear that further elaboration of the process of assimilation is necessary in order to more fully describe the dynamics involved.

It is here contended that socioeconomic assimilation is analytically separable from the other two major dimensions, and moreover, that it operates as an intermediate step in the overall process. The reasoning is straightforward. First, since cultural assimilation refers primarily to an acceptance of, and perhaps commitment to, societal values and norms, it may involve only *token* participation in society. Certainly, it cannot be said to require full and equal participation in the public educational system and the occupational

15. See for example, Milton Gordon, *Human Nature, Class, and Ethnicity* (New York: Oxford University Press) pp. 167 and 174–75. He notes that variations in cultural assimilation exist with respect to class. This holds regardless of the ideological position one takes with respect to assimilation—"Americanization," "Melting Pot," or "Cultural Pluralism." For example, Gordon takes the position that the development of class divisions within ethnic groups "tend to restrict primary group relations." However, his focus is primarily on such relations *within the ethnic group*, and not the likelihood of greater intergroup primary relations.

16. Gordon, *Human Nature*, p. 169.

structure, with their consequent effects on income distribution. This is supported by the high drop-out rates among nonwhite youths, and the very existence of businesses owned and operated by ethnics, for ethnics, and located in ethnic neighborhoods. Similarly, for structural assimilation to take place, it is necessary for socioeconomic assimilation to have already occurred. How can intergroup contacts of a primary nature occur among people with widely variant educational backgrounds, occupational interests, or income levels? Without question, this precludes the possibility of "large-scale entrance into cliques, clubs, and institutions of the host society."[17]

SEGREGATION AND ASSIMILATION

Gordon and others have provided the underlying logic for the overall process of assimilation simply as a movement from cultural to structural assimilation. This is obviously consistent with the historical patterns of immigration, and racial and ethnic group settlement in the United States. We contend, however, that a more complete elaboration of the process requires the inclusion of socioeconomic assimilation and segregation as intermediary factors. Thus, we view assimilation as a sequence of events which proceeds in much the following manner: (1) the first step toward full and equal participation in society for any racial or ethnic group is cultural assimilation; (2) cultural assimilation, in turn, is necessary before any group can make substantial improvement in their socioeconomic status; (3) advancement in socioeconomic status facilitates residen-

17. Ibid.

tial mobility, and is thus a necessary and prior condition to reduction in residential segregation; and (4) substantial reduction in racial and ethnic residential segregation is a necessary precondition to structural assimilation.

Cultural and socioeconomic assimilation

The relationship between cultural and socioeconomic assimilation is, of course, more complex than indicated above. We can posit a reciprocal relationship such that certain aspects of socioeconomic assimilation may actually accelerate the pace of cultural assimilation. For example, while educational improvement is not only one indicator of cultural assimilation, it is also a mechanism through which minority members can rapidly achieve that goal. However, despite the positive relation between the two dimensions of assimilation, we would argue that cultural assimilation is not simply dependent upon the prior socioeconomic assimilation of a minority group. This is especially true for groups in an urban context. We do recognize, though, that advancement in socioeconomic status can positively influence both the rate and the extent to which groups may become culturally assimilated.

Segregation and cultural assimilation

Gordon argues that segregation probably retards the process of cultural assimilation. Acquiring citizenship, learning to speak English, and other aspects of cultural assimilation may well occur regardless of residential location. Yet, it is reasonable that the process is slower in some areas than in others, depending on the presence of various formal and informal mechanisms. The presence of relatively large ethnic concentrations, for example, may have persistent deterrent effects on cultural assimilation. There is evidence that the existence of an "institutionally complete" set of activities and services (ethnic goods, stores, churches, and foreign language newspapers) facilitates the maintenance of ethnic subcultural lifestyles and, therefore, slows the process of cultural assimilation.[18] Still, segregation does not appear to operate as an impermeable barrier to cultural assimilation. Participation in the basic institutional activities, and acceptance of society's basic value orientations and related normative systems, are necessary facts of life for ethnic groups, no matter the degree of their segregation.

Lieberson dealt directly with this relation in his research on white ethnic groups in the United States. He showed that the degree of segregation among these groups is clearly associated with their rate of cultural assimilation into American society. For example, the ability to speak English and American citizenship were both positively linked to reductions in residential segregation. In many instances the relationships were not strong, however, indicating that segregation does not preclude their assimilation.[19]

18. See for example, Herbert Gans, *The Urban Villagers* (New York: Free Press, 1962); Raymond Breton, "Institutional Completeness of Ethnic Communities and Personal Relations to Immigrants," *American Journal of Sociology* 70 (September 1964): 193–205; Leo Driedger and Glenn Church, "Residential Segregation and Institutional Completeness: A Comparison of Ethnic Minorities," *Review of Canadian Sociology and Anthropology* 11 (February 1974): 30–52.

19. Stanley Lieberson, "Impact of Segregation." It should be noted that Lieberson did not distinguish among the various dimen-

Segregation and socioeconomic assimilation

Most empirical studies of residential segregation emphasize socioeconomic factors, virtually excluding consideration of the overall assimilation process. More specifically, they generally attempt to assess the impact of residential segregation upon socioeconomic advancement. The evidence thus far, however, is contradictory. On the one hand, there is support for the position that segregation plays a crucial role in restricting socioeconomic opportunities. On the other hand, some argue that the effects of segregation are easily overrated.

In one of the earlier studies of segregation and socioeconomic differentiation, Bahr and Gibbs argue that residential segregation is *not* significantly related to income, educational, or occupational differences between blacks and whites.[20] Their conclusion was that residential segregation may not be as basic to other forms of racial differentiation as is commonly believed. Similarly, Jiobu and Marshall suggest that segregation does not, by itself, have much effect on assimilation.[21] They too find that the level of segregation between blacks and whites is not meaningfully related to racial differences in socioeconomic indicators, leading them to question the spatial determinants of black assimilation.

In contrast, in an analysis of southern cities, Roof suggests that residential segregation functions as an "intervening" variable between certain structural characteristics of cities (age and percent nonwhite) and the structure of socioeconomic inequality.[22] In a causal analysis, he argues that segregation directly affects educational inequality, and through it occupational inequality, which in turn affects income inequality. In addition, he reports other direct consequences of segregation on occupational inequality, apart from those directly related to educational opportunities.

Economists have also provided support for the view that segregation impedes socioeconomic advancement. Their focus, though, has primarily been on the degree that residential *de*segregation would increase income opportunities. Steger, for example, estimates that the effects of income opportunity deprivation due to residential segregation exceed 10 billion dollars annually.[23] He further offers the following set of consequences which might result from substantial residential desegregation: (1) black families would move closer to areas with more job opportunities, and spend less time and money commuting to work; (2) employee and employer discrimination would probably diminish; (3) black representation in most occupations would increase; (4) the participation of blacks in the

sions of assimilation in his research. Although speaking English and citizenship are both indicators of cultural assimilation, he also found segregation to be similarly related with intermarriage, educational improvement, and occupational improvement. In ours and Gordon's terms, the former of these is clearly an indicator of marital assimilation (or indirectly of structural assimilation), while the latter are indicators of socioeconomic assimilation.

20. Howard Bahr and Jack Gibbs, "Racial Differentiation in American Metropolitan Areas," *Social Forces* 45 (June 1967): 521–32.

21. Robert Jiobu and Harvey Marshall, "Urban Structure and the Differentiation Between Blacks and Whites," *American Sociological Review* 36 (August 1971): 638–49.

22. Roof, "Residential Segregation."

23. Wilbur Steger, "Economic and Social Costs of Residential Segregation" in *Modernizing Urban Land Policy* ed. Marion Clawson (Baltimore: Johns Hopkins University Press, 1973) pp. 83–113.

labor force would increase; (5) there would be an increase in the volume of migration of higher-skilled blacks from the ghetto; and (6) black mean earnings would increase.

In regard to these contradictory findings, it is important to note that racial segregation is currently quite high across American cities, and has been for several decades. Thus, it is possible that the narrow range in intercity segregation scores is insufficient for there to be any substantial impact on socioeconomic assimilation. Conceivably, the impact of segregation on assimilation may be no different in a city with a segregation score of, say, 70 than in a city with a score of 96 (on a scale from 0 to 100). If a reasonable number of cities with lower scores did exist, one might expect the process of black socioeconomic improvement in those cities to register more than in cities with traditionally high scores. The point is, once the level of segregation climbs very high, further increases in segregation may have little additional effect on restricting socioeconomic assimilation. Lieberson's analysis of white immigrant groups (which tend to have substantially lower segregation scores), indirectly suggests this possibility. He discovered that the relationship between the mean level of occupational achievement of immigrant groups and their level of residential segregation was strong and negative. That is, the higher the degree of occupation achievement, the lower the level of segregation.[24]

Segregation and structural assimilation

While it is clear that segregation has retardant effects on both cul-tural and socioeconomic assimilation, its impact on structural assimilation is even stronger. As suggested earlier, segregation appears to be fully sufficient to prevent structural assimilation to any meaningful extent. It may even be argued that the perpetuation of minority residential segregation has been, and continues to be, one of the primary mechanisms for restricting intergroup personal contact.[25] The specific impacts of residential segregation on structural assimilation, however, should be looked at from two quite disparate positions: (1) from the perspective of the *dominant* groups, and (2) from the perspective of the *subordinate* groups.

"The view from the top"

Van den Berghe initially noted the importance of residential segregation under a "competitive" as opposed to a "paternalistic" form of race relations."[26] More recently, Roof has amplified van den Berghe's argument:

25. This position also seems to suggest that residential *de*segregation would bring about structural assimilation. Such an assertion requires clarification, however. First, we have contended that the specific households involved must be of similar socioeconomic status; otherwise the status differences alone will serve to inhibit structural assimilation. In addition, though, it would appear that there also must be substantial similarity with respect to family composition. See Ozzie Edwards, "Family Composition as a Variable in Residential Succession," *American Journal of Sociology* 77 (January 1972): 731–41. Finally, Harvey Molotch presents a convincing argument that the neighborhoods involved must be truly desegregated and not merely experiencing racial succession; "Racial Integration in a Transition Community," *American Sociological Review* 34 (December 1969): 878–93.

26. Pierre Van den Berghe, *Race and Racism: A Comparative Perspective* (New York: Wiley, 1967) p. 30.

24. Lieberson, "Impact of Segregation."

Physical distance replaces "social" distance as a decisive regulatory mechanism in the transition from paternalistic to competitive race relations. Spatial concentration, by ensuring greater institutional separation and minority visibility, imposes barriers to effective economic competition and thereby aids in preserving dominant group privileges.[27]

While the latter author is referring primarily to the effects of segregation on socioeconomic assimilation, the argument is even more persuasive in terms of the effects of segregation on intergroup personal contact (in Gordon's terms, structural assimilation). Segregation encourages the emergence of institutional separation, the development of subcultural styles, and heightens minority group visibility and distinctiveness. These conditions, plus the direct inhibiting effect of residential isolation, are sufficient to prohibit face-to-face intimate exchanges between those living within an ethnically segregated area and those living outside.

The direct inhibiting effect of residential segregation on primary social contact is critically important, for the impact appears to be independent of social class, race or ethnicity, age, and other such factors. Sheer distance and time constraints, plus the reduced likelihood of spontaneous encounters, mean that some effort must go into sustaining primary contact. Such efforts are made, it is true; but most of them appear to be among persons at the same social class level and of the same racial or ethnic status.[28]

To the extent it occurs across groups, it is mainly among members of the same social standing.

Another important consideration concerns the status and symbolic aspects of segregation. Guest and Weed, for example, argue that the residential location decision is based on the individual's knowledge of the average status of potential neighbors. This, in turn, is a consequence of their perceived ethnic characteristics.

Thus, a high-status German views the status of his potential neighbors, not on a basis of their individual incomes, but on his perception of the average income of their ethnic group. He will be willing to live next door to Poles, regardless of individual incomes, if he perceives the Polish ethnics as a whole to be relatively similar in status to his group.[29]

Ethnic segregation of this kind, thus, does not rest on negative attitudes or prejudice towards individuals of a different ethnic group. Rather, it is a function of the relative positions of ethnic groups in the stratification system. This offers a reasonable explanation of why whites often tend not to want to live in the same neighborhood as blacks, even those of the same economic standing. No matter what their socioeconomic level, blacks tend to be viewed by whites as significantly lower in social status.

In addition to the status value of a given residential location, it is also the case that people consider the type of day-to-day contacts they and their children will encounter, when deciding upon a neighborhood in which to live. While this may not always be explicitly verbalized, parents often prefer homogene-

27. Roof, "Residential Segregation," p. 396.

28. Edward Laumann, "The Social Structure of Religious and Ethnoreligious Groups in a Metropolitan Community," *American Sociological Review* 34 (April 1969): 182–197.

29. Guest and Weed, "Ethnic Residential Segregation," p. 1092.

ous neighborhoods, with respect to age, social class, and ethnicity, because such a social environment facilitates greater parental control, not only over the playmates, but the general social influences their children will encounter.[30]

"The view from the bottom"

In the previous discussion, we have stressed the perspective of society's dominant groups: namely, that dominant-group members play an active role in restricting the emergence of racially and ethnically heterogeneous neighborhoods. There is, of course, another side to this issue, the voluntary and strategic aspects of segregation as they are seen from the standpoint of subordinate racial and ethnic groups. Here, residential segregation is viewed as an important requirement in the effort to develop and maintain separate and distinct racial or ethnic identities, subcultures, and life styles, that is, cultural pluralism. More specifically, segregation is perceived not only as helpful but as *necessary* if a group is to provide an "institutionally complete" set of activities and services for its members. This was demonstrated, for example, by Driedger and Church in a study of six ethnic groups.[31] We would expect this to be the case particularly in metropolitan areas where the number of people of the same ethnic group are sufficient to produce the "critical mass" necessary for the establishment and perpetuation of ethnic subcultural activities and institutions.

The larger the ethnic group, the greater . . . is the possibility of supporting institutions that reinforce ethnicity: churches, newspapers, stores, clubs, political organizations. These institutions link people to their groups, exercise authority over the members, protect them from outsiders, help attract fellow ethnics, and constantly remind them of the identity. . .[32]

This combination of "critical mass" and residential segregation is especially significant in characterizing the experience of the Jews in the United States and Canada. They live almost exclusively in urban areas, especially the larger ones, and are highly segregated, despite widespread movement to the suburbs in recent years.[33] Accessibility to the synagogue and the importance of their children marrying "within the group" have been important features of Jewish life, giving rise to the perpetuation of predominantly Jewish neighborhoods. Furthermore, residential concentration bolsters the defense against outside prejudice and discrimination, and serves to constantly remind them of their identity.

Along similar lines, it can be argued that segregation results in other positive functions for blacks in the United States. One argument in support of "voluntary" segregation of blacks is that their concentration in urban areas facilitates the emergence of black pride.[34] Institu-

---

30. Richard Sennett, "The Brutality of Modern Families," *Transaction* (September, 1970): 29–37.

31. Driedger and Church, "Residential Segregation and Institutional Completeness."

32. Claude Fischer, *The Urban Experience* (New York: Harcourt, Brace, Jovanovich, 1976) p. 131.

33. See Wilfred Marston, "Social Class Segregation Within Ethnic Groups in Toronto," *Canadian Review of Sociology and Anthropology* 6 (May 1969): 65–79; and Erich Rosenthal, "Acculturation Without Assimilation? The Jewish Community of Chicago, Illinois," *American Journal of Sociology* 66 (November 1960): 275–88.

34. See William Wilson, *Power, Racism, and Privilege* (New York: MacMillan, 1976).

tional separation and restricted inter-group interaction facilitate group consciousness and identity. It might also be said that the persistence of segregation aids in the development of black political power, which in turn, often translates into socioeconomic advancement. This, of course, is based on the premises that the segregation of blacks within a city ensures the emergence of a "black voice" in local government, and that political structures exist for these voices to be heard.

Positive consequences of racial segregation also follow in the sense that it can result in increased opportunities for leadership positions in the institutional sectors, religion, business, education, or politics, within the black community and, to a degree, in the larger society. In addition, segregation often produces a strategic population which is more easily amenable to mobilization—a factor of some importance, especially in times of racial conflict. Some blacks, in fact, argue that the net effect of wide-ranging desegregation might actually be dysfunctional for the black population. It would undercut an important source of political socialization, and reduce the powerful—and growing—political force that blacks are able to marshall in the nation's cities.

CONCLUDING REMARKS

In the preceding discussions of segregation and its relation to the various dimensions of assimilation, the focus was upon the overall extent of residential separation and the degree to which it exists among various groups. While this aspect of segregation clearly has implications for the assimilation process, there are also other aspects that play important roles. In addition to the overall segregation of blacks from whites in American metropolitan areas, for example, the location of blacks in the *inner city* serves as an added barrier to their socioeconomic assimilation. This is true especially in light of the continuing decentralization of economic activity in metropolitan areas. Since 1948, suburban areas have received over 80 percent of the new employment in manufacturing, retail and wholesale trade, and selected services.[35] Thus, even as the nation's central cities become increasingly black, the newer and better job opportunities are locating farther away from them, toward the urban periphery. This not only makes it difficult for many blacks to find out about job opportunities, it also creates an excessive transportation burden for those inner city residents who are successful in finding work.

Another aspect of residential segregation that bears directly on structural assimilation is the *geographic pattern* of racial or ethnic residence. In some cities, blacks are located primarily in a single concentrated area; while in others, they reside in several smaller, noncontiguous areas. Therefore, while the overall level of segregation, and its consequences, may be similar or even identical in both situations, the implications with respect to interracial contact may be quite different. In the former case, residents are statistically less likely to come into contact and interact with whites. Of greater importance, though, the possibility of a political power base

35. Neil Gold, "The Mismatch of Jobs and Low-Income People in Metropolitan Areas and Its Implications for the Central City Poor," *Report of the Commission on Population Growth and the American Future* Volume 5 (Washington, DC: USGPO, 1972) pp. 443–86.

and an institutionally complete set of services and functions are both greater in a single concentrated area, due to the larger "critical mass" available in an accessible location.

There is no question that the impact of residential segregation upon the assimilation process is complex indeed. It is for this reason that the question of the residential patterning of racial and ethnic groups is clearly one of the most significant and sensitive problems facing society today. In fact, it qualifies as one of the basic urban dilemmas. On the one hand, the persisting residential segregation of blacks in America will almost assuredly contribute to the perpetuation of long-standing prejudices, discriminatory practices, and forms of inequality. Not even the most ambitious of legislative and judicial efforts have had more than cosmetic effects on the underlying structural condition. Yet, on the other hand, any considerable reduction in the degree of overall segregation (or the dispersal of black populations living in concentrated areas) might seriously undermine recent attempts at maintaining black consciousness, subculture, and political and economic power.

What then are the prospects for metropolitan racial desegregation in the immediate future? We think, unfortunately, that they are not good. Although it is clear that the majority of blacks would prefer living in integrated neighborhoods, other evidence indicates that most whites still prefer to live in racially homogeneous neighborhoods.[36] It seems that there is a continuing reluctance among whites to occupy the same residential areas as blacks. According to Brian Berry and his associates, "Across the range of white responses . . ." is the general conclusion that at each income level and regardless of socioeconomic characteristics, a concentration of black families is perceived negatively by whites.[37]

In addition, recent attempts to reduce racial inequality may have given rise to even stronger resistance on the part of whites to the residential desegregation of blacks. At one time in the past social distance between blacks and whites was so great that physical distance was irrelevant to status considerations. Today, this is no longer the case. With the continuing pressures for racial equality, it is now reasonable to argue that residential propinquity symbolizes status equality. Under these circumstances, it seems clear that whites, especially those whose economic position is similar to that of the growing, black middle-class, will undertake strong and persistent measures to prohibit any significant influx of blacks into their neighborhoods. For, if physical distance is no longer available as a mechanism, they will have little else on which to base their self-perceived superior status position.

Sciences, 1973) pp. 21–84; Brian Berry, Carole Goodwin, Robert Lake, and Katherine Smith, "Attitudes Toward Integration: The Role of Status in Community Response to Racial Change" in *The Changing Face of the Suburbs*, ed. Barry Schwartz (Chicago: University of Chicago Press, 1976) pp. 221–264.

37. Brian Berry et al., "Attitudes Toward Integration," p. 222 (italicized in the original). See also Guest and Weed, "Ethnic Residential Segregation," for a similar argument.

36. See for example, Thomas Pettigrew, "Attitudes on Race and Housing: A Social-Psychological View" in *Segregation in Residential Areas*, ed. A. Hawley and V. Rock (Washington, DC: National Academy of

ANNALS, AAPSS, 441, Jan. 1979

Housing, Neighborhoods, and Race Relations: Recent Survey Evidence

By D. GARTH TAYLOR

ABSTRACT: This essay looks at the various uses which have been made of public opinion data in explaining and predicting patterns of racial residential segregation. Public opinion is central to understanding the process of housing discrimination because housing market behavior is difficult to monitor and police in any official or bureaucratic fashion. Current poll results show that racial attitudes or preferences for segregated neighborhoods by whites (or by blacks) are not the central stumbling blocks in desegregating American neighborhoods. Rather, shifts in the nature of the housing market in an area reflect responses to a broader, more complex set of neighborhood processes. Factors causing neighborhood change vary greatly in their effects depending on the kind of neighborhood "at risk" and the amount of integration which is likely to occur. Simple calculations of the future of integrated neighborhoods or the amount of segregation due to preferences are in error unless they take these complexities into account.

D. Garth Taylor is currently an Assistant Professor in the Department of Political Science at the University of Chicago and a Senior Study Director at the National Opinion Research Center. Recent publications or essays include: several case studies of public reactions to school desegregation and busing in American cities; trends in American racial attitudes since World War II; studies of the relation between fear of crime, fear of the ghetto and white racial attitudes; and a general treatment of the progress of Myrdal's predictions for the American Creed since World War II.

IN the 1973 National Academy of Sciences report on housing integration, Thomas Pettigrew summarized the results from several studies of white and black attitudes toward integration as follows: "The paucity of optimal interracial contact at the neighborhood level, the perceived intimacy of housing and the assumption of dissimilarity [between black and white characteristics of culture and social life] erode the more abstract beliefs in equality held by most white Americans when the issue of race and housing is made directly relevant to the individual."[1] This article builds on Pettigrew's review in several ways. First, there have been studies done in the 1970's which allow us to compare trend data for evidence of change in the psychological aspects of interracial housing. Second, studies have been done in recent years which have further refined our understanding of the process which Pettigrew summarized. Third, new issues and different theoretical approaches have arisen in the analysis of segregation in the housing market and the role of public opinion in that process.

ATTITUDES TOWARD INTEGRATED HOUSING

In the last few years housing segregation has displaced other concerns to become the central issue in the

struggle to end racial inequality. Even though the optimal trend data are lacking, a compelling argument can be made that this is recognized in both black and white American public opinion. In 1963 the National Opinion Research Center (NORC) asked a national sample of whites the following question: "In recent months a lot of attention has been paid to what has been called the Negro Civil Rights Movement. In your opinion what are the main things that Negroes are really trying to get?" About half of the white population said that the main goals of the Civil Rights movement were economic equality (45 percent) and educational equality (41 percent). Much further down the list of visible public demands were housing equality (21 percent) which shared the same level of perceived importance as access to public places (21 percent). Since then the relative importance, or the visibility, of the housing issue has changed. A recent Harris survey shows that in 1977 more whites thought that blacks are discriminated against in getting decent housing (34 percent) than in almost any other sphere. The exact question was: "Let me ask you about some specific areas of life in America. For each, tell me if you think blacks are discriminated against in that area or not." Other areas where discrimination was the most visible are: getting white collar jobs (34 percent) and getting full equality (33 percent). Each of these areas is currently seen as more of a social problem than: wages paid (21 percent), getting quality education (19 percent), and getting manual jobs (10 percent).

The same pattern of change is found in studies of black opinion. Another 1963 NORC survey posed the following question to a black national sample: "Here is a list of things Negro

1. Thomas Pettigrew, "Attitudes on Race and Housing: A Social-Psychological View" in *Segregation in Residential Areas*, ed. Amos Hawley and Vincent Rock (National Academy of Sciences, 1973). Throughout this essay I will use the phase "white attitudes toward integration" to refer to attitudes toward moving into an integrated neighborhood as well as attitudes toward having blacks move into a previously less integrated neighborhood. In places where it is necessary to analyze each process separately, I will use more precise terminology.

groups working for equal rights frequently want. . . . Which do you think is the most important to work for now?" Equal job opportunities topped the list with 58 percent, desegregated schools and voting rights were a distant second with 13 percent each, and no discrimination in housing was considered the most important goal by 1 percent of the black population. In 1977 the Harris poll found that the housing market was nearly at the top of the list of areas where blacks perceived discrimination (74 percent), only ranking less than getting white collar jobs (76 percent) and getting full equality (75 percent). As with the white population, the perception of discrimination in these areas is greater than in wages paid (66 percent), getting quality education (61 percent), and getting manual jobs (54 percent). The rank order in perception of discrimination in these areas (and for the other areas on the Harris list) is nearly the same for the black and white populations. The difference is that the blacks are much more aware of discrimination in any particular area. This is the same pattern of issue awareness as was reported by Sheatsley.[2] The difference between the time Sheatsley wrote and the present is that the central focus of the campaign for civil rights has shifted to issues which can only be solved with a nondiscriminatory housing market.

Sheatsley argued that the ease with which desegregation can be accomplished depends on black and white agreement on the importance of various goals in the civil rights movement and white willingness to compromise on the rights which blacks consider to be the most im-

portant. The question for the present, then, is whether or not whites are favorable to housing integration.

Figure 1 shows trends in the percent of the white population giving a pro integration reply to a number of queries. There are two dimensions which seem particularly relevant to understanding white housing attitudes. The first is that whites are sensitive to the *amount* of integration implied in a question. There are some whites, although fewer and fewer, who object to small amounts of integration, particularly if it is made clear that the invading blacks are of equal social status (which is the way it actually happens). From items 3, 5, and 6 it seems clear that the less integration in the question, the more likely a favorable response.

The second dimension is the amount of legitimacy whites will extend to an actively integrationist black perspective. Question number 1 asks whether whites are willing to reserve for themselves the right to actively discriminate against potential black neighbors. Over half do not reserve this right and the trend is in the liberal direction. On the other hand, question 4 (and question 2 to some extent) asks about legitimating black pressure on the housing market. Whites are much less willing to do this and, furthermore, there is no apparent trend toward the liberal position for *these* questions. So, although whites are less and less willing to reserve the right to affirmatively discriminate against blacks, they are not willing to go so far as to grant the legal rights which would legitimate an aggressive black position in the housing market.

It is interesting to note that there is a similar kind of ambivalence in the black population. Several studies have shown that blacks almost unanimously support the position that

2. Paul B. Sheatsley, "White Attitudes Toward the Negro," Daedalus 95 (1966): 217–38.

FIGURE 1

THE PERCENT GIVING THE PRO-INTEGRATION RESPONSE TO SEVERAL HOUSING
(NATIONAL SAMPLES, WHITES ONLY)

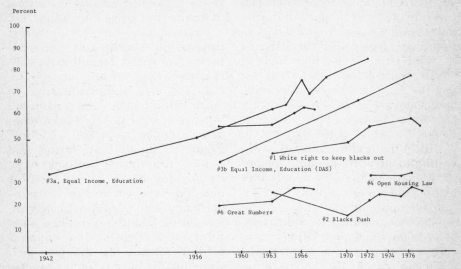

Items:
1. "White People have a right to keep Negroes out of their neighborhoods if they want to, and Negroes should respect that right."
2. "Negroes shouldn't push themselves where they're not wanted."
3a. "If a Negro with the same income and education as you have moved into your block would it make any difference to you?"
3b. Same question, Detroit Area Study
4. "Suppose there is a community-wide vote on the general housing issue. There are two possible laws to vote on. Which law would you vote for?" (A homeowner cannot refuse to sell to someone because of their race or color.)
5. "If colored people came to live next door, would you move?" ("No")
6. "Would you move if colored people came to live in great numbers in your neighborhood?" ("No")

whites *should* not discriminate. There is less agreement, however, when the issue moves to the guarantee of legal rights which might be evoked against an unwilling white homeowner. Marx reports that in 1964, 50 percent of the blacks in his sample of nonsouthern metropolitan areas agreed with the statement that "an owner of property should not have to sell to Negroes if he does not want to." In Detroit, in 1968, 38 percent of the black population agreed with the same statement.[3]

3. Gary Marx, *Protest and Prejudice* (New York: Harper, 1969). This idea was also sug-

A 1939 Fortune survey forced whites to choose among three general ways of handling blacks in the housing market. Forty-one percent believed that there should be laws compelling Negroes to live in certain districts; forty-two percent thought there should be no laws, but there should be an unwritten understanding backed up by social pressure to keep Negroes out of the neighborhoods where white people live;

gested by Robert A. Levine, "The Silent Majority: neither simple nor simple-minded," Public Opinion Quarterly 35 (1971–72): 571–77.

while 13 percent were willing to say that Negroes should be allowed to live wherever they want to live and there should be no laws or social pressures to keep them from it. The impression we gain from the data in Figure 1 is that since World War II the public has rejected housing laws which would force segregation but that the third category—affirmative open housing advocates—has only grown by 15 percent or so. This means the bulk of the population is still in the middle category—unwilling to advocate possibly unconstitutional practices to avoid integration, but uneasy with the implication for one's neighborhood of an out-and-out guarantee of equal treatment to the black population.

Recent research has shown that the major reasons for change in the racial attitudes are cohort succession and the development of a general climate of liberal opinion where Americans are less likely to refuse rights to certain disadvantaged or minority groups, blacks, women, or politically unpopular groups. The continuation of either of the latter sources of change in American public opinion depends greatly on continued moral leadership by key actors in the judicial and political system. As certain values, such as integration, become dominant in the political process, the climate is created in which these values seem moral and right, particularly by the young. These values are first taken up by the young and well-educated and then gradually diffuse to other sections of the society.[4] An important source of change in housing attitudes,

then, would be a resurgence or reaffirmation of interest by visible political leaders, or by the Supreme Court, in the continued pursuit of the goal of a fully desegregated society.

From the time of World War II through the middle 1960's the Supreme Court and the national political leadership unambiguously upheld the idea of desegregation in most realms which were considered important, such as public accommodations, employment, and schooling. Figure 1 shows that during that period Americans became more racially tolerant in those areas. A detailed examination of the patterns of change shows that American opinion during that time exhibited what Riley and Pettigrew call a "counter-ceiling" effect.[5] The groups which were initially most favorable to integration became more favorable at a much faster rate than those groups which were opposed (some of which even changed in a negative direction). When opinions change in this way the population becomes increasingly divided. As the pressure for change continues, more and more groups find that they have had enough and fall into the alienated category. Eventually the groups which were left behind form a large enough block in the population that they begin to win elections, thus elevating political leaders who will no longer affirm the goals which the new majority find repugnant or threatening. An analysis of the elections after the middle 1960s shows that the winning coalitions have been disproportionately made up of those groups which were left behind during the period of rapid change in American racial attitudes in the 1960s.

4. D. Garth Taylor, Paul B. Sheatsley, and Andrew M. Greeley, "Attitudes Toward Racial Integration," *Scientific American* 238 (1978): 42–49; D. Garth Taylor "The Diffusion and Change of Public Attitudes Toward Some Social Issues in Recent American History" (PhD diss., University of Chicago, 1976).

5. D. Garth Taylor, "Attitudes Toward Integration"; Robert Riley and Thomas Pettigrew "Dramatic Events and Attitude Change," Journal of Personality and Social Psychology 34: 5 (1976): 1004–1015.

One of the reasons that the Supreme Court and the current political leadership have so gingerly approached the racial issues which are most important today (busing, metropolitan desegregation, and housing) is that these have become the central issues in American race relations during a historical moment when the political center of gravity has shifted from an activist approach. If Americans overcome their current crisis of confidence in national institutions, and if the national political leadership becomes more willing to take risks in espousing black people's rights, then it is possible that the Supreme Court or the Congress could exercise sufficient moral leadership to facilitate further change in American racial attitudes, and housing attitudes in particular.

RACIAL ATTITUDES AND THE HOUSING MARKET

There have been four general approaches to the question of how racial attitudes and racial prejudice actually operate in the housing market. The first simply documents the dimensions and changes in various forms of prejudice, without specifically addressing the question of how these attitudes relate to behavior in the housing market. This leads to interesting, noncommittal essays but does not address urgent policy concerns.

The second approach is to attempt to directly measure the role of prejudice in the decision of when and where to move. One of the problems with this approach is that it is hard to define the exact moment that someone enters the housing market and impossible to draw a representative sample of people whose housing and mobility decisions might or might not be influenced by racial prejudice. One strategy for confronting

this problem is to determine the motivations and prejudice of a sample of people who either say they might move, who have already moved, or who moved during the course of a panel study. This strategy of direct measurement has consistently shown no effect of racial prejudice on housing choices. For example, Bradburn et al found that whites who moved into an integrated neighborhood are not distinguished from those who moved into segregated neighborhoods in any of the criteria they applied in selecting new homes. Mayer reports a study of a tipping neighborhood in Detroit where neither the degree of prejudice nor the stated intention to move was a reliable indicator of who actually moved during the course of the invasion. And finally, Taylor and Stinchcombe find that the decision to move out of predominantly white census tracts in Boston, between September 1973 and July 1975, was only marginally related to people's personal orientations to the busing conflict— and then in the opposite direction than expected. Those who moved out of the city were younger, better educated and therefore, on balance, slightly *more* in favor of busing than those who stayed in the city.[6]

The third strategy is another kind of direct measurement. People are asked to imagine that they are going to move and then the investigator attempts to determine the effect of racial prejudice on their choice of *where* they would like to move. This method has been used recently in

6. Norman Bradburn, Seymour Sudman, and Galen Gockel, *Racial Integration in American Neighborhoods* (National Opinion Research Center, 1970); Albert Mayer, "Russell Woods: Change Without Conflict" in Studies in Housing and Minority Groups, ed. Nathan Glazer and Davis McEntire (Berkeley: University of California Press, 1960).

the Detroit Area Study. With this approach, there is no attempt to address the relation between prejudice and *actual* housing market behavior. This is an important point because it means that strong qualifications must continually be made as to the exact nature of the dependent variable. In particular, the results from the study in Detroit suggest that it is quite difficult to ask questions about *hypothetical* housing situations which do not also cause people to answer in terms of general racial attitudes which in reality, might not predict behavior in an *actual* housing situation.

The fourth approach to studying the effect of racial attitudes in the housing market does not measure attitudes directly or even indirectly. With this approach, the researcher writes equations showing the hypothetical effects of racism on white people's distribution of housing choices, propensity to move, willingness to pay extra to avoid racial contact, and so on. These equations are then used to simulate and predict the pattern of neighborhood change given different kinds of housing markets. If the pattern of change under the simulation study is about what we observe or think we should observe in real life, then the argument is made that the theories about prejudice and attitude-behavior relations implied by the equations were correct. The final step is then to show what would happen in the housing market if there were no discrimination or prejudice.

To summarize the four approaches, it is difficult to analyze the role of racial attitudes in the housing market in any great detail. There are difficult methodological and conceptual issues in isolating the topic for study. The research so far has not succeeded in going beyond simple

models of prejudice, simple models of the relation between prejudice and housing market behavior, and has only recently begun to recognize the great diversity in the housing market and the array of neighborhood reactions to integration. What follows is a review of the few areas where enough research has been done to begin to think formally about how to incorporate racial attitudes into policy models of the housing market.

Housing preferences: buying and selling

Attitude studies have shown that the negative white reaction to neighborhood integration depends less on the amount of integration taking place at any particular time than it does on the amount of integration (or neighborhood change) that whites believe will *eventually* occur. A detailed analysis by Bradburn, Sudman and Gockel showed that whites' future expectations for a desegregating neighborhood were influenced not so much by racial prejudice as by: (1) the perception of the level of black demand for housing in the neighborhood; and (2) by a subtle process which depends on whether the white reaction during the initial stages of desegregation was violent or peaceful. Berry et al observed a wide range of responses from different neighborhoods within the same SMSA. They agree that the white response to black invasion is based on the expected *future* state of the neighborhood. They argue, however, that the effect of black immigration on white reactions depends on the social status of the neighborhood (high status neighborhoods are less threatened by black residents). Similarly, the Taeubers argue that only in the north, where the black population was growing rapidly, did black residential patterns resemble the invasion-succession sequence characteristic of tipping neighborhoods. Northern cities not experiencing large-scale black immigration, and hence where the perceived demand for housing was low, did not display a high prevalence of neighborhood turnover.[7]

Judging from Figure 1, only about 5 percent of the white population currently objects to a new Negro neighbor of equal income and education. This view is nearly unanimously held because it does not imply giving up any rights whites want to reserve for themselves, because the amount of integration implied is quite low, and because the question reminds respondents that integration generally occurs along equal class lines. Whites are very tolerant of the idea (and the reality) of integration when these three criteria are met. Integration is more likely to be opposed when the number of invading black families (or when the *threatened* number) is much higher and when the integration threatens to involve groups of different social status as is especially the case when whites fear that housing projects will be built in middle and upper middle class parts of the city.

When asked in a 1965 Gallup poll what they would do if a Negro family actually moved next door, the percent of the white population saying

they would move out was equal to about half the percent who said they would object. If we make a moderately strong assumption about the continued relationship between these variables, then at present there are about 2 or 3 percent of the white population who would say they would move if an equal status black family moved in next door. The percent who actually *would* move for this reason is even lower, but how much lower we cannot say because the studies of the relation between attitudes and behavior in the housing market usually find the percent of moves attributed to this cause is so low that it cannot be distinguished from sampling error.

In the 1976 Detroit Area Study, white residents were asked a series of question which were most likely interpreted by them as questions about what they would do if they were residents of neighborhoods which were at various levels of threat from ghetto expansion. Respondents were shown a series of cards portraying a neighborhood of 15 houses, each looking exactly the same, arranged in a 3×5 grid with the respondent's house in the middle. The racial composition of the neighborhood was varied by making different cards showing 1, 3, 5, and 8 of the houses painted black. Each white respondents was asked how uncomfortable he or she would feel "with the situation" if they lived in the pictured neighborhood and another black family moved in; if they would move out of the neighborhood if that happened; and, finally, if they would consider moving into a neighborhood with such a racial composition. It was found that as the percent black in the neighborhood goes up, so does the percent of whites who are uncomfortable with the situation, the percent of whites who would move out

7. Norman Bradburn, Seymour Sudman, and Galen Gockel, *Racial Integration in American Neighborhoods* (National Opinion Research Center, 1970); Karl Taeuber and Alma Taeuber, *Negroes in Cities* (Chicago: Aldine, 1965); Brian J. L. Berry, Carole Goodwin, Robert W. Lake, and Katherine Smith, "Attitudes Toward Integration: The Role of Status in Community Response to Racial Change," in The Changing Face of the Suburbs, ed. Barry Schwartz (Chicago: University of Chicago Press, 1976).

of the neighborhood, and the percent of whites who would not consider moving into the neighborhood even if there was a nice, affordable house available. At each level of racial composition the percent who did *not* say they would consider moving in is about the same as the percent uncomfortable, and both percents are higher than the percent who say they would move out.

Why should the percent not moving in be higher than the percent moving out? Those not moving in are reacting not only to the *current* percent black in each neighborhood, but also to what they think the current percent black implies for the *future* of the neighborhood. Thus, even though the amount of ghetto expansion is low, and therefore quite tolerable for those in neighborhoods with a low percent black, those who might move in have to calculate what the present percent black implies for the future of the neighborhood, and so are much more uneasy with the situation than those who are already in the neighborhood.

In sum, if all racial barriers were removed from the housing market, most whites would be in the situation of receiving a small number of black families of equal social status into their neighborhoods. Among white Americans today, 59 percent report that there are no blacks in their neighborhood, 9 percent report blacks in the neighborhood but 4 or more blocks away, 13 percent are 1 to 3 blocks away from black families and only 15 percent live on integrated blocks. In such a "truly open" housing market, the amount of further racial integration which would occur would be upsetting to only a very small minority of the white population.

The studies of neighborhood tipping do not, at first, seem consistent with this observation. What they have shown, however, is that white fears of neighborhood integration stem from a fear of racial engulfment when ghetto expansion is a serious possibility. One of the unfortunate results of the tipping studies is that they have led to the idea of a white preference function for neighborhoods based on the current and anticipated percent black. For most possibilities under a truly open housing market, the data indicate that this preference function is quite flat. It is only when the expansion of the ghetto threatens that whites become alarmed—and most likely even before many blacks have moved into the neighborhood.

Blacks also fear ghetto expansion. The same Detroit Area Study found that 31 percent of the blacks in the SMSA would not be willing to move into an all-black neighborhood. At the other end of the continuum, 62 percent of the blacks in the SMSA were not willing to take the risks involved in being the first to move into an all-white neighborhood. Both of these two extreme poles have particular symbolic meaning beyond the fact that they happen to represent the two ends of the distribution of possible racial mixtures. Between these poles, black housing preferences are not related to the racial mixture of the neighborhood. Almost 100 percent would be willing to move into neighborhoods which are 20, 53, and 73 percent black. When blacks are asked to choose an *optimal* racial mix (usually in a questionnaire emphasizing several different aspects of black-white relations), they usually say "half and half," choosing neighborhoods about 50 percent white, and give race-related reasons for their choice; "it's better to learn how to get along with whites." Other data show, however, that this is a ranking of objects which do not differ in their overall utility vis à vis housing choices. Most blacks are willing to live in any kind of good neighborhood; some are hesitant about moving into a ghetto, and even more are hesitant about block busting.[8]

THE EFFECTS OF REAL AND ANTICIPATED RACIAL CHANGE ON WHITE HOUSING ATTITUDES

The most well-documented and well-replicated finding in research on the effect of interracial housing and neighborhood integration is that white prejudice declines with interracial contact, particularly when the interracial contact occurs in a situation where whites and blacks are of equal social status and are aware that they share similar values.[9] But the accumulated survey data do not all fit this hypothesis. At the aggregate level, areas of the metropolis where racial contact is quite high do not necessarily show the highest levels of racial tolerance. Similarly, as we saw in Figure 1, the recent liberalization of American racial attitudes has not held across all types or domains of racial attitudes equally.

One of the earliest generalizations to arise from American urban research

is that there are "natural areas" of the city where the level of disorganization of daily social life (indicated by such statistics as crime and delinquency rates) is quite high. Whites who fear ghetto expansion are afraid of the increase in real risk to life, limb, and property which results from the increased social disorganization of the ghetto. For a variety of reasons, natural areas of the city which are characterized by higher rates of social disorganization often come to be identified with the lower status members of particular racial and ethnic groups.

White racial attitudes should, therefore, be distinguished into two kinds. First, there are some whites who are aware of the fact that black people live in areas where social disorganization is greater. A rejection of black neighbors is based on a rejection of the social disorganization of ghetto life. The attitude linking race and disorganization is nothing more than an awareness of the general statistical relation between racial composition and life style in various American neighborhoods. Whites who would not choose to live in areas where there is a high percentage of blacks may well be reacting to the social organization which is *usually* characteristic of such neighborhoods and not to the actual presence of black neighbors. Whites who are aware that black neighborhoods are often disorganized, but who do not attribute the disorganization to the race of the inhabitants, cannot be said to be prejudiced. If anything, they are well-informed.

The effect of anticipated racial change can be studied by looking at the areas where blacks are likely to move in. Because of the relation between race and social class in this society, the pressure of black housing demand is the greatest in white

8. This observation is particularly damaging for a direct application of Schelling's models for simulating the effect of housing preferences on patterns of neighborhood change. If black preferences are not well-defined and not accurately represented by a point on a desegregation curve, then the applicability of the model to the *actual* process of neighborhood change breaks down.

9. Pettigrew, "Attitudes on Race and Housing"; Gordon W. Allport, *The Nature of Prejudice* (New York: Addison Wesley, 1954); Arnold Rose, Frank Atelsels and Lawrence McDonald, "Neighborhood Reactions to Isolated Negro Residents: An Alternative to Invasion and Succession," *American Sociological Review* 18 (1953): 497–507.

lower-middle and working class neighborhoods. Many observers have noted that there is substantial segregation by occupation within *both* the black and the white community, and that there has been little tendency for this pattern to change.[10] The amount of occupational segregation *within* either racial community is about the same, and is about half as great as the segregation *between* blacks and whites for any occupational group. The result is that American cities, in general, are segregated along class lines. Overlaid on this pattern is the racial segregation which results from a discriminatory housing market. Residential mixing is a particularly salient threat to whites' status and neighborhood values because blacks *of the same social status* are usually believed to have value characteristics of persons of lower social status. So, even though the blacks who enter a neighborhood are usually of slightly higher social status than the whites who live there,[11] the whites who are already in the neighborhood may react negatively because they are prepared to believe that the style of life and the social honor of attachment to the neighborhood are going to change.

Analysis of several national surveys done between 1972 and 1977 finds that, controlling for region and location of the neighborhood within the urban area, occupational groups do not differ in the likelihood that they live in a neighborhood which is integrated. This finding is similar to Simkus' observation that all white occupational groups are about equally segregated from blacks in similar status levels.[12] But the argument here is that, although white occupational groups are about equally segregated from blacks, the *middle* occupational groups experience the greatest pressure from black housing demand. NORC data show that although white occupational groups do not differ in the likelihood of exposure to integration, they differ substantially in what they believe to be the implications of integration in their neighborhoods. Figure 2 shows that, controlling for size of place, there is a great difference by occupational group in a person's belief that his integrated neighborhood will remain integrated for the next 5 years. The middle occupation groups are much more likely to believe that if their neighborhood becomes integrated, it will tip. Furthermore, this pattern is more pronounced in the central cities of large SMSA's than it is in other locations.

Because of this fear, those in the middle occupation groups are less likely to be willing to grant blacks the legal rights which would allow them to push further into white neighborhoods. Figure 3 shows the pattern in the percent giving liberal or pro-integration responses to the housing referendum and the "push" questions. This reluctance to affirm black rights does not stem from general racism, however, since the responses to the "equal income and education" question show no difference by occupational group. To summarize this point, the effect of a high anticipated black demand for housing in a particular market area is to make the belief more widespread that a neighborhood will tip. This

---

10. Albert A. Simkus, "Residential Segregation by Occupation and Race in Ten Urbanized Areas, 1950–1970," *American Sociological Review* 43 (1978): 81–93.

11. Taeuber and Taeuber, *Negroes in Cities.*

12. National Opinion Research Center Cumulative Codebook for the 1972–1977 General Social Surveys, Chicago 1977; Albert Simkus, "Residential Segregation."

FIGURE 2

OCCUPATIONAL DIFFERENCES IN THE PROPORTION THINKING THAT A NEIGHBORHOOD WITH SOME BLACKS WILL STAY INTEGRATED FOR THE NEXT 5 YEARS

Question Wording: Are there any (Negroes/Blacks) living in this neighborhood now? (IF YES) Do you think this neighborhood will become all (Negro/Black) in the next few years, or will it remain integrated?

LOCATION OF RESPONDENT'S NEIGHBORHOOD	OCCUPATION				
	PROFESSIONAL, MANAGERIAL	CLERICAL, SALES	SKILLED BLUE COLLAR	UNSKILLED BLUE COLLAR	SERVICE
Within Central City of one of the 100 largest SMSA's	.915 (329)	.816 (223)	.800 (115)	.674 (175)	.736 (144)
Suburb of a City	.947 (228)	.926 (136)	.891 (64)	.833 (96)	.938 (48)
Other	.945 (362)	.955 (198)	.923 (168)	.893 (244)	.907 (140)

DATA SOURCE: NORC General Social Surveys for 1972, 1973, 1974, 1975, 1976, 1977 (pooled).

makes the whites who live there less willing to extend further rights to blacks to enable the desegregation of the housing market even though it does not appear to affect the acceptance of small amounts of integration on an individual basis.

If a black presence does threaten neighborhood values and social status, then it is clear that the proc-

FIGURE 3

OCCUPATIONAL DIFFERENCES IN PROPORTION WILLING TO GRANT BLACKS RIGHTS TO PUSH THEIR DEMANDS IN THE HOUSING MARKET (QUESTIONS 2 AND 4 FROM TABLE 1)

Question 2: Negroes should not push themselves where they are not wanted. Proportion "disagree slightly" or "disagree strongly."

REGION OF RESIDENCE	OCCUPATION				
	PROFESSIONAL, MANAGERIAL	CLERICAL, SALES	SKILLED BLUE COLLAR	UNSKILLED BLUE COLLAR	SERVICE
Non-South	.405 (1389)	.277 (1002)	.190 (448)	.248 (644)	.280 (553)
South	.239 (498)	.198 (344)	.111 (244)	.134 (387)	.158 (183)

DATA SOURCE: Pooled 1972, 1973, 1975, 1976, 1977 NORC General Social Surveys.

Question 4: Suppose there is a community-wide vote on the general housing issue. There are two possible laws to vote on. Which law would you vote for? Proportion supporting "a homeowner cannot refuse to sell to someone because of their race or color."

REGION OF RESIDENCE	OCCUPATION				
	PROFESSIONAL, MANAGERIAL	CLERICAL, SALES	SKILLED BLUE COLLAR	UNSKILLED BLUE COLLAR	SERVICE
Non-South	.420 (807)	.404 (547)	.311 (289)	.360 (444)	.429 (347)
South	.236 (309)	.256 (223)	.233 (150)	.201 (234)	.217 (120)

DATA SOURCE: Pooled 1973, 1975, 1976 NORC General Social Surveys.

ess is somewhat more complicated than the stimulus-response imagery which is embodied in current conceptions of the housing market and the process of residential segregation. Residential segregation cannot be understood without also considering the dynamics of neighborhood segregation and change along class as well as racial lines. The status implications of a black neighborhood presence are different for different classes in the white population; the norms of violence which guide community behavior are different for different classes; and the perceived amount of competition for white housing will clearly be different for different classes.

Furthermore, if racial residential segregation subsides, it will be *within* similarly situated economic groups. It is already the case that blacks tend to move into white neighborhoods where the current inhabitants are of approximately equal *objective* social status. Because of the spatial sorting in American cities, it cannot be expected that this pattern will change. When (or if) residential desegregation occurs it will be due to the intermingling of similar social classes in the black and white populations.

THE FUTURE FOR RESEARCH AND FOR HOUSING INTEGRATION

The opinion studies show that white Americans are in the middleground on housing desegregation. They are willing to live with what they perceive to be a reasonable amount of it—a small influx of black neighbors with minimal threat of engulfment by ghetto expansion. Although they will tolerate desegregation, whites resist granting formal recognition to the black rights which are necessary for desegregating all housing markets. The likelihood of change in this profile of American

public opinion depends on continued white experience with desegregated housing, the reestablishment of a social movement for achieving black housing rights—or at least the discouragement of anti-open housing groups—and a reaffirmation by American political and judicial leadership of the goal of integrated neighborhoods.

Within this climate of general opinion, whites and blacks react to their neighborhoods and make the decentralized, individual decisions which produce the collective result of extremely segregated housing patterns in the American landscape. The bulk of the theoretical and empirical analysis in this essay has focused on how those individual decisions are made, with particular emphasis on the role of prejudice relative to the role of other factors which people might consider when reacting to the neighborhoods in a city, and in deciding whether to move into (or out of) one of those neighborhoods.

Housing segregation and race relations are intertwined in a complex way. Except for extreme cases, involving threatened ghetto expansion or location of public housing projects, the role of black and white neighborhood preferences in residential segregation is quite minimal. Most whites have no objection to the level of integration which would occur if their neighborhood were desegregated in what has been described as a reasonable manner. Most black neighborhood preferences are formed independently of the racial composition of the neighborhood except, of course, for the extreme cases of all-white and all-black neighborhoods. An individual black person, although he or she may say it is better to live in a mixed or 50:50 neighborhood when forced to make choices, most likely does not have a well-formed preference for neighborhood racial composition.[13]

The second major finding of this review, and the second charge against the current models of neighborhood change, is that a simple prejudice-flight view of white housing behavior is not a differentiated enough view of what actually happens. When whites respond to an integrated neighborhood they do not respond directly to the percentage black. They respond to the current style of life (or "social organization" or "status honor") in the neighborhood and to what they believe will happen to the style of life in the neighborhood over the next several years. The actual social psychological changes which occur with an increasing percent black are more complicated than the simple assertion that people become more or less prejudiced. The actual relation between black inmigration and a white person's decision to move is different from what might be expected from some simple formulations of the white flight hypothesis. The factors which contribute to the shared neighborhood perception that "it is time to leave" ought to be studied carefully, from a perspective which takes account of the important role of neighborhood dynamics in forming public opinion.

The third major finding of this review is that there is a great deal of heterogeneity between neighborhoods of different class levels in the inhabitants' interpretations of and

13. Paul Courant and John Yinger, "On Models of Racial Prejudice and Residential Structure," *Journal of Urban Economics* 4 (1977): 272–91 states that: "Surveys reveal that most whites prefer not to live with blacks and that a majority of blacks prefer to live in integrated neighborhoods." The data summarized in this essay show that this statement is wrong on several counts.

perceived implications of black inmigration. The level of black demand for housing, the status implications of black inmigration, and the receptivity to certain principles of integration are quite different for neighborhoods of different class levels. Furthermore, there is heterogeneity in neighborhood reactions, which depends on the location of the neighborhood in the metropolitan area and whether the neighborhood is in the North or the South. Each of these sources of heterogeneity should be included in models of the housing process which are used for policy purposes.

If there are more than enough receptive whites available to desegregate the society fully, if whites do not become more prejudiced by exposure to integration, and if whites do not leave integrated neighborhoods because they are prejudiced, then why is the amount of segregation so high and why are the prospects for change so slim?

One reason for continued segregation is that neighborhood integration often does not come about in a "reasonable" way. There are only certain areas of the city where black housing demand is great. This is partly because of the class-based differentiation of the housing market—blacks, by and large, are moving into working class and middle class neighborhoods. Within the class-based restriction of potential housing areas, black demand is further bottlenecked by racial discrimination. It is typically the case that of the appropriate neighborhoods for black integration, the ones which actually receive the inmigration are the neighborhoods adjacent to the ghetto. This creates the conditions for ghetto expansion and substantiates the white fears of a decline in neighborhood quality and housing value.

Because the typical pattern of neighborhood is not a "reasonable" one, the second factor which keeps whites from buying into or staying in integrated areas is their uncertainty about what will happen to them if they live in an area where there are a few black families. Housing decisions are difficult to police and desegregation will occur when individuals refuse to discriminate. But when there is uncertainty about the goodness of the outcome, it is unlikely that individuals will rigorously adopt and adhere to this personal moral code. In this kind of situation, small amounts of information about the outcome of neighborhood policies which insure that the outcome will be positive can have a great deal of impact. Thus, neighborhood realtors have been able to influence the process of neighborhood change by diffusing information about the housing market. On the other hand, community groups have been able, in various ways, to insure against negative results and thereby stabilize neighborhood change and avoid tipping in areas where the black demand is high enough that this is a possibility. One of the most recent in this series of experiments is the "housing value insurance" program instituted in a suburb of Chicago which guarantees that white property will not suffer from integration.

It is clear that, because of the nature of the anxieties about neighborhood integration, buyers will not act individually to promote integration. If the notion that the housing market should consist of individual decisions persists, then it is clear that progress will be slow for integration and will only be fitfully achieved, if at all in an open market situation. The hope for change in the pattern of personal decisions in the housing market depends on: diffusing accurate information about the market in American neighborhoods; taking steps ("concerted action" in the economists' terminology) to insure that neighborhoods will not be damaged by desegregation; and an affirmative, moral leadership at the national level supporting the means and ends of neighborhood integration.

ANNALS, AAPSS, 441, Jan. 1979

Racial and Ethnic Residential Segregation in Boston 1830–1970

By NATHAN KANTROWITZ

ABSTRACT: Residential segregation in Boston between European ethnic populations has declined little during the 20th century. Racial segregation rose during the 19th and early 20th century, but has remained stable since about 1940, prior to the expansion of the city's Negro population. These conclusions indicate that racial segregation is but an extension of the pattern of ethnic separation, especially since Asian and Latin ethnics show similar patterns in the contemporary city. Moreover, segregation levels are only slightly lower in the 1970 SMSA suburban ring than they are in the central city. We suggest that this demographic record is relevant to issues of Boston's public school desegregation controversy.

Nathan Kantrowitz is Professor of Sociology, Kent State University. He has been employed at Columbia and Fordham Universities, as well as with State Government in Illinois and New York.

RESIDENTIAL segregation between Negroes and whites, or rich and poor, in cities of the United States has always been acknowledged as a pervasive fact of urban life. This recognition has not always been accorded the European ethnics; for example, that Irish and Italian Catholic populations maintained some voluntary self-segregation from each other. Generally, sociologists after World War II tended to regard residential segregation between European ethnics as no longer of importance; more recently, however, their segregation has been recognized.[1] As a textbook example, Gist and Fava's 1974 edition mentions them in a separate section entitled "Race and Ethnicity" which was not present in the 1964 edition.[2] An account of this disappearance and rediscovery of ethnic segregation is the subject of research in progress, but it is sufficient to say that there is little in the way of historical research into the relationship of racial and ethnic segregation.

Although this study includes but one city, with special ecological qualities,[3] comparative studies which include Boston indicate its segregation patterns are not unique.[4] The conclusion drawn here is that Negro-white segregation is but one aspect of Boston's pervasive ethnic and racial residential segregation. This conclusion is reached by way of the following points. Historically, it is argued that European interethnic segregation has declined little in Boston City, while in the contemporary metropolis the 1970 census reveals only slightly lower averages as we go from the central city to the ring of the Boston Standard Metropolitan Statistical Area (SMSA). Moreover, contemporary European, Latin, and Asian ethnics all show great similarities in their segregation, which in many cases are as high as the black-white levels. This leads us, finally, to infer that while racial segregation is generally higher than interethnic segregation, it is hardly a singular or solely a modern phenomenon. This conclusion supports a similar one made for New York,[5] but has greater historical depth.[6]

There are three steps to the argument. The first will put the contemporary city in historical perspective, with a summary of the record of racial and ethnic segregation levels since 1830. After this a more detailed focus on the 20th century

1. Nathan Kantrowitz, *Ethnic and Racial Segregation in the New York Metropolis: Residential Patterns Among White Ethnic Groups, Blacks, and Puerto Ricans.* (New York: Praeger, 1973), chaps. 1 and 2.

2. Noel, P. Gist and Sylvia F. Fava, *Urban Society.* (New York: Thomas Y. Crowell, 1974), pp. 186–187.

3. Walter Firey, *Land Use in Central Boston,* (Cambridge, MA: Harvard University Press, 1947).

4. Stanley Lieberson, *Ethnic Patterns in American Cities.* (New York: Free Press, 1963); Karl E. Taeuber and Alma F. Taeuber, *Negroes in Cities: Residential Segregation and Neighborhood Change.* (Chicago, Aldine Press, 1965); Sharon E. Bleda, "Bases of Ethnic Residential Segregation: Recent Patterns in American Metropolitan Areas," (Paper presented at the annual meeting, American Sociological Association, San Francisco, 1975); Avery M. Guest and J. A. Weed, "Ethnic Residential Segregation: Patterns of Change," *American Journal of Sociology* 81: 1088–1111.

5. Kantrowitz, *Ethnic and Racial Segregation.*

6. For related studies, see Lieberson, *Ethnic Patterns in American Cities*; Karl E. Taeuber and Alma F. Taeuber, "The Negro as an Immigrant Group: Recent trends in Racial and Ethnic Segregation in Chicago," *American Journal of Sociology* 69 (1964):374–382; Eugene S. Uyeki, "Ethnic and Race Segregation, Cleveland 1910–1970," (Paper presented at the annual meeting, Population Association of America, Montreal, 1976).

city is provided, to argue that even were Negroes another white ethnic group suffering no discrimination, they would still be highly segregated. Finally it will be shown that different parts of the metropolis are similar; on average, the SMSA suburban ring's ethnic and racial segregation levels are not drastically lower than those of the central city.

There are three basic problems of evidence: the quality of the census enumerations themselves, the limitations of our basic segregation measurement index, and the crazy-quilt of geographical areas such as city wards or census tracts.[7]

Our data are the racial and ethnic enumerations of the U.S. decennial census: race has always been a socially defined attribute, in which the interviewer (and more recently the respondent) made a personal judgment; ethnicity was defined by the respondent's place of birth until the 1960 and 1970 censuses when it became redefined as "foreign stock" (the place of birth of respondent or parents). Given what we know of the errors of enumeration in contemporary censuses on a national level, it is the better part of valor to assume that any 19th or 20th century census of Boston failed to count at least 5 to 10 percent of any racial or ethnic population, an error which probably varies by population group and by city ward or census tract.

The U.S. Census Bureau actually does an outstanding job of both counting people and self-criticism. The inescapable fact is that enumerating great urban warrens, especially their slums, is incredibly difficult and prone to error. On occasion, administration of the effort may simply collapse, which is

what seems to have happened in the Census of 1960 in parts of Chicago.[8] It is only conjecture, but the 19th century and early 20th century censuses seem certainly no better, at the same time only marginally worse. Neither complex computer technology nor esoteric statistical methodology overcome these basic flaws; only common sense helps.

The basic measure of segregation utilized here is the one most commonly used by sociologists, the Index of Dissimilarity, a variant of Lorenz Curve analysis long used by economists. It is as good as any other, and better than some. As with any index, such as the Bureau of Labor Statistics Consumer Price Index, it has no inherent validity but is useful primarily for comparative purposes. It varies from 0 to 100, but its numerical values are only approximation (in technical terms, it is at best an ordinal scale). My own judgment of how researchers really interpret the scale is that indexes below 30 are considered "low," those over 70 as "high," with changes of 5 points or less considered minor.[9] Since there is only

7. A more detailed explanation of these problems is in Kantrowitz, *Ethnic and Racial Segregation*, chap. 2.

8. U.S. Bureau of the Census, U.S. Censuses of Population and Housing: 1960. *Census Tracts*. Final Report PHC(1)-26. Chicago, Illinois, Standard Metropolitan Statistical Area. (Washington, DC: USGPO, 1962), 18.

9. Further discussions are in Hubert M. Blalock, Jr., *Toward A Theory of Minority-Group Relations* (New York: John Wiley, 1967); and in Kantrowitz, *Ethnic and Racial Segregation*. Technical material will be found in many places, for example, Taeuber and Taeuber, *Negroes in Cities*; Karl E. Taeuber and Alma F. Taeuber, "A Practitioner's Perspective on the Index of Dissimilarity," *American Sociological Review* 41 (1976):884–89; Charles F. Cortese, R. Frank Falk, and Jack Cohen, "Further Consideration on the Methodological Analysis of Segregation Indices," *American Sociological Review* 41 (1976):630–637; Jack K. Cohen, R. Frank Falk, and Charles F. Cortese, "Reply to Taeuber and Taeuber," *American Sociological Review* 41 (1976):889–93.

limited consensus among sociologists on its use, so assumptions and definitions should be made explicit.

AN OVERVIEW OF RACIAL AND ETHNIC SEGREGATION IN BOSTON CITY, 1830–1970

During the 140 years for which some record of segregation exists, Boston City's population growth has been similar to that of the nation's other larger cities. The central city has declined in population since the high of 801,444 in 1950; also, it has been displaced by the SMSA as the most meaningful demographic unit. The surrounding area has grown to the extent that the Boston SMSA's 2,899,000 population in 1970 makes it the 8th largest in the nation. However, the central city contains only 22.1 percent of its population, one of the lowest such percentages for the United States.[10]

A focus on the city itself is still warranted for several reasons; it is still a social unit in such fields as political control and education. Moreover, we can use existing data to trace the demographic history of segregation, back to 1830, in order to comprehend the contemporary SMSA.

The percentage of foreign born within Boston peaked prior to the Civil War; since then it has declined to one-third at the beginning of the 20th century, and to 13.1 percent in 1970. This decline in the percentage of foreign born does not necessarily mean, however, the elimination of European heritage; "Italian" or "Irish" Bostonians exist, although they may be a far different social group than either their forebears or

their kin in Italy or Ireland today. Moreover, the "foreign stock" in 1970 still constituted 37.0 percent of the city's population and, together with the 16.3 percent Negro, 1.8 percent "other nonwhite," and 1.1 percent Puerto Rican, constituted a majority of the city's population.[11]

Numerically, the Negro population of the city has differed from the European ethnic because it was comparatively small until the period after World War II. It grew largely by natural increase from 1900–1940, and by migration since 1940. Recently, a combination of white suburbanization and black migration into the central city (plus of course, the natural increase of births over deaths among inner city blacks), has raised the Boston black population to 16.3 percent as of 1970. This is nevertheless small in comparison with other cities, as for example, Chicago's 32.7 percent.

This relatively small size and recent growth of the black population should be kept in mind as we view the segregation indexes of Figure 1. This Figure indicates that white-black segregation rose during the century prior to 1940 (before the black population expanded greatly), and has stabilized since.

Before the Civil War black-white segregation rose sharply: from 44.4 in 1830, to 52.4 in 1840, to 59.1 in 1850. Schnore and Knights,[12] who compiled this data, infer (errone-

10. U.S. Bureau of the Census, *Statistical Abstract of the United States: 1974* (Washington, DC: USGPO, 1974).

11. Third and subsequent generation ethnicity is not tabulated by the census. Our own conclusion, based on work in progress, is that they constitute at least another 20 percent of the city's population.

12. Leo F. Schnore and P. R. Knights, "Residence and Social Structure: Boston in the Ante-Bellum Period," in *Nineteenth Century Cities: Essays in the New Urban History*, Ed. Stephan Thernstrom and Richard Sennet, New Haven: Yale University Press, 1969), p. 252.

FIGURE 1.
RACIAL SEGREGATION[1], BOSTON CITY, 1830–1970.

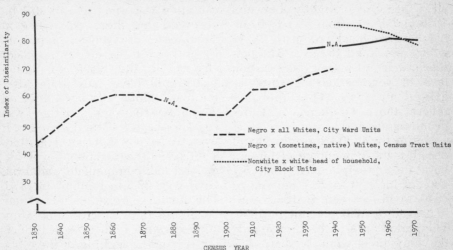

SOURCES: U.S. Bureau of Census (Washington, D.C.: USGPO. *The Eighth Census of the United States, 1860: Population*, 1864; Ninth Census-Volume I, *The Statistics of the Population of the United States*, 1872; *Statistics of the Population of the United States at the Tenth Census (June 1, 1880)*, 1883; *Compendium of the Tenth Census, Part I*, 1883; *Report on Population of the United States at the Eleventh Census: 1890, Part I*, 1895; Census Reports, Volume I, *Twelfth Census of the United States, Population, Part I*, 1902; *Thirteenth Census of the United States, Volume II, Population*, 1913; *Fourteenth Census of the United States, Volume III, Population*, 1922; *Fifteenth Census of the United States: 1930, Population, Volume III, Part I*, 1932; *Sixteenth Census of the United States: 1940, Population*, Volume II, Part 3, 1943; U.S. Census of Population: 1950, Volume II, *Characteristics of the Population*, Part 21, Massachusetts, 1952; U.S. Census of Population and Housing, *Census Tracts*. Final Report PHC(1). Boston, Mass. Standard Metropolitan Area, 1952; U.S. Censuses of Population and Housing: 1960. *Census Tracts*. Final Report PHC(1)-18. Boston, Mass. Standard Metropolitan Statistical Area, 1962; Census of Population: 1970. Vol. 1, *Characteristics of the Population*, Part 23, Massachusetts, 1973. Also: Annemette Sorensen, K. E. Taeuber, and J. Hollingsworth, Jr., "Indexes of Residential Segregation for 109 Cities in the United States, 1940 to 1970", *Sociological Focus*, 8 (April 1975), 125–42; Leo Schnore and P. R. Knights, "Residence and Social Structure," *Sociological Focus*, p. 247–257.

[1] With city wards as the basic geographic units, segregation indexes for each year are listed in the order of Negroes × all whites/Negroes × native whites: 1830, 44.4/n.a.; 1840, 52.4/n.a.; 1850, 59.1/51.2; 1855, n.a./51.2; 1860, 62.3/n.a.; 1870, 62/62; 1880, n.a./50.6; 1890, 56/57; 1900, 56/57; 1910, 63/64.1; 1920, 65/65.3; 1930; 68/68; 1940; 73/73.

With census tracts as the basic geographic units, segregation indexes for each year for Negroes × native whites are 1930, 77.9; 1950, 80.1; for Negroes × all whites, 1960, 82; 1970, 81.

With city blocks as the basic geographic units, segregation indexes for each year for nonwhite × white heads of household are 1940, 86.3; 1950, 86.5; 1960, 83.9; 1970, 79.9. In 1970, Negro × white head of household index was 84.3.

ously, we think) from this an intensification of racial segregation only during the antebellum period. However, other data assembled by Lieberson support the conclusion that much of this rise probably was the result of the foreign born influx.[13] For example, if differentiation is made between all whites and native

13. Lieberson, *Ethnic Patterns in American Cities*, p. 78.

born whites, it can be seen that while the segregation between blacks and all whites rose slightly between 1850 and 1860, (from 59.1 to 62.3), that between blacks and native born whites remained stable at 51.2, approximately the same segregation level of Negroes and all whites as existed in 1840. This probably reflects the consequence of European migration.

During the 1830's and subsequent decades, the percentage of foreign born rose precipitously, from 5.7 percent in 1830 to 23.7 percent in 1840, to 45.7 percent in 1850, until it peaked at 53.0 percent in 1855. The period prior to the Civil War is the only time when a sharp differentiation of foreign born and native born whites may be justified; by the time of the Civil War, the second generation would have expanded rapidly, and the clear distinction between foreign and native born would be obscured by the importance of native born children of migrants. Schnore and Knights', and Lieberson's data indicate that the foreign born were highly segregated from the black population. For example, the highest racial levels were German-Negro segregation at 67.9 in 1850 and 73.1 in 1855. (Much higher than the black-native white levels of those years just cited above.) In comparison, German-Irish segregation was relatively low, at 36.1 in 1850, and 44.7 in 1855.[14]

In summary, for 1830–1860 it is hypothesized that the influx of European migrants coincided with an overall rise in residential segregation, and perhaps were part of its causes; and as one consequence, the

black population became even more segregated. Whether this analysis of causation is correct, it can still be observed that there was a rise in racial segregation during this period. There seem to have been no major changes in the black population that would have caused the rise: the total number of blacks hovered around two thousand, so if there was any appreciable natural increase, it was eroded by net out-migration. The racial segregation level remained stable immediately after the Civil War: 62.3 in 1860; 62 in 1870. The drop in segregation in 1890 may be an accident of city annexation and redrawn ward boundaries affecting the index; nothing in the city's social history indicates less discrimination against the population.[15] After 1900, as demonstrated in Figure 1, black-white segregation increased steadily until the end of World War II, after which it stabilized, and even decreased slightly thereafter.

It is worthwhile to emphasize that neither stability nor increase in the Negro population seems to have caused change in segregation levels. Each decade from the Civil War to 1900 saw about a 50 percent increase in Boston's Negro population, while for 1900 to 1940, each decade saw only a 20 percent increase. In effect, a century's rapid then slow rate of increase in the Negro population was not paralleled by changes

---

14. J. R. Wilkie, "Racial and Ethnic Segregation in Boston, 1850," manuscript, 1975. Table 1 shows different levels, but a similar pattern. The difference stems from a different definition of the population tabulated.

15. Perhaps the fact that the number of city wards increased from 12 in 1850 and 1860, to 16 in 1870, to 25 in 1880 (the number of wards remained at this approximate number at least until World War II) may have helped cause this fluctuation. We know of no historical set of actual maps of either ward boundary changes or of block-by-block locations of the black population. We have assumed that each census year's ward (and census tract and city block) boundaries encompasses a separate ecological reality.

in segregation levels: this suggests no causal relationship.

In considering the 20th century, we have separated the period prior to World War II (to 1940) from the period of 1950 and after. This dichotomy does not give us two homogeneous categories in every respect, but it does provide a division which is related to the rate of increase in Boston's black population. During 1900–1940, each decade saw the black population increase by about one-fifth, something which could reflect natural increase with little migration. It appears likely from the histories of this period that this is what actually happened. The second period, from 1940, saw a dramatic shift in the rate of increase in the black population: each of the decades ending in 1950, 1960, and 1970 saw an increase of about two-thirds, the result of a large net inmigration. White-Negro segregation stabilized during this period, or, if anything, possibly decreased after 1940, during this period of large black increase.

Actually, it could be argued that racial segregation has remained fairly stable since the depression of the 1930's, and that some of the observed rise is an artifact of measurement; that is, the transition from indexes calculated from larger city wards to those calculated from smaller census tracts. Generally, the larger the area unit used, the lower the index number. How, for instance, to judge the fact that the 1920 index of 65.3 rises to 77.9 in 1930; how much is a "real" rise, how much the consequence of the switch from city ward to census tract statistics? Fortunately it is possible to gauge empirically some part of this by calculating the same 1930 segregation indexes both by wards and by census tracts. Segregation of Negro from native born whites is 68 when calculated by wards, and 77.9 by census tracts.

It is reasonable to consider this difference of 10 points as a general rule of thumb;[16] it is then possible to go back to 1910, add ten points to the segregation levels, and find stable levels, with the 1910 64.1 counted as 74.1, 1920 65.3 counted as 75.3, then to (by census tracts) 1930 and 77.9, 1950 and 80.1. In 1950 another complication occurs with the slight rise associated with

16. The limited empirical evidence which is available indicates that our splice of Boston's ten point difference between indexes calculated by census tracts and those calculated by city wards is fair. Lieberson calculated indexes of segregation between blacks and native whites for nine other cities in 1930 (p. 122) which provides some basis for judgment. Although Lieberson was concerned with the problem of changing areal units, he, like many researchers who have studied Chicago, was content to group that city's hundreds of census tracts into 75 community areas as a matter of convenience in calculation. He calculated indexes for the remaining eight cities by census tracts; of these, the Census Bureau published statistics by groupings of census tracts (which they labeled "statistical areas") in two cities. Indexes for 1930 between blacks and native whites shown as—calculated by census tracts/calculated by "statistical areas"—are 85.0/80 for Cleveland, 82.1/76 for St. Louis. These small differences could be attributed to the fact that the "statistical areas" are combinations of census tracts. However, the remaining six cities for which Lieberson used census tracts, had city ward data published, and these can be shown as, calculated by census tracts/calculated by city wards; Buffalo 80.5/81, Cincinnati 72.8/66, Columbus 62.8/59, Philadelphia 63.4/52, Pittsburgh 61.4/53, Syracuse 86.7/82. We think this evidence suggests Boston's ten point difference is a reasonable rule of thumb.

An additional fragment of evidence is available from the 1940 census. Here, Taeuber and Taeuber, *Negroes in Cities*, p. 39 shows an index of 86.3 for nonwhite versus white heads of household by city blocks. In comparison, the index for the black-white population by city wards was 73.0, a difference of 13.3 points.

the use of city blocks. But for this period there are calculations both by city blocks and by census tracts shown in Figure 1. A more conservative view dates stability from World War II. For this most recent period it is clear, whether census tracts or city blocks are used, that racial segregation levels have been relatively stable since 1940, while the black population has increased considerably.

ETHNIC AND RACIAL SEGREGATION IN THE 20TH CENTURY CITY

Has there been a decline in interethnic segregation during the 20th century, and does this throw any light on racial segregation? Table 1 indicates that neither interethnic nor racial segregation has declined, and presents reasonable evidence from which to conclude that racial segregation may be reasonably considered as quite similar to the ethnic rather than as a separate phenomena.

Since 1930 calculations are available from census tracts, providing a more precise demographic reflection of the social reality that Irish, Italians, Russians, or Cubans are different kinds of people. The segregation of blacks from all European ethnics remained relatively stable between 1930 (at 79.9 or 81.4) and 1970 at 85. These racial levels vary little when considered separately for old and new immigrant groups. When European ethnics are considered among themselves, little change can be seen between the 1970, 55 and the 1930, 54.2 or 52.7. Among the Europeans it can be seen that the old vs. old levels are lower than the other regional comparisons,

a division which is stable over time.[17]

Moreover, this series can be extended back to 1910, or to 1880, to encompass indexes calculated by census tracts, if additional assumptions are made. The approximate 10 points mentioned in relationship to Figure 1's splice between indexes calculated by census tracts and city wards, allows the conclusion that there has been a slight rise in the segregation of Negroes from ethnics between 1910, 1920, and 1930, an imputed 1910 value of 75.1 from the 65.1 calculated, and an imputed 1920, 75.8 from the calculated 65.8 for Negroes versus all European ethnics. Note also there was a slight rise from 1880 to 1910. All in all, there appears to have been a slight rise in the segregation of the Negro population from European ethnics from the end of the 19th century, and then another slight rise after the first World War to the beginning

17. Parenthetically, our data sometimes point to unexplained areas of social history and mobility. For example, the 1930 census tabulated some ethnicities which maintained a separatism from the 10 we have relied on for our analysis. Examples of average segregation from European ethnics are 48 for Armenians, 68 for Syrians, 74 for Lithuanians. Who were these people, and what became of them? We guess they are a few among many ethnics whose social cohesion is expressed both in residential segregation and social mobility. An examination of a number of these groups might tell us much about social mobility. Some suggestive information along these lines exists: for example, *Five Ethnic Groups in Boston: Blacks, Irish, Italians, Greeks, and Puerto Ricans*, ed. Charles M. Sullivan et al. (Boston: Action for Boston Community Development, Inc., and United Community Services of Metropolitan Boston, 1972) pp. 148–56. Unfortunately this is a small and truncated sample of central city Greeks and excludes what I suspect is a vigorous, wealthy, and segregated suburban population.

of the depression of the 1930's, followed by stability.

If one does not wish to engage in the additional assumptions necessary to go back to the end of the 19th century, the heart of the argument still holds. That is, any rise in segregation levels by race versus ethnicity occurred long before the Negro population of Boston began to increase rapidly after World War II. Similarly, it is argued that the European interethnic segregation levels have remained stable since 1930, (or since 1880, if 10 points are added to the indexes calculated by city ward to make them equivalent to the tract index calculations.

Given such stable time series it seems reasonable to raise the question, what is unique about racial as compared with ethnic segregation? Obviously, it is its higher level; in 1970 the European interethnic average was 55, a good deal lower than the 85 between Negroes and European ethnics. But if the Negro population were another white ethnic group, and suffered no racial discrimination, their segregation levels from other white ethnics would be at least 55, the current white average.

Some basis for this can be found in a consideration of selected ethnic groups in 1970: Eire, a Roman Catholic northern European group; Italy, a southern European Roman Catholic group; USSR, basically slavic Jews; and Sweden, a Protestant Northern European group. It is clear that each of these groups maintains an appreciable level of segregation from other groups, ranging from a figure of 50 for the Irish or the Swedes, to 53 for the USSR slavic Jews, to 61 for the Italians. Some are higher than these averages, some lower, but the point is that the

claimed minimum level of 55 is reasonable.

Further evidence of this is provided in Table 2, where individual segregation index numbers are shown. It is important to note, in passing, the stability between 1960 and 1970 before focusing on 1970. Also notable is that the 1970 overall segregation figure of blacks from whites of 81 (footnote b) shows considerable variation for individual ethnics—from 79 with United Kingdom, Germany or USSR, to 94 with Hungary. The very low level of 59 with Puerto Ricans possibly stems from the appreciable minority of Negro Puerto Ricans,[18] as well as the recent large scale migration of both Negroes and Puerto Ricans.

But of primary concern here is the segregation between similar groups, for example, a group of primarily Roman Catholic white populations. Here the 51 between Ireland and Italy is a benchmark for the durability of separatism: for nearly half a century after the end of the large scale migration from Europe ended, two white Roman Catholic populations would need to move 51 percent of their population to achieve exact integration. It should not be surprising then that the Irish are highly segregated from the Latins: Mexicans (83), Cubans (70), and Puerto Ricans (79); we find this phenomenon repeated with the Italian segregation from the Mexicans (89), Cubans (80), and Puerto Ricans (85). To some extent these populations are similar in race and religious heritage, but no matter what

18. Nathan Kantrowitz, *Negro and Puerto Rican Populations of New York City in the Twentieth Century* (New York: American Geographical Society, 1969).

TABLE 1

UNWEIGHTED AVERAGES OF INDEXES OF SEGREGATION BY RACE AND EUROPEAN ETHNICITY[a]:
1880, 1910, 1920 (BY CITY WARDS); 1930–1970 (BY CENSUS TRACTS), BOSTON CITY[b]

POPULATIONS COMPARED	1970 AVERAGE	1960 AVERAGE	1950 AVERAGE	1930 FOREIGN BORN AVERAGE	NWFMP AVERAGE	1920 AVERAGE	1910 AVERAGE	1880 AVERAGE
Negro to European Ethnics[c]								
Negro vs. All	85	80	81.5	79.9	81.4	65.8	65.1	56.7
Negro vs. Old	84	82	80.4	78.6	79.8	65.5	62.1	53.3
Negro vs. New	85	78	82.7	81.2	83.1	66.3	69.6	63.6
Inter Ethnic[c]								
All	55	51	50.6	54.2	52.7	43.0	46.2	45.2
Old vs. Old	41	35	28.5	29.8	23.9	27.2	27.0	28.0
New vs. New	62	55	61.5	61.2	64.4	44.2	52.2	40.3
Old vs. New	55	55	55.0	61.2	59.5	52.5	56.7	60.3

SOURCES: U.S. Bureau of the Census, 1972, 1962; Lieberson, 1963: 28–29, 57, 79, 84.

[a] Foreign Stock in 1960 and 1970, Foreign Born Whites in all other years (except where in 1930, NWFMP = Native Whites of Foreign or Mixed Parentage). See text for definition of "old" and "new" distinctions.

[b] Census tract grouped because of boundary changes for 1930 and 1950 only. Otherwise no groupings for census tracts in 1960 and 1970, or wards in 1880, 1910, or 1920.

[c] Statistics of Norway in 1970 not in published volume. So our data is taken from tabulation from Fourth Count File A computer tapes. See Table 9 for index numbers. Excluding those foreign stock which have under 1,000 enumerated populations: Norway, Czechoslovakia, and Hungary in 1970, and Czechoslovakia and Hungary in 1960 results in slightly lower averages (which can be calculated from Table 9). The 1970 Norway × Negro uses Native Born Nonwhites for Negro population.

reasons one posits, race could not be the crucial one.

One may turn to segregation between small populations of Roman Catholic Latins themselves; the segregation of Mexicans from Cubans is 80, from Puerto Ricans is 86, and that of Cubans from Puerto Ricans is 79. Finally, that between the small populations of Chinese and Japanese foreign stock is 72.

The conclusion is simple: black-white segregation is hardly a unique phenomenon, although it differs from the interethnic in degree. If blacks were white, and thus were not subject to racial discrimination, but perhaps had some large recent migration volume, and were possibly burdened by some disadvantages in language or education, it could hardly be argued that the figure would be lower than the 55 average level among the Europeans

themselves. Blacks *are*, however, subject to discrimination, a fact obvious to any American. What the figure might be, in the absence of discrimination, can only be guessed. Some feel it could be as high as the 72 between Japanese and Chinese, or the 86 between Mexicans and Puerto Ricans.

THE 1970 BOSTON SMSA: CENTRAL CITY AND SUBURBAN RING

Some territorial separatism seems a normal and tenacious fact of urban life for most of the people of the inner city. But the city is old and cramped, and by 1970 encompassed but 22.1 percent of the SMSA's people. (Table 3)

Generally, there is litle difference between the segregation characteristics of the central city and the SMSA ring. As a preface, it can be noted

TABLE 2

INDEXES[a] OF SEGREGATION BETWEEN SELECTED ETHNICITIES AND RACE, BOSTON CITY, 1960 (ABOVE DIAGONAL), 1970 (BELOW DIAGONAL)

Ethnicity and Race	United Kingdom	Ireland (Eire)	Norway	Sweden	Germany	Poland	Czecho-slovakia	Austria	Hungary	USSR	Italy	Mexico	Cuba	Puerto Rican	Negro	Other Races
European Foreign Stock																
United Kingdom	—	26	38	26	28	41	50	44	51	59	51	X	X	80	81	58
Ireland (Eire)	28	—	44	38	39	48	60	59	65	68	52	X	X	82	86	69
Norway	50	48	—	37	39	54	56	57	64	69	56	X	X	83	83	67
Sweden	38	42	49	—	33	51	54	50	56	65	55	X	X	83	83	60
Germany	29	36	47	43	—	46	53	47	52	59	56	X	X	79	79	61
Poland	39	45	55	46	43	—	56	34	52	38	57	X	X	87	81	69
Czechoslovakia	68	74	69	67	60	74	—	56	52	65	70	X	X	81	84	70
Austria	42	46	55	44	44	43	61	—	46	32	66	X	X	87	82	68
Hungary	68	73	67	61	66	67	72	61	—	53	76	X	X	86	84	68
USSR	48	56	57	47	47	42	69	40	60	—	74	X	X	90	81	74
Italy	47	51	61	60	54	55	82	59	81	63	—	X	X	88	88	76
Western Hemisphere Foreign Stock																
Mexico	80	83	84	87	80	84	71	80	85	78	89	—	X	X	X	X
Cuba	67	70	76	70	69	71	72	67	78	72	80	80	—	X	X	X
Other																
Puerto Rican Birth or Parentage	75	79	X	81	75	80	89	77	93	81	85	86	79	—	68	73
Negro[b]	79	84	91	85	79	80	93	80	94	79	88	93	82	59	—	71
Other Races (Oriental)	X	X	X	X	X	X	X	X	X	X	X	X	X	X	X	—

SOURCE: U.S. Bureau of the Census, 1962, 1972; 1970 Norwegian statistics not published, so all Norwegian indexes calculated from Computer Tape Fourth Count File A, with Native Born Nonwhites × Norway used for Negro × Norway.
[a] Averages calculated in preceding tables from worksheets carried out to two additional digits past decimal point, so any averages calculated from present table may differ slightly.
[b] Index of Negro × All Whites equals 82 in 1960, 81 in 1970.
X Data not available.

TABLE 3

UNWEIGHTED AVERAGES OF INDEXES OF SEGREGATION BY RACE AND ETHNICITY (FOREIGN STOCK),
TOTAL BOSTON STANDARD METROPOLITAN STATISTICAL AREA,
CENTRAL CITY AND SMSA RING, 1970

POPULATIONS COMPARED	TOTAL SMSA AVERAGE	CENTRAL CITY ONLY AVERAGE	SMSA SUBURBAN RING ONLY AVERAGE
European Inter-Ethnic[a]			
All	63	65	62
Old vs. Old	55	58	54
New vs. New	67	69	66
Old vs. New	63	65	63
China vs. European Ethnic[b]			
All	76	77	73
Old	76	76	72
New	76	78	73
Japan vs. European Ethnic[b]			
All	79	76	80
Old	77	75	78
New	80	77	81
Mexico vs. European Ethnic[b]			
All	82	82	81
Old	80	82	80
New	83	83	83
Cuba vs. European Ethnic[b]			
All	79	74	78
Old	79	73	79
New	79	74	77
Native Born Nonwhites vs. European[b] Ethnic			
All	87	86	75
Old	87	87	74
New	87	85	76

SOURCE: Table 4, 6, 1970 Census, Fourth Count File A: Population.
[a] (Number of Comparisons) among European Interethnics are All vs. All (210), Old vs. Old (36), New vs. New (66), Old vs. New (108).
[b] (Number of Comparisons) vs. European Ethnics are vs. All (21), vs. New (9), vs. Old (12).

that, as with the overall population, the various European foreign stocks are predominantly located in the SMSA ring. Only the Cubans (61.8 percent), Chinese (57.9 percent) and native born nonwhites are still based in the central city. Finally, the various foreign stocks are overwhelmingly native born, except for the Orientals and Latins.

Viewing European interethnic segregation as a baseline reveals some interesting patterns. The higher averages shown here, when compared with Table 1, are a function of a larger variety of ethnic populations which have higher segregation levels. Since the main concern is a comparison between central city and suburban ring, this, of course, causes no problem.

The European interethnic averages show little difference between central city (65) and the suburban ring (62), a fact which remains essentially the same when the "old" and "new" ethnic groups are considered separately.

Just as the SMSA ring's average is slightly lower than that for the city, so it is true for the Chinese and the Europeans in the central city (77) as compared with the ring (73), and the Mexicans in the central city (82) compared to the ring (81). There is slight movement in the opposite direction with the Japanese and the Cubans. In fact, the only group with a discernable lessening of segregation from the Europeans is the black population, where the suburban ring at 75 is much lower than the central city at 86.[19] Given the stability of all other groups compared to the Europeans, it seems that those Negroes who live in the SMSA ring are less segregated than those in the central city. This may be only an accident of land development or the vagaries of our index number. On the other hand, it might indicate greater racial tolerance and lessened discrimination.

Two groups go counter to the general decline between the central city and ring, the Japanese and the Cubans. For each, out of 21 possible comparisons with individual European ethnic groups, the Japanese showed increased segregation in 16, the Cubans in 19. For example, comparing Japanese with the United Kingdom, the segregation index for the city itself was 70, while that for the SMSA ring was 10 points higher. Possibly the Japanese and the Cubans are developing even more distinct territorial separateness as they suburbanize. With the limited demographic data at hand, however, this can only be a guess.

19. This is segregation of Negroes from ethnics. The segregation of all Negroes from the total white population shows even sharper shifts. From Thomas Van Valey, Wade Clark Roof, and Jerome E. Wilcox, "Trends in Residential Segregation: 1960–1970," *American Journal of Sociology* 82 (1977):826–844; the 1970 Negro-white indexes are 79.3 for the entire SMSA, 81.2 for the central city, and 54.4 for the SMSA ring.

CONCLUSIONS

No claim is made that Boston's segregation is typical of all cities although, as was mentioned earlier, the available comparative studies of segregation in American cities indicate Boston is not unusual. In Boston city itself, it is evident that racial segregation is but an extreme extension of ethnic segregation; if Boston's blacks were a white ethnic group, instead of the actual level of segregation of around 80 found now, a level of at least 60 could be expected. Moreover, the metropolis as a whole, for 1970, seems similar to the city alone.

The evidence is indirect but compelling. Segregation between European ethnicities has remained stable or has declined little; the evidence demonstrates this clearly since 1930, is reasonable for the period since 1910, and is suggestive in showing only slight declines since the 19th century. Currently, Asian and Latin populations show similar patterns vis-à-vis the Europeans; even when considering individual ethnicities with much in common, one finds relatively high levels between groups such as Japanese and Chinese, or Mexicans and Cubans. Some of the differences, such as the white Roman Catholic Irish and Italians, in 1970, whose indexes declined from 51 in the central city to 32 in the SMSA ring, suggest the need to follow specific groups in detail, beyond the coarse accounting of the decennial population census.

Returning to school desegregation in the city, it can be seen that given the high and continuous level of ethnic and racial segregation in Boston City itself, one would hardly expect to disturb any facet of life based on territorial organization without an upheaval. Moreover, there is only slight hope from the averages that the suburbs are different. However, the drop in segregation, from the central city to the suburbs, between a few similar ethnics such as the Irish and Italians, and between dissimilar populations such as blacks and European ethnics, offers some possibility that territorial cohesiveness may change. But certainly within the city itself (the arena of the school desegregation dispute), there is no lessening.

Finally, there is fragmentary evidence that the public schools of Boston City were less segregated than its residences. We know from comparative research[20] that, in general, racial segregation in United States public elementary schools is at least shaped by residential segregation. Specifically, for Boston City, on a school-by-school basis, the 1970 Index of Dissimilarity between white and black public school children

was 74.[21] What level of segregation should one expect if the schools were "ideal neighborhood" schools? As a hypothetical comparison, the Index of Segregation between black and nonblack children ages 5–14 was calculated by census tracts, to arrive at an index of residential segregation of 89.[22] This can be only an approximate comparison, but the difference between 89 residential and 74 school segregation is so large as to be persuasive. A conclusive accounting would require an investigation into segregation in both public and private schools, as well as the history of Boston education. But the fact that residency dominates elementary public school segregation is clear.

20. Reynolds Farley and Alma Taeuber, "Racial Segregation in the Public Schools," *American Journal of Sociology* 77 (1974): 888–905; Reynolds Farley, "Racial Integration in the Public Schools, 1967 to 1972: Assessing the Effect of Governmental Policies," *Sociological Focus* 8 (1975):3–26.

21. Reynolds Farley, "Racial Integration in the Public Schools," p. 10.

22. From the published census tract report: U.S. Bureau of the Census, Census of Population and Housing: 1970. *Census Tracts*. Final Report PHC(1)-29, Boston, Mass. SMSA. (Washington, DC: USGPO, 1972). Table P-5, Negro Children aged 5–14 years, in Census Tracts with 400 or more Negro population was used in conjunction with Table P-1, all children aged 5–14. The 24,429 Negro children aged 5–14 in Table P-5 constituted 93.4 percent of the 26,147 Negro children aged 5–14 enumerated by the 1970 census in Boston city.

A Tale of Three Cities: Blacks and Immigrants in Philadelphia: 1850–1880, 1930 and 1970

By Theodore Hershberg, Alan N. Burstein, Eugene P. Ericksen, Stephanie Greenberg, and William L. Yancey

ABSTRACT: Determining whether the black experience was unique, or similar to that of earlier white immigrant groups, is central to the debate over whether blacks should be the beneficiaries of special compensatory legislation in the present. To answer this question requires interdisciplinary research that combines a comparative ethnic, an urban, and a historical perspective. Thus we observe the experience of three waves of immigrants to Philadelphia: the Irish and Germans who settled in the "Industrializing City" of the mid-to-late nineteenth century; the Italians, Poles and Russian Jews who came to the "Industrial City" at the turn of the twentieth century; and blacks who arrived in the "Post-Industrial City" in their greatest numbers after World War II. Analysis of the city's changing opportunity structure and ecological form, and the racial discrimination encountered shows the black experience to be unique in kind and degree. Significant changes in the structures that characterized each of the "three cities" call into question our standing notion of the assimilation process.

Theodore Hershberg is Associate Professor of History and Public Policy in the School of Public and Urban Policy at the University of Pennsylvania where he directs the Philadelphia Social History Project and the newly established Center for Philadelphia Studies.

Alan N. Burstein is Assistant Professor of Sociology and Urban Studies at Washington University in St. Louis.

Eugene P. Ericksen is Associate Professor of Sociology, and sampling statistician, Institute for Survey Research, Temple University.

Stephanie W. Greenberg is Research Sociologist at the Center for the Study of Social Behavior at the Research Triangle Institute.

William L. Yancey is Professor of Sociology at Temple University.

The Philadelphia Social History Project, part of the School of Public and Urban Policy at the University of Pennsylvania, is funded by the Center for Studies of Metropolitan Problems, NIMH (MH 16621); Division of Research Grants, NEH (RC 25568-76-1156); and the Sociology

Program, Division of Social Sciences, NSF (SOC 76-20069), Theodore Hershberg, principal investigator. Research underway at Temple University is also supported by the Center for Studies of Metropolitan Problems, NIMH (MH 25244), William L. Yancey and Eugene P. Ericksen, co-principal investigators. A special note of thanks is due to the many PSHP Research Associates and to Henry Williams and Richard Greenfield.

SIGNIFICANT differences in socioeconomic condition characterize the experience of black and white Americans. Why and how this happened, and what if anything should be done about it, are among the central questions of our time. Their answers have important implications for public policy. The crux of the matter can be put this way: were the burdens and disabilities faced by black Americans peculiar to their historical experience or were they simply obstacles which every immigrant group entering American society had to overcome?[1]

Over the years we have come to see how the study of the black experience requires a broader context than gross comparisons of whites with blacks. Recent research has finally recognized that white America consists of diverse groups and that the study of their distinct experiences requires a comparative ethnic perspective. While this constitutes a major advance, what remains conspicuously absent from the literature —especially from the history of blacks in cities—is an awareness that the study of the black experience necessitates an urban perspective as well.[2] Two distinct environ-

---

1. This essay is based on the research of five authors, all Research Associates of the Philadelphia Social History Project which collected and made machine-readable the data for the nineteenth century. For further information about the PSHP and its interdisciplinary approach to research see Theodore Hershberg, "The Philadelphia Social History Project: A Methodological History" (Ph.D. diss., Stanford University, 1973), and "The Philadelphia Social History Project: A Special Issue," *Historical Methods* 9 (1976): 2–3. The twentieth-century data were collected by William Yancey and Eugene Ericksen. PSHP data form the basis for Alan N. Burstein, "Residential Distribution and Mobility of Irish and German Immigrants in Philadelphia, 1850–1880," (Ph.D. diss., University of Pennsylvania, 1975); the nineteenth and twentieth-century data were used in Stephanie Greenberg, "Industrialization in Philadelphia: The Relationship between Industrial Location and Residential Patterns, 1880–1930," (Ph.D., diss., Temple University, 1977).

"A Tale of Three Cities" attempts to synthesize the findings reported in these dissertations and in a number of separate journal articles and unpublished papers; reference to these will be made at appropriate points in the

text. Many of these papers will appear in *Toward an Interdisciplinary History of the City: Work, Space, Family and Group Experience in Nineteenth-Century Philadelphia*, ed. Theodore Hershberg (New York: Oxford University Press, forthcoming, 1979); hereafter cited as *Interdisciplinary History of the City*.

2. Recent monographs on urban black communities provide an ethnic and racial perspective on the black experience but fail to adequately treat its urban context. See Gilbert Osofsky, *Harlem: The Making of a Ghetto: Negro New York, 1890–1920* (New York: Harper and Row, 1963); Allan H. Spear, *Black Chicago: The Making of a Negro Ghetto, 1890–1920* (Chicago: University of Chicago Press, 1967); Seth M. Scheiner, *Negro Mecca: A History of the Negro in New York City, 1865–1920* (New York University Press, 1965); David M. Katzman, *Before the Ghetto: Black Detroit in the Nineteenth Century* (Urbana: University of Illinois Press, 1973); John W. Blassingame, *Black New Orleans, 1860–1880* (Chicago: University of Chicago Press, 1973).

An exception is Kenneth L. Kusmer, *A Ghetto Takes Shape: Black Cleveland 1870–1930* (Urbana: University of Illinois Press,

ments embrace much of Afro-American history: plantation and ghetto.[3] Once the most rural of Americans, blacks are today the most urbanized. Unfortunately, the histories that have been written treat the city in passive terms, as a kind of incidental setting for the subject at hand; in order to learn how the "city" affected blacks it is necessary to construct a history which treats the city in dynamic terms. Such a history would conceive of "urban" as a "process" linking the experience of people to aspects of the particular environment in which they lived.[4] In this essay a comparative ethnic and an urban perspective are combined to further understanding of the black experience.

This essay will focus on Philadelphia's "opportunity structure." Such a term encompasses a wide variety of factors; although much more than the hierarchy of occupations define an opportunity structure, the distribution of occupations is certainly central to the concept and may be considered its most important single attribute. For the sake of brevity, a vertical distribution of occupations will be used as a proxy measure for a group's place in the

larger opportunity structure. The term "ecological structure," or the distribution in space of people, housing, jobs, transportation, and other urban elements is understood as the material expression of the opportunity structure. A city's ecological structure can thus be considered as a major determinant of differential "access"—to jobs, housing, transportation, and services. Finally, the term "structural perspective" encompasses both the opportunity structure and its ecological form and is used here to characterize our overall conceptual approach.

The experience of black and white immigrant groups, then, must be understood within a changing urban environment, recognizing the effects that such environments had upon different groups of people at different points in Philadelphia's past. The ecological "rules" that explain important elements of the white immigrant experience do not explain, for most of Philadelphia's history, what happened to blacks. Where blacks were concerned the rules were inoperative, suspended as it were by the force of racism. Racism, particularly its manifestation in discriminatory hiring and housing practices, is the final dimension in the explanatory framework. The subsiding of the worst of racial discrimination in contemporary American life suggests that blacks will at last begin to be treated as other people. But the potential gains will not be realized because other offsetting changes have occurred simultaneously. Philadelphia's opportunity structure has altered radically for the worse, and the ecological manifestations of these changes leave blacks at a severe disadvantage: they find themselves in the wrong areas of the wrong city at the wrong time. Despite the les-

1976). Following in the tradition of W.E.B. DuBois, the *Philadelphia Negro: A Social Study* (Philadelphia, 1899; New York: Schocken Press, 1965) and St. Clair Drake and Horace R. Cayton, *Black Metropolis: A Study of Negro Life in A Northern City* (New York: Harper and Row, 1945), Kusmer discusses how the urban environment affected the collective experiences of blacks in late nineteenth and early twentieth-century Cleveland.

3. For an interpretative overview of Afro-American history that develops this theme see August Meier and Elliot Rudwick, *From Plantation to Ghetto*, 3d. ed. rev. (New York: Hill and Wang, 1976).

4. The concept "urban as process" is elaborated in Theodore Hershberg, "The New Urban History," *Journal of Urban History* 5 (November 1978).

sening of racial discrimination, major changes in Philadelphia's opportunity and ecological structure prevent today's blacks from experiencing the successes enjoyed by the city's earlier immigrant groups.

UNIQUE ASPECTS OF THE BLACK EXPERIENCE

Those who argue that the black experience was not unique fall into two categories. The first explanation of the socioeconomic differentials can be captured in single words—bootstraps—or opportunities. According to this point of view, blacks, like all immigrant groups, had equal access to opportunities. If they took advantage of these opportunities—that is, if they pulled long enough and hard enough on their bootstraps they made it. The bootstraps argument claims that everybody had it tough and that the problems faced by blacks were no tougher than those encountered by other immigrant groups entering American society. The message of this view for contemporary public policy is obvious: if blacks did not have a uniquely discriminatory past, they do not deserve to be the beneficiaries of compensatory legislation in the present.

The second explanation, known as the "Last of the Immigrants," rejects the bootstraps view of the past and concedes that blacks—in cities such as Philadelphia—were the victims of a peculiarly racist past. Such a concession, however, only documents how racist America was "back then," and suggests that time will be sufficient remedy. As late as 1910, the well-meaning holders of this viewpoint remind us, 90 percent of black Americans were rural and 80 percent were southern. Of all American blacks ever to live in cities, the vast majority settled in

them after World War II: thus, in demographic terms, blacks can be considered as the last of the immigrants. Although this explanation differs from the notion of bootstraps in its view of the black past, its implications for public policy in the present are identical. We need not undertake any special legislation to ameliorate the condition of blacks today because the same process of assimilation through which European immigrants were integrated into the urban American mainstream will take care of black urban immigrants. Since the process of assimilation worked for other groups, it will work for blacks: all we need to do is stand by and give it time.[5]

THE ASSIMILATION PROCESS

Unfortunately, viewing blacks as the last of the immigrants is inac-

5. This point of view is held by many in positions of considerable influence in our society. In discussing the impact of the Bakke case with a black clerk in a Washington, D.C. bookstore, no less than Chief Justice Warren E. Burger was quoted as saying that ". . . his grandparents had come from Europe and were illiterate and it had taken 150 years for his people to improve themselves." Miss Audrey Hair, the bookstore clerk, said: "I asked him if he didn't think 300 years was enough time for my people?" New York Times, 5 November 1978, p. 6. The "Last of the Immigrants" explanation is cogently presented by Nathan Glazer, "Blacks and Ethnic Groups: The Difference, and the Political Difference it Makes," in Key Issues in the Afro-American Experience, ed. Nathan I. Huggins, Martin Kilson, and Daniel M. Fox (New York: Harcourt Brace Jovanovich, 1971), pp. 193–211. A more popular expression can be found in Irving Kristol, "The Negro Today is Like the Immigrant of Yesterday," New York Times Magazine, 11 September 1976.

No particular author is identified with the Bootstraps explanation; rather it is considered endemic in American culture and is associated with a racist interpretation of the black experience; that is, blacks failed because they are racially inferior.

curate and, in its false optimism, may ultimately prove to be as pernicious as the bootstraps explanation. Assimilation is not a mysterious process rooted in the individual, but is a combination of factors: opportunities available at a given time; housing stock; the nature and condition of the local, regional and national economy; the number of skilled and unskilled positions available in the laborforce; the location of jobs; the transportation facilities; the fiscal circumstances of the local government; and the degree of discrimination encountered. Nor is there much validity in dealing with the assimilation process at the individual level; every immigrant group has its specially gifted members who "make it" despite the barriers erected by the host society. The concern here is with the experience of entire groups, rather than the exceptionally talented few, and the focus is on the opportunity structure which affected all people and which regulated the degree of group progress.

The experience of blacks and immigrants will be compared at three points in Philadelphia's history. Although blacks were present in the city over the entire period, the reference to three cities reflects temporally distinct waves of immigrants to Philadelphia: the "Old" immigrants—Irish, Germans and British—who settled in the 1840's and 1850's; the "New" immigrants—Italians, Poles and Russian Jews—who arrived in the years between 1885 and 1914; and the "newest" immigrants—blacks—who came in their greatest numbers after 1945 (see Table 1).[6]

6. Sam Bass Warner has also described "three" Philadelphias: "The Eighteenth-Century Town" of 1770–1780; "The Big City" of 1830–1860; and "The Industrial Me-

What happened to these groups depended not only upon what they brought with them from the Old World and the South—values, language, skills, urban and industrial experience—but what awaited them upon arrival in Philadelphia. It was not only that people with different backgrounds came to the city, but that the structure of opportunities that they found in Philadelphia was

tropolis" of 1920–1930; *The Private City: Philadelphia in Three Periods of Its Growth* (Philadelphia: University of Pennsylvania Press, 1968); see also Warner, "If All the World Were Philadelphia: A Scaffolding for Urban History, 1774–1930," *American Historical Review* 74 (October 1968).

A more recent study also identified "three cities": the "commercial" city of the eighteenth and early nineteenth centuries, the "industrial" city of the late nineteenth and early twentieth centuries, and the "corporate" city of the post World War II period; see David Gordon, "Capitalist Development and the History of American Cities," in *Marxism and the Metropolis: Perspectives in Urban Political Economy*, ed. Larry Sawers and William K. Tabb (New York: Oxford University Press, 1978).

The differences here reflect purpose. Warner initially wanted to demonstrate to historians that systematic data were available with which to document the major changes that occurred in the urban environment over the last two centuries. His major purpose in *The Private City*, however, had far less to do with changes in the city's opportunity and ecological structure than with the failures of urban life in a capitalist economy; he attributes urban problems to the pursuit of private profit at the expense of the public good. Where these once coincided in the colonial city, they diverged permanently with the emergence of the urban-industrial order in the nineteenth century. Gordon's purpose was to classify cities according to stages in their historical economic development, arguing that urban form and the requirements of capitalism are inextricably linked to each other. Our purpose differs; we wished to characterize the particular kind of economy and environment that awaited the settlement of three temporally distinct waves of immigrants. Thus we have designated our three cities as "The Industrializing City," "The Industrial City," and "The Post-Industrial City."

TABLE 1

ETHNIC COMPOSITION OF PHILADELPHIA: 1850–1970
(AS PERCENT OF TOTAL POPULATION)

	1850	1880	1900	1930	1970
Blacks	4.8	3.6	4.8	11.3	33.6
Ireland*					
Born	17.6	11.9	7.6	2.7	0.4
2nd		15.1	13.6	6.8	1.9
Stock		27.0	21.2	9.4	2.3
Germany					
Born	5.6	6.6	5.5	1.9	0.6
2nd		9.6	9.6	4.8	1.4
Stock		16.2	15.1	6.7	1.9
Great Britain†					
Born		3.8	3.6	1.9	0.4
2nd			4.8	3.2	1.1
Stock			8.4	5.1	1.5
Italy					
Born		0.2	1.4	3.5	1.3
2nd			0.9	5.8	4.0
Stock			2.2	9.3	5.3
Poland					
Born		0.1	0.6	1.6	0.6
2nd			0.3	5.8	1.8
Stock			0.9	7.4	2.4
USSR°					
Born		0.03	2.2	4.5	1.3
2nd			1.3	5.3	3.2
Stock			3.6	9.9	4.5
Total Foreign					
Born	29.0	24.2	22.8	18.9	6.5
2nd		30.4	32.1	31.7	16.6
Stock		54.6	54.9	50.6	23.1
Total Population	408,081	840,584	1,293,697	1,950,961	1,950,098

* Includes Northern Ireland.
† Includes England, Scotland, Wales.
° Includes Russia, Lithuania, Estonia, Latvia.

NOTE: In 1880, "2nd generation" refers to native-born with *fathers* born in specified country. Native-born with native fathers and foreign-born mothers are classified as native. In 1900, 1930, and 1970, "2nd Generation" refers to native-born with *fathers* born in specified country or, if father is native, with *mother* born in specified country. If parents are born in different foreign countries, birthplace of father determines parentage of native-born. "Stock" includes foreign-born plus 2nd generation.

SOURCES: Figures for 1850 and 1880 are computed primarily from Philadelphia Social History Project compilations of the United States manuscript censuses of population. In 1880, figures for Italy, Poland, and USSR are taken from published United States Census totals. See Department of the Interior, Census Office, *Census of Population: 1880,* v.1, "Statistics of the Population of the United States at the Tenth Census," (Washington, D.C.: U.S. Government Printing Office, 1883), 540. Figures for 1900, 1930 and 1970 are computed from published United States Census totals. See Department of the Interior, United States Census Office, *Census of Population: 1900,* v.1, pt. 1, "Population," (Washington, D.C.: U.S. Census Office, 1901), 780, 866–905; U.S. Department of Commerce, Bureau of the Census, *Census of Population: 1930,* v.III, pt. 2, "Population," (Washington, D.C.: U.S. Government Printing Office, 1932), 701–708: U.S. Bureau of the Census, *Census of Population: 1970,* v.1, "Characteristics of the Population," pt. 40, Pennsylvania—Section 1, (Washington, D.C.: U.S. Government Printing Office, 1973), 356.

different as well; each time period represented a different stage in the city's urban-industrial development. And it was these differences that shaped a wide range of subsequent experience for each immigrant group. A full treatment of these differences would require discussion of a breadth of topics. This essay will focus on the changing opportunity structure and the residential experience of the black and white immigrants who lived in the designated three cities.

According to the accepted notion of the assimilation process, upon arrival in America immigrants settled in densely populated urban ghettoes among friends and neighbors of the same ethnic background. A few, the most successful among them, were able to move out of the ghetto within their own lifetime, but for most others, integration into the fabric of the larger society was the experience of their children and grandchildren. Several generations were required to complete the process. This point of view pervades our culture; we find it embedded in our literature, film and folklore. Its most recent and popular expression is found in Irving Howe's best-selling study, *World of Our Fathers*.[7]

Settlement in dense urban enclaves made sense. It was seen as the logical response of the newcomers to the hostility of the native population and to the strangeness of white Anglo Saxon Protestant culture at the societal core. It was rational as well—when understood as the natural tendency of the immigrants, faced with an unfamiliar new setting—to establish a secure and friendly place, to create a sense of the old Country in the new. A piece of Europe was transplanted in the streets of America.

The pervasiveness of this notion, however, did not rest solely on logic or cultural trappings. With the nation absorbing twenty million immigrants in thirty years at the turn of the last century, some scholars, particularly a group of sociologists at the University of Chicago, undertook major

studies of the immigrant experience.[8] Their empirical observations corroborated those of the social reformers who were dealing with the problems of the immigrants, as well as those of the writers and artists who were capturing the immigrant saga in word and on canvas.

RESIDENTIAL SEGREGATION

Sociologists have maintained that the degree of residential segregation is an acceptable indicator of, or a proxy for, assimilation. An ethnically enclosed residential experience insulates a group from important mechanisms of assimilation, limits cross-cultural contacts that affect the socialization of the young, and has serious implications for subsequent experiences such as intermarriage, upward job mobility, and the formation of social ties. Thus, the lower the degree of segregation the greater the likelihood that a group is experiencing assimilation. The accepted notion of the assimilation process found what appeared to be scientific confirmation in the levels of segregation observed for northern and midwestern cities in 1930. Expectations based on the accepted model were apparently confirmed by the data: old immigrants from Ireland, Germany and Britain, who had arrived in America in the 1840's and 1850's, were the least segregated residentially (20–30); while new immigrants from Italy, Poland and Russia, who came

8. See for example Robert E. Park, "The Urban Community as a Spatial Pattern and a Moral Order," in *The Urban Community*, ed. Ernest W. Burgess (Chicago: University of Chicago Press, 1926); Louis Wirth, *The Ghetto* (Chicago: University of Chicago Press, 1928); Ernest W. Burgess, "Residential Segregation in American Cities," *Annals of the American Academy of Political and Social Science*, 140 (1928): 105–115; Robert E. Park, *Human Communities* (Glencoe, IL: Free Press, 1952).

7. (New York: Harcourt Brace and Jovanovich, 1976).

between 1885 and 1914, were considerably more segregated (50–60).[9] Here was proof—or so it seemed— that an assimilation process was operating in American cities; with the passage of time immigrants were being integrated into the mainstream. When the logic of this argument is applied to the high levels of segregation for urban blacks (70–80) observed in 1970, one is left with a comforting conclusion. With time, these latest newcomers will assimilate, as did earlier groups. The optimistic implications of this viewpoint for public policy are obvious: no legislation need be passed when a social process operates to generate the desired results.

Unfortunately, while the segregation scores are accurate, the interpretation is not. The data on white immigrant residential segregation are cross-sectional for 1930; when cross-sectional data are used to infer historical process they can distort history and lead to an erroneous conclusion. The low scores for the Irish and German immigrants—half the level observed for the Italians,

Poles and Russian Jews—are not indicative of change over time from high to low segregation, and thus proof of an assimilation process; rather, they are the *retention* of segregation levels experienced by the Irish and German immigrants upon initial settlement (see Table 2).[10] In other words, the low segregation scores for the old immigrants, the higher scores for the new immigrants, and the highest scores for the blacks are not evidence for the existence of an assimilation process rooted in the individual and responsive to the passage of time, but are a reflection of changing structural conditions that awaited each wave of immigrants who settled in Philadelphia at three different points in time.[11]

9. Stanley Lieberson, *Ethnic Patterns in American Cities* (Glencoe, IL: Free Press, 1963). The Index of Segregation expresses the percentage of a group that would have to move to another location in the city to achieve a distribution throughout each areal unit equal to their proportion of the city's total population; the Index measure is often expressed as a whole number ranging from 0 (no segregation) to 100 (complete segregation). For a detailed explanation of the Index of Segregation, see Otis Dudley Duncan and Beverly Duncan, "Residential Distribution and Occupational Stratification," *American Journal of Sociology* 60 (1955): 493–503; Otis Dudley Duncan and Beverly Duncan, "A Methodological Analysis of Segregation Indexes," *American Sociological Review* 20 (April 1955): Karl E. Taeuber and Alma F. Taeuber, *Negroes in Cities: Residential Segregation and Neighborhood Change* (Chicago: Atheneum, 1965), pp. 195–245.

10. The dissimilarity scores reported in Table 2 are calculated in the same manner as the Index of Segregation but describe the degree of difference from native-whites as opposed to the remainder of the city's population. The scores reported in Tables 2 and 8, moreover, *are based on identical areal units*.

Tract level data were not collected by the nineteenth-century U.S. Census Bureau. For the 1930 and 1970 censuses, Philadelphia was divided into 404 and 365 tracts respectively. To achieve compatible boundaries, it was necessary to collapse these into 248 tracts. The much smaller PSHP areal units for the nineteenth century—7,100 rectangular grids one and one-quarter blocks square— were aggregated up to the level of the 248 census tracts. Areal compatibility was thus achieved across the entire 120 year period. For information on the construction of the PSHP grid areal unit, see Hershberg, "The PSHP: A Methodological History," pp. 150– 87; and "The PSHP: A Special Issue," pp. 99–105.

11. Given the standing notion of the assimilation process, moreover, the decline in residential segregation over the period 1930– 1970 is less than might be expected: the greatest decline was found among Polish stock (55% in 1930 to 35% in 1970), but Italian stock fell only slightly (58% to 48%), and Jewish stock did not change (53% to 52%). See Table 2.

TABLE 2

INDICES OF DISSIMILARITY FROM NATIVE WHITES: 1850, 1880, 1930–1970 (248 TRACTS)

	1850	1880	1930	1940	1950	1960	1970
Blacks	47	52	61	68	71	77	75
Puerto Ricans							
Stock						81	82
Ireland							
Born	30	32	28	32	29		
2nd		31					
Stock		31	21			24	28
Germany							
Born	33	36	32	35	31		
2nd		33					
Stock		34	27			25	26
Great Britain							
Born			24	23	22		
Stock			22			21	22
Italy							
Born			59	60	54		
Stock			58			47	48
Poland							
Born			54	55	46		
Stock			55			32	35
USSR							
Born			56	57	54		
Stock			53			50	52
Foreign							
Born	21	26					
2nd		25					
Stock		25					
Other Foreign							
Born		27					
2nd		21					
Stock		24					

NOTE: See Note for Table 1. "Stock" for 1960 includes foreign-born plus 2nd generation which is defined as for.1900, 1930 and 1970. "Other Foreign-Born" refers to all immigrant groups except Irish and Germans.
SOURCES: Figures for 1850 and 1880 are computed from Philadelphia Social History Project compilations of the United States manuscript censuses of population. Figures for 1930–1970 are computed from tract-level data taken from the United States censuses.

THE NINETEENTH-CENTURY
CITY: 1850–1880

Immigrant ghettoes did not form in the nineteenth century manufacturing city. In simplest terms, no supply of cheap, concentrated housing existed to quarter the thousands of Irish and Germans who poured into the city seeking work in the 1840s and 1850s. As the manufacturing center of America and one of the largest in the Atlantic community, Philadelphia's job market was a magnet not only for immigrants, but for large numbers of native whites from the surrounding countryside.[12] The rapidly expanding population, which doubled between 1840 and 1860, reaching 565,000 by the latter year, far outstripped growth in the city's housing supply.

12. Bruce Laurie and Mark Schmitz, "Manufacture and Productivity: The Making of an Industrial Base in Nineteenth-Century Philadelphia," in Hershberg, Interdisciplinary History of the City.

Thus newcomers found housing wherever they could. Since the large homes which faced each other on the main streets were expensive, most new settlement occurred in the smaller, cheaper houses and shanties that sprang up in sidestreets, lanes and back-alleys. Boarding with other families was quite common; one household in four took in lodgers. Population expansion in the pre-Civil War years, led to sharply increased density, and growth in general was characterized by a "filling-in" process which ensured socioeconomic heterogeneity within a geographically compact city. The Irish and German immigrants, 18 and 6 percent of the 1850 population, respectively, were dispersed across the face of the city.

By 1880, when data are available to identify the American-born children of the immigrants, Irish stock were 30 percent and German stock 16 percent of the city's population. With these data, the residential patterns of the immigrants and their children can be reconstructed in detail. There were five identifiable clusters of Irish stock and one of German stock. However, only one person in five of Irish background and one person in eight of German background lived in such clusters. What is more, even in these areas which represented the heaviest concentrations of Irish and German stock in the city, each group composed only half of the population in their respective clusters.[13]

In 1850, the city's rudimentary transportation system—the horse-drawn omnibus lines which operated

over mud and cobblestone streets— was irregular in service and prohibitively expensive for all but the wealthiest. Almost everyone lived within walking distance of their workplaces; indeed, for many at mid-century, home and work were not yet separated. Most blue-collar workers appear to have lived within a radius of half a mile of their jobs in 1850 with a median distance of two blocks.[14]

Most jobs were concentrated within the city's historic core. Half of all manufacturing jobs, which accounted for one male worker in two, and an even greater proportion of nonmanufacturing jobs, were found within a few square blocks of Philadelphia's downtown. Industry—the location of manufacturing jobs—dominated the organization of the city's spatial arrangements. Workers' residential patterns reflected the spatial characteristics of their industries. For example, the residences of workers in concentrated, centralized industries were clustered in or adjacent to the city's core; those who labored in dispersed industries lived scattered across the city.[15]

Industry was more important than ethnicity in organizing the city's residential patterns. Workers of different ethnic groups employed in

13. Hershberg, "The PSHP: A Methodological History," pp. 285–323; see especially Tables 21 and 23; A. Burstein, "Patterns of Segregation and the Residential Experience" in Hershberg, "The PSHP: A Special Issue," pp. 105–113.

14. Hershberg, Harold Cox, Richard Greenfield and Dale Light, Jr., "The Journey-to-Work: An Empirical Investigation of Work, Residence, and Transportation in Philadelphia, 1850 and 1880," in Hershberg, Interdisciplinary History of the City. Although the estimated journey to work doubled between 1850 and 1880, reaching a radius of one mile and a median of one-half mile, the absolute distances involved remained quite short.

15. Greenfield, Hershberg, and William Whitney, "The Dynamics and Determinants of Manufacturing Location: A Perspective on Nineteenth-Century Philadelphia"; Greenberg, "Industrial Location and Ethnic Residential Patterns" both in Hershberg, Interdisciplinary History of the City.

the same industry had residential characteristics—segregation, clustering, density and centrality— more in common with each other than with members of their own ethnic group. German leather workers, to choose a representative example of an ethno-industrial type, were distributed over space more like Irish or native-white leather workers than like Germans in other industries. Under conditions of limited transportation and housing availability, workers had more in common residentially with coindustrial workers than with those of common cultural background.[16]

Another way of making this point is to examine the socioeconomic and demographic characteristics of the Irish population who lived in ethnic clusters. If ethnicity rather than industry were determining the organization of residence, the Irish in these areas should have resembled each other; the areas should have been similar pieces from a common cultural nucleus that was prevented from forming by the state of the housing market. Yet, when the areas are empirically examined, they turn out to be thoroughly distinct from each other. The characteristics of the Irish in each of the five clusters match the industrial opportunities available there; thus they differed markedly in occupational structure, unemployment rates, property holding, age and sex structure, household and family types.[17]

The only major exception to the above generalizations were blacks. They were marginal to the rapidly industrializing urban economy of this period, and were considerably more segregated than white immigrants. They had few manufacturing jobs, even though they lived within easy access to more jobs of this type than any other ethnic group. Although the typical black worker lived within one mile of 23,000 manufacturing jobs—half again as many as were accessible to the typical Irish, German or native-white worker —he was refused employment (see Table 3).[18] Racism proved more powerful than the rules that normally governed spatially conditioned job access. In the few instances when blacks did obtain manufacturing jobs, they did not live close to their white coworkers. Rather they tended to live close to one another, regardless of industrial affiliation.[19]

It is fundamental to understand that, as the result of the new industrial order and the emergence of the factory system, all of this occurred within a context of widening occupational opportunity for whites. This is especially significant because the manufacturing sector has traditionally provided the first step up the occupational ladder to new arrivals to the city. Opportunities for upward mobility created by an expanding economy—which provided the bootstraps for the Irish and German immigrants—were so limited for blacks that they were virtually nonexistent. In 1847, for example, less than one-half of one percent of the adult black

16. Greenberg, "Industrialization in Philadelphia."
17. Miriam Eisenhardt, Jeffrey Sultanik, and Alan Berman, "The Five Irish Clusters in 1880 Philadelphia," unpublished PSHP paper.
18. Greenberg, "Industrial Location and Ethnic Residential Patterns," in Hershberg, *Interdisciplinary History of the City*; and Greenberg, "Industrialization in Philadelphia."
19. On the other hand, given black overrepresentation in such service occupations as waiter and porter, their residential pattern was functional: the single large black residential concentration was located adjacent to the city's largest concentration of hotels, restaurants and inns in the downtown area.

male workforce could find jobs in the economy's dynamic new sectors such as iron and steel and machine tools. During the antebellum years, blacks were not only excluded from the new and well-paying positions, they were uprooted as well from many of their traditional unskilled jobs, denied apprenticeships for their sons, and prevented from practicing the skills they already possessed.[20] Little changed between 1850 and 1880; although the number and proportion of skilled positions

20. Hershberg, "Free Blacks in Antebellum Philadelphia: A Study of Ex-slaves, Freeborn and Socioeconomic Decline," *Journal of Social History* 5 (December 1971); and "Freeborn and Slaveborn Blacks in Antebellum Philadelphia," in *Slavery and Race in the Western Hemisphere* ed. Eugene Genovese and Stanley Engerman (Princeton: Princeton University Press, 1975).

The characteristic difficulties that blacks faced in finding employment were described by Joshua Bailey, member of the Board of Managers of the Philadelphia Society for the Employment and Instruction of the Poor. Bailey wrote in his diary that "Employers express themselves willing to receive such an one (a young 'colored' man) into their shops, but they cannot dare to do it knowing the opposition such an act would meet from their workmen who will not consent to work with colored persons." (10 January 1853).

The process of adjustment to conditions in the New World was a difficult one for all newcomers—black and white immigrants alike. Yet the historical record makes clear that much about the black experience was different—some times in degree, other times in kind. Blacks were the victims of frequent race riots and saw their homes, schools and churches burned again and again. Though legally a free people and citizens, only members of the black race were denied the right to vote in the State of Pennsylvania after 1838. They occupied the worst housing in the Moyamensing slum and suffered from the greatest degree of impoverishment. Their mortality rate was roughly twice that of whites, and the death of black men early in their adult lives was the major reason that blacks were forced, far more often than whites, to raise their children in fatherless families; see F. F. Furstenberg, Jr., Hershberg and J. Modell, "The Origins of the Female-Headed Black Family: The Impact of the Urban Experience," *Jour-*

increased significantly with the economy's expansion, which benefitted the immigrants and especially their American born children, blacks experienced little or no progress (see Table 4). Thus, at least as far back as the mid-nineteenth century, the position of blacks in the city was unlike that of any other group.

Rapid growth in the years between 1850 and 1880 affected Philadelphia's ecological structure. The traditional view of immigrant residential settlement is firmly rooted in the original Park-Burgess notion of concentric zones, in which socioeconomic status of the population increases with increasing distance from the center of the city.[21] It is this model which describes a city with a low status core and a high status periphery, and it is in the low status core that the immigrant ghettoes are to be found. It is clear, however, that such a model did not fit the preindustrial city. In the preindustrial setting, transportation was poor and did not facilitate movement within the city. Since jobs and services were relatively centralized, the most desirable residences were those close to the center of the city. Thus the preindustrial model, postulated by Sjoberg, describes a city in which the most affluent live close to the center while the impoverished live on the periphery.[22]

nal of Interdisciplinary History 6 (September 1975).

For the occupational experience of the white immigrant workforce, see B. Laurie, Hershberg and G. Alter, "Immigrants and Industry," *Journal of Social History* 9 (December 1975) and B. Laurie and M. Schmitz, "Manufacture and Productivity."

21. Robert Park, Ernest W. Burgess, and Roderick D. McKenzie, eds., *The City* (Chicago: University of Chicago Press, 1928).

22. Gideon Sjoberg, "The Preindustrial City," *American Journal of Sociology* 60 (1955): 438–45; Gideon Sjoberg, *The Preindustrial City: Past and Present* (Glencoe, IL: Free Press, 1960).

TABLE 3

DISTRIBUTION OF ETHNIC GROUPS BY ACCESSIBILITY TO MANUFACTURING JOBS: 1880 (MALES, 18+)

	BLACKS	IRISH	IRISH-2ND	GERMAN	GERMAN-2ND	NATIVE-WHITES	TOTAL
Mean Jobs within 1 mile	23,289	15,179	14,985	18,894	17,863	15,313	16,074

NOTE: See Table 1.
SOURCE: Figures are computed from Philadelphia Social History Project compilations of the United States manuscript census of manufactures.

In 1850, the residential pattern in Philadelphia could still be partially described by the pre-industrial model. But in 1854, the City of Philadelphia merged with twenty-seven other political sub-divisions within Philadelphia County and the greatly enlarged city (it grew from 2 to 130 square miles) rapidly changed; consolidation led to the professionalization of the police and fire departments and the expansion of the public school system. But more importantly for what concerns us here, governmental rationalization facilitated the implementation of critical technological innovations in transportation and building construction. That, in turn, dramatically accelerated Philadelphia's transition to the modern form. Iron track was laid in the streets of the city in 1857; when the horse-drawn cars were hauled over the rail instead of street surfaces, the decline in friction made it possible to carry three to four times more passengers than had the omnibus. The effects of this transportation breakthrough were felt after the Civil War. The war brought boom times to certain sectors of the city's economy, but it retarded building construction as it accelerated capital accumulation. By the late 1860s the building industry, spurred by the new transportation technology, exploded in a surge of construction that continued into the twentieth century. The horse-car lines, which carried some 99 million passengers in 1880, led the way to residential and commercial deconcentration, while growth in the city's railroad network led to manufacturing decentralization; though the city's population more than doubled between 1850 and 1880, reaching 845,000 by the end of the period, the rate of building growth after 1870 far surpassed population growth.[23]

Population density declined; the average dwelling by 1880 (roughly 6 persons) contained almost one person less than it had in 1850. The modal housing type shifted from the free-standing or semi-detached three and four story dwelling to the two story row home. Moreover, houses that previously were erected by carpenters on demand were now built by large contractors anticipating the form of the modern tract development. Some 50,000 homes—one-third of the 1880 housing stock—were built in the preceding decade. The ratio of new population to new homes was 8 to 1 in the 1840s; by the 1870s, it had declined to 4 to 1.[24]

23. Hershberg, et al., "The Journey-to-Work."
24. Ibid. We do not wish to leave the impression that the decline in population densities over the period was due solely to the increased availability of housing. Declining population densities were also tied to declining fertility, a process experienced over at least the last century in Western Europe and North America.
   When the city is divided into concentric rings of roughly one mile, the inner two rings lost population consistently over the period. The first ring fell from 206,000 persons in 1880 to 67,000 in 1970; and in the second ring population fell from 241,000 in 1880 to 135,000 in

THE ANNALS OF THE AMERICAN ACADEMY

TABLE 4

OCCUPATIONAL DISTRIBUTION OF MALES, 18+, BY ETHNICITY: 1850, 1880
(AS PERCENT OF ETHNIC GROUP)

	BLACKS	IRISH	GERMAN	FOREIGN-BORN°°	NATIVE-WHITES**
1850					
High White Collar and Professional	1.1	1.4	2.6	1.8	8.9
Low White Collar and Proprietary	4.2	11.2	13.6	12.0	23.2
Artisan	17.1	42.1	67.3	49.6	57.0
Specified Unskilled	44.0	11.2	3.9	9.1	6.3
Unspecified Unskilled	33.3	33.9	12.3	27.6	4.3
Totals	4245	25389	10633	36022	51930
(Row %s)	(4.5)	(27.5)	(11.5)	(39.1)	(56.3)
Dissimilarity from all Native-Whites**	67	34	18	26	—

	BLACKS	IRISH	IRISH-2ND	GERMAN	GERMAN-2ND	FOREIGN-BORN°°	NATIVE-WHITES††	NATIVE-WHITES**
1880								
High White Collar and Professional	1.0	1.2	1.7	1.9	1.8	1.5	5.5	4.6
Low White Collar and Proprietary	6.6	18.3	22.4	23.6	26.0	20.5	33.7	31.2
Artisan	14.0	31.8	43.5	57.9	54.0	42.6	42.7	43.8
Specified Unskilled	52.2	19.5	18.4	10.5	13.0	15.8	12.8	13.7
Unspecified Unskilled	26.2	29.2	14.0	6.1	5.2	19.7	5.3	6.7
Totals	9043	38035	21780	26780	12690	64743	105165	139635
(Row %s)	(4.2)	(17.8)	(10.2)	(12.5)	(5.0)	(30.3)	(49.3)	(65.4)
Dissimilarity from Native-Whites of Native-White Parents††	60	31	15	16	12	17	—	—
Dissimilarity from all Native-Whites**	58	28	12	14	10	15	—	—

†† Excludes 2nd Generation Irish and Germans.
** Includes 2nd Generation Irish and Germans.
°° Includes Irish and Germans Only.
NOTE: See Note for Table 1.
SOURCES: Figures are computed from Philadelphia Social History Project compilations of the United States manuscript censuses of population.

The dramatic growth during the latter period did not result in a duplication of the spatial patterns that characterized the 1850 city; the decade of the 1870's can be considered the beginning of modern urban form in Philadelphia. The shuffling of the occupational universe brought about by the process of industrialization — the creation of jobs with new skills and the dilution of others, the

---

1970. Although contemporary population density gradients from the center outward are not level, their smoothing over time is one of the striking changes in urban population structure.

emergence of bureaucracy and a managerial class—coincided with the city's ability to accommodate wholly new changes in landuse specialization. Not only did industry and commerce accelerate their carving up of urban space, but social differentiation and spatial differentiation proceeded in tandem. Social differences in work—wages, status and work environments—now began to be mirrored in increasingly homogeneous residential settings. The supervisors and clerks who left the shop floor for woodpaneled offices now sought to leave their older heterogeneous neighborhoods for new residential areas where they could live with people more like themselves. The differentiation of residential areas along class, racial-ethnic and life-cycle lines accelerated. The more affluent Irish and German immigrants and their children started to join native-whites in an exodus from the city's center to new modern neighborhoods developing at its peripheries. Over the ensuing thirty years, large residential areas of cheap concentrated housing in the old city center were vacated, making room for the next wave of immigrants and ensuring that the residential patterns of the new immigrants would be far more segregated than those experienced by the old immigrants.

THE EARLY TWENTIETH-CENTURY CITY: 1900–1930

The availability of cheap, old housing concentrated in close proximity to plentiful manufacturing jobs contributed to the considerably higher levels of residential segregation of the Italians, Poles, and Russian Jews who settled in the industrial city of the early twentieth

century.[25] The forces set in motion in the 1870's proceeded apace, led by the tract development of the row house, and major changes in transportation technology. The trolleys were electrified in the 1890's, the elevated train and subway were introduced in the early decades of the next century, and the automobile made its appearance shortly thereafter.

The new means of transportation made it possible to open large outlying areas of the city for residential settlement.[26] Unlike building practices in other major cities, Philadelphia's landlords erected few tenements at this time. The row house remained the modal-housing type; in 1915, roughly nine houses in ten were of this architectural form.[27] The emergence of the street car suburbs and the row house ensured the continued decline in residential density. Despite an increase in the city's population to almost two million by 1930, the average density per dwelling fell to 4.2 persons. Philadelphia richly deserved its nickname as "The City of Homes."

The city's economy did not change dramatically over the half century between 1880 and 1930.[28] Its most

25. For an excellent discussion of the Polish experience in Philadelphia in the first two decades of the twentieth century, and less detailed but useful information on other immigrant groups in the city at the same time, see Carol Golab, *Immigrant Destinations* (Philadelphia: Temple University Press, 1978).
26. Sam Bass Warner, Jr., has described this process for late nineteenth-century Boston, *Street Car Suburbs: The Process of Growth in Boston, 1870–1900* (Cambridge, MA: Harvard University Press, 1962).
27. Golab, *Immigrant Destinations*, p. 153.
28. Greenberg, "Industrialization in Philadelphia," see Chap 6, "Changes in the Location of Jobs Between 1880 and 1930 and the

salient feature remained its diversi-
fication. Despite the entrance of
some new industries, most notably
in the electronics field, Philadelphia's economy was characterized
by the same range of activities found
in the nineteenth century: textiles, ap-
parel, printing, publishing, foundry,
and machines. Two important changes
were noticeable in 1930. First, although the number of manufacturing
jobs increased 60 percent over the
period, it fell as a proportion of all
jobs (from 48 to 31 percent) and increased far less rapidly than did the
population as a whole; second,
changes in transportation and production technologies began to accelerate the shift of manufacturing activity from the city's center to outlying areas. The full impact of these
changes, however, would not be felt
until the 1960s and 1970s.[29]

The new occupational opportunities that emerged tended to be located in the economy's white-collar
sector (see Table 5). By and large,
expanding jobs were found in the
professional, white collar or service
categories; faced with discrimination, language difficulties and limited educational backgrounds, few
blacks and immigrants worked in
these desirable positions. As a result, "New" immigrants found their
occupational opportunities more limited in this period than the "Old"
immigrants had encountered in the
nineteenth century; improvements
in the overall occupational distribution of black workers during these
years were at best marginal.

The socioeconomic differentiation
of the city's space that resulted from
transportation innovation, the decentralization of manufacturing and
greater housing availability produced an urban form well described
by the Chicago School model of concentric zones. At furthest remove
from the center, in the street-car
suburbs, lived white-collar and
highly skilled "aristocrats of labor";
largely, these groups were composed
of native-whites and the success-
full descendants of Irish, German
and British immigrants. Although
the automobile suburbs would not
emerge until after World War II,
roughly one person in seven in Philadelphia was sufficiently well-off to
commute regularly to work by auto
in 1934 (this is almost the same proportion of the workforce that could
afford regular use of the horse-
drawn street cars in their "journey-
to-work" in 1880).[30]

In the zones surrounding the
manufacturing and retailing core
lived the bulk of the working classes, largely "new" immigrants and
blacks, roughly one-third of whom
walked to work. In general, ethnic
concentrations were located near
concentrations of industrial employment.[31] This is particularly true of
the Italian and Polish areas. Workers
living in these neighborhoods were
overrepresented in industrial occupations. Once again, the relationships between the occupational distribution of immigrant groups and
the location of their jobs and residences can be seen.[32] The principal

Composition and Stability of Urban Areas in
1930," pp. 139–182.
29. Eugene P. Ericksen and William L.
Yancey, "The Location of Manufacturing Jobs
in Philadelphia: Changes in the Pattern,
1927–1972," unpublished paper, (Temple
University, 1976).

30. Greenberg, "Industrialization in Philadelphia," Chap 6; Hershberg, et. al., "The
Journey-to-Work."
31. Ericksen and Yancey, "Work and Residence in an Industrial City," Journal of Urban
History (Forthcoming, 1979).
32. The relationship between work and
residence was for Polish immigrants in 1915

TABLE 5

OCCUPATIONAL DISTRIBUTION OF MALES AND FEMALES, 10+, BY ETHNICITY: 1900, 1930
(AS PERCENT OF ETHNIC GROUP)

	BLACKS	IRELAND	GERMANY	GREAT BRITAIN	ITALY	POLAND	RUSSIA	WHITE FOREIGN-BORN	2ND GENER-ATION FOREIGN-BORN	NATIVE WHITE OF NATIVE PARENTS
				1900						
Professional	1.6	2.8	3.7	5.2	3.5	0.6	2.0	2.5	4.5	7.5
Owners and Executives	1.5	5.6	8.6	8.3	7.0	3.7	12.6	8.0	7.1	9.6
Clerks and Sales	1.0	8.9	8.6	10.4	1.6	2.3	6.9	4.2	13.6	17.4
Trade and Transportation	10.8	11.5	7.0	7.0	6.4	4.4	7.5	6.9	9.9	10.3
Manufacturing	8.2	40.2	54.3	56.2	32.6	55.5	62.8	47.3	49.2	40.4
Domestic and Personal Service	54.1	18.0	11.1	8.2	12.4	4.8	4.5	17.4	8.9	8.8
Laborers	21.6	10.7	4.0	3.2	34.8	25.9	3.0	11.0	4.6	3.4
Agriculture	0.6	1.0	1.0	0.9	1.4	1.4	0.4	1.2	0.7	1.1
Other	0.6	1.3	1.5	0.6	0.3	1.4	0.3	1.5	1.5	1.5
Dissimilarity from Native-Whites of Native-White Parents††	64	18	17	16	35	38	25	23	10	—

	BLACKS	WHITE FOREIGN-BORN	TOTAL NATIVE WHITE
		1930	
Professional	2.4	3.9	8.5
Owners and Executives	1.5	13.6	8.6
Clerks and Sales	2.6	9.3	27.8
Trade and Transportation	17.1	7.9	9.3
Manufacturing	12.6	42.8	33.7
Domestic and Personal Service	43.4	12.4	6.0
Laborers	17.6	7.3	2.5
Agriculture	0.6	0.9	0.4
Other	2.1	2.0	3.2
Totals	118890	203692	565481
(Row %)	(13.4)	(22.9)	(63.7)
Dissimilarity from all Native-Whites**	61	26	—

†† Excludes 2nd Generation.
** Includes 2nd Generation.
NOTE: See Note for Table 1.
SOURCES: Figures are computed from published United States Census totals. See Department of the Interior, United States Census Office, *Census of Population: 1900*, v.II, pt. II, "Population," (Washington, D.C.: U.S. Census Office, 1902), 583, 585; U.S. Department of Commerce, Bureau of the Census, *Census of Population: 1930*, v.IV, "Population," (Washington, D.C.: U.S. Government Printing Office, 1933), 1412– 1415.

what it had been for the Irish and German immigrants in the nineteenth century. Golab summarizes their experience in these words: "Each Polish settlement (and there were nine such areas) directly reflected the industrial structure of the neighborhood in which it was located. It was the availability of work that determined the location of the Polish colony,

for the Poles were invariably employed in the neighborhoods where they resided." *Immigrant Destinations*, p. 113.

A similar conclusion was reached by E. E. Pratt in his study of immigrant worker neighborhoods: *Industrial Causes of Congestion of Population in New York City* (New York: Columbia University Press, 1911).

TABLE 6

LOCATION OF ETHNIC POPULATIONS BY DISTANCE FROM CITY CENTER AND ACCESS
TO INDUSTRIAL JOBS: 1930 (PERCENT OF FOREIGN STOCK LIVING IN
CENSUS TRACT WITH THE FOLLOWING CHARACTERISTICS)

	WITHIN 3 MILES OF CITY CENTER	WITHIN 1 MILE OF 5,000 OR MORE INDUSTRIAL JOBS	OF THOSE WHO ARE WITHIN 3 MILES OF CITY HALL, PERCENT WITH ACCESS TO 5,000 OR MORE INDUSTRIAL JOBS	OF THOSE WHO ARE BEYOND 3 MILES OF CITY HALL, PERCENT WITH ACCESS TO 5,000 OR MORE INDUSTRIAL JOBS
British	.305	.614	.816	.520
Irish	.411	.610	.791	.483
German	.336	.633	.838	.529
Polish	.404	.815	.943	.724
Russian	.565	.537	.778	.223
Italian	.794	.714	.801	.627
Blacks	.786	.799	.882	.489
Native Whites	.393	.593	.803	.489
Total	.469	.643	.829	.473

NOTE: See Note for Table 1.
SOURCE: Figures are computed from tract-level data taken from the United States Census.

exception were Russian Jews who, after initial settlement in South Philadelphia, established neighborhoods in the nonindustrial street-car suburbs in the west and northwestern areas of the city. Workers here were disproportionately found in wholesale and retail rather than industrial jobs. [33]

By 1930 native whites and old immigrants had moved into better jobs and were able to use their greater income to ensure more housing choice; they lived in many different areas of the city characterized by greater housing value and distance from the center. As a result, they were less segregated. The relationship between occupational segregation and residential segregation was a close one. The data suggest that the segregation of newer immigrants was not complete because their occupational segregation was not complete; and, as in the nineteenth century, work location took prece-

dence over the desire to live in an ethnic neighborhood in the residential location decision. [34]

Blacks again stand in sharp contrast. Although they continued to live in and near areas characterized by high industrial concentrations, blacks were excluded from industrial work. Although 80 percent of the blacks in the city lived within one mile of 5,000 industrial jobs, less than 13 percent of the black work force found gainful employment in manufacturing. Blacks earned their livelihood as best they could, concentrating as they had in the last century, in menial, domestic and largely unskilled low-paying occupations (see Tables 5 and 6). [35]

THE MODERN CITY: 1970

Modern Philadelphia bears little resemblance to earlier periods. Tech-

33. Yancey and Ericksen, "The Structural Antecedents of Ethnic Communities," unpublished paper, (Temple University, 1976).

34. Yancey and Ericksen, "The Structural Antecedents.

35. Yancey and Ericksen, "The Structural Antecedents; Greenberg, "Industrialization in Philadelphia."

TABLE 7

PERCENT MANUFACTURING JOBS AT GIVEN DISTANCES (IN MILES)
FROM CENTER OF PHILADELPHIA: 1850–1970

	1850*			1880†			1930°			1970°		
DISTANCE	#	%	CUM %	#	%	CUM %	#	%	CUM %	#	%	CUM %
0–0.99	30,366	60.9	60.9	78,111	47.2	47.2	52,794	18.8	18.8	32,380	15.7	15.7
1.00–1.99	15,576	31.3	92.2	44,848	27.1	74.3	62,062	22.1	40.9	26,812	13.0	28.7
2.00–2.99	1353	2.7	94.9	20,521	12.4	86.7	48,582	17.3	58.2	23,305	11.3	40.0
3.00–3.99	192	0.4	95.3	4,634	2.8	89.5	39,596	14.1	72.3	31,143	15.1	55.1
4.00–4.99	387	0.8	96.1	3,806	2.3	91.8	42,404	15.1	87.4	37,536	18.2	73.3
5.00+	1959	3.9	100.0	13,570	8.2	100.0	35,384	12.6	100.0	55,067	26.7	100.0
Total Jobs:	49,833			165,489			280,823			206,243		

* Center is 3rd and Market.
† Center is 7th and Market.
° Center is 14th and Market.
SOURCES: Figures for 1850 and 1880 are computed from Philadelphia Social History Project compilations of the United States manuscript censuses of manufactures. Figures for 1930 and 1970 are computed from tract-level data taken from the Pennsylvania Industrial Directory.

nological change has continued to alter urban form and the means of crossing its increasingly inhabited spaces. Automobile suburbs have emerged in all directions and a wide-range of choice characterizes the housing market. Philadelphia's population peaked in 1950 at 2.1 million and was, in 1970, exactly as it had been in 1930: 1.95 million. Population density, however, continued its decline reaching three persons per dwelling in 1970—almost exactly half of what it had been in 1850.

Significant changes affected the city's economy. Some 75,000 manufacturing jobs were lost between 1930 and 1970, and the appearance of new jobs in the service sectors have not made up the loss.[36] In this regard, Philadelphia's experience resembles that of many older industrial cities in the Northeast. Large manufacturing employers have abandoned the city for regions with lower taxes, and a work force of nonunionized labor. The location of the remaining manufacturing activity has changed significantly. The

earlier shift in production technology, from coal and steam to electricity, combined with important changes in transportation technology in the post-World War II years, produced a marked decentralization of manufacturing jobs. The advent of the interstate highway system, connecting with urban expressways—and the emergence of the trucking industry—has led to the suburbanization of manufacturing activity in industrial parks in the surrounding SMSA. Of every ten manufacturing jobs in the city, the three-mile ring from the city's center held nine jobs in 1880, six in 1930 and four in 1970 (see Table 7).

These changes have had important consequences for Philadelphia's blacks—the city's most recent immigrants. Their numbers increased from 221,000 in 1930 to 645,000 in 1970, and their proportion of the city's population increased from one-tenth to one-third. Today's blacks inherit the oldest stock of deteriorated housing once inhabited by two earlier waves of immigrants, but the jobs which once were located nearby and provided previous newcomers with avenues for upward mobility are gone. Precisely at the mo-

36. Ericksen and Yancey, "The Location of Manufacturing Jobs, in "The Structural Antecedents."

ment in time when the worst of the racist hiring practices in industry appear to have abated, the most recent black immigrants find themselves at considerable remove from the industrial jobs that remain and thus are unable to repeat the essential experience of earlier white immigrants. When understood in light of changes in the city's economy as a whole, especially the decline of manufacturing activity and the demand for unskilled labor, it is plain to see that blacks in 1970 Philadelphia are faced with a very different set of circumstances from those which existed in the nineteenth and early twentieth centuries.[37]

The uniqueness of the black experience can be understood in yet another way. Blacks have always been the most segregated group in Philadelphia; this was true in the years 1850–1880, when blacks constituted but 4 percent of the city's population; in the years 1900–1930, when they were roughly 8 to 12 percent; and in 1970, when 33 percent of the city was black. Thus population size alone cannot explain their consistently higher levels of segregation; indeed, despite the fact that smaller groups requiring less housing are often the most segregated, as the size and proportion of the black population increased over time, so did their segregation from native whites: 47 (1850), 52 (1880), 61 (1930), 75 (1970) (see Table 2). This development is tied to the rapid growth of new suburban housing after World War II; whites settled in these automobile suburbs, and in classic "trickle down" manner, blacks inhabited the older housing vacated by whites.[38]

What sets the contemporary black experience off from that of earlier white immigrants (and earlier black Philadelphians), however, is not simply the consistently higher level of segregation. A new measure of residential experience has been developed that asks what proportion of a typical person's census tract consisted of the same group; for example, what percentage of the population in the typical black person's census tract was black? In this measure of "dominance," the composition of the areal unit is sought.[39] On the other hand, the Index of Segregation asks what percentage of a group would have to move to another location in the city to achieve a distribution throughout each areal unit in the city equal to their proportion of the city's total population.

Using the dominance measure, the striking differences that distinguish blacks from white immigrants can be seen.[40] The typical Irish

Structural Theories of Urban Form: Their Implications for Urban Renewal," in Charles Tilly, ed., *An Urban World* (Boston: Little-Brown, 1974), 442–446.

39. The dominance measure is an "experiential" rather than a "distribution" measure; it expresses "the proportion of the population in the mean individual's areal unit comprised by his group. . . ." The measure is calculated as a weighted arithmetic mean:

$$I_{dom} = \frac{1}{G} \sum_{i=1}^{n} \left(g_i \frac{g_i}{P_i} \right) = \frac{1}{G} \sum_{i=1}^{n} \frac{g_i}{P_i}^2$$

where G is the total population of the group whose residential pattern is being examined; g_i is the population of that group residing in the ith areal unit; p_i is the total population of the ith areal unit; and n is the total number of areal units; A. Burstein, "Patterns of Segregation and the Residential Experience," p.111.

40. The "dominance" measure not only operates to homogenize the experience of the two earlier waves of white immigrants, it also calls into question too great a reliance on the Index of Segregation as a useful tool to infer social experience. To the extent that cross-cultural contacts are central to our thinking about

37. Ericksen and Yancey, "Work and Residence," in "The Structural Antecedents."
38. William Alonso, "The Historic and the

immigrant in 1880 and the typical Italian immigrant in 1930, for example, shared a similar aspect of their residential experience. When the hypothetical immigrant in each era walked through his neighborhood, what kind of people might he have met? The Irishman in 1880 lived with 15 percent other Irish immigrants, 34 percent Irish stock, 26 percent all foreign born persons and 58 percent all foreign stock. The

typical Italian immigrant in 1930 had an almost identical experience. He lived with 14 percent other Italian immigrants, 38 percent Italian stock, 23 percent all foreign born persons and 57 percent all foreign stock.[41] In striking contrast, the typical black in 1970 lived in a census tract in which 74 percent of the population was black (see Table 8). What is more, the "dominance" of blacks has risen steadily since 1850 when it was 11 percent; it was not until 1950, however, that the typical black lived in a census tract with a black majority. Ghettoes are the product of the post-World War II city.

The black residential experience, differs from that of white immigrants in yet another important regard. As ethnic occupational segregation decreased over time—that is, as white immigrant groups gained access to a broader range of occupations—their residential segregation decreased. Quite the opposite was true for blacks: despite the occupational desegregation produced in recent decades by the opening of new job opportunities for blacks, their residential segregation has increased over time.

As measured by the Index of Dissimilarity, the differences between the occupational distributions of blacks and native-whites did not fall below 60 percent until 1940 when it reached 52 percent. After 1930, comparisons can be made only with all whites (native and foreign-born combined); it fell to 42 percent in 1950, 29 percent in 1960 and 25 percent in 1970. The significance of the

the socialization of the young and subsequent mobility and assimilation experience, the dominance measure, in getting more directly at who lives near whom, may be a better measure than the Index of Segregation; indeed we have seen that although some groups can be twice as segregated as others—as the new immigrants were compared to the old—they can display identical levels of dominance. Although the thrust of this essay is not methodological, we think it time that the uses of the Index of Segregation, particularly the assumptions that underlie its correlation with a wide range of social behaviors, be carefully reconsidered. We are not claiming that the Index of Segregation is without value, but rather that in many instances it may be (and has been) inappropriately applied. The socioeconomic correlates of the Index of Segregation and our new measure of dominance remain a topic for empirical investigation.

Although when compared to the black experience the differences between the old and new immigrants appear small indeed, there were differences nonetheless. While the dominance measures for the white immigrant groups were approximately equal, this does not mean that they had the same residential *pattern*. In order for the new immigrants, proportionally smaller than the old immigrants, to achieve so much higher measures of segregation than, and measures of dominance equal to, the old immigrants, they would have had to be considerably more clustered. Thus, relative to the entire settled area of the city, the residential pattern of the new immigrants must have been much more compact than that of the old. Accordingly, an examination of the dimensions of segregation reveals that while the very localized experiences of the old and new immigrants may have been the same, the old immigrants had access to more diverse areas of the city. See Burstein, "Patterns of Segregation."

41. Golab's description of 1915 immigrant residential patterns corroborates the argument presented here: "No immigrant group in the city ever totally monopolized a particular neighborhood to the extent that it achieved isolation from members of other groups." Golab, *Immigrant Destinations*, p. 112.

TABLE 8

INDICES OF DOMINANCE: 1850, 1880, 1930–1970 (248 TRACTS)

	1850	1880	1930	1940	1950	1960	1970
Blacks	11	12	35	45	56	72	74
Ireland							
Born	24	15	3	2	2		
2nd		19					
Stock		34	8			5	3
Germany							
Born	9	11	4	3	2		
2nd		14					
Stock		25	11			5	3
Great Britain							
Born			4	3	2		
Stock			12			5	3
Italy							
Born			14	13	9		
Stock			38			23	21
Poland							
Born			7	6	4		
Stock			20			9	8
USSR							
Born			14	12	9		
Stock			28			17	14
Foreign							
Born	32	26	23				
2nd		32	34				
Stock		58	57				
Native-White	68	44					
Other Foreign							
Born	7	8					
2nd		7					
Stock		14					

NOTE: See Notes for Tables 1 and 2.
SOURCES: See Sources for Table 2.

relatively sharp decline in occupational dissimilarity between blacks and whites after World War II, expecially in the decade of the 1950's, however, should not be exaggerated (see Table 9). In a 1975 survey of adult males in the Philadelphia Urbanized Area, blacks reported a mean income of $3,000 below whites even after the effects of age, education and occupation were controlled.[42]

42. Ericksen and Yancey, "Organizational Factors and Income Attainment: Networks, Businesses, Unions," unpublished paper (Temple University, 1978). This result is con-

SUMMARY AND CONCLUSIONS

Systematic data on levels of segregation, as measured by the index of dissimilarity and our measure of ethnic dominance, make clear that a "Tale of Three Cities" is the story of three distinct waves of immi-

sistent with those reported in many national studies.

The occupational dissimilarity scores are reported at the bottom of each occupational table. The scores can be interpreted in the same manner as the segregation scores: the percent of blacks who would have to shift to another occupational strata in order to approximate the same distribution as whites.

TABLE 9

OCCUPATIONAL DISTRIBUTION OF MALES AND FEMALES, 16+, BY ETHNICITY: 1970
(AS PERCENT OF ETHNIC GROUP)

	BLACKS		PUERTO RICANS		WHITES*	
	CITY	SMSA	CITY	SMSA	CITY	SMSA
Professional	7.7	8.1	4.4	5.3	15.1	17.2
Owners and Executives	2.5	2.5	1.4	1.9	7.0	8.8
Clerks and Sales	21.6	20.4	14.7	13.2	32.7	29.9
Trade and Transportation	5.2	5.3	4.3	3.4	3.8	3.4
Manufacturing	30.1	30.1	52.8	49.3	27.6	27.6
Domestic and Personal Service	22.7	23.1	13.8	14.2	8.0	7.8
Laborers	8.0	8.0	6.8	8.4	3.1	3.0
Agriculture	0.6	0.8	0.8	3.9	0.1	0.6
Other	1.7	1.6	0.8	0.5	2.5	1.5
Totals	232,192	279,703	6270	10,749	525,058	1,570,045
(Row %)	(30.4)	(15.8)	(0.8)	(0.6)	(68.8)	(83.6)
Dissimilarity from *All* Whites	24	25	36	37	—	—

* Includes a small number of non-Black non-Whites, i.e., Chinese, etc.
SOURCES: Figures are computed from published United States Census totals. See U.S. Bureau of the Census, *Census of Population: 1970*, v.I, "Characteristics of the Population," pt. 40, Pennsylvania—Section 1, (Washington, D.C.: U.S. Government Printing Office, 1973), 395, 400, 451, 456, 499, 504.

grants, three distinct opportunity structures and ecological forms, and three distinct settlement patterns. In each of the three cities, immigrants interacted with the urban structure they encountered and produced markedly different residential patterns.

The first city—the industrializing city of the mid-nineteenth century—was settled by large numbers of Irish, Germans and British of the "Old" immigration. They established integrated residential patterns which have persisted throughout the twentieth century.

The second city—the industrial city of the early twentieth century—was home for even greater numbers of Italians, Poles, and Russian Jews of the "New" immigration. The residential patterns they formed were much more segregated than those of their predecessors. Yet even here the

stereotypic notions of settlement and adjustment to conditions in the New World require some qualification. The experience of initial segregation in working and lower class ghettoes and subsequent occupational and residential mobility, as Sam Warner and Colin Burke pointed out, is a limited case in American history: limited to the "New" immigrants in the largest cities at the turn of the last century.[43] And, as the dominance data make clear, most immigrants never lived in ghettoes if they are understood as places inhabited only, or largely, by a single ethnic group.

The third city—"post-industrial" modern Philadelphia—was the destination for thousands of black migrants largely from the Southeast.

43. Sam Bass Warner and Colin Burke, "Cultural Change and the Ghetto," *Journal of Contemporary History* 4 (1969): 173–187.

Their segregation and dominance scores have increased steadily from 1850. Unlike earlier groups, today's blacks live in isolated ghettoes.[44]

Changes in the patterns of ethnic settlement, can only be fully understood within the context of an ecological explanation that focuses upon changes in the housing market, industrial base, transportation, production, and communication technologies. The ecological perspective makes it possible to explain the changing measures of segregation and dominance, important aspects of the ethnic experience, and the uniqueness of the black experience.

The many significant changes in the relationship between work and residence that characterized Philadelphia's growth over the last century had direct implications for the location, character and stability of ethnic communities. Under constraints of expensive transportation and limited housing, industrial affiliation had a greater impact on the residential choice of immigrants than did their ethnicity.

To the degree that specific ethnic neighborhoods were based on their concentration in nearby industrial employment, the stability of these neighborhoods has depended upon the stability of jobs. When contemporary observers seek explanations for stable neighborhoods, for example, they find strong ethnic ties; yet their analyses all too often confuse causes with effects. The strong ethnic ties are themselves the product of stable neighborhoods; the stability of the neighborhood results from the continuing presence of industrial employment opportu-

nities. The black slums in 1970, for example, were located primarily in areas that had no manufacturing jobs in 1930.[45]

This structural view then suggests that the presence of nearby industrial employment reinforces the stability of white ethnic communities, and it is the industrial concentrations of white ethnics rather than ethnic culture or historical accident that underlies resistance to black invasion. Previous research by Burgess and Duncan and Lieberson has suggested that historical accidents or differences in ethnic tolerance for blacks accounts for their differential resistance to black settlement.[46] The results presented here indicate that the frequently expressed stereotypes of resistant Poles, Italians, and fleeing Russian Jews are applicable only when one does not consider the impact of the ecological structure of the city, the position of these groups in the occupational structure, and their location and access to industrial employment. The reason that white ethnics on Chicago's South Side were able for so many years to prevent black residential penetration has more to do with the continued presence of their job opportunities in the nearby stock yards and steel mills than with cultural factors. The lack of adjacent industrial turf explains the rapid racial turnover that characterized Harlem's transition from an upper middle-class suburb

44. Puerto Ricans, a much smaller group than blacks, are in fact the most recent immigrants to the city and are also slightly more segregated than blacks, see Table 2.

45. Gladys Palmer, *Recent Trends in Employment and Unemployment in Philadelphia* (Philadelphia: Works Project Administration, Philadelphia Labor Market Studies, 1937); Ericksen and Yancey, "The Location of Manufacturing Jobs."

46. Burgess, "Residential Segregation;" Otis Dudley Duncan and Stanley Lieberson, "Ethnic Segregation and Assimilation," *American Journal of Sociology* 64 (January 1959): 364–74.

to a lower-class slum in the early decades of the twentieth century.[47] These same factors emerge from an examination of the ghettoes of blacks and Puerto Ricans in comtemporary Philadelphia; unlike the earlier white ethnic villages, these racial ghettoes have not formed around abundant employment opportunities; they emerged instead in economically depressed residential areas which were abandoned by affluent whites who moved to more distant suburbs seeking greater socioeconomic homogeneity, better schools, and more spacious housing.

A decade ago the *Report of the National Advisory Commission on Civil Disorders* asked why "the Negro has been unable to escape from poverty and the ghetto like the European immigrants?" Their answer stressed historical factors.[48]

47. Gilbert Osofsky, *Harlem: The Making of a Ghetto*. While carefully documenting the real estate boom and bust that followed the construction of the elevated lines which connected Harlem with lower Manhattan, Osofsky overlooked entirely the significance of the work-residence relationship in his explanation of the dramatic changes in Harlem's racial demography.

48. (New York: Bantam Books, 1968); see chapter 9, "Comparing the Immigrant and Black Experience," pp. 278–282. For a convincing critique of the "Last of the Immigrants" theory that focuses on patterns of intra- and inter-generational oecupational mobility and supports our argument nicely, see Stephan Thernstrom, *The Other Bostonians: Poverty and Progress in the American Metropolis* (Cambridge, Mass.: Harvard University Press, 1973), chapter 10, "Blacks and Whites," pp. 176–219. "By now . . . ," Thernstrom concluded, somewhat too optimistically in our opinion, "American Negroes may face opportunities and constraints that are fairly analogous to those experienced by the millions of European migrants who struggled to survive in the American city of the late nineteenth and early twentieth centuries. But until very recently, the problems of black men in a white society were different in kind from those of earlier newcomers . . . the main factor that will

They pointed to the changing nature of the American economy, to slavery and its legacy of racial discrimination, and to the decline of patronage and services when urban black voters win political power.

To the arguments of the Kerner Commision, three further points can be added. First, it is clear that the changing opportunity structure and the different ecological arrangements of the city provide the basic parameters within which the experience of white ethnics and blacks must be understood. To assume a constant opportunity structure and an unchanging ecological form is to seek explanations for differences in ethnic settlement and adjustment in the cultural origins of ethnic groups and thus to misdirect inquiry from the obvious. Cultural factors come into play only within the larger structure of the urban environment.[49] Second, the impact of housing and industrial location—the constraints that work and residence imposed on earlier immigrants—are significant. Western European immigrants came at the most propitious time; both the highly skilled Germans and British, and the relatively unskilled Irish, found ample opportunities. Even though the industrial base of the city began to decline at the turn of this century, it is clear that Eastern European immigrants, when compared with post World War II blacks, settled in what must be considered the "ghettoes of opportunity." Finally, the experience of blacks stands in sharp contrast to that of white

impede black economic progress in the future will be the forces of inertia that have been called passive or structural discrimination" (pp. 218–219).

49. Yancey, Ericksen and Richard N. Juliani, "Emergent Ethnicity: A Review and Reformulation," *American Sociological Review* 41 (June, 1976): 3.

ethnics. Not only has their segregation increased over the last century
—contrary to the standing theory of
assimilation—but it is also clear that
blacks have been forced to settle in
the oldest industrial and residential
areas of the city—areas which have
been left behind by the processes of
modern urban-industrial development.

There is little to be gained by continuing a debate among advocates of
structural and cultural points of view
where one is posed to the exclusion of
the other. Both play critical explanatory roles. Structural considerations
explain well the occupational and residential experience of white immigrants who settled in mid-nineteenth
and early twentieth-century Philadelphia; they do not explain the
black experience. Here the explanation must be racism. If it is understood as a cultural factor, then culture explains why blacks who lived
in Philadelphia at the same time
fared so badly despite the twin
structural advantages of abundant
industrial opportunities and residential location where these opportunities were particularly plentiful. If racial descrimination had been
absent in earlier Philadelphia, blacks
should have done at least as well if
not better than their white immigrant contemporaries.

In modern Philadelphia racism has
somewhat abated, but the twin structural advantages of the past have disappeared. Thus structural constraints
loom large today; though different
from the racial barriers that prevented
advancement in the past, they function just as effectively. They retard the
economic progress of all groups—
blacks and whites alike—who still
inhabit the depressed areas of a
city with a declining opportunity
structure.

Although the Bootstraps and the
Last of the Immigrants explanations
for the socioeconomic differential
that characterize blacks and whites
today are of markedly different
types, they have the same implications for public policy: do nothing.
Both explanations are false and
based on a mistaken understanding
of our history. Why these points of
view persist is important to comprehend. They are accepted in large
part because they justify things as
they are now. And in legitimating
the status quo, these two views demonstrate how what is believed about
the past affects the present—not in
abstract scholarly logic, but in the
material daily life of real people, not
only in Philadelphia, but across the
nation. Since our sense of history—
conscious or not—exercises a real
power in the present , it should sensitize us to the dangers of ahistorical social science.[50] This essay provides an empirically-grounded and
interdisciplinary historical perspective so often absent in discussions of
contemporary social problems and
their solutions.

The Bootstraps explanation looks
to the past, but however heroic the
sound which comes from praising
the courage and stamina of earlier
white immigrants, it rings totally un-
true when applied to the historical
experience of blacks. The Last of the
Immigrants explanation looks to the

50. See Stephan Thernstrom, "Further reflections on the Yankee City series: the pitfalls
of ahistorical social science," *Poverty and
Progress: Social Mobility in a Nineteenth-
Century City* (Cambridge, Mass.: Harvard
University Press, 1964), pp. 225–239; and
Michael B. Katz, "Introduction," *The People
of Hamilton, Canada West: Family and Class
in a Mid-Nineteenth-Century City* (Cambridge, Mass.: Harvard University Press,
1975), p. 1.

future, but the conditions that blacks face in modern Philadelphia are so different from those which earlier groups found that the analogy is thoroughly inappropriate. Unless major structural changes and perhaps some form of preferential treatment are undertaken at all levels of public and urban policy, it is doubtful that assimilation and economic progress for blacks will be possible. The approaches which blacks utilize to enter the American mainstream will certainly not be the same as those used by white immigrants; of necessity, they may have to be devised in ways yet unanticipated. As a national policy is formulated to revitalize our cities, it must be remembered that racial discrimination, though less pervasive, persists. The challenge is to recognize how our cities have changed and to use this understanding to provide real bootstraps for blacks so that they may indeed become the last of the immigrants.

ANNALS, AAPSS, 441, Jan. 1979

Race Relations and Residential Segregation in New Orleans: Two Centuries of Paradox

By DAPHNE SPAIN

ABSTRACT: Because of its origins as one of the oldest slave trading centers in the country, New Orleans has a unique history in both race relations and residential segregation. Slavery required blacks to live in close proximity to their white owners. This created a mixed residential pattern that was characteristic of other southern cities in the nineteenth century. The rigid caste/race system defined social distance when physical distance was lacking. In the twentieth century, the advent of civil rights and equality for blacks has led to less patriarchal race relations but, paradoxically, greater residential segregation. Blacks have become more residentially isolated since the turn of the century. This essay documents the disappearance of the classic "backyard pattern" in New Orleans.

Daphne Spain received her B.A. from the University of North Carolina, Chapel Hill, in 1972 and her Ph.D. from the University of Massachusetts in 1977. She taught at the University of New Orleans for a year before joining the Population Analysis Staff at the Census Bureau in 1978. She is currently investigating the effects of migration on career development; racial succession in housing; and black suburbanization.

NEW ORLEANS has the reputation of being the least American of American cities. Its European origins in the early eighteenth century are still most visible in the Vieux Carre, the French Quarter, and it is this tourist area that is romantically visualized when one mentions New Orleans. Even its slogan, "The city that care forgot," reinforces the image of New Orleans as a city untroubled by mainstream America's urban problems. If these urban problems can be partially defined in terms of race relations, however, New Orleans is very much in the mainstream.

A city so famous for its French and Spanish cosmopolitan aura must also be remembered for its role as the largest slave-trading center of the United States. A city that claims to be the "birthplace of jazz" is also the place about which the phrase "being sold down the river" was originated by slaves farther up the Mississippi, fearful of the hard life on Louisiana sugar and cotton plantations. Over one hundred years after slavery, New Orleans has its first black mayor with the election of Ernest "Dutch" Morial. But when Morial takes office there will still be private clubs, like the Mirabeau Bar and Clematis Restaurant, where one must ring a buzzer to be admitted. And there may still be the painted sign on the wall of a warehouse on Governor Nicholls Street near the French Market, "Colored Entrance Only," as a vestige of the Jim Crow era.

New Orleans in the 1970s is a pastiche—like other cities—of its past and present. What makes it atypical of other cities is its strange blend of European culture with the "peculiar institution" of slavery in its early stages of development. New Orleans has historically had a reputation of maintaining liberal race relations. Supposedly the close residential proximity of Creoles, Americans, and slaves, enforced by limited land area, contributed to a high tolerance for racial and ethnic differences. But before the Civil War and again after Reconstruction, legally enforced segregation between whites and blacks pervaded the social structure. Whatever tolerance there was thus existed within the strict norms of southern race relations. The "backyard" pattern of slave residences prevented social and economic segregation from being translated into housing segregation until the turn of the twentieth century. The Jim Crow era, from the 1890s until the 1950s, was the period in which New Orleans began adopting the residential patterns of large northern cities. Blacks became increasingly concentrated in the central city while whites settled the newly drained land surrounding the initial settlement.

The lack of urban riots in the 1960s and the election of black politicians in the 1970s indicate that New Orleans has a workable interracial community. But as race relations have improved, residential segregation has worsened. Social and economic conditions are combining to create racial enclaves of larger magnitude than previously were known in this city. Thus while other cities may be experiencing slight decreases in levels of residential segregation, New Orleans is experiencing slight increases in segregation because: 1) it started from a relatively low nineteenth century level, and 2) its black population is exceedingly poor and does not have the socioeconomic ability to move to the suburbs. The ways in which the special history of New Orleans has shaped existing residential patterns and race relations are the topic of this essay.

HISTORICAL BACKGROUND

The social history of New Orleans is a history of successive cultural layerings dating from its founding by the French in 1718. By 1763 New Orleans had become Spanish Territory, only to be returned to French rule in 1800. When the Louisiana Territory was sold to the United States in 1803, the city had already experienced nearly a century of European culture.

The Spanish and French were not the only residents of eighteenth century Louisiana. There were native Indians, whom Bienville tried to enslave as early as 1708; when that failed he attempted an exchange of Indians for blacks from the West Indies. Although their origins are unclear, there were reported to be approximately twenty blacks in Louisiana by 1717. The formal African slave trade began soon thereafter when a ship arrived in Pensacola in 1719 and slaves were sent to plantations outside New Orleans. The 1726 Census recorded 1,540 slaves for Louisiana (out of a total population of 3,997), 300 of whom lived in New Orleans; by 1732 there were nearly 1,000 slaves in New Orleans. With the erection of the first sugar mill, and the invention of the cotton gin in 1793, there was an increased demand for labor which translated into an increased demand for slaves. Between 1732 and 1785, therefore, the number of blacks in Louisiana grew from 2,000 to 16,500; between 1785 and 1810, the slave population more than doubled.[1]

Added to this mix of Spanish, French, and slave blacks were the free blacks, or "free people of color." By the census of 1788, their number amounted to 1,500.[2] By 1803 there were 1,335 free blacks in the city, or one-ninth of its total population.[3] A large part of that increase was due to the slave insurrection in Haiti in 1791 and the black uprising in San Domingo in 1796.[4] Despite legislation prohibiting it, there was a large influx of free people of color to New Orleans after this West Indian turmoil.

At the end of the eighteenth century, New Orleans society was thus characterized by several layers of ethnicity and race. Spanish and French composed the white society, while slave and free blacks composed the black society. The black society was not a united one, however. There were sharp class distinctions between free and slave blacks. Many forms of public entertainment and accomodations that were open to free men of color were closed to slaves.[5]

When the Americans arrived in 1803 there was yet another layer added to the city's already diverse culture. The Americans were confronted with not just a frontier town, but with a highly cultured "foreign" city. The French and Spanish were confronted with the brash vulgarities and backwoods manners of the "Americains." Instant antipathy developed. The city

1. John S. Kendall, "New Orleans' 'Peculiar Institution,'" *The Louisiana Historical Quarterly* 23 (1940): 868.

2. Grace King, *New Orleans: The Place and the People* (New York: Macmillan, 1915), p. 334.

3. James E. Winston, "The Free Negro in New Orleans, 1803–1860," *The Louisiana Historical Quarterly* 21 (1938): 1075.

4. Constance M. Green, *American Cities in the Growth of the Nation* (New York: Harper and Row, 1965), p. 71.

5. Winston, "The Free Negro in New Orleans," p. 1082.

soon became commercially and politically split between the old-line
Creoles (those of French and Spanish
heritage) and the new Americans.

On the eve of the War of 1812,
New Orleans was a predominantly
black city. There were 10,824 slaves,
5,727 free blacks, and 8,000 whites
living in New Orleans in 1810.[6]
The War of 1812 was particularly
important for the free colored population because they helped defend
the city. Forming a separate bat-
talion, they fought alongside whites
under General Jackson. After the
victory Jackson promised them re-
wards equal to those for white
soldiers; but many in New Orleans
felt Jackson had overstepped his
bounds. Whites perceived free Negroes as little different from slaves.
By 1816 such public sentiment resulted in legislation that segregated
nearly every conceivable facility in
New Orleans: theatres; the French
Opera House; public exhibitions;
hotels; Charity Hospital; public
schools; restaurants and saloons.
Jails were segregated, with different
uniforms for blacks and whites (a
seemingly redundant measure).
Streetcars were segregated and cars
for blacks were marked with a star
on all sides; hence the term "star"
evolved to denote all varieties of
segregation in New Orleans, much
as "Jim Crow" was used throughout the United States after 1890.

SLAVERY IN THE CITY

Congress outlawed the importa-
tion of slaves in 1808, but aboli-

tion of foreign slave trading simply
meant that Louisiana turned to the
interstate market for its labor supply.
In 1812, Louisiana was admitted to
the Union as a slave state, and some
of the largest slave auctions in the
country took place in New Orleans.
Richard C. Wade reports that the
"conveyance records show over
4400 sales in 1830, and, though the
figures fluctuated annually, over
3000 transactions took place in the
last antebellum year."[7] The most
famous auctions occurred at the St.
Charles Hotel. One account documents twenty-five slave pens within
one-half mile of the hotel, most of
them on Baronne, Gravier, Magazine, and Esplanade streets.[8] Wade
found the highest concentration in
1854 with seven slave dealers located in a single block of Gravier.
Orleans Parish was the third largest
slave-holding parish in the state,
with 18,068 slaves in 1850 and
13,385 in 1860.[9] Approximately one-
third of the New Orleans population owned one slave in 1860. These
figures were slightly lower than for
1820, since in that year "slavery
was as much a part of life in the
city as on farm and plantation."[10]

There were two types of slaves in
New Orleans at this time: those
waiting to be sold at auction and
those owned by residents. Slaves
in the city performed primarily
domestic tasks and were often hired
out for a day, month or even year
to defray the costs of their upkeep.
Some slaves lived away from their
master's house. But most lived in

6. In 1840, the free colored population
reached its peak of 20,000, Roger Fischer,
"Racial Segregation in Antebellum New Orleans" *American Historical Review* 74 (February, 1969): 929; The city remained black
from 1810 until 1840, when the white
population finally exceeded the black population. Kendall, "New Orleans' "Peculiar
Institution'," p. 869.

7. Richard C. Wade, *Slavery in the Cities*
(New York: Oxford University Press, 1964),
p. 199.
8. Robert Reinders, *End of an Era: New
Orleans 1850–1860* (New Orleans: Pelican,
1964), p. 25.
9. Reinders, *End of an Era*, p. 27.
10. Wade, *Slavery in the Cities*, p. 4.

close proximity to their owners, in compounds composed of the main house and slave quarters enclosed by walls. Fire insurance maps of New Orleans during this period show the city was interlaced with brick walls that divided each block into smaller sectors. There were few alleys because those became the focal points for slave life outside of white supervision.[11]

Housing for urban blacks during slavery was cramped and sparse, but seldom geographically segregated. Both slaves and free blacks were intermingled with whites throughout the city in what Demerath and Gilmore called the "backyard pattern."[12] The purpose of this mix was hardly to promote racial integration, but to keep an eye on blacks and prevent the growth of a cohesive black community. The limited land space in New Orleans also dictated such close living quarters. Wade interpreted this housing pattern as the physical manifestation of prevailing racial policy.[13]

New Orleans conformed to the backyard pattern very closely. Every area of the city had some blacks. The western part of the city had only 6,250 slaves to a total population of 35,000 in 1847, but they were evenly distributed throughout the seven wards.[14] Blassingame credits this residential integration with the easy race relations that existed during the nineteenth century. The interracial housing pattern often led to a disregard of the color line in such activities as drinking, eating, and gambling.[15]

New Orlean's special adaptation of the backyard pattern was the "superblock." In the American sector, the richest whites were located along the major boulevards, which were in turn separated by ten or fifteen smaller streets. Blacks who lived behind the big house lived several blocks behind the main boulevard on one of the interior streets. Thus "superblocks" about one-half mile square, with white perimeters and black cores, developed along such boundaries as St. Charles, Jefferson, and Napoleon Avenues.[16] Since not all whites could afford to live in mansions, however, the cores of superblocks were never entirely black. The remnants of this pattern can still be observed today with small four-room houses backed up behind nineteenth century mansions.

As urban slavery became less viable, housing arrangements began to disintegrate as well. Small black sections began to appear in southern cities by 1840, most of which were concentrated at the edge of town. The tendency for blacks to cluster together at the periphery was more pronounced in 1860 than in 1820. Thus on the eve of the Emancipation Proclamation, the segregation that pervaded other areas of life was finally instituted in housing.

DISEASE AND DIVISIONS

Between the War of 1812 and the Civil War, two major events affected the population and its dis-

11. Wade, *Slavery in the Cities*, p. 60.
12. N. J. Demerath and Harlan Gilmore, "The Ecology of Southern Cities," in *The Urban South*, ed. Rupert Vance and N. J. Demerath (Chapel Hill: University of North Carolina Press, 1954), p. 155.
13. Wade, *Slavery in the Cities*, p. 75.
14. Wade, *Slavery in the Cities*, p. 76.

15. John W. Blassingame, *Black New Orleans: 1860–1880* (Chicago: University of Chicago Press, 1973), p. 16.
16. Peirce F. Lewis, *New Orleans: The Making of an Urban Landscape* (Cambridge, MA: Ballinger, 1976), p. 44.

tribution in New Orleans. The first was a series of epidemics which started in the 1820s and culminated in 1832 with a combination of yellow fever and cholera that killed 5,000 people in ten days. Another major yellow fever outbreak struck in 1847, leaving over 2,000 dead. Neither of these was as bad as 1852, however, when 1,365 died in one week, with the toll for that summer at 8,000.[17] Until the swamps were drained and filtered water introduced in 1910, New Orleans had a well deserved reputation as the most deadly city in the U.S.

While epidemics were affecting the population size of the city, events on the political front were affecting the distribution of that population. In 1836, relations between the Creoles and the Americans had deteriorated to such an extent that the city was actually split into three municipalities: that between Canal and Esplanade Streets to be governed by the Creoles; west of Canal by the Americans; and east of the Quarter by immigrant truck farmers. Each sector had its own fiscal system and its own currency (called "shin plasters") with which to pay employees. The Americans moved ahead with street and wharf repairs, public school building, and numerous other civic improvements, and by the time the three sectors recombined in 1852, New Orleans was an American city.

During this sixteen year period ethnic loyalties were so great that the Creole and American societies rarely mixed. The Americans created separate churches, cemeteries, canals, and public parks in parallel development to the old French Quarter. As they moved farther

west, they constructed the Garden District as a counterpart to the fine homes in the Quarter. Canal and Esplanade Streets were perceived almost as national boundaries, and people of one political sector rarely lived in the other sector. Well before the outbreak of the Civil War, therefore, New Orleans had experienced not only legal segregation between races, but had formalized ethnic segregation as well. The Civil War separating North and South was thus just another schism in the history of New Orleans.

THE CIVIL WAR

Between 1860 and 1870, the white population of New Orleans declined from 144,601 to 140,923, but the black population doubled from 24,074 to 50,456. This large growth began when the city fell to the Federals in 1862. Although the rate of black increase declined steadily after 1870, it never fell below twelve percent in any decade before 1900.[18] It was just after the Federal victory that the free black population mounted sustained protests against the color barrier. In a battle that was to last fifteen years, free blacks fought all forms of public segregation: in schools (for which they paid taxes but could not let their children attend); in theatres; in hotels and in restaurants. The first of four black newspapers was formed at this time, L'Union (1862–1864), to be followed by the Tribune (1864–1870), the Louisianian (1870–1882), and the Pelican (1886–1889). Despite the public pressure exerted by the black media, the fight for civil rights made little headway until the Radical Republicans cleared the

17. Charles N. Glaab and Theodore A. Brown, *A History of Urban America* (New York: Macmillan 1967), p. 89.

18. Dale A. Somers, "Black and White in New Orleans: A Study in Urban Race Relations, 1865–1900," *The Journal of Southern History* 40 (February 1974): 21.

way for Congressional Reconstruction in March 1867, by granting blacks the right to vote.

A massive demonstration in May of 1867 led to the desegregation of city streetcars. The Louisiana Constitution of 1868 (known as the "black and tan" constitution due to its creation by Negroes and Republicans) wrote desegregation of public schools and accommodations into Louisiana law. Blacks attended public schools from 1871 to 1877, and sometimes ate and drank in white restaurants and saloons.[19] These laws never really took effect in rural parishes, but New Orleans blacks could demand desegregation of their Radical representatives, and the Federal soldiers stood by to support them. The war against the color line in Louisiana was fought "in the streets and saloons and schools of New Orleans."[20]

By 1870, however, blacks had still not achieved full equal rights. The private school system was revived from pre-Civil War days so that white children could avoid attending integrated schools. In 1868 there were only ten private schools in the city; by 1871 there were over one hundred. In September of 1874 a white supremacist organization, the White League, led a three-day outbreak that temporarily overthrew the Radical government. That was followed shortly by the great school riots of 1874.[21] Although the Civil Rights Act of 1866 helped put some force behind the state constitution,

the days of black equality were numbered. Federal troops were withdrawn from New Orleans in 1877 and the Democratic "redeemers" who came to power soon reestablished the black person's inferior status in Louisiana.

THE INTRODUCTION OF JIM CROW

The Democrats passed discriminatory legislation in the 1890s when it appeared that they would no longer face interference from the federal government. Interracial marriages that had been legalized in 1870 were prohibited in 1894. The *Plessy* v. *Ferguson* ruling endorsing "separate but equal" facilities was a Louisiana case settled by the Supreme Court in 1896.[22] Blacks were disenfranchised by the state constitutional convention in 1898. By 1902, Jim Crow laws were in full effect with the resegregation of city streetcars.

The only apparent exception to the interracial schisms of the 1890s was the labor movement in New Orleans. There was a strike of both black and white longshoremen in 1865, and a Negro Longshoremen's Protective Union was formed in 1872 to divide jobs with whites.[23] The Knights of Labor organized associations of skilled and unskilled, black and white workers into geographic districts, and by 1887 there were twelve such associations in

19. Somers "Black and White in New Orleans," p. 24; Fischer, "Racial Segregation in Antebellum New Orleans," p. 936.

20. Roger Fischer, "The Post-Civil War Segregation Struggle," in *The Past as Prelude: New Orleans 1718–1968*, ed. Hodding Carter (New Orleans: Pelican, 1968), p. 295.

21. Fischer, "The Post-Civil War Segregation Struggle," p. 300.

22. Homer Adolph Plessy, one-eighth Negro and seven-eighths white, was arrested for refusing to ride in the "colored" section of a train from New Orleans to Covington, La.; this violated the Louisiana law requiring "equal but separate accomodations for the white and colored populations." Albert P. Blaustein and Robert L. Zangrando, eds., *Civil Rights and the American Negro: A Documentary History* (New York: Washington Square Press, 1968), p. 189.

23. Somers, "Black and White in New Orleans," p. 30.

New Orleans and thirty outside the city. This interracial labor activity culminated in the three-day General Strike of 1892, which was "the first general strike in American history to enlist both skilled and unskilled labor, black and white, and to paralyze the life of a great city."[24] More than 20,000 men participated in the strike. Counting their families, they equalled nearly one-half of the city's population.

This form of racial cooperation soon ended, however, and by 1900 Jim Crow was as prevalent in the city as in the country. The turn of the century in New Orleans was ushered in by a race riot that was to "establish the pattern for Negro-white relations for the next half century."[25]

TWENTIETH CENTURY—THE FIRST HALF

The New Orleans Race Riot of 1900 was precipitated by the police questioning of a black man, Robert Charles, who was active in the Liberian emigration movement. The police and Charles exchanged shots; Charles killed several officers and a three-day riot ensued in which whites killed over 30 blacks; three whites were wounded in the rioting, and Charles killed and wounded fifteen more people before he was shot. The riot was partially attributable to economic conditions in New Orleans at the time. There had been several years of heavy black inmigration from the plantations, and blacks were displacing whites in unskilled jobs. Over 90 percent of the labor force in public works was black in 1900. The level

of prejudice had intensified to such an extent that Mayor Capdeville won the 1900 election on the promise that "public works must be done by whites."[26]

Two technological inventions combined at the turn of the century to help shape the racial geography of New Orleans. The first was the Wood Pump. Invented in 1917, it was the first effective means of draining the large swampy areas surrounding the city. The city then expanded in directions thought previously impossible. Because the land was opened up during the Jim Crow era, however, only whites could take advantage of the newly available housing. Thus the Wood Pump was an unwitting agent of residential segregation in New Orleans.[27]

The other event was the expansion of the city streetcar system. With public transportation available, blacks no longer had to live near their white employers and they began moving back toward the central business district, into formerly swampy areas.[28] Public transportation also meant that whites could move farther out of the city and still be within reasonable commuting distance of the business district. The two opposite directions in which the races moved set the stage for the development of racial enclaves.

24. Roger W. Shugg, "The New Orleans General Strike of 1892," *The Louisiana Historical Quarterly* 21 (April, 1938): 547.

25. Somers, "Black and White in New Orleans," p. 42.

26. Parkash Kaur Bains, "The New Orleans Race Riot of 1900" (Diss., University of New Orleans, 1970), p. 10.

27. Lewis, *New Orleans: The Making of an Urban Landscape*, p. 63.

28. H. W. Gilmore, "The Old New Orleans and the New: A Case for Ecology," *American Sociological Review* 9 (1944): p. 393; Zane Miller, "Urban Blacks in the South, 1865–1920: The Richmond, Savannah, New Orleans, Louisville, and Birmingham Experience," in *The New Urban History*, ed. Leo Schnore (Princeton, NJ, Princeton University Press, 1975) p. 200.

The beginning of this clustering did not become evident until the 1930s. Levels of residential segregation, as calculated by the index of dissimilarity, working from census tracts and ward data when it became available, indicate that scores were fairly stable until 1930 and then began to increase gradually to their highest level in 1960. These calculations reveal modern levels of segregation that surpass those of seventy years ago.

Scattered literature about New Orleans during the first half of the twentieth century suggests that although there was a Negro "Main Street"—Rampart, on the edge of the French Quarter—there were no neighborhoods in the city with a concentration of a majority of blacks.[29] But by 1950 there were numerous segregated blocks emerging in the city. Fifty-seven percent of all blocks had less than one percent black housing units, while eight percent had less than one percent white.[30] This could be interpreted to mean that thirty-five percent of all blocks were integrated. A housing profile for New Orleans blacks in 1950 shows that such integration did not insure equality, however. Fewer than twenty-five percent of blacks were home owners compared to forty-four percent of whites; median rent for blacks was $13 less per month than for whites; and black owner-occupied homes were valued

at $3,800 as compared with $10,000 for whites. Four-fifths of all black dwellings were dilapidated or lacked plumbing, and forty percent were overcrowded. "Nonsegregation for Negroes in New Orleans seemed to mean the right to crowd into old and poor dwellings as whites left them for new housing."[31]

It may be true that there were few neighborhoods or blocks that were completely white or completely black between 1900 and 1950. But if the distribution of the black population is examined by wards, it becomes clear that over twenty-five percent of all blacks in the city were concentrated in two or three out of a total of seventeen wards during this period, as shown in Table 1.

TWENTIETH CENTURY—THE SECOND HALF

Ironically, an effort to supply good, inexpensive public housing began the process which put an end to the relative integration of New Orleans neighborhoods. The Housing Authority of New Orleans was created in 1937, and was the first such agency in the United States to receive federal funds for slum clearance and publicly subsidized housing. By the end of 1941, the Housing Authority had built two white projects (with 1,826 units) and three black projects (2,309 units), with another black one under construction. By 1956, when the Desire Project was completed, there were 3,102 units for whites and 7,173 units for blacks.[32] The projects were eventually integrated but remained predominantly black.

29. John H. Rohrer and Munro S. Edmonson, *The Eighth Generation* (New York: Harper, 1960); Henry Allen Bullock, "Urbanism and Race Relations", in *The Urban South*, ed. Rupert Vance and N. J. Demerath (Chapel Hill: University of North Carolina Press, 1954) p. 222.

30. Forrest E. LaViolette, "The Negro in New Orleans," in *Studies in Housing and Minority Groups*, ed. Nathan Glazer and David McIntire (Berkeley: University of California Press, 1960), p. 116.

31. LaViolette, "The Negro in New Orleans," p. 117.

32. LaViolette, "The Negro in New Orleans," p. 119.

The areas in which these projects were built have become the current areas of greatest black concentration. (Table 1). In 1960, LaViolette wrote that residential segregation in New Orleans was increasing, but was paradoxically increasing the potential political power of blacks by making it easier to organize the community. But, he predicted, as blacks gained in power, that power would be turned against the segregation that originally made it possible. Later events tended to support his prediction.

The Seventh Ward has consistently contained over 10 percent of the black population, while the Third and Eleventh overlap as areas of high black concentration. The emergence of the Ninth Ward in 1960, as an area in which nearly 25 percent of all blacks lived, is largely due to urban renewal. Not only is the city's largest housing project (Desire/Florida) located in the Ninth Ward, but blacks displaced by other types of urban renewal, for example the Interstate and the Superdome, were forced into the Ninth Ward as one of the few remaining low rent areas. The area is now almost 90 percent black and has some of the city's highest unemployment, illiteracy, and poverty rates. Thus, in 1960 over 40 percent of all blacks lived in only two wards, the Seventh and the Ninth, compared to the 27 percent to 36 percent concentrated in two wards in earlier years.

Although data by ward are not available after 1960, it is possible to get a current estimate of black population distribution by ward using the voter registration lists for 1977. These records for the 1977 mayoral election indicate that the black population has become even more segregated since 1960. Twenty-

nine percent of all black registered voters lived in the Ninth Ward in October, 1977, and seventeen percent in the Seventh Ward, for a total of forty-six percent of the black registered population of voters.[33]

There are obvious drawbacks to the use of voter registration data rather than actual population. Blacks are historically underregistered compared to whites. The percent of the black population registered to vote in 1960 varied from 10.2 to 25.5 compared to 36.7 to 64.6 percent for whites the same year. In 1960, registered voters constituted 18.5 percent of the black population in the Seventh Ward and 12.7 percent in the Ninth Ward. Whites registered to vote equalled 39.6 percent in the Seventh and 37.6 percent in the Ninth Wards.[34]

Voter registration figures actually underestimate the amount of racial segregation because the Ninth Ward has one of the lowest voter registration rates due to its high incidence of poverty and illiteracy. But with a black candidate in the 1977 election there is reason to believe there was higher black registration than in 1960. If that were the case, the estimate might be closer to the actual population figures than in 1960. Whatever adjustments are made, however, figures still indicate that blacks have become increasingly residentially isolated since the turn of the century.

The *Brown* v. *Board of Education* decison in 1954 marked the legal end of the Jim Crow era. Segregation of public schools ended in New Orleans in 1960 with a federal

33. Mr. Joseph Givens, "Total Community Action, New Orleans, Louisiana," April 1978, personal communication.

34. Wards of New Orleans, Bureau of Governmental Research, New Orleans, Louisiana, 1961, p. 40.

decree from Judge J. Skelley Wright. A poll taken just after his ruling revealed that 82 percent of New Orleans parents would rather see the schools closed than desegregated.[35] Disputes over the progress of integration continued until 1966. Many parents opted out of the fray by sending their children to private schools set up exclusively to avoid desegregation. New Orleans today has a high proportion of its school age population in private schools; thirty-one percent of the high-school students attend nonpublic institutions in the city.[36] There are still occasional racial upheavals in high schools which cause them to be shut down; a student was killed in one such incident. But the frenzy of the "cheerleaders" of the early 1960s has ebbed, in New Orleans as elsewhere.

The 1960s were relatively calm in New Orleans. There were no riots in the mid-60s as there were in other large cities, although the socioeconomic conditions for blacks were as bad or worse than elsewhere. That the city expected the possibility of riots is evidenced by a project, funded by the New Orleans Human Relations Committee, on the establishment of black-white sensitivity groups. It was an effort to bring blacks and whites into contact with one another to reduce racial tensions in the community. The results were inconclusive and the attempt was apparently abandoned when things cooled off in the rest

of the country.[37] Such a small-scale attempt (only 40 people were involved) at remedying a 200 year-old problem seems desperately naive in retrospect.

New Orleans began the decade with the fifth highest level of poverty in the country. It also had the highest amount of sub-standard housing of any city. Unemployment was high, varying from 3 to 7 percent throughout the 1960s; among blacks rates varied from 10 to 35 percent, depending on age and sex.[38]

Three largely black areas emerged as "target areas" for the newly created Model Cities Program: the Desire-Florida Housing Project; Central City Housing Project; and the Lower Ninth Ward. Although voter registration has been very low—13 percent in both the 1950 and 1960 elections among blacks in the Ninth Ward,[39] LaViolette's thesis regarding the relationship of residential segregation and political power appears to have been supported in the 1960s with the election of the first black to the Louisiana legislature since Reconstruction.[40] That man was E. N.

37. City of New Orleans Human Relations Committee, "Report to the Committee: A Pilot Study for the Establishment of Black-White Sensitivity Groups in the City of New Orleans," New Orleans, Louisiana, 1969.

38. New Orleans City Demonstration Agency, "First Year Action Plan for New Orleans' Model Cities Program," March 1970.

39. Leonard Reissman, K. H. Silvert, and Cliff Wing, Jr., "The New Orleans Voter: A Handbook of Political Description," *Tulane Studies in Political Science*, vol. II, (New Orleans, LA: Tulane University, Urban Life Research Institute, 1955) p. 17; Bureau of Governmental Research, 1961, p. 40.

40. Martin Siegel, *New Orleans: A Chronology and Documentary History, 1539–1970* (Dobbs Ferry, New York: Oceans Publications, Inc., 1975), p. 55.

35. Warren Breed, "The Emergence of Pluralistic Public Opinion in a Community Crisis," in *Applied Sociology*, ed. Alvin Gouldner and S. M. Miller (New York: The Free Press, 1965), p. 130.

36. *Louisiana School Directory*, State Department of Public Education, Baton Rouge, Louisiana, 1977.

TABLE 1

NEW ORLEANS WARDS WITH THE HIGHEST PROPORTIONS OF THE TOTAL BLACK POPULATION:
1900–1930; 1960*

WARD NUMBER	3	7	9	11	TOTAL %
1900	.146	.124			.270
1910	.136	.114		.112	.362
1920	.109	.114		.121	.344
1930		.137		.135	.272
1960		.166	.249		.415

* Calculated by dividing the number of blacks in each ward by total number of blacks in the city.[34]

Morial, who has now been elected mayor of the city. It was estimated that approximately ninety-five percent of the black vote went to Morial as did only twenty percent of the white vote.[41] Morial could not have won on black votes alone; he needed the coalition of both blacks and whites. But he also could not have won without the solid support of the black community, the successful organization of which may have been the result of encroaching residential segregation.

Studies conducted during the 1960s reflect an awareness of the problem of race relations and housing discrimination in New Orleans. The Urban League catalogued a list of grievances against banks, the FHA, VA, and realtors as agents of housing discrimination.[42] Another study found that blacks paid a greater proportion of their income for housing than any other group in the city; lived in overcrowded conditions more frequently; and were less satisfied with their living arrangements. The same study documented

covert racial discrimination among realtors and lending agencies.[43] A more optimistic report found no evidence of concerted price discrimination in black housing, but acknowledged that blacks got less quality (in both housing and neighborhood) for their money than whites.[44]

Although the city escaped riots, there was racial unrest due to the poor housing and socioeconomic status of blacks. The 1970s were ushered in by a particularly violent incident. A branch of the Black Panther Party set up headquarters in an apartment in the Desire Housing Project. On 16 September 1970, the New Orleans police were involved in a shoot-out with the group which resulted in the death of a black youth, the wounding of three, and the arrest of fourteen other blacks. Three months later local clergymen protested that the police had gained entry to the apartment by wearing clerical garb. Mayor Landrieu pledged that such tactics would

41. The New Orleans States-Item, 10 December, 1977, p. A-5.
42. Urban League of Greater New Orleans, "To House a City: An Introductory Handbook on Housing in New Orleans," Division of Community Services, Department of Housing, New Orleans, Louisiana, November 1967.

43. Leonard Reissman, "Housing Discrimination in New Orleans: Summary and Recommendations," New Orleans, Louisiana Tulane University, Tulane Urban Studies Center, 1970.
44. Larry Smith and Company, New Orleans Community Renewal Program, Report Series #4, "Minority Housing Patterns, Needs, and Policies," Report to the City Planning Commission, City of New Orleans, May 1970.

not be permitted again, possibly an admission that such had actually been used.[45] Black Panther activities dissipated after the confrontation and the organization is no longer highly visible in New Orleans.

In 1970, New Orleans was 45 percent black, with projections of a black majority by 1980. But economic conditions for blacks failed to improve over the 1960 level. Forty-four percent of the city's blacks earned incomes below the poverty level, compared to 10 percent of the whites. Blacks below the poverty level made up fully 20 percent of the New Orleans population in 1970, and the housing projects showed the highest overlap of percent black and four poverty indicators: highest percentage of families below the poverty level; lowest median family income; highest percentage receiving public assistance; and highest unemployment.[46]

Approximately 70 percent of the housing in New Orleans was over twenty-one years old in 1970, and it is estimated that 25 percent of the housing was substandard at that date.[47] Homeownership rates are currently low for the city as a whole —35%—and blacks average only a 10 percent ownership rate.[48]

Previously small and scattered all-black residential areas have begun to expand. The number of census tracts with over 80 percent black nearly doubled between 1940 and 1970.[49] As they increase in land area, the black areas are beginning to merge toward each other. It appears that by 1980 there could be a black residential belt following the curve of the river, in the area that was undesirable backswamp one hundred years ago.

Other forces are coalescing to relocate the black population and in the process destroy what viable communities once existed. In 1965 a new Interstate highway was built through the middle of Claiborne Avenue, a main thoroughfare in the central city black community. Where there were once old oaks comparable to the ones on St. Charles, there are now concrete posts holding up more concrete. A Cultural Center was located just outside the French Quarter in the old black community of Treme. The plans called for the demolition of eight square blocks; by the time construction began in the early 1970s, 410 families had been displaced.[50] The Cultural Center is surrounded on all sides by six-foot barbed wire fences and one must park inside the gates to attend any functions. Thus the Center has been effectively cut off from the French Quarter which it was meant to border. The Louis Armstrong Park, on the site of the former slave dancing grounds called Congo Square, is practically inaccessible to the surrounding black community.

Aside from the efforts of city officials to improve New Orleans at the seeming expense of blacks, private investors are having an impact as well. The "renovation boom" experienced

45. Siegel, *New Orleans: A Chronology and Documentary History*, 1539–1970, p. 57.
46. Total Community Action, *Profile of Poverty in New Orleans* (April 1973), p. 1.
47. New Orleans City Planning Commission, "New Orleans Housing, 1973: Problems, Goals, Programs." (1973), p. 1.
48. Office of Policy Planning and Analysis, Needs Assessment, City of New Orleans, 2 June 1977.

49. Lewis, *New Orleans: The Making of an Urban Landscape*, p. 98.
50. Beverly G. Andry, "The Impact of Civic Decisions on Treme: A Community in Transition," (Diss., University of New Orleans, 1976).

by other large central cities has hit New Orleans with a vengeance. Colliseum Square, the Irish Channel, Algiers Point all are previously black neighborhoods with good housing stock which have become targets of upper middle class white renovators. Housing prices in some of these areas have doubled within a year or less. Many blacks, the elderly, and the poor are being displaced.[51] And there is evidence that the renovators expect their neighborhoods to become increasingly white over the next five years.[52] Although some houses of valuable architectural design are being salvaged, there is local concern over the fate of those displaced. What is good for the city is not always good for the poorer citizens, of whom New Orleans has a large proportion.

All these factors have led to increasing levels of residential segregation for the city. Indexes of segregation show an increase from 1940 (81.0) to 1960 (86.3) and then a slight decline for 1970 (83.1).

The decline from 1960 to 1970 is probably a result of the development of a new section of the city known as "New Orleans East." Although suburban in character, it is within the city limits and provides inexpensive housing and a large number of rental units. This is also the same area where a privately

developed all-black upper middle class neighborhood (Pontchartrain Park) was built in the 1950s. Since New Orleans East was only sparsely populated in 1960, the introduction of a black suburban enclave contributed to increasing the index of segregation. After whites and other blacks started moving out to the surrounding area, however, which occurred during the 1960s, the index declined. New Orleans East now has an even racial balance, but the belief among realtors and New Orleans residents who live there is that it will eventually become mostly black. When and if that happens, the index of segregation will probably rise once again.

CONCLUSIONS

New Orleans in the late 1970s is catching up with the rest of the country in both race relations and residential segregation. A largely black city has finally elected a black mayor, and black residential enclaves are merging into the ghettos characteristic of other large cities. As Taeuber says of old southern cities with remnants of the backyard pattern, urban renewal is completing the process of "racial modernization."[53]

In 1980, the residential segregation score for New Orleans will no doubt be higher than previous scores. It cannot increase indefinitely, of course, but if current trends persist the score may reach the low 90s. A growing black population with nearly half of its members in poverty does not bode well for the integration of blacks into white middle class neighborhoods. The

51. Ralph E. Thayer and Paul Waidhas, "What do In-Town Investors Want?," *Urban Land* 37 (June, 1977): 19–21; Helen Rosenberg, "Areas of Relocation of Displaced Lower Garden District and Irish Channel Residents," (Diss. University of New Orleans, 1977); Andry, "The Impact of Civic Decisions on Treme."

52. Shirley Laska and Daphne Spain, "Impact on New Orleans of 'Back to the City' Movement: Implications for Future Urban Problems," paper presented at the Southern Sociological Society, March, 1978.

53. Karl E. Taeuber, "Racial Segregation: The Persisting Dilemma," *Annals of the American Academy of Political and Social Science* 422 (November 1975) p. 95.

suburban parishes around New Orleans have been increasing in population while New Orleans has lost population, and the white inner-city renovators are a small minority compared to the white migrators to the suburbs. If blacks cannot join that suburban push, the central city will not only become more black, but more segregated as well.

The forecast is gloomy. Many in New Orleans are putting their faith in the new black administration. But the city is in such poor financial condition that it will take years to implement programs aimed at improving the socioeconomic status, and hence, the housing conditions, of blacks. As New Orleans joins mainstream America, it also joins the ranks of cities with severe residential segregation.

ANNALS, AAPSS, 441, Jan. 1979

Barriers to the Racial Integration of Neighborhoods: The Detroit Case

By REYNOLDS FARLEY, SUZANNE BIANCHI, and DIANE COLASANTO

ABSTRACT: This paper reports findings from a 1976 study of the causes of racial residential segregation in the Detroit metropolis. One of the reasons for the persistence of high levels of segregation is white ignorance of the changing values of other whites. If all whites— especially real estate dealers and lenders—recognized the willingness of most whites to accept black neighbors, to remain in racially mixed areas and even to consider purchasing homes in neighborhoods which have black residents, the pattern of whites fleeing when blacks enter their neighborhood might be altered. Blacks overwhelmingly prefer mixed neighborhoods but are somewhat reluctant to move into a neighborhood where they would be the only black family because they fear the hostile reactions of whites. Blacks may also be ignorant of the changing racial attitudes of whites and may overestimate the difficulties which would arise if they entered a white neighborhood.

Reynolds Farley is an Associate Director of the University of Michigan's Population Studies Center and chairman of the Department of Sociology. He is continuing to analyze the causes of racial residential segregation in the Detroit area and is conducting an investigation of changing levels of racial segregation in the nation's public schools.

Suzanne Bianchi recently completed a dissertation at the University of Michigan which determined how changes in the family living arrangements of blacks and whites affected their economic well-being. She is now employed in the Education and Social Stratification Branch of the Population Division of the United States Bureau of the Census.

Diane Colasanto completed a dissertation at the University of Michigan which described the relationship between the attitudes of Detroit area blacks and whites and their residential preferences. She is presently developing models of racial residential segregation in American cities, using both demographic and attitudinal data, and is an Assistant Professor of Sociology at the University of Wisconsin in Madison.

S INCE the early 1960s there have been important changes in the opportunities available to blacks in the United States. Courts have overturned segregationist practices and numerous laws have been enacted at the local, state, and federal level to encourage a more racially integrated society. There is ample documentation that blacks have made significant gains since 1960 in the economic and political spheres.[1]

Despite legislation and economic improvements, levels of racial residential segregation in 1970 were approximately as great as they were decades earlier.[2] The Taeubers' investigation demonstrated that stable interracial neighborhoods were extremely rare in American cities of all sizes and in cities of each region.[3] Long documented the continued growth of the black population in the largest urbanized areas from 1960 to 1970—a growth that has been con-

centrated within central cities.[4] In 1970, a very small proportion of blacks lived in suburbs and those few who resided there tended to be concentrated in largely black neighborhoods.[5]

The residential segregation of blacks from whites remains the principal barrier to further racial progress. Residence patterns have the capability of aiding or hindering the achievement of racial equality of opportunity—a fact explicitly recognized in the use of busing to integrate schools. To the extent that residential segregation impedes equal access to educational and employment opportunities, it is an important social policy consideration. In addition, being neighbors affords a realm of contact quite different from contact on the job or at school. A fully integrated society—if that is the goal—necessitates opportunities for contact at such a level.

If policies are to be developed which will decrease racial residential segregation, it is necessary to investigate those social processes and beliefs which currently confine whites and blacks to different neighborhoods. Traditionally there have been three explanations for racial residential segregation: economic, institutional discrimination, and the preferences of blacks.

Economic argument

The economic argument contends that racial residential segregation

1. U.S., Commission on Civil Rights, *Social Indicators of Equality for Minorities and Women* (August, 1977); R. Freeman, "Black Economic Progress Since 1964," *Public Interest* (Summer 1978): 52–68; S. Levitan, W. Johnston, and R. Taggert, *Still a Dream: The Changing Status of Blacks Since 1960* (Cambridge: Harvard University Press, 1975); U.S., Bureau of the Census, "The Social and Economic Status of the Black Population in the United States, 1974," *Current Population Reports*, Series P-23, No. 54 (July, 1975); R. Hauser and D. Featherman "White-Nonwhite Differentials in Occupational Mobility Among Men in the United States, 1962–1972," *Demography* (May 1974): 247–266.

2. A. Sørensen, K. Taeuber and J. Hollingsworth, "Indexes of Racial Residential Segregation for 109 Cities in the United States, 1940 to 1970," *Sociological Focus* (April 1975) Tables 1 and 2; T. Van Valey, W. Roof and J. Wilcox, "Trends in Residential Segregation: 1960–1970," *American Journal of Sociology* (January 1977) Tables 1 and 2.

3. K. and A. Taeuber, *Negroes in Cities* (Chicago: Aldine, 1965), 105–114.

4. L. Long, "How the Racial Composition of Cities Change," *Land Economics* (August 1975).

5. B. Berry and J. Kasarda, *Contemporary Urban Ecology* (New York: Macmillan, 1977) 23–47; A. Hermalin and R. Farley, "The Potential for Residential Integration in Cities and Suburbs: Implications for the Busing Controversy," *American Sociological Review* (October 1973): 605–608.

exits primarily because blacks cannot afford more integration. That is, blacks do not have the financial resources to purchase or rent housing in white areas of central cities or in suburban rings. While it is true that even in 1977 black family income was, on average, only 57 percent that of white families,[6] it is also true that blacks can afford a much more integrated situation than currently exists. The Taeubers demonstrated that income differences do not produce the segregation of blacks from whites.[7] High income whites, for instance, live in different neighborhoods than do high income blacks; and poor whites generally do not have poor blacks as their neighbors.

It is also the case that whites in all income brackets are well represented in the suburbs while blacks, regardless of their income, tend to live within the central city. In 1970, 12 percent of all blacks in the Detroit urbanized area actually lived in the suburbs. However, if blacks had been represented in the suburbs in the same proportion as were whites with comparable incomes, one would have expected 67 percent of the black families to reside in the suburbs.[8]

Figure 1 shows the proportion of families at each income level living within the suburban ring of Detroit in 1970 and 1974. The proportion of white families in the ring is much higher than the proportion of blacks at each income level. Also, as the income of white families rises, so does the proportion living in the suburban ring. For blacks, the proportion in the suburbs is essentially constant for all income levels. Even though there is still a sizable racial gap in average family income, black families already have sufficient income to allow a much greater representation of blacks in white neighborhoods than currently exists.

Institutional discrimination

A second perspective is that there is a pervasive "web of discrimination" that prevents blacks from freely competing for housing.[9] There is ample evidence that real estate agents, apartment managers, landlords and suburban developers have denied blacks access to housing in white areas. In addition, the practices of banks, financial institutions, local governments—through their control of zoning, building regulations and land development—and the federal government, through FHA and VA regulations, have contributed to racial residential segregation. In the past, violence[10] and legal requirements, such as restrictive covenants,[11] were used to keep blacks in certain neighborhoods and exclude them from white areas.

Since the end of world War II a variety of discriminatory policies have been overturned by the Federal

6. U.S., Bureau of the Census, "Money Income and Poverty Status of Persons in the United States: 1977," *Current Population Reports*, Series P-60, No. 116, Table 1.

7. Taeuber and Taeuber, *Negroes in Cities*, Chap. 4; K. Taeuber, "The Effect of Income Redistribution on Racial Residential Segregation," *Urban Affairs Quarterly* (September 1968).

8. Hermalin and Farley "The Potential for Residential Integration in Cities and Suburbs: Implications for the Busing Controversy," Table 4.

9. National Academy of Sciences, *Freedom of Choice in Housing* (Washington: National Academy of Sciences, 1972).

10. A. Spear, *Black Chicago* (Chicago: University of Chicago Press, 1967), 20–27; Chicago Commission on Race Relations, *The Negro in Chicago* (Chicago: University of Chicago Press, 1922), Chap. V.

11. C. Vose, *Caucasians Only* (Berkeley: University of California Press, 1967).

FIGURE 1

PROPORTION OF TOTAL DETROIT METROPOLITAN AREA BLACKS AND WHITES
WHO LIVED IN THE SUBURBAN RING, 1970 AND 1974

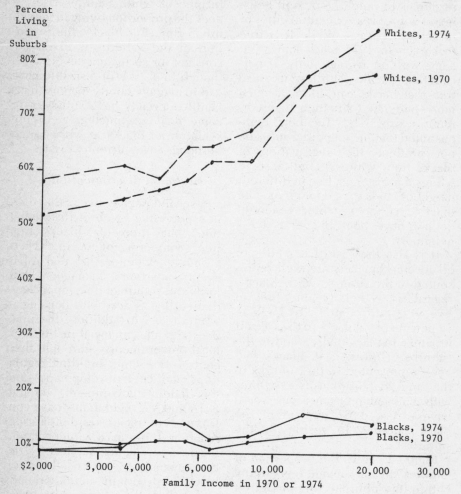

Source: U.S., Bureau of the Census, *Annual Housing Survey*, 1974, Series M-170-74-5:
Tables B-1, B-4, C-1, and C-4.

courts, and the Civil Rights Act of 1968 barred discrimination in the sale or rental of most housing. As a result, exclusionary tactics have come to depend more heavily upon subtler tactics such as the selective steering of blacks to some neighborhoods and whites to others.[12]

12. J. Saltman, "Implementing Open Housing Laws Through Social Action," *Journal of Applied Behavioral Science* (October 1975).

A Department of Housing and Urban Development study conducted in 1977 discovered that in about one-quarter of the instances that prospective black renters or buyers approached a realtor, they were subject to discrimination.[13]

13. U.S., Department of Housing and Urban Development, "Background Information and Initial Findings of the Housing Market Practice Survey," (1978), mimeographed. See

The continued operation of a web of discrimination is based upon the supposition that there is a strong demand on the part of almost all whites for racially segregated neighborhoods. However, institutional practices may remain in effect long after they are desired.

White attitudes have become progressively more liberal with regard to housing opportunities for blacks. Not only do whites endorse the ideal of residential integration, they have become much more willing to live in integrated neighborhoods themselves. The proportion of whites in national samples who said they would not be upset if a black with an income and education similar to their own moved onto their block rose from 35 percent in 1942 to 84 percent in 1972.[14]

Increasingly, whites report they are willing to accept black neighbors and there is a growing recognition by whites that they do not have the prerogative of excluding blacks.[15] When asked to decide whether "whites have the right to keep blacks out of their neighborhood if they want to" or whether "blacks have a right to live wherever they can afford to, just like white people," only 9 percent of the whites in the Detroit area in 1976 answered that they had the right to keep blacks out. If realtors and public officials continue to encourage residential segregation, they may not be reflecting the values of the white public.

The preferences of blacks

There is also the view that residential segregation results largely from the preferences of blacks to live with other blacks. Such a view is not supported by empirical investigations. A national study conducted in 1969, for instance, found that three-quarters of the black respondents wished to live in integrated neighborhoods, while only one black in six expressed a preference for an all-black area.[16]

The riots of the 1960s and the emergence of separatism and militancy among blacks apparently did not reduce the desire of many blacks for mixed residential neighborhoods. An analysis which focused upon post-riot changes in the attitudes of Detroit blacks revealed that between 1968 and 1971, the proportion of blacks preferring racially mixed neighborhoods increased from 57 to 62 percent.[17]

The reality of, on the one hand, a highly segregated metropolitan area such as Detroit and, on the other hand, the increasing acceptance of integrated living on the part of both blacks and whites invited a more thorough investigation of the attitudes and preferences of Detroit area residents in 1976. Detroit is a particularly suitable location for such a study. It is the nation's sixth largest city and is the hub of a highly segregated

also: D. Pearce, "Black, White and Many Shades of Gray: Real Estate Brokers and their Racial Practices," (Ph.D. diss., University of Michigan, Ann Arbor, 1976).

14. P. Sheatsley, "White Attitudes Toward the Negro," *Daedalus* (Winter 1966) Table 1; National Opinion Research Center, *National Data Program in the Social Sciences*, Tape File of 1972 General Social Science Survey, Question 46.

15. D. Taylor, P. Sheatsley and A. Greeley, "Attitudes Toward Racial Integration," *Scientific American* (June 1978): 43.

16. T. Pettigrew, "Attitudes on Race and Housing: A Social Psychological View," in *Segregation in Residential Areas*, ed. A. Hawley and V. Rock (Washington: National Academy of Sciences, 1973) p. 44.

17. H. Schuman and S. Hatchett, *Black Racial Attitudes: Trends and Complexities* (Ann Arbor: Institute for Social Research, 1974), Table 1.

metropolitan area.[18] About 45 percent of the city's 1.5 million residents were black in 1970 but only 4
percent of 2.5 million suburban residents were black.[19] Since 1970, the
city has become even more black.
One indicator of this is the racial
composition of the public schools.
The proportion black in the city's
schools rose from 64 percent in 1970
to 80 percent in 1976.[20] In es-
sence, it appears that Detroit is becoming a black city imbedded in a
white suburban ring.

Data for this study were gathered
in the spring and summer of 1976.
The target population consisted of
heads of households or their spouses
living in year-round housing units
in the Detroit area. From the total
of 1503 sample households selected,
1134 interviews were obtained.
Seven hundred and thirty-four whites
and 400 blacks were interviewed
yielding response rates of 78 percent and 71 percent respectively.
Race of interviewer was controlled
such that black respondents were
always interviewed by blacks and
white respondents by whites.[21]

The geographic distribution of the
sample mirrored that of the area.
Eighty-five percent of the white respondents lived in the suburbs but
only 11 of the 400 blacks were
suburban residents. The average age
of respondents was 45 years for
whites and 43 for blacks. On the average, white household heads or their
spouses completed 12.1 years of

school white blacks completed about
one year or less. Median household
income was about $18,500 for whites
and $12,500 for blacks. Income
levels are relatively high in Detroit
and thus the average income of
white households exceeds the national average by about $4,000 while
among blacks, the Detroit advantage
is $2,500. The demographic char-
acteristics of the respondents in this
study correspond closely to independent estimates of the same characteristics developed by a March,
1976 Bureau of the Census survey.[22]

The interview contained a variety
of questions assessing black and
white receptiveness to differing
levels of integration, knowledge of
the area's housing market and open
housing laws, perceptions of the
opposite race and perceptions of
how one's neighbors would react to
integration.

THE NEIGHBORHOOD
PREFERENCES OF BLACKS
AND WHITES

One of the primary aims of this
study was to devise better measures
of the neighborhood preferences of
blacks and whites so that we could
more completely describe those factors which impede residential integration. We assessed neighborhood
preferences of blacks and whites by
presenting them with a series of
cards depicting neighborhoods of
differing racial composition. Each
cord had 15 houses drawn on it.
Some of the houses were white,
some were black and one house—
the most central house—was designated as "your house." A picture
of these cards is shown in Figure 2.

18. U.S., Bureau of the Census, *Statistical Abstract of the United States: 1977*, Table 33.
19. U.S., Bureau of the Census, *Census of Population*: 1970, PC(1)-B24, Table 24.
20. U.S., Office for Civil Rights: *Fall 1976 Elementary and Secondary School Civil Rights Survey* (Tape file).
21. S. Bianchi, "Sampling Report for the 1976 Detroit Area Study," (Ann Arbor, University of Michigan Detroit Area Study, 1976) Mimeograph.
22. R. Farley, H. Schuman, S. Bianchi, D. Colasanto and S. Hatchett, "Chocolate City, Vanilla Suburbs: Will the Trend Toward Racially Separate Communities Continue?" *Social Science Research* (forthcoming, 1978).

FIGURE 2

PICTURES OF NEIGHBORHOOD DIAGRAMS PRESENTED TO BLACK AND WHITE RESPONDENTS

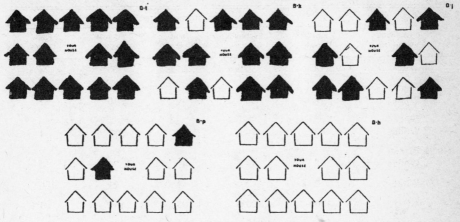

Neighborhood Diagrams for Black Respondents

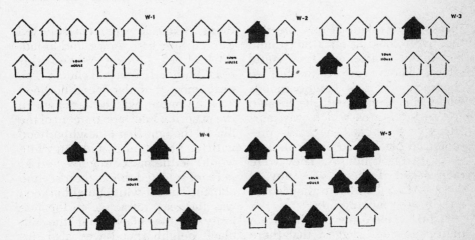

Neighborhood Diagrams for White Respondents

Using these cards, respondents were asked several questions about a hypothetical situation. Whites were to imagine that they were living in a neighborhood with no black families and then to imagine that one black family moved in. How comfortable would they feel in that situation? This question was repeated for three more neighborhood cards, each showing more and more black families: three, five, and eight black houses. After these questions, white respondents were asked whether they would try to move out of any of the neighborhoods where they indicated they would feel uncomfortable.

Black respondents were presented with slightly different neighborhood cards and a different hypothetical situation (also shown in Figure 2).

TABLE 1

NEIGHBORHOOD PREFERENCES OF *BLACK* RESPONDENTS

NEIGHBORHOOD COMPOSITION	ATTRACTIVENESS RATINGS				
	FIRST CHOICE	SECOND CHOICE	THIRD CHOICE	FOURTH CHOICE	FIFTH CHOICE
All-Black	12%	5%	21%	35%	27%
10 Blacks– 4 Whites	14	55	18	10	2
7 Blacks– 7 Whites	63	20	14	2	1
2 Blacks– 12 Whites	8	17	40	32	3
All-White	2	3	7	21	66
Total	100%	100%	100%	100%	100%
N =	392	392	391	382	382

Blacks were asked to imagine that they were looking for a house and had found a nice one they could afford. They were requested to choose among five neighborhoods where this house could be located and pick the area which was most attractive to them. The cards presented to blacks had either 0, 2, 7, 10 or 14 black houses. They were then asked if there were any of these five neighborhoods they would not consider moving into.

At first glance, the findings from these questions suggest that there will be few integrated neighborhoods since blacks and whites prefer areas with very different racial compositions. However, closer inspection reveals that certain types of racially mixed neighborhoods may be appealing to both races.

Table 1 presents the residential preferences of blacks in terms of how they ranked the hypothetical neighborhoods. Blacks prefer to live in a neighborhood that has an equal number of black and white residents. Sixty-three percent selected this as their first choice and an additional 20 percent ranked this neighborhood as second choice. The next most popular neighborhood was the one in which blacks are in the majority. Fourteen percent of the blacks thought that a neighborhood with ten black houses and four white would be the most attractive and 55 percent selected this as their second choice. The all-white neighborhood was the least attractive to the majority of the blacks but the all-black neighborhood was also unpopular. Only 17 percent selected it as their first or second choice.

When blacks were asked which of the five neighborhoods they would consider moving into, almost all of them—more than 90 percent—said they would move into a neighborhood that was already integrated; that is, a neighborhood which already contained either 10, 7 or 2 blacks. There was much greater reluctance to entering an all-black or an all-white neighborhood. Sixty

TABLE 2

NEIGHBORHOOD PREFERENCES OF *WHITE* RESPONDENTS

| NEIGHBORHOOD COMPOSITION | COMFORTABLENESS RATING | | | | | |
	VERY COMFORTABLE	SOMEWHAT COMFORTABLE	SOMEWHAT UNCOMFORTABLE	VERY UNCOMFORTABLE	TOTAL	N
1 Black– 13 Whites	43%	33%	18%	6%	100%	706
3 Blacks– 11 Whites	26	33	26	15	100	705
5 Blacks– 9 Whites	18	26	27	29	100	703
8 Blacks– 6 Whites	11	15	25	48	100	706

nine percent would consider the all-black area and 37 percent, the all-white.

Whites are not as amenable to residential integration as are blacks. Table 2 presents the neighborhood preferences of whites. Although three-quarters of the whites would feel more comfortable with one black family in their neighborhood, this percentage drops steadily as the number of black families increases. Fifty-nine percent would be comfortable with three blacks in their neighborhood; 44 percent would feel comfortable if whites were slightly in the majority but only 26 percent of the whites would be comfortable if there were more blacks than whites living in their neighborhood.

The majority of black respondents viewed a 50/50 racial mix as most desirable but such a mix would make the majority of whites uncomfortable. That is, even though whites were not presented with the choice of a 50/50 racial mix, the majority said they would be uncomfortable in a neighborhood where five of the fifteen houses were occupied by blacks.

A consideration of what whites say they would do in the various situations reveals that whites will generally tolerate some black neighbors but will leave if there are numerous blacks living close to them. Only 7 percent of the whites would try to move upon the arrival of the first black family; with three black families, an additional 16 percent would try to move. The percentage of whites who would move increases as more blacks are pictured and two-thirds of the whites would try to move by the time their neighborhood becomes majority black; that is, eight black families and seven white.

The neighborhood preferences of blacks and whites seem incompatible. Blacks favor living in numerically integrated neighborhoods; in fact, a neighborhood that has an equal number of black and white families is the one they see as most attractive. For whites, on the other hand, desirable levels of racial mixture in neighborhoods are those situations in which whites are in the overwhelming majority.

Three quarters of the whites would feel comfortable in neighborhood A—an area with one black— but only 5 percent of the blacks saw this type of area as attractive, that is, as their first or second choice. When we consider a neighborhood with three black families— neighborhood B—its attractiveness for blacks increases but the proportion of whites who would feel comfortable decreases to 59 percent. Neighborhood C—eight blacks and seven whites—is very attractive to blacks but only a little more than one-quarter of the whites would feel comfortable in such an area.

Although blacks and whites clearly have different, and apparently incompatible, preferences, it is possible to interpret the data a bit more optimistically. To do this it is necessary to consider how blacks and whites claim they would behave in various situations: would they move in or move out?

The overwhelming majority of whites do not object to one black family in their neighborhood and would not move away were one home sold to a black. In addition, there are a number of blacks—over one-third—who say they would be willing to be "pioneers" in an all-white area and for a few blacks, this type of neighborhood is most attractive. Thus, it appears that the prospects for minimally integrating some neighborhoods in the Detroit area are good.

A similar situation exists when the prospects for a slightly greater degree of integration are considered. Once there are blacks already living in a neighborhood, almost all blacks say they would move in. Ninety-five percent of the blacks, for instance, would consider moving to a neighborhood which already contained two black families. Even though a neighborhood with this number of blacks is not as attractive

to whites, 76 percent of the whites say they would *not* try to move away from such an area. Any vacancies that occur in such a neighborhood might be filled by either whites or blacks since half of the whites said they would actually consider moving into a neighborhood which contained three black families.

Without a more detailed examination of the preferences of whites and blacks, it is impossible to predict the degree of neighborhood integration that we can expect or to specify how stable such integrated neighborhoods might be. It is reasonable to conclude that, despite the large differences between blacks and whites in what they define as the most desirable situation of neighborhood integration, both groups would accept a much greater degree of integration than currently exists.

WHITE PERCEPTIONS OF THE ATTITUDES OF OTHER WHITES

To better understand the issues involved in the neighborhood choices of whites, those who said they would try to move from one of the racially integrated neighborhoods were asked to state their reasons. The most frequent response—given by 40 percent of the 401 whites who said they would try to move— was that blacks would not keep up their property or that property values would decrease once blacks arrived. Approximately one-sixth of the whites thought the crime rate would go up or that they would not be safe living with blacks. Another one-sixth thought that blacks moving into the neighborhood signaled the beginning of an inevitable transition to an all-black neighborhood. The remainder of the whites expressed a variety of other reasons for leaving the integrated area.

The concerns of whites, therefore, stem primarily from two sources: their perception of the process of neighborhood racial transition and their perception of the characteristics of black neighbors. Many whites think that if one black enters a neighborhood, the area will soon become all black. They may opt to move out sooner rather than later to minimize the racial difficulties and financial losses they anticipate. Thus when asked why he would leave an integrated neighborhood, one respondent replied: "Because if I stayed any longer, my house wouldn't be worth anything." One key component of this prediction is the belief that other whites do not want to live in integrated neighborhoods. Many whites may assume that once a black moves into their area, that their white neighbors will quickly put their homes up for sale and that other whites who are looking for housing will not consider the neighborhood.

In the 1976 Detroit Area Study, whites were asked what they thought the reaction of their neighbors and other whites in the metropolitan area would be to neighborhood integration. In doing so, it was possible to assess the degree to which an individual's perception of other whites affects his or her own neighborhood preferences.

In general, respondents viewed their neighbors as much less liberal on racial issues than they considered themselves to be. When asked if they would sell their own home to a black couple, 71 percent of the whites chose the liberal alternative —they would sell to a black. In addition, when asked what they would do if their neighbors objected, 56 percent of the whites claimed they would go ahead with the sale. By comparison only 31 percent thought that their neighbors would sell to a black in the same situation.

This finding is consistent with earlier investigations which show that whites underestimate the willingness of their white neighbors to accept close interracial contact.[23] Eighty eight percent of the whites thought that a white child and a black child should be allowed to play together in the white child's home, but only 37 percent of the whites thought that their neighbors would approve of such interracial contact.

These perceptions of what other whites would do, and how other whites feel about integrated neighborhoods, shape the residential preferences of whites. Whites see their neighbors as less tolerant of blacks than they are and this increases their likelihood of moving from a neighborhood blacks have entered. As evidence of this, it was found that 69 percent of the whites who thought that their neighbors would not sell to a black couple say they would try to move away from an integrated neighborhood compared to 59 percent of the whites who think their neighbors would be liberal and sell to a black. In addition, the perceived attitudes of other whites in the metropolitan area—those who are potential homebuyers—affect whether or not an individual will try to move from an integrated neighborhood.

Both the Department of Housing and Urban Development study and private investigations demonstate that, despite the 1968 Civil Rights Act, many realtors treat prospective black clients differently and steer

23. O. D. Duncan, H. Schuman and B. Duncan, *Social Change in a Metropolitan Community* (New York: Russell Sage, 1973), Table 43.

them away from white areas.[24] Realtors may also misperceive the racial attitudes of whites and may underestimate the frequency with which whites would accept a black neighbor or move into an area where blacks are already living.

WHITE PERCEPTIONS OF THE CHARACTERISTICS OF BLACKS

Many whites think that having blacks in their neighborhood will have negative consequences for the quality of life in their area. They may think that the appearance of the neighborhood will deteriorate, that crime will rise and that the social class will change. Each of these potential consequences would make life in the neighborhood unpleasant and cause property values to decline. Therefore the degree to which the perception of blacks by whites affects their willingness to live in racially integrated neighborhoods was investigated.

Whites were asked to evaluate several characteristics of the average black person and to compare them with those of the average white. It was found that many whites view blacks as having undesirable characteristics relative to whites. Half of the white respondents thought that blacks were not as quiet as whites; 48 percent thought that blacks were not as moral as whites; and 59 percent claimed that blacks were more prone to violence than whites. Most importantly, 70 percent of the whites felt that blacks were not

as likely as whites to take good care of their house and yard.

In every instance, those who perceive blacks as having negative characteristics are more likely to say that they would try to move out of a racially integrated neighborhood than those who do not perceive blacks negatively. These data are presented in Figure 3. The biggest difference, as expected, is for those who have varying perceptions of the ability of blacks to take good care of their property. Three-quarters of the whites who think that blacks take less good care of their house and yard than whites say they would move out of a racially integrated neighborhood. By comparison, only 42 percent of the whites who think that blacks will take good care of their property say that they would move away.

Many of these attitudes of whites are based upon the assumption that if blacks come to live in their neighborhood, the blacks will be poorer and less well educated than the whites who already live there. Whites may feel that since the prospective black neighbors are in a lower social class, both the visible and intangible qualities of their neighborhood will be destroyed.

This perception of the characteristics of blacks who enter white areas is erroneous. The Duncans' investigation of Chicago[25] and the Taeubers[26] study of ten major cities show that blacks who move into white neighborhoods are similar in social and economic status to whites who already reside there. The process of neighborhood integration is definitely not led by poor blacks who

24. U.S., Department of Housing and Urban Development, "Background Information and Initial Findings of the Housing Market Practice Survey," pp. 6–18; Saltman, "Implementing Open Housing Laws Through Social Action," pp. 41–54; Pearce, "Black, White and Many Shades of Gray: Real Estate Brokers and their Racial Practices."

25. O. D. and B. Duncan, *The Negro Population of Chicago* (Chicago: University of Chicago Press, 1957); Chap. VII.

26. Taeuber and Taeuber, *Negroes in Cities*, pp. 154–173.

enter well-to-do white areas. Rather, the blacks who replace whites have the financial ability to purchase better housing and their educational attainment typically exceeds that of the whites in the areas they enter. These investigations demonstrate that even in census tracts undergoing substantial racial change, the socioeconomic status of black residents at the end of a decade compared favorably to that of the whites who lived in the area at the start of the ten-year span.

Several barriers which prevent whites from accepting integrated neighborhoods have been identified. Whites perceive that other whites are opposed to residential integration and feel that they will suffer personally if they do not move out of their neighborhood shortly after blacks enter. Many whites think that blacks would be undesirable neighbors because of differences in social class and in behavior. They fail to realize that the blacks who enter their neighborhoods would resemble them in social and economic standing.

THE RELUCTANCE OF BLACKS TO ENTER WHITE AREAS

Blacks are quite favorable to residential integration, overwhelmingly prefer mixed neighborhoods, but are somewhat unwilling to move into a neighborhood where they would be the only black family. When asked why they would not move into an all-white neighborhood, blacks generally responded that they were concerned about the reactions of the whites who lived in the neighborhood. Thirty-four percent of the 215 black respondents who would not consider moving into a white area thought that white neighbors would be unfriendly to them and make the lone black family feel unwelcome. An additional 37 percent

thought they would feel uncomfortable for other reasons ("I don't like people looking at every move you make"). One-sixth of the blacks expected even more serious consequences of being the first black to integrate a neighborhood—they anticipated that there would be violence and a real danger of physical harm to themselves, their families or their homes.

It is possible that blacks overestimate white hostility to neighborhood integration. Although many blacks thought that a black family would not be welcome in the suburbs of Detroit, 73 percent of the suburban whites in this study said they would feel either very or somewhat comfortable with one black family in their neighborhood. It appears that blacks are not aware that many whites would accept residential integration and that a major reason why blacks are unwilling to seek out housing in predominantly white neighborhoods is that they fear the reaction of their new white neighbors.

Not only do blacks perceive whites as unwilling to tolerate neighborhood integration, they also think that *white home owners* discriminate against blacks. Blacks were asked the following question: "Do you think that in the Detroit area many, some or only a few blacks miss out on good housing because white owners won't rent or sell to them?," Forty-seven percent of the blacks thought that many blacks missed out on good housing because of discrimination of this type. Those blacks who thought that there was discrimination by individual whites were less likely to want to move into an all-white neighborhood.

Interestingly enough, there was no relationship between the willingness to move into an all-white area and the perception that blacks

FIGURE 3

PERCENT OF WHITES WHO WOULD MOVE OUT OF AN INTEGRATED NEIGHBORHOOD
BY THEIR PERCEPTION OF THE CHARACTERISTICS OF BLACKS

Neighborhood A	Neighborhood B	Neighborhood C
1 black house	3 black houses	8 black houses
14 white houses	12 white houses	7 white houses

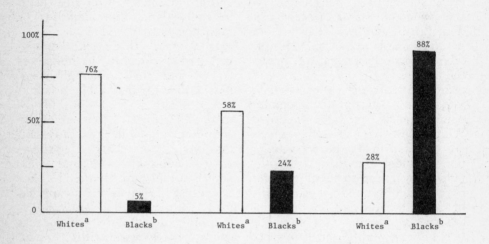

[a] Percent of whites who would feel very or somewhat comfortable in this neighborhood

[b] Percent of blacks who would prefer this type of neighborhood (first or second choice)

missed out on good housing because of the discriminatory practices of *white real estate agents*. Half of the blacks thought that many blacks missed out on housing because of discrimination by realtors. However, they were just as likely to consider moving into an all-white neighborhood—63 percent would consider this—as were blacks who thought that discrimination by real estate agents was not so widespread. It is the perception of the reacion of individual whites—specifically those whites who are potential neighbors—that is important in determining whether or not a black will consider moving into a particular neighborhood. While blacks see institutional discrimination as an important problem, this perception does not determine whether they view white areas as desirable. Rather, it is the perceived characteristics of white residents of those areas that is the important determinant. If blacks view whites as receptive, then they will consider being "pioneers" in a white area. If they think that the white residents of the neighborhood would react negatively, they do not want to move into the neighborhood.

At the beginning of this study, we thought that two other barriers might prevent blacks from considering housing in white areas; first, a misperception of their own economic abilities and, second, a commitment to live within the black community.

Demographic studies show that economic differences between the races do not account for residential segregation, but we do not know if blacks are knowledgeable about their ability to purchase homes in white areas of the city and in the suburban ring. It was thought that they might overestimate the cost of such housing and fail to seek housing that they could actually afford. To determine whether this was true, Detroit area respondents were asked how much they thought a single family home would cost in a largely white section of the city and in several suburbs. They were then asked if they thought that many blacks could afford to live in each area. Blacks quite accurately assessed the cost of housing and realized that very many blacks could afford to live in those areas of middle-class housing. If blacks fail to live in white neighborhoods it is not because they overestimate the cost of housing.

Some blacks may feel that for ideological or cultural reasons it is undesirable to live in a neighborhood where one has only white neighbors. They may perceive that they have a responsibility to the black community. Detroit area blacks were asked the following question: "Suppose a black person moved out of his all-black neighborhood into a mostly white neighborhod. What do you think other black people would say about this person? Would they say he was moving into that mostly white neighborhood because he wanted a better home, or that he was deserting the black community, or what?" Four-fifths of the blacks chose the first alternative and only one-fifth said that a black moving to a white area was deserting the black community. In addition, the perception of the reaction of other blacks to this issue is not important in determining whether or not the respondent would consider moving into an all-white neighborhood. Thirty-seven percent of the blacks who chose the first alternative would consider an all-white neighborhood, as would the same percentage of blacks who thought that the black person would be deserting the black community.

Therefore, neither the perception of the cost of housing in white areas nor the perception of the reactions of other blacks is an effective barrier to the willingness of blacks to live in white neighborhoods. The primary factor was the perception of the reaction of whites to having black neighbors.

During the three decades since the end of World War II, there have been substantial changes in racial attitudes and real improvements in the status of blacks. Almost all state imposed policies of racial discrimination and racial isolation have been overturned by federal court rulings. Barriers to political participation have been removed and, in all sections of the nation, blacks serve on juries, act as judges, and are elected to office. Although the income of blacks lags far behind that of whites—black families in 1977 had an average purchasing power equivalent to that of white families in 1954—occupational gains are evident and many more than token numbers of blacks work at prestigious jobs once reserved for whites.[27]

The area in which the least progress has been made is neighborhood segregation since racial isolation in cities is almost as great now as it was at the end of the

27. U.S., Bureau of the Census, "Money Income and Poverty Status of Families and Persons in the United States: 1977," Table 3.

great Depression; and suburbs are approximately as white now as they were prior to the post World War II building boom. In 1954, the Supreme Court stated that racial segregation in schools may affect the hearts and minds of black children in ways unlikely ever to be undone.[28] Although we do not know that residential segregation has similar deleterious consequences for all blacks, it contributes to the segregation of schools and may severely restrict occupational choices for many blacks. Residential segregation, we presume, also has adverse consequences for whites by encouraging prejudice and stereotyping.

Programs to guarantee equal opportunities in housing should, on the one hand, capitalize upon the changing racial attitudes and, on the other, stress enforcement of existing laws. Whites are increasingly willing to accept black neighbors. One important reason for the persistence of high levels of neighborhood racial segregation is white ignorance of the changing values of other whites. If all whites—especially real estate dealers and lenders—recognized the willingness of most whites to accept black neighbors, to remain in racially mixed areas and even to consider purchasing housing in neighborhoods which have black residents, the pattern of whites fleeing when blacks enter their neighborhood might be altered. Furthermore, if whites realized that the blacks who are likely to move into their neighborhoods will be their socioeconomic equals, their objections to residential integration might decline.

Blacks may also be ignorant of the changing racial attitudes of whites and may overestimate the hostility they would confront if they entered

28. Brown v. Board of Education, 347 U.S. 483 (1954).

a white neighborhood. There is a long history of violence in the Detroit area and knowledge of past harassment of blacks who dared to move into white neighborhoods is likely more widespread and, perhaps, more influential than is knowledge of current attitudes of whites. In addition, blacks may underestimate the pervasive endorsement of racially mixed neighborhoods by their own black peers.

The Civil Rights Act of 1968 bans discrimination in the sale or rental of housing. This law, at best, has been partially effective. Practices of steering whites and blacks to distinct neighborhoods occur frequently in Detroit and other metropolitan areas. Few individuals or realtors have been prosecuted and convicted of violating the civil rights of prospective black buyers. Furthermore, the general public appears rather ignorant of open housing laws. In this Detroit study, respondents were asked if they knew of any laws which prohibit discrimination in the sale or rental of housing. Thirty-seven percent of the whites and more than one-half of the blacks— 52 percent—did not know of such laws, although they had been on the books for almost a decade. If a national program publicized the existing open housing laws and censured violators, racial residential segregation might decline.

In addition to enforcing current laws against housing discrimination, special police protection should be provided to newly integrated neighborhoods. Black fears of integration may be prompted by the violent reactions of a few whites who strongly oppose the entry of blacks. In such circumstances, strong steps should be taken to ensure the civil rights of all concerned.

Current levels of racial residential

segregation reflect not only the discriminatory tastes of individuals but the explicit policies of a panoply of governmental authorities: FHA and VA decisions not to loan money to blacks who wished to enter white areas; the National Defense highway system which made suburban and exurban commuting easy; zoning laws which restricted housing choices for a large segment of the population, and numerous school boards which designated some schools and areas for blacks and others for whites.[29] Although the ideal of equal opportunities in housing is consistent with the basic constitutional values which are widely endorsed in our society, there has never been a national commitment to overcome the legacy of past discriminatory policies. Seldom, if ever, have the presidents of the United States, the secretaries of HUD, top administrators at the FHA or VA, mayors, or school officials stressed the importance of providing equal housing opportunities for all

29. For a description of many of these practices see: D. L. Foley, "Institutional and Contextual Factors Affecting the Housing Choices of Minority Residents," in Hawley and Rock, *Segregation in Residential Areas*, pp. 85–148.

citizens. If leaders spoke out forcefully and frequently on this topic, attitude changes would occur more rapidly and future censuses would report that many more blacks and whites live in the same neighborhoods.

In summary, six policy recommendations are offered which have been derived from this investigation of racial attitudes and residential segregation:

Make whites aware that other whites are not as prejudiced as they may think.

Make whites aware that blacks of equal status will be their new neighbors if residential integration becomes a reality.

Make blacks aware that whites are not as hostile to neighborhood integration as they may think.

Make both blacks and whites aware that it is illegal to discriminate in the sale or rental of housing.

Prosecute realtors or home owners who violate the Civil Rights Act of 1968 or who threaten the civil rights of those blacks who enter a white area.

Have national and local leaders stress the importance of equal housing opportunities.

ANNALS, AAPSS, 441, Jan. 1979

Racial Change and Social Policy

By THOMAS F. PETTIGREW

ABSTRACT: Five major trends in contemporary American race relations are specified and discussed: (1) the discontinuities of social change, with uneven progress within and across institutions; (2) two contrasting processes, one benefitting the black middle class and the other restraining the black poor; (3) the altered nature of racial discrimination, from blatantly exclusionary practices to more subtle, procedural, ostensibly "non-racial" forms centered upon demographic trends, housing patterns, and spatial arrangements; (4) racial attitude changes, with greater rejection of racial injustice among whites combined with continued resistance to the measures needed to correct the injustice; and (5) the shifting demographic base of American race relations, from the national era of 1915–1945, through the metropolitan era of 1945–1970, to the present era of movement away from large cities, the Northeast, and the Midwest. Each of these trends are shown to intersect in important ways with the structural linchpin of modern race relations: the maldistribution of blacks and whites throughout metropolitan areas. Finally, six practical guidelines for future racial policies in urban areas are offered.

Thomas Pettigrew is Professor of Social Psychology and Sociology at Harvard University. A native southerner, he received his B.A. from the University of Virginia in 1952 and his Ph.D. from Harvard in 1956. A specialist in race relations throughout his career, Pettigrew has focused on black-white issues in the United States, together with comparative work in South Africa and the United Kingdom. He is the author of A Profile of the Negro American *(1964) and* Racially Separate or Together? *(1971); and editor of* Racial Discrimination in the United States *(1975).*

An extended version of this paper appears as a chapter in a volume edited by Arthur P. Solomon from a Conference on Alternative Forms of Urban Growth and Development at the Joint Center of Urban Studies at M.I.T. and Harvard University in 1977.

AMERICAN race relations have experienced dramatic changes, especially since World War II. And even the basic outlines of the field that were valid in the 1960s are questionable now. From the dual macro and micro perspectives of demography and social psychology, this paper will focus on these rapid racial shifts and their policy implications.

FIVE MAJOR TRENDS

The discontinuities of social change

Race relations of the United States have undergone profound alterations in the last third of a century. But no social change of such proportions occurs smoothly and consistently either within or across institutions. Sweeping and fundamental alterations necessarily entail considerable confusion and ambiguity; indeed, the discontinuities of traditional customs side-by-side with new practices is the hallmark of transitional periods between two radically diverse eras. Obviously, America has been transversing precisely such a transitional period in race relations during the past generation.

As with adolescence, transitional periods are awkward. The society must haltingly develop a new equilibrium and a new, at least partial, consensus. The political left views the process as too slow; the right as dangerously rapid. Moreover, the awkwardness and controversy are exacerbated when, as with race relations, both national symbols and social structure are deeply implicated. The treatment of black Americans has been a national issue since our beginning; it has been persistently our key domestic issue of conflict; and it has shaped and

contorted much of our social structure. Understandably, then, the end of this transitional period is not yet in sight.

This perspective emphasizes that Gunnar Myrdal's hopeful model of a "benign circle" was only partially accurate. Myrdal, in his classic An American Dilemma,[1] argued that America's institutional racism constituted a "vicious circle" where each of the major social institutions, through its own discriminatory practices, contributed to the discrimination and exclusion of blacks in other institutions. But, he pointed out, once racial change began there should emerge a "benign circle," with the same cumulative effect of interlocking institutional practices that produced the "vicious circle" now operating in reverse.

Myrdal's hope for the future, as with most of his insights, proved in large part correct. But experience taught us an important qualification. The reverse action of the "benign circle" does not flow irresistably. Progress in one realm, say industrial jobs, will mean little as long as gains are not forthcoming in another realm, say the ability to reside in the suburbs near the jobs. These discontinuities across institutional sectors can greatly impede social change. And they can raise and later frustrate the hopes of black people—a situation that contributed directly to the urban riots of the 1960s.[2]

1. Gunnar Myrdal, An American Dilemma (New York: Harper & Row, 1944), pp. 75–78.
2. Thomas F. Pettigrew, A Profile of the Negro American (New York: Van Nostrand-Reinhold, 1964), chap. 8; Thomas F. Pettigrew, "Social Evaluation Theory: Convergences and Applications," in Nebraska Symposium on Motivation, 1967, ed. David Levine (Lincoln: University of Nebraska Press, 1967), pp. 241–311; Thomas F. Pettigrew, Racially Separate or Together? (New York: McGraw-Hill, 1971), chap. 7.

Levitan, Johnston, and Taggart provide an assessment of differential black gains during the 1960s.[3] By their indicators, black progress was greatest in employment and earnings and next greatest in education. Blacks actually gained on whites in absolute as well as relative terms in these realms. Next these authors list income advances, though the absolute dollar gap between the races actually widened. Health is fourth in the order of improvements. Yet black health may not have improved in comparison to white health; life expectancies over the decade rose for black women but actually declined slightly for black men. Some political gains were made, though they hardly constitute a black breakthrough into the circles of power and decision-making. The Voting Rights Act of 1965 led to dramatic rises in black voters and officeholders, especially in the South. Yet today, after a more than six-fold increase since 1967, the over 4,500 black elected officials comprise less than one percent of the nation's elected officials. And the number of black-owned businesses has actually declined since 1960. Finally, housing is judged to be the institution witnessing the least racial improvement. While housing quality advanced markedly for blacks during the 1960s, this gain remained less than that of whites and took place within the context of an intense and unremitting pattern of residential segregation by race throughout urban America.

Farley reviews these same trends during the 1970s.[4] In general, Farley finds that many of the favorable trends for blacks—such as the education of the young, occupations of the employed labor force, and female earnings—continue through the lean early seventies. But Farley also finds the continuation of a number of negative trends that disproportionately affect lower-status blacks—a sharp rise in the number of female-headed households, and extremely high rates of unemployment and nonparticipation in the labor force among black men. These dual considerations introduce the next of the five trends.

Two contrasting processes

Andrew Brimmer writes, "Within the Negro community, there appears to be a deepening schism between the able and the less able, between the well-prepared and those with few skills."[5] While some economists have challenged Brimmer's evidence of a growing schism among blacks in income, occupational and educational trends tend to support his general argument. The civil rights movement of the sixties *did* make a fundamental difference in the lives of younger, educated blacks, but it achieved only modest gains for older, less-educated blacks. The movement's goals were generally status and dignity oriented for the black middle class rather than bread-and-butter issues for the black working class.

The black middle class has markedly expanded in recent years. If

3. Sar A. Levitan, William B. Johnston, and Robert Taggart, *Still a Dream: The Changing Status of Blacks Since 1960* (Cambridge, MA: Harvard University Press, 1975).

4. Reynolds Farley, "Trends in Racial Inequalities: Have the Gains of the 1960s Disappeared in the 1970s?" *American Sociological Review* 42 (April 1977): 189–208.

5. Andrew F. Brimmer, "Economic Progress of Negroes in the United States: The Deepening Schism," Unpublished Speech at Tuskegee Institute (22 March 1970), p. 3.

one adopts a rough definition of middle-class status in terms of employment, education, and real income, then about two-fifths of blacks are now middle-class, contrasted with only one-twentieth of blacks in 1940, and about two-thirds of whites at present. Hence, 38 percent of employed blacks in 1974 were either in white-collar or skilled blue-collar occupations; 64 percent of employed whites had such positions. The 1970 percentages of adult blacks and whites who were high school graduates were 38 and 65. Likewise, 38 percent of black families had incomes over $10,000 during 1974 compared to 67 percent of white families.[6]

Given this phenomenal growth in the black middle class, combined with an almost doubling of the black population since 1940, it is safe to estimate that over 90 percent of black families of middle-class status today are first generation middle class. And like other first generation middle-class families, they are typically anxious to consolidate their newly-gained status and pass it on to their children. Indeed, Duncan demonstrates with 1962 census data how difficult it has been in the past for the black middle class to retain their status across generations.[7] Black men who originated in upper status families tended to slide down, Duncan found, while such white men tended to retain their status. And black men who originated in lower status families

were likely to remain there, while similar white men were likely to move up.

The rapid growth of the black middle class raises a methodological point for comparative racial research. Social scientists often deceive themselves and others into thinking that they have "equated" for socioeconomic status across race by controlling solely for present education, occupation, and/or income, without checking on wealth and recency of status.

Other implications are political. Militant black ideology today emphasizes group unity, precisely because unity is increasingly difficult to achieve as the growing middle class acquires interests that conflict with those of poor blacks. Dr. Martin Luther King, Jr. was probably the last black national leader who could appeal to a wide spectrum across black America.

A further political effect involves white Americans. Black poverty is largely beyond the purview of most whites. But the enlarging black middle class, with its new jobs in formerly all-white settings, is highly conspicuous to whites. This differential association process lends visible support to the widely-held white contention that the critical aspects of racial injustice were corrected during the civil rights era of the 1960s.

This sanguine fiction is further supported by the arguments of conservatives who wish to give racial change a low national priority. These observers select data that reflect the expansion of the black middle class. Liberals counter by selecting data that reflect the insignificant changes in the lives of the majority of black citizens. Both are partly right and partly wrong. The full evidence is more complex.

6. U.S. Bureau of the Census, *Current Population Reports*, Series P-23, No. 38 (Washington, D.C.: USGPO, 1971), p. 79; U.S. Bureau of the Census, *Current Population Reports*, Series P-23, No. 54 (Washington, DC: USGPO, 1975), pp. 27, 75.

7. Otis Dudley Duncan, "Pattern of Occupational Mobility Among Negro Men," *Demography* 5 (1968): 11–22.

We have been witnessing two diverging processes within black America, and projections of race relations into the future must consider both.

The altered nature of racial discrimination

Growing class disparities within black America do not imply that race relations problems are evolving into economic problems. Racial discrimination lives on in many forms, but its character has fundamentally changed since World War II.

Older forms of institutional discrimination generally invoked total exclusion of blacks or a rigid color line above which blacks could not rise. Such blatant mistreatment became relatively easy to attack in the federal courts and later in the 1964 Civil Rights and 1965 Voting Rights Acts. Consequently, over recent decades, these older, direct, primary forms have been replaced by secondary racial discrimination that is more indirect, more subtle, more procedural, more ostensibly nonracial, and more centered upon spatial arrangements, demographic trends, and housing patterns.

The counterattack to this proliferation of secondary discriminatory forms has necessarily emphasized results and outcomes through affirmative recruitment, enrollment, and hiring programs. Earlier case-by-case enforcement of antidiscrimination laws proved ineffective because complaints were typically nonstrategic.[8] Systematic patterns of discrimination require systematic patterns of reform and enforcement. The relative success of these new

8. Leon Mayhew, *Law and Equal Opportunity: A Study of the Massachusetts Commission Against Discrimination* (Cambridge, MA: Harvard University Press, 1968).

procedures, at least for middle-class goals, is amply attested to by the ferocity of the attacks upon affirmative action procedures and what is misperceived to be "racial quotas" and "reverse discrimination."[9] The mixed judgment in *Bakke* leaves the future status of these procedures in question; but there is no question as to the need for them if positive racial change is to continue in America.

Racial attitude changes

White resistance to many forms of racial change has declined while black insistence has risen over the past two decades. But these broad generalizations require qualification.

White America's attitudes on a wide range of racial issues have modified sharply. These modifications are especially notable in the improved stereotypes of blacks and in support of the eradication of the more direct forms of racial discrimination. For example, in 1942 only 42 percent of whites believed that blacks had the same intelligence as whites; but by 1956 this per-

9. "Misperceived" is employed because of the conceptualization problems involved in these two terms. To use "quota" recalls the blatant exclusionary practices of rigid *ceiling limits*. Today's affirmative action goals set *floor targets*. The two are barely related unless there is a strict zero-sum situation in operation—not a typical situation yet in America. "Reverse discrimination" implies a mirror-image reversal of the traditional patterns of discrimination against black Americans—clearly a notion divorced from history. In a less strict sense, the term has been loosely used to describe poorly structured and administered affirmative action programs, such as the dual track, fixed number of slots system of the medical school of the University of California at Davis that was struck down in *Bakke*. But such questionable procedures are neither inherent in nor typical of affirmative action programs.

centage had risen to 78 where it has remained. Likewise, where back in 1942 only 30 percent of whites felt blacks "should go to the same schools as whites," this figure rose steadily to 49 by 1956, 70 by 1965, and 86 by 1972.[10] And while only 42 percent of whites in 1942 thought "Negroes should have as good a chance as white people to get any kind of job," 81 percent thought so by 1965 and 95 percent by 1972.[11]

But there are revealing exceptions to this general trend. "Negroes shouldn't push themselves where they are not wanted" was disagreed with by only 27 percent of whites in 1963 and 23 percent in 1977.[12] Another striking example is afforded by the issue of "busing." While 41 percent of a national sample of adult Americans told Harris Survey interviewers in early 1971 that they were unwilling to have school children bused for integration in their communities, 69 percent were unwilling by March 1972 following then President Nixon's televised attacks upon the process. These and other exceptions to the trend of improving racial attitudes suggest a general principle: *white Americans*

increasingly reject racial injustice in principle but are reluctant to accept the measures necessary to eliminate the injustice.

Some of this long-term improvement is accounted for by population replacement: older, bigoted whites have been dying over these years and have been replaced by younger, more tolerant whites. But most of this change actually reflects shifting positions of whites who have lived through the period as adults.[13] And social psychological research has repeatedly shown that these individual shifts typically take place after—not before—major structural changes have occurred in American race relations.[14] Thus, only 38 percent of white southern parents sampled by Gallup in 1963 had no objection to their children attending school with "a few" black children. But court-ordered school desegregation soon after began to sweep through the region, and white southern parents steadily changed their minds after the accomplished fact: 62 percent had no objections two years later in 1965, 78 percent by 1969, 83 percent by 1976.[15] Notice that this fait accompli phenomenon contradicts the popular misconceptions that attitude change must always precede behavioral change or that successful institu-

10. Mildred A. Schwartz, *Trends in White Attitudes Towards Negroes*, (Chicago, IL: National Opinion Research Center, 1967); and Andrew M. Greeley and Paul B. Sheatsley, "Attitudes Toward Racial Integration," in *Social Problems and Public Policy: Inequality and Justice*, ed. Lee Rainwater (Chicago, IL: Aldine, 1974), pp. 241–50.

11. Schwartz, *Trends in White Attitudes*; and James A. Davis, *1972 General Social Survey* (Chicago, IL: National Opinion Research Center, 1973).

12. Paul B. Sheatsley, "White Attitudes Toward the Negro," in *The Negro American*, ed. Talcott Parsons and Kenneth B. Clark (Boston, MA: Houghton Mifflin, 1966), pp. 303–24; and James A. Davis, *1977 General Social Survey* (Chicago, IL: National Opinion Research Center, 1978).

13. Roberto Fernandez, Cohort Replacement and Racial Attitude Change, 1956–1976-7, (Honors Thesis, Department of Sociology, Harvard University, 1978).

14. Herbert H. Hyman and Paul B. Sheatsley, "Attitudes Toward Integration," *Scientific American* 211 (July 1964): 16–23; and Thomas F. Pettigrew, "Complexity and Change in American Racial Patterns: A Social Psychological View," in *The Negro American*, pp. 325–59.

15. Pettigrew, *Racially Separate or Together?*, p. 176; and *Gallup Poll Index*, Report No. 127 (Princeton, NJ: American Institute of Public Opinion, February 1976).

tional reforms must await massive attitude support. Notice, too, that this same fait accompli effect can also operate in reverse direction; thus, there may well be some retrogression in white racial attitudes following the Supreme Court's publicized ruling in the 1978 *Bakke* case.

Dramatic racial events, such as the tragic assassination of Dr. King in 1968, have also been shown to alter positively white racial attitudes.[16] But even in this extreme situation, the particular whites who changed the most were those who were already the most open to racial alterations.

Black attitude shifts need to be qualified in terms of age and region. The 1954 Supreme Court ruling against school segregation had an enormous effect on raising the hopes of black Americans of all ages.[17] But heightened militancy and alienation from white society is most notable among young blacks who were born after the decision, grew up with the civil rights movement, and never experienced the full force of traditional American racism. Similarly, black northerners never knew the full depths of southern racial oppression, and have in recent years witnessed less structural improvement in their region than black southerners.[18] Consequently, just as the relative deprivation hypothesis would predict,[19] younger black

Northerners represent the most militant sector and older black southerners the least. But, as Schuman and Hatchett properly warn, "talk centers too much on sweeping transformations of the total black population."[20] Though these investigators themselves found significant shifts among Detroit blacks between 1968 and 1971, they point out that opinion changes among blacks have largely moved the group politically from a conservative stance to the center rather than any massive radicalization process.

The shifting demographic base of American race relations

The most fundamental alterations involve the demographic base that undergirds race relations. Broadly speaking, there have been three overlapping demographic racial eras in the twentieth century, the third of which we are now entering. Each has contributed to the present racial scene.

1915–World War II. Following the Civil War, there was relatively little black migration out of the rural South for half a century. But 1915 was a watershed year that initiated the first of the three demographic eras in this century. World War I abruptly ended European immigration while it simultaneously led to new war orders. Industry turned to the South with its labor surplus, and began to recruit furiously among poor whites and blacks alike. A train ticket combined with a guaranteed job at what looked to southern eyes as big wages represented a powerful temptation to leave the

16. Robert T. Riley and Thomas F. Pettigrew, "Dramatic Events and Attitude Change," *Journal of Personality and Social Psychology* 34 (November 1976): 1004–15.

17. Pettigrew, *A Profile of the Negro American*, pp. 184–5.

18. Peter Goldman, *Report From Black America* (New York: Simon & Schuster, 1970).

19. Pettigrew, *Racially Separate or Together?*, chap. 7.

20. Howard Schuman and Shirley Hatchett, *Black Racial Attitudes: Trends and Complexities* (Ann Arbor: Institute for Social Research, University of Michigan, 1974), p. 118.

region. And millions did for the next half century. This massive, long-distance migration of blacks from farm to city and from south to north made race relations not just a provincial concern of the former Confederacy, but for the first time an urban and national concern.

1945–1970. The second era involved the spatial separation of the races across the central city and suburban line, together with a continuation of the urbanizing migration to the North. The boom in housing construction following World War II basically established our present pattern of intrametropolitan segregation of the races. And the largest force in this process of residential separation was the Federal Government itself.[21]

Since 1950, one Federal housing program after another—public housing, Federal Housing Administration and Veterans Administration mortgages, urban renewal, model cities, even taxation policy—have exacerbated this trend. Within this national structure, of course, the many discriminatory practices of the banking and real estate industries cemented housing segregation at the local level. Just as the first demographic era established race relations as a national issue, this second era established race relations as a metropolitan issue.

1970–present. Before the nation has come to grips with the metropolitan scope of its racial problems, the third demographic era has arrived. We are only now beginning to learn about its radically different dimensions and to appreciate its sweeping implications for the future.

Other papers in this collection detail this new era. Here we shall only summarize its principal features.[22]

Nonmetropolitan areas are now growing faster than metropolitan areas for the first time in many years. The reason for this new trend is twofold: outmigration from metropolitan areas is now often in excess of inmigration; and natural population increases no longer offset the deficit because of the markedly lower birth rate.

The largest Standard Metropolitan Statistical Areas (SMSAs), with over three million people each, account for most of the drop in the growth rate. Medium sized SMSAs (one to three million) are still growing, though region is a critical mediating factor. In the Northeast and Midwest, these intermediate SMSAs are not growing, and some are actually losing population. In the West and South, these SMSAs are continuing to grow but at reduced rates with much of the inmigration centered in three retirement areas: Miami-Fort Lauderdale, Phoenix, and Tampa-St. Petersburg.

In marked contrast, small SMSAs (under one million) have experienced accelerated rates of growth and inmigration during the 1970s.

Regional redistributions of both races are considerable. The Northeast and Midwest are both losing black and white residents through more outmigration than inmigration. The West continues to gain both races through migration. And even the South has a net inflow of both

21. Charles Abrams, "The Housing Problem and the Negro," in *The Negro American*, pp. 512–24; and Theodore J. Lowi, "Apartheid U.S.A.," *Trans-action* 7 (April 1970); 32–39.

22. G. Sternlieb and J. W. Hughes, eds., *Post-Industrial America: Metropolitan Decline and Inter-Regional Job Shifts* (New Brunswick, NJ: Center for Urban Policy Research, Rutgers University, 1975); Wilbur Zelinsky, "Is Nonmetropolitan America Being Repopulated? The Evidence From Pennsylvania's Minor Civil Divisions," *Demography* 15 (February 1975): 13–59; and C. Jack Tucker, "Changing Patterns of Migration Between Metropolitan and Nonmetropolitan Areas of the United States: Recent Evidence," *Demography* 13 (November 1976): 435–43.

blacks and whites.[23] Definitive answers
as to the characteristics of these blacks
coming into the South must await the
1980 Census. But fragmentary evidence
suggests that many of these inmigrating
blacks are relatively well educated,
southern born, and returning to their
vastly altered hometowns either to retire
or to continue their professional careers.

Jobs and income are also on the move.
Between 1967 and 1972, the growth rate
of total employment was five times
greater in the South Atlantic than in the
Middle Atlantic states. Consequently,
projections to 1990 indicate a pronounced movement of income away
from the Northeast and Midwest to the
West and South.

THE STRUCTURAL LINCHPIN OF AMERICAN RACE RELATIONS

Each of these five major racial
trends intersects with the structural
linchpin of modern American race
relations: the intrametropolitan distribution of blacks and whites. The
basic facts of this urban spread of
the races across urban areas should
be reviewed briefly before we discuss these intersections.

Blacks live in metropolitan areas
more than whites, 76 percent to 67
percent in 1974, and they are far
more likely to be living inside central cities than in the suburban rings.
In 1974, 77 percent of metropolitan
blacks resided in central cities
(down from 79 percent in 1970)
compared to only 38 percent of
metropolitan whites (down from 41
percent in 1970).[24] Hence, blacks
are twice as likely as whites in
these areas to live inside the core
city. This doubled proportion of
blacks in central cities is the basic
fact underlying the spatial maldistribution of the races; and it is the

largest single reason for the vast
residential separation of black and
white citizens in America today.

Other related phenomena exacerbate this situation further. Blacks
are more likely to reside in the
very largest metropolitan areas.
They constituted 27 percent of the
central city populations of SMSAs
over one million in 1974 contrasted
with 16.9 percent of the central
cities of smaller SMSAs.[25] More
dramatically stated, there are more
black citizens today in the New York
SMSA than in *any* southern state,
more in the Chicago SMSA than in
either Mississippi or South Carolina,
and more in the Philadelphia SMSA
than in Arkansas and Kentucky combined. And it is in these huge SMSAs
where blacks in the past have comprised smaller proportions of the
metropolitan rings. This situation
has been slowly easing (4.0 percent
in 1960, 4.5 percent in 1970, and 4.9
percent in 1974), largely due to
recent gains in the rings around New
York City, Los Angeles, and the
District of Columbia.

Residential segregation is also intense within both the core cities
and the suburbs. Utilizing an index
of dissimilarity, the Taeubers' analyses of central city block data from
the Censuses of 1940, 1950, and
1960 lead to stark conclusions.[26]
By 1960, seven out of every eight
nonwhite families living in nonwhite blocks of central cities would
have had to move to a white block
to attain a random racial pattern.
A similar analysis of 1970 data reveals only a slight overall decline,
with six out of every seven nonwhite families needing to move to

23. U.S. Bureau of the Census (1975), p. 13.
24. *Ibid.*, pp. 9, 14.
25. *Ibid.*, p. 15.
26. Karl E. Taeuber and Alma F. Taeuber, *Negroes in Cities* (Chicago, IL: Aldine, 1965).

attain randomness.[27] These studies show that housing segregation during the 1940s increased throughout the country; and during the 1950s continued to spread in the South while receding slightly elsewhere. The 1960s appear to have witnessed a dual process in accommodating expanding black city populations. While there was some movement of blacks to previously all white neighborhoods that helped to lower the Taeubers' index, there was also an enlargement and increasing density of distinct black areas in cities ranging from Buffalo to Shreveport to Sacramento.[28]

There are three popular misconceptions concerning this phenomenon. Black-white residential separation in housing is often thought to be largely a function of differential racial incomes, to be similar to the patterns of residential separation between other ethnic and social class groups, and to be currently breaking down into salt-and-pepper patterns in the suburbs. The Taeubers counter each of these comforting misconceptions. They state flatly, "Economic factors cannot account for more than a small portion of the observed levels of racial residential segregation."[29]

Moreover, black-white housing segregation is so much more extreme than any other urban group patterns as to be qualitatively distinct. Within central cities, using the dissimilarity index, it is almost three times that of white ethnic

groups and double both that of social classes and even that of Chicanos and Anglos in the urban Southwest. The Taeubers have shown, too, that in Chicago such late-arriving minorities as Puerto Ricans, Mexican-Americans, and Japanese-Americans dispersed more residentially in a few years despite discrimination than black Americans had in two generations.[30] Clearly the force of racial discrimination in housing practiced against blacks has no parallel in the United States (save, perhaps, for the isolation of Native Americans on reservations).

Nor are most blacks in the suburbs in any salt-and-pepper pattern. The Taeubers made a detailed analysis of the 34,000 increase in the black population in Chicago's suburbs during the 1950s.[31] They found that 83 percent of this apparent improvement occurred either in heavily black suburbs or in industrial suburbs with black ghettos of their own. Much of the 1970–74 black suburban growth of two-thirds of a million is similarly distributed. Precise determinations must again await the 1980 Census; but predominantly black suburban areas—such as Compton, California and East St. Louis, Illinois—are absorbing a significant portion of this increase. Salt-and-pepper residential patterns do exist in many suburban neighborhoods, and there are reasons to believe that they are increasing. Yet such patterns do not predominate.

There are two important differences between black metropolitan housing units within and outside

27. A Sorenson, Karl E. Taeuber, and L. G. Hollingworth, "Indexes of Racial Residential Segregation for 109 Cities in the United States," *Sociological Focus* 8 (1975): 125–42.

28. T. G. Clemence, "Residential Segregation in the Mid-Sixties," *Demography* 4 (1967): 562–68.

29. Taeuber and Taeuber, *Negroes in Cities*, p. 2.

30. Karl E. Taeuber and Alma F. Taeuber, "Is the Negro an Immigrant Group?" *Integrated Education* 1 (June 1963): 25–28.

31. Taeuber and Taeuber, *Negroes in Cities*.

the central city. According to data from the 1973 Annual Housing Survey, 56 percent of black housing units in the suburbs were owner-occupied compared to only 36 percent of black units in the core city. Furthermore, suburban black housing units were far more likely to have been built since April 1970. Though 13 percent of all metropolitan housing units in 1973 were occupied by blacks, only 7 percent of these new units were black occupied. Yet black owner-occupied units in the suburban rings were just as likely as white units to be new. Suburban renters were not as fortunate, but they were still far more likely to occupy new housing than black renters within the central city.[32]

The discontinuities of social change

This massive metropolitan pattern of housing segregation has now become the principal barrier to progress in other realms. Indeed, the residential segregation of blacks and whites has emerged as a functional equivalent for the explicit state segregation laws of the past in that it effectively acts to limit the life chances and choices of black people generally.

Roof developed a path model that links housing segregation with racial inequities in other realms.[33] He analyzed 1960 Census data from 39 southern cities with at least 1,000 nonwhite housing units. Controlling for each city's age, size, and nonwhite percentage, Roof found significant relationships between the intensity of a city's residential

32. U.S. Bureau of the Census (1975), pp. 133–36.
33. Wade Clark Roof, "Residential Segregation of Blacks and Racial Inequality in Southern Cities: Toward a Causal Model," *Social Problems* 19 (1972): 393–407.

segregation and its racial disparities in education, occupation, and income. His best-fitting model suggests that housing segregation acts directly to widen racial inequalities in both education and occupation, which in turn lead to racial inequality in income.

Roof's work formalizes relationships that have long been suggested by observers. Poorer schools and city services restrict initial black opportunities; jobs increasingly leaving the city for suburban belts become harder to retain or obtain when black workers cannot follow them residentially; ghetto dollars often buy less as spending options are limited; and many other disruptive processes are established by residential separation of the races. Note, too, that not only are these problems made worse by housing segregation, but remedies for these same problems are also made more costly and politically difficult. Consider the so-called "busing" controversy in this perspective. A majority of whites today simultaneously support public school desegregation and oppose the transportation made necessary to achieve it by our extensive system of housing *apartheid*. Ways out of this apparent dilemma must involve metropolitan approaches to the problem together with solid progress in eroding residential segregation.

Two contrasting processes

The metropolitan housing patterns of the sixties and seventies are part of the diverging processes within black America described earlier. Younger, educated black families are beginning to buy new homes in the suburbs as well as continuing the older black middle-class pattern of living on the outer boundaries of the ghetto. These are the people whom middle-class white suburbanites are generally willing to greet as neighbors.

The poorly educated and older families, however, are largely still part of the growing densities of central black areas in the core cities. Thus, the diverging housing developments mirror the diverging socioeconomic developments among blacks. This relationship is imperfect, to be sure; some poor blacks in such places as East St. Louis are recorded as "suburban," and most middle-class blacks still reside in the central city. But as both of these processes proceed, a geographical as well as socioeconomic distance is likely to develop between the two status poles of the black world. Such a development is, of course, comparable to that of the white world; but it will be novel for black America and carries considerable implications for the future.

The altered nature of racial discrimination

We have noted that racial discrimination has become more indirect, subtle, procedural, and ostensibly nonracial. We see now how housing segregation and the establishment of white rings around black cores undergird this trend. In fact, there is a broad consensus today among race relations specialists that urban development has shaped, and will shape even more in the future, the course of American race relations.

Once again, however, the difficulty of achieving the needed remedies is evident. Blatant denial of voting rights complete with the defiant symbols furnished by a Governor Wallace struck easily at the nation's sense of fairness and simple justice. And the resulting

Voting Rights Act of 1965 is the most effectively designed anti-discrimination legislation ever written in the United States.

But equally debilitating racial discrimination that indirectly results from housing segregation and the maldistribution of the races throughout metropolitan areas does not evoke the same notions of fairness and justice. The effects of the discrimination are less obvious, and easy rationalizations abound that attribute all educational and occupational handicaps to blacks themselves. The connection between the handicaps and barriers, such as the central city and suburban boundary, are less understood. And structural problems are harder to analyze than simple denial of the vote; faceless, traditional structures do not arouse the white public like a Wallace or a Sheriff Clark. Consequently, the remedies themselves—more metropolitan cooperation, scattered site public housing in the suburbs—often seem unfair and unjustified. The white Palo Altos of America would rather conceive of themselves as islands without ties to the black East Palo Altos. Racial justice arguments alone will not win majority support for these needed structural alterations. Future urban development planning must keep racial considerations in the fore while packaging structural changes in a much broader context.

Changes in racial attitudes

This conclusion fits with the summary principle that emerged from a review of attitude trends: white Americans increasingly reject racial injustice in principle but are reluctant to accept the measures necessary to eliminate the injustice.

In the housing discrimination realm, this tendency takes the form of 85 percent of white adults by 1972 reporting that it would not make any difference to them "if a Negro with just as much income and education" moved onto their block contrasted with consistent majorities throughout the 1960s and 1970s who oppose "a Federal law forbidding discrimination in housing against Negroes."[34] Basically, these data represent a conflict between two widely held beliefs.

On the one hand, many feel that whites have the "right" to restrict blacks from their neighborhoods. On the other hand, many feel that blacks have the "right" to live where they wish and can afford. What is more, many of the same white Americans hold *both* of these beliefs. One study in a New Jersey suburb confronted its middle-class respondents with this conflict directly, and found both the inconsistency and similar means of handling it to be widespread.[35] Often whites assume that their values are entirely different from those of blacks. Hence, 61 percent in 1963 agreed that "Negroes are not ready to live in better neighborhoods"; and three-fourths of urban northerners in 1968 believed that blacks have "worse jobs, education, and housing than white people" at least in part because of "something about Negroes themselves."[36]

Blacks are also wary.[37] They list better housing as one of their most pressing needs, and are far more dissatisfied with their present housing than whites. Only a minority feel better off personally from recent improvements in the housing stock of blacks. Most would prefer a thoroughly racially mixed neighborhood, yet they are reluctant to seek housing in white areas in part because of anticipated discrimination and abuse. Furthermore, it is precisely those blacks— the young, well-off, and living in the North—who otherwise are the most likely to seek interracial housing, who most often harbor these fears. Thus, those blacks most able to test the limits of the dual housing markets appear to be the most reluctant to do so.

In addition, the black community has differential access to negative information. One Boston study found that the great majority of middle-income black families who had moved to white suburbs had been well received, but their favorable experiences were little known in Boston's black community. Instead, the unfavorable experiences of the few families who had met suburban abuse and had moved back to the ghetto were widely known in the community.[38]

Another point with policy significance also emerges from these national survey data. When whites report acceptance of interracial neighborhoods, they typically have in mind a token number of black families. When blacks report acceptance, they typically prefer mixed areas with approximately half of each race. Stable neighborhoods might best compromise between

34. Thomas F. Pettigrew, "Black and White Attitudes Toward Race and Housing," in *Racial Discrimination in the United States* ed. T. F. Pettigrew (New York: Harper & Row, 1975) pp. 92–105; and James A. Davis, *1975 General Social Survey* (Chicago, IL: National Opinion Research Center, 1976).

35. Robert W. Friedrichs, "Christians and Residential Exclusion: An Empirical Study of a Northern Dilemma," *Journal of Social Issues* 15 (1959): 14–23.

36. Pettigrew, "Black and White Attitudes," p. 101.

37. *Ibid.*, pp. 105–23.

38. Lewis G. Watts, et al., *The Middle-Income Negro Family Faces Urban Renewal* (Boston: Massachusetts Dept. of Commerce and Development, 1965).

these positions with roughly 20 to 35 percent black proportions, as some successful planned interracial developments have done.[39] Bradburn, however, did find stable interracial neighborhoods of varying proportions.[40]

Survey research in metropolitan Detroit conducted in 1976 puts the problem into perspective.[41] It found that many blacks can afford suburban housing, and that both races are knowledgable about the housing market. Furthermore, black respondents tended to prefer mixed neighborhoods and indicated willingness to enter such neighborhoods. Yet metropolitan Detroit reveals an intense pattern of residential segregation by race. Why? The Michigan researchers concluded that white prejudices supply a principal answer. Their white respondents tended to be reluctant to stay in neighborhoods where blacks are moving in and to buy homes in interracial areas. Detroit area whites tend to believe that black entry automatically lowers property values and increases crime. This white resistance is conditioned by racial proportions. Two-fifths of the white

respondents say they would move, for example, from a one-third black neighborhood whereas two-thirds say they would move from a neighborhood with a slight black majority.

Attitudes must be seen in their full social context. The views of both whites and blacks are more derivative than causal in the process of how shelter is distributed by race in the United States. Both white and black Americans are more willing to reside in an interracial neighborhood if they have experienced integration previously, though the dual housing markets have long prevented most citizens from having had such experience. As social psychology has repeatedly demonstrated, behavior change typically precedes rather than follows attitude change.[42] Therefore, the most effective way to alter opposition, black and white, to interracial housing is to have them live successfully in such housing. Segregated housing has caused today's fear of and opposition to interracial neighborhoods in both races; only a single housing market, free of "redlining" and "bluelining," and spread throughout the metropolitan area, can begin to develop its own acceptance.

The shifting demographic base of American race relations

Housing segregation is, in large part, a legacy of the post-World War II period. But what about the strikingly new demographic trends on the 1970s? How will they affect this situation?

The new trends have already made some difference.[43] Whereas nonmetropolitan areas lost almost a

39. A similar racial proportion appears optimal at this time in schools as well. See: Thomas F. Pettigrew, "The Racial Integration of the Schools," in *Racial Discrimination in the United States*, pp. 224–239. This proportion reflects the country's racist past, and it should ease upward over time as racial fears subside. For now, however, this proportion seems to avoid blacks' fears of tokenism and whites' fears of being in an unaccustomed minority status.

40. Norman M. Bradburn, S. Sudman, and G. L. Gockel, *Racial Integration in American Neighborhoods* (Chicago, IL: National Opinion Research Center, 1970).

41. Reynolds Farley et al., "Chocolate City, Vanilla Suburbs: Will the Trend Toward Racially Separate Communities Continue?" Unpublished paper presented at the Annual Meeting of the American Sociological Association, Chicago, Illinois, 1977.

42. Pettigrew, *Racially Separate or Together?*

43. U.S. Bureau of the Census (1975), pp. 14–15.

third of a million blacks during the sixties (−323,000), their black populations grew slightly from 1970 to 1974 (+34,000). Within SMSAs, the growth of the black population was more evenly divided between the central city and the suburbs. Whereas only 19 percent of the black metropolitan increase in the 1960s occurred in the suburbs, 43 percent did during 1970–1974. Put differently, the absolute increase in the black population of metropolitan rings in just the first four years of this decade (+668,000) almost equaled the increase of the entire previous decade (+758,000). While these trends slowed the increase in the black proportions of core cities in SMSAs with over a million people, blacks still constituted only 5 percent of metropolitan rings in 1974. Even at the accelerated black growth rate in the suburbs during the 1970–1974 period, it would require roughly 80 years before blacks acquired their true metropolitan proportion in the suburbs.

A small advance in interracial neighborhoods during the 1970s is suggested by data from the General Social Surveys conducted by the National Opinion Research Center.[44] While only 29 percent of a national sample of whites in 1972 told interviewers that blacks lived in their neighborhood, 35 percent did so by 1977. And the percentage of whites who reported that blacks resided on their block rose from 11 percent in 1972 to 14 percent in 1977.

In broader terms, these new trends imply for the future a more extensive spread of blacks across communities of varying size, with somewhat less piling up in the largest central cities. They further point to the South as likely to remain the dominant regional home of black Americans. As recently as 15 years ago, one leading demographer predicted that 75 to 85 percent of blacks would live outside of the South.[45] Such a situation seems less likely now since jobs have increased in the revived region and the percentage of blacks residing in the South has remained constant at 53 through the seventies.[46]

Not all of the effects of the new demographic trends have positive implications. If it is the rising middle-class blacks who are disproportionately leaving the northern core cities for the suburbs and for the South, this exodus could strip urban black communities of their major leadership. Worse, the new population trends are in many ways too little and too late to prevent massive concentrations in a small number of the biggest central cities, many of which are losing both jobs and their tax bases. By 1970, one in every three blacks lived in just 15 central cities, a list that includes such troubled municipalities as New York, Detroit, Philadelphia, Baltimore, Cleveland, and Newark.[47] The spectre of widespread structural unemployment of poorly educated blacks in these cities, far worse than even that experienced in recent years, seems a genuine possibility that informed planning must face and attempt to thwart.

44. Davis, *General Social Survey*, 1973; and Davis, *General Social Survey*, 1978.

45. Horace C. Hamilton, "The Negro Leaves the South," *Demography* 1 (1964): 273–295.

46. U.S. Bureau of the Census (1975), p. 13.

47. U.S. Bureau of the Census (1971), p. 17.

SOME COMMENTS ON POLICY

Some commentators today question why a high priority should be granted to the alleviation of racial segregation in housing. Most ethnic groups in this country have concentrated together from either choice or force, goes the argument, so what is so different about blacks? Two centuries of legalized slavery and a century more of legalized segregation, of course, are unique to blacks and make such comparisons with white ethnic groups dubious at best. In addition, an array of special factors have been discussed in this paper. Residential separation of blacks and whites, we noted, is so much more vast than that between other groups as to be a qualitatively different phenomenon. This separation is in large part a creation of explicit federal policy, and therefore can best be untangled by federal policy. Its existence has built its own acceptance among both races until now Americans are conditioned to think in terms of two housing markets. And, most important, residential segregation is linked to inequalities in education, employment, and income. Indeed, it has now emerged as the chief obstacle to further progress in solving America's oldest domestic problem.

There are other reasons for assigning high priority to this issue. One involves the delivery of services to a relatively powerless group. When blacks are concentrated in tightly confined areas, it has proven historically easier to discriminate against them in a variety of city services ranging from public schools to garbage collection. Redlining difficulties in obtaining mortgages and property insurance offer another example of this concentration principle.

A further consideration concerns how group separation leads to diverging values. White and black citizens living apart over generations establish increasingly diverse values that in turn make interracial interaction in the future all the more strained and difficult.[48] Finally, as the race riots of the 1960s tragically demonstrated, the present maldistribution of the races contributes to long-term conflict. Interracial communication is limited; interracial comparisons and stereotypes become divorced from reality; interracial rumors spread rapidly. If we wished to design metropolitan areas in such a way as to maximize the probability of racial strife, we would be hard pressed to improve on present patterns.

Detailed policy ideas are provided in the accompanying articles. Suffice it here to mention six general guidelines that follow from this discussion and characterize many of the more promising proposals.

The problems are structural, so their remedies must also be structural. Fair housing laws and antidiscrimination commissions that have relied exclusively upon individual complaints have failed to dent the problem.[49] And "brotherhood weeks" and other attempts merely to change attitudes do not directly address the basic issues.

Successful remedies at the local level must be planned within the larger national scene. The total supplies of housing and jobs offer illustrations. In times of acute shortages of low- and medium-income housing, efforts to combat housing segregation are severely restricted. But times of significant increments to the housing stock are precisely the

48. Pettigrew, *Racially Separate or Together*, chap. 12.
49. Mayhew, *Law and Equal Opportunity*.

crucial times for action. The immediate post-World War II building boom was one such time, and our failures during that period are at the root of our problems now. Hopefully, the opportunity for long-lasting remedies will be seized during the next such boom. Similarly, the national employment picture is a critical consideration. Our refusal to supply federal travel funds to move workers to where the jobs are retards beneficial demographic movements and undercuts job training programs.

Piecemeal efforts within a metropolitan area are generally ineffective and may even prove counterproductive. Opening one suburb or previously all-white section of the central city for black residents, for example, frequently funnels the pent-up demand overwhelmingly in one direction and simply extends the ghetto. Not unlike the negative results of the bluelining and steering practices of many banks and real estate firms, such efforts leave bitterness in their wake and serve to bolster the worst fears and prejudices of both races.

Despite substantial positive changes in white racial attitudes, structural reforms in this domain will continue to be strongly resisted if they are advanced only in terms of racial justice. Since these reforms must in any event be systemic and patterned, they necessarily will be part of a larger package the goals of which are in fact far broader than racial concerns. Race relations are now so intertwined with urban growth and development that virtually all urban planning decisions, from mass transit to property taxes, carry vital significance for the future intrametropolitan distribution of black Americans.

Another side of this same point concerns incentives for the suburbs.

"What's in it for us?" understandably ask suburbanites, when virtually all state and federal aid now comes to their communities uncontingent upon their cooperation with the metropolitan area. Refusal to allow small public housing developments, for instance, may well remain a right of suburbs. But the exercise of this veto option should entail a heavy cost in outside aid for other programs. If an area chooses to secede from the society's central problems, then the society should financially secede from it.

The intense pattern of today's black-white residential separation did not emerge simply from undirected individual choices. Entrenched policies of governmental and private agencies carefully shaped, reinforced, and legitimized it. This suggests that these structurally effective policies for developing segregation might usefully be reversed. Consider the time-honored mortgage practices of the F.H.A., V.A., and many private lenders. Whites often obtained mortgages more easily and at better terms if they bought in the suburbs rather than in the core city. Blacks, if they could secure mortgages at all, got them only for designated portions of the inner city. Reversing this process, whites could be routinely given unusually attractive, subsidized terms to own housing in mixed areas of the central city, and blacks routinely given such terms to own housing in mixed areas of the suburbs. Some limited housing programs do the equivalent of this now. But, if we are serious about eroding the legacies of past policies, we must make such subsidized transactions a routine part of the housing market's operations.

Often remedies fashioned in the race relations domain visualize a single desired end state. For instance, private fair housing groups in the suburbs often aim only for salt-and-pepper patterns. But there are, of course, a great range of options, from "mini-ghettos" in the suburbs to continued and heightened migration trends away from the largest metropolitan centers to smaller cities. No single option need predominate, as long as they all contribute in their own manner to the larger interrelated goals of a wider black residential distribution and greater black choice in housing.[50]

50. Two specific objections—one from blacks, the other from whites—have often been raised concerning these goals. Politically concerned blacks, noting the development of black political strength in central cities, question the wisdom of metropolitan efforts at this time. However, the suggestions in this paper involve metropolitan cooperation, not political consolidation. Black mayors, from Bradley and Jackson to Hatcher and Gibson, realize the necessity of such cooperation for the viability of their own cities; nor are their political bases threatened by any foreseeable degree of black suburbanization. Some whites object to the goal of broadening black housing options at the expense of what they perceive to be their option to live in an all-white neighborhood. But, obviously, the two situations are not comparable. Whites are free now to exercise their option to live in all-black areas; and neither blacks nor whites have any "right" to reside in exclusively uniracial areas.

ANNALS, AAPSS, 441, Jan. 1979

Patterns of White Avoidance

By FRANKLIN D. WILSON

ABSTRACT: This paper addresses the issue of whether whites' utilization of alternate forms of schooling is racially motivated. More specifically, an effort is made to determine whether residence in census tract units of varying racial composition influences white outmigration and utilization of nonpublic schools. Results are reported and summarized for sixty-three public school districts serving central cities. It is found that residential populations living within individual school districts differ with respect to the extent of racial selection in residential relocation and nonpublic school utilization, according to region, percentage of public school pupils black, type of district, and implementation of school desegregation programs.

Franklin D. Wilson is Associate Professor of Sociology and a member of the Research Staff of the Institute for Research on Poverty at the University of Wisconsin. He is the author of Residential Consumption, Economic Opportunities and Race, *and has written articles on metropolitan structure and change. He is currently studying the demographic impacts of school desegregation policy.*

This article is based on Discussion Paper 78-500 which, complete with tables, is available from the Institute for Research on Poverty, University of Wisconsin, Madison.

PUBLIC policies directed toward reducing the extent of racial isolation within the nation's school districts have provoked a great deal of controversy among parents, politicians, and academicians. One of the most controversial aspects of school desegregation programs has been the necessity of reassigning large numbers of pupils to schools located away from their immediate residential areas. It is questioned whether such programs are producing their intended outcome.[1]

This concern has stimulated interest in the identification of factors causally related to school segregation, and in finding alternate ways of reducing the extent of racial isolation in the nation's public school systems. Two of the main issues under scrutiny are the extent of correspondence between residential and school segregation, and whether the attainment of racially mixed neighborhoods promotes desegregated school environments.[2] This paper focuses on the second of these issues, and assesses the potential for school desegregation in selected central city school districts based on the residential patterns of black and white pupils. The current effort to illuminate this issue asks whether neighbor-

hoods of varying racial composition influence whites to seek alternate forms of schooling either by migrating or through increased utilization of nonpublic schools.

The necessity of implementing school desegregation programs is premised on the supposition that acceptable levels of interracial contact cannot be expected when the attendance zones of schools embrace contiguous residential areas that are homogeneous in racial composition; that is, observed levels of racial isolation in public schools are thought to reflect the extent of prevailing racial residential segregation.[3] Thus it would seem to follow that interracial contact in public schools could be enhanced significantly if residential neighborhoods were racially mixed.

REVIEW OF PREVIOUS STUDIES

If one were to employ existing estimates of racial residential segregation for central cities of metropolitan areas as a baseline for assessing the potential for school desegregation based on residential patterns, approximately three-fourths of the whites or blacks would have to shift their residential location in order to achieve maximum school desegregation.[4] However, there is

1. Martin T. Katzman, *The Quality of Municipal Services, Central City Decline, and Middle Class Flight* (Boston: Department of City and Regional Planning, Harvard University, 1977); Karl E. Taeuber and Franklin D. Wilson, "The Impact of Desegregation Policies on Population Redistribution in Metropolitan Areas," In *Population Policy Analysis: Issues in American Politics*, ed. Michael Kraft and Mark Schneider (Lexington Books, 1978) pp. 135–53.

2. Franklin D. Wilson and Karl E. Taeuber, "Residential and School Segregation: Some Tests of their Association" in *Demography of Racial and Ethnic Groups*, ed. Frank Bean and W. Parker Frisbie (New York: Academic Press, 1978, forthcoming).

3. Reynolds Farley, "Residential Segregation and Its Implications for School Integration," *Law and Contemporary Problems* 39 (Winter 1975): 164–94; Eleanor P. Wolf, "Do School Violations Cause School Segregation? Can Metropolitan Busing Correct It?" (Paper presented at the Annual Meeting of the American Sociological Association, New York City, 1 September 1976).

4. Annemette Sørensen, K. E. Taeuber, and L. J. Hollingsworth, Jr., "Indexes of Racial Residential Segregation for 109 Cities in the United States, 1940 to 1970," *Sociological Focus* 8 (April 1975): 125–42; Ann B. Schnare, Residential Segregation by Race in U.S. Metropolitan Areas: An Analysis

one basic flaw in this line of argument: racial composition of public schools does not depend exclusively on that of residential areas. Both school district administrative policies and the availability of alternate schooling without a change of residence can act to distort the correspondence between the racial composition of schools and residential areas. Evidence for the first source of distortion is indicated by the large number of court rulings in favor of plaintiffs who have charged that the extent of racial isolation prevailing within a given district was partially related to specific acts perpetrated by school boards and administrators.

The effect that utilization of alternate forms of schooling has on attenuating the extent of correspondence between racial residential and school segregation has yet to be thoroughly investigated. At issue is whether whites' utilization of alternate schooling is racially motivated. The logical point of departure with respect to finding an answer to this question would be to analyze the responses of whites living in racially mixed residential areas. A search of the relevant literature uncovered only a few studies that have attempted to address the question of whether racially mixed neighborhoods lead to similar mixing in schools. Bradburn, Sudman and Gockel report that they could find little support for the notion that white parents shift their children from one school to another (public or private) in response to the racial

composition of their neighborhood.[5] On the other hand, they do note that there appears to be a slight increase in the relationship between the willingness of white parents to send their children to integrated schools and the proportion black in those schools.[6]

The Bradburn, Sudman, and Gockel study focused on integrated neighborhoods that were stable in racial composition. These types of neighborhoods are only a small fraction of the neighborhoods located within large urban areas. The literature on residential succession indicates that most neighborhoods with black and white households in residence are in various stages of racial succession.[7] The process of residential succession based on race has a major impact on the structure of neighborhood institutions and organizational forms.[8] The neighborhood-based elementary school is one organizational form whose population composition is affected by that of the population it serves.

Wegmann notes that in neighborhoods undergoing racial transition the proportion of blacks in public elementary schools tends to exceed the proportion they represent of the population residing within the attendance area of individual schools.[9]

Across Cities and Over Time (Washington, D.C.: The Urban Institute, Contract Report No. 246-2, 1977); Thomas Van Valey, W. C. Roof, and J. E. Wilcox, "Trends in Residential Segregation: 1960–1970," *American Journal of Sociology* 82 (January 1977): 826–44.

5. Norman Bradburn, Seymour Sudman and Galen Gockel, *Racial Integration in American Neighborhoods: A Comparative Study* (Chicago: National Opinion Research Center, 1970), p. 302.
6. Ibid., p. 294.
7. Howard Aldrich, "Ecological Succession in Racially Changing Neighborhoods: A Review of the Literature." *Urban Affairs Quarterly* 10 (March 1975): 327–48.
8. Harvey Malatch, *Managed Integration: Dilemmas of Doing Good in the City* (Berkeley: University of California Press, 1972).
9. Robert G. Wegmann, "Neighborhoods and Schools in Racial Transition," *Growth and Change* 6 (July, 1975): 3–4.

Wegmann speculates that white out-migration and nonpublic school utilization, and the higher fertility rate of black households are the major factors associated with this differential.[10] The findings of a recent case study of the Los Angeles school district are consistent with this observation. That study provides the conceptual framework for the analysis reported in this paper.

Wilson and Taeuber sought to determine whether the increased presence of minorities in residential areas invokes avoidance responses among whites, as in the increased utilization of private and parochial schools or the outmigration of families with school age children.[11] It was suggested that avoidance was likely if whites desire to minimize the extent of contact their children have with blacks because of perceptions of the lowering of educational standards, breakdown of discipline, and/or because of racially prejudiced attitudes. These authors found that even after controlling for the general ecological and socioeconomic characteristics of attendance areas, the percent black among the school age populations of attendance zones was substantially associated with private school utilization, the outmigration of white families with school age children, and a lower representation of whites in public schools.[12]

The data used in the Wilson-Taeuber analysis predate the desegregation controversy in Los Angeles, and provide direct evidence on the residence/school link as a component of the general process of white avoidance of racially mixed housing and schools. Although limited in universe of coverage, two important (but tentative) conclusions are indicated by the findings of this study, both of which should be reviewed further. First, it is clear that some whites seek to avoid attending schools with blacks regardless of the form or instrument of racial contact. This observation is consistent with the literature on racial residential succession, which indicates that most racially mixed residential areas are unstable and are likely to become uniracial at some point in the future. The second conclusion is that the racial composition of some public schools at a given point in time may already bear the imprint of white avoidance even in the absence of the implementation of desegregation programs. This conclusion is consistent with findings reported in the literature on residential differentiation, which indicates that people respond to the racial identification of their neighbors in making a residential decision.[13] Thus the possibility of achieving racially mixed school environments, based on the residential patterns of blacks and whites, appears less likely in communities whose residential structure already bears the imprint of racial selection.

10. See also Aldrich, "Ecological Succession in Racially Changing Neighborhoods," p. 337.

11. Wilson and Taeuber, "Residential and School Segregation."

12. Ibid., pp. 16–20.

13. Thomas F. Pettigrew, "Attitudes on Race and Housing: A Social-Psychological View" in *Segregation in Residential Areas*, ed. A. H. Hawley and V. P. Rock (Washington, DC: National Academy of Sciences, 1973) pp. 21–84; Reynolds Farley et al, "Chocolate City, Vanilla Suburbs: Will the Trend Toward Racially Separate Communities Continue?" (Paper presented at the Annual Meetings of the American Sociological Association, Chicago, 31 August 1977); Diane L. Colasanto, The Prospects for Racial Integration in Neighborhoods: An Analysis of Residential Preferences in the Detroit Metropolitan Area (Ph.D. Diss. University of Michigan, Ann Arbor, 1977).

DATA AND METHODS

The findings from the Los Angeles case study must be regarded as highly tentative, since they are based on the experience of only one large central city, and thus may not be representative of other communities. This investigation is an extension of the Los Angeles study, and applies a similar conceptual framework to further explore the association between the racial composition of residential areas and white nonpublic school utilization and outmigration for sixty-three central city school districts.

The analysis makes use of data from the 1970 census tapes for census tracts (fourth count). For each central city school district the unit of analysis is a census tract containing residential populations. It is important to note that these census tracts reflect the boundaries of school districts and not those of the politically defined central city.[14]

Attention is focused on the black and Anglo (white) residential population age 5–13 years, the age span covered by elementary schools. The white population was obtained by subtracting persons of Hispanic origin from the category of persons designated as "white" on the census tapes. This adjustment is necessary because the fourth count census data only distinguish between blacks and whites as ethnic categories, and the latter category includes persons of Spanish surname or Spanish language.

The sixty-three school districts in-

cluded in this study represent a convenience sample, as they were selected primarily on the basis of data availability and the fact that blacks represented at least 10 percent of public school enrollment in 1970. However, the similarities and differences between them are relevant for the analysis. For example, each of the four major regions are represented, there are county-wide as well as central city districts, and 59 percent of the districts had implemented some form of desegregation program on or before 1970.

It was hypothesized that if many Anglo parents seek to avoid sending their children to schools in which the potential for contact with black pupils is great, or which are perceived to be poor schools because of the presence of black pupils, then we should find evidence of one or both of the following: (1) enhanced Anglo enrollment in private or parochial schools; (2) lower percentage of the Anglo population of elementary school age. These are the direct indications of white avoidance that are employed as dependent variables, hypothesized as being affected by the racial, socioeconomic, and housing characteristics of populations living within census tracts.

It can be suggested that if whites with school-age children respond to the presence of blacks in their neighborhood by migrating, the net effect ceteris paribus, would be to lower their representation in the population remaining. Unfortunately, residential areas with fewer whites of school age are also more likely to attract black families because of the availability of low-cost housing, or because they live in the path of expanding black residential areas.[15]

14. The determination of the school district boundaries was made possible by the use of a special census tape which contains geographic identification codes for census tracts, block groups, and enumeration districts associated with individual school districts. The census tract codes were matched with those on the fourth count population and housing files.

15. Aldrich, "Ecological Succession in Racially Changing Neighborhoods."

Housing variables were included to take account of the first source of bias, and the percent of the black population living in the same house in 1965 and 1970 was included to identify areas of rapid black influx.

In the Los Angeles study, private and parochial schooling were combined into a single category. They are analyzed separately here to determine whether they are used differentially by whites in responding to the presence of blacks of school age. Private schooling is primarily a southern phenomenon, whereas parochial schooling, although national in scope, tends to predominate in the nonsouth regions. Another reason for performing separate analyses for each type of schooling relates to their differential utilization by blacks as alternatives to public schools. An average of 98 percent of all children in private elementary schools are white for the sample of cities as a whole. In the case of parochial elementary schools, the proportion black varies substantially by school districts.

Finally, parochial elementary schools, like their counterparts in the public sector, tend to draw their pupils from particular residential areas. The attendance boundaries of most parochial elementary schools correspond to those of the church parishes. If black and white pupils attending parochial schools are segregated residentially, the potential for interracial contact is no greater than is the case in public schools. The potential for an average white child in parochial schools having contact with a black child is substantially less than one would expect, given the overall proportion black in parochial schools in each school district. This has caused great concern among some church officials, because the tuition cost of parochial schools may encourage whites to use them as "safe havens," particularly when the public schools are threatened with desegregation.[16]

A multiple regression equation was estimated for each of the three dependent variables. Each equation included selected characteristics of residential populations living within census tracts believed to be associated with each dependent variable, but is not reported here in detail.[17] The discussion of results focuses only on the net effects of the percentage of the population age 5–13 years in census tracts who are black (hereafter referred to as percent black) on private and parochial school utilization and outmigration.

RESULTS

It can be noted that the effect of percent black varied enormously between districts. Baltimore and Pittsburgh are the only districts in which the effects of percent black are statistically significant and in the predicted direction for each of the measures of white avoidance.

The substantial variation observed in the effect of percent black merely

16. David V. Sarahan, "What About Desegregation in Catholic Schools?" *Momentum* (December 1977): 10–15.

17. The full multiple regression equations included the following variables: a Gini index of similarity of the income distribution of black and Anglo families; median years of schooling completed for the Anglo population; median occupational status score of the employed Anglo population; median family income of the Anglo population; percentage of the black population living in the same house in 1965; percentage of the population age 5–13 years who are black; percentage of housing units that are owner-occupied; median age of occupied dwelling units; median value of occupied dwelling units. The equations for private and parochial school utilization included the percentage of the Anglo population age 5–13 years, and the equation for parochial school utilization also included an estimate of the percentage of the Anglo population that is Catholic.

confirmed what some researchers have suspected; namely that simplistic interpretations of the residence/school linkage, as constant across places, conceal a great deal of complexity resulting from historical circumstances, as well as systematic differences between school districts that arise from the effects of racial, socioeconomic, political, and demographic factors. An attempt was made to determine whether interdistrict variations in the effects of percent black on the measures of white avoidance are associated with several variables believed to affect the linkage between the racial composition of schools and residential areas. The·limited number of school districts affects the type of groupings and cross-classifications that can be performed, and limits the generalizability of the results.

School districts were divided along a south-nonsouth axis, with respect to all the classification variables. Attention is focused on variation in the effect of percent black on migration and private school utilization, since few of the districts achieved significant coefficients for parochial school utilization.

The county-central city district dichotomy is only relevant for the southern region of the country, as there are few districts outside the south which serve both county populations and black pupils in significant numbers. A slightly higher percentage of central city districts show indications of their white school age populations being reduced as a result of the increased concentration of blacks in residential areas. This is to be expected when the availability of predominantly white suburban areas provides a variable long-term alternative to continued residence in central cities. County school districts,

on the other hand, effectively reduce the likelihood of whites using migration as a means of avoiding interracial contact in public schools, since cities and suburbs are likely to be served by the same district.

The fact that percent black has significant effects on private school utilization in a greater percentage of central city districts is contrary to conventional wisdom. It is often assumed that private schooling provides the only viable alternative in a county district, since residential relocation would require, in some instances, a move to another labor and housing market area.[18] The districts included in these tabulations are simply too few to allow further partitioning in order to determine whether this association is spurious or reflects a genuine differential in pattern of response with respect to type of district.

It can be hypothesized that school districts with higher percentage black are more likely to exhibit patterns of white avoidance, since the opportunity for interracial contact increases with percent black enrolled in public schools.[19] This pattern can be observed among the southern districts both with respect to outmigration and private school utilization. In the case of nonsouth districts, the pattern is slightly curvilinear with respect to migration, and private school utilization is inversely related to percent black. Again a word of caution should be interjected, as the number of cases involved is simply too small to warrant anything other than a cautionary observation.

18. David J. Armor, "Declaration of David J. Armor," *Carlin et al v San Diego Board of Education* (San Diego, 1977).
19. Michael W. Giles, "Racial Stability and Urban School Desegregation," *Urban Affairs Quarterly* 12 (June 1977): 499–510.

A final classification of these districts is presented according to whether they had implemented any form of desegregation program prior to the 1971 school year.[20] Sixty-nine percent of the south and 46 percent of the nonsouth districts had implemented some form of desegregation program. Although the school segregation scores are moderately high for practically all of the districts, the desegregated district average score is ten points lower than the nondesegregated districts (70 versus 80).

The most interesting aspect of the pattern is the fact that a higher percentage of the nonsouth desegregated districts had significant coefficients for the effect of percent black on both migration and private school utilization than is true of the southern districts. In fact, the percentage differences between the southern districts is small. It would be remiss not to point out, however, that a higher percentage of the nonsouth districts showed significant effects of percent black on both private school utilization and migration even in the absence of controls. This is somewhat surprising, considering that efforts to desegregate southern districts have a longer history than is true of nonsouthern districts.

DISCUSSION

This paper began by posing the question of whether whites' utilization of alternate forms of schooling was racially motivated. The analysis presented may be viewed as an attempt to broaden the scope of inquiry to include the general area of residential selection and differentiation. In this regard, attention is focused on whether neighborhoods of varying racial composition within selected central cities influence whites to seek alternate forms of schooling, either by migrating or through increased utilization of nonpublic schools.

The results obtained from analyzing the effects of percent black on several indicia of white avoidance are varied and complex, and are not amenable to unequivocal interpretation. In the nonsouth region of the country, a strong case can be made for racial selectivity, both with respect to residential relocation and private school utilization. These regional differences persisted even after controlling for the percentages of public school pupils that are black and the implementation of desegregation programs.

The racial selectivity in residential relocation, as evidenced by the effect of percent black on the percentage of the white school age population living within census tracts in nonsouthern districts, is probably the result of the general process of ghetto formation and expansion.[21] No cross-sectional analysis of the kind presented here can adequately take account of the forces that shape the dynamics of racially changing neighborhoods. The expansion of black residential areas at their periphery can influence whites

20. Information on school desegregation activities was obtained from the following sources: Christine Rossell, "Measuring School Desegregation," pp. 171–202. In David J. Kirby, T. Robert Harris, and Robert L. Crain, *Political Strategies in Northern School Desegregation.* (Lexington, MA: Lexington Books, 1973); and U.S. Commission on Civil Rights, *Reviewing a Decade of School Desegregation 1966–1975* (Washington, DC, January 1977).

21. Gary Orfield, "White Flight Research: Its Importance, Perplexities and Possible Policy Implications," Symposium on School Desegregation and White Flight. (Notre Dame, IN: Center for Civil Rights, 1975), pp. 48–49.

to relocate, or to place their children in private schools until they can afford to do so. Southern cities have only recently begun to experience the growth of black residential areas as a result of their expansion into previously all white residential areas.[22] This may partially explain why only the largest and oldest of the southern districts also show substantial effects of percent black on outmigration.

The utilization of private schooling as a means of minimizing interracial contact is apparently not limited to the implementation of extensive district-wide desegregation programs. This is clearly indicated by the fact that in a significant number of school districts the increased potential for interracial contact, in residential neighborhoods with increased percent black, tends to invoke avoidance responses in whites similar to those believed to be associated with school desegregation.

One important question that remains to be answered in regard to the effect of percent black on private schooling is why whites in nonsouthern districts use this form of avoidance at the neighborhood level more frequently than whites in southern districts. As in the case of outmigration, one could speculate that historical differences in the spatial dynamics of the expansion of black residential areas may be the major factor operating. For some whites, the avoidance response may be temporary in nature until a more permanent solution is obtainable; for others, this may be the only alternative available because of employment immobility. For example, public service employment is a large component of the local economy in central cities. In many of these cities, private schooling may be the only alternative available because of employment related residency requirements.

The utilization of parochial schooling in the majority of districts analyzed does not appear to be racially motivated, at least at the neighborhood level. Several factors can be suggested as contributing to this outcome. First, attendance at parochial schools, even with respect to non-Catholics, may be influenced more by such factors as size of classes, discipline, religious instruction, and academic standards, than by racial background of peers. Indeed, many parents with children in parochial schools argue that these are their strongest attractions as an alternative to public schools.[23] Second, open attendance policies and tuition costs may jointly discourage whites from using parochial schools in order to avoid interracial contact. This applies particularly to local areas in which parish boundaries are likely to cut across residential areas of varying racial composition.

It is surprising that current discussion of the efficacy of desegregation programs has been uninformed as to the impact that community context can have on the relative success or failure of such programs.[24] The effort to explain inter-

22. Karl E. Taeuber and Alma Taeuber, *Negroes in Cities* (Chicago: Aldine Press, 1965); Leo F. Schnore and Philip C. Evenson, "Segregation in Southern Cities," *American Journal of Sociology* 72 (July 1966): 58–67.

23. Andrew M. Greeley, William C. McCready, and Kathleen McCourt, *Catholic Schools in a Declining Church* (Kansas City, MO: Sheed and Ward, 1976) pp. 3–27; 222–43.

24. Robin M. Williams, Jr., "Conflict Resolution and Mutual Accommodation: The Case of the Schools," (A paper presented at the 71st Annual Meeting of the American Sociological Association, New York City, 30 August 1976).

district variations in the indicia of white avoidance needs to be expanded to include a larger array of school districts and the addition of other relevant variables, such as the rate of city-to-suburb migration, the rate of growth of the black population, and whether the communities served by these school districts experienced racial disturbances during the 1960s decade. The results of such an analysis could provide an early warning as to what types of desegregation programs will or will not work within particular types of communities.

The implications of the results of this analysis for school desegregation policy are direct. One of the main reasons given for reassigning pupils to schools on the basis of racial backgrounds, under a desegregation program, is that school racial isolation is in part a consequence of residential location. The results reported here clearly indicate that the process of racial selection is an important component of residential location and differentiation in some urban areas. Thus the possibility of achieving stable racially mixed school environments, independent of the residential patterns of blacks and whites, appears less likely in cities in which residential structures already bear the imprint of racial selection.

ANNALS, AAPSS, 441, Jan. 1979

Racial Transition and Black Homeownership in American Suburbs

By ROBERT W. LAKE

ABSTRACT: Home ownership has traditionally served as an efficient wealth generating mechanism for the American middle class. Recent data indicating an increase in the metropolitan area black population living in the suburbs raise two questions: is black suburbanization equivalent to home ownership, and does black suburban homeownership lead to equity accumulation and the generation of wealth? These questions are addressed through analysis of a national sample of suburban housing units surveyed in 1974, and again in 1975, as part of the Census Bureau's *Annual Housing Survey*. As of the mid-1970s, black suburbanization has not been entirely synonymous with homeownership nor has homeownership automatically served the wealth generating function for blacks that it has provided for earlier suburbanizing aspirants to the middle class.

Robert W. Lake is an Assistant Research Professor at the Rutgers University Center for Urban Policy Research, New Brunswick, New Jersey. He has published several articles on race and housing, and is currently directing a two-year study of institutional barriers to black suburban homeownership.

This analysis is part of a larger study financed by the U.S. Department of Health, Education, and Welfare, National Institute of Mental Health.

I wish to thank George Sternlieb for comments and suggestions on this paper and William Dolphin for invaluable computer programming assistance.

ACCUMULATION of equity through homeownership is perhaps the most widespread and successful means of wealth generation available to the American middle class. The inflation of housing values in the post-world war II era has been a particular boon to the largely suburbanized homeowning middle-class white population. The nation's black population, however, comprised of renters rather than owners and generally confined to portions of older urban areas that have not experienced the inflation of housing values characteristic of suburbia, has been less able to benefit from the wealth generative potential of suburban homeownership. Recent trends, since 1970, show a slight increase of black population in the suburbs, and a corresponding decrease in the proportion of the black population remaining in the central cities. It is therefore instructive to consider, first, the extent to which increase in the rate of black suburbanization is synonymous with increased homeownership, and secondly, whether black suburban homeownership is synonymous with equity accumulation and the generation of wealth.

In addressing these issues, this paper examines the extent to which racial transition from white to black or black to white occupancy accompanies the turnover of suburban housing units. Analysts have long stressed the importance of existing housing stocks, as opposed to new construction, as a source of homeownership possibilities for blacks and other minorities.[1] The transfer of existing units from white to black

occupancy is thus a necessary concomitant of black suburban population growth. The suburban focus is justified since it is there that ownership possibilities are most concentrated.

Data made available through the U.S. Census Bureau's *Annual Housing Survey* permit year to year tracing of unit and household characteristics in a national sample of housing units resurveyed each year.[2] Utilizing data for 1974 and 1975, three aspects of suburban racial and tenure transition are analyzed in terms of their impact on black homeownership in the suburbs.

2. Our discussion of post-1970 suburban housing characteristics is based on published and unpublished data from the U.S. Bureau of the Census *Annual Housing Surveys* for 1974, 1975, and 1976. The *Annual Housing Survey* comprises a national sample of some 84,000 housing units resurveyed each year, and weighted to represent the national housing stock.

The Census Bureau's confidentiality requirements restrict identification of intra-metropolitan location of sampled housing units in some cases. Unless otherwise indicated, our analysis of "suburban" housing units is therefore limited to units in the noncentral city portions of fifty SMSA's for which intrametropolitan location is identified on AHS computer tapes. These fifty SMSA's which contained 74.8 percent of the nation's black metropolitan occupied housing units in 1970 are: Akron, Albany-Schenectady-Troy, Anaheim-Santa Ana-Garden Grove, Atlanta, Baltimore, Birmingham, Boston, Buffalo, Chicago, Cincinnati, Cleveland, Columbus, Dallas, Denver, Detroit, Ft. Worth, Gary-Hammond-East Chicago, Greensboro-Winston Salem-High Point, Honolulu, Houston, Indianapolis, Jersey City, Kansas City, Los Angeles-Long Beach, Louisville, Miami, Milwaukee, Minneapolis-St. Paul, New Orleans, New York City, Newark, Norfolk-Portsmouth, Oklahoma City, Paterson-Clifton-Passaic, Philadelphia, Phoenix, Pittsburgh, Portland (Ore.), Providence-Warwick-Pawtucket, Rochester, Sacramento, St. Louis, San Bernardino-Riverside, San Diego, San Francisco-Oakland, San Jose, Seattle-Everett, Tampa-St. Petersburg, Toledo, and Washington, D.C.

1. See, for example, John Kain, "Theories of Residential Location and Realities of Race," in *Essays on Urban Spatial Structure* (Cambridge: Ballinger, 1975), pp. 139–40.

First, what is the magnitude of transition from white to black occupancy in suburban housing units? Disaggregating this overall transition rate into renter and owner components provides a measure of availability of homeownership opportunities for blacks in the suburbs.

Second, what are the characteristics of suburban housing units acquired by blacks? Here, differentiation between units initially occupied by whites and those units which turn over within the black housing market provides evidence of the significance of white to black transition as a source of quality owner-occupied suburban units. While earlier studies have examined the characteristics of *neighborhoods* or *areas* experiencing white to black racial succession, data on the individual housing units involved have heretofore not been available.[3]

Thirdly, what are the housing market dynamics confronting the suburban black homeowner seeking to recapture stored equity through resale? Earlier studies, not focused primarily on suburbia, have demonstrated that a black-occupied housing unit infrequently reverts to white occupancy.[4] If this pattern is replicated in the suburbs, then black homeowners wishing to sell will be at a distinct disadvantage: adequate market demand is required if homeownership is to function as a path to capital accumulation. The suburban dream will be less golden if other-

wise equivalent units owned by blacks and whites are funnelled into dual resale markets leaving blacks with inferior rates of economic return and equity recapture.

Initial findings suggest that white to black transition in suburban rental units far outpaces that in owner occupancy, extending the central city disparity in homeownership rates for whites and blacks into the suburbs. Those black suburbanites who do own their own homes are far more dependent on black replacements than are whites, saddling black owners wishing to sell with the consequences of lesser black buying power. Complicating the picture, however, is the finding that more black-owned suburban units are turned over to whites than to other blacks, suggesting that the market for black-occupied units may be more open in the suburbs than has previously been reported for central city areas.

Property value is found to be a significant feature, with the lowest value black-owned suburban units yielding the least likelihood of equity return upon transfer to another household. The findings suggest the need for policy initiatives aimed at stimulating the demand for black-owned suburban units, for it is only in this way that suburban homeownership will provide blacks with the wealth generative function it has traditionally served for earlier aspirants to the middle class.

In assessing these trends, the following discussion focuses first on the rate of black suburbanization since 1970 and the characteristics of black suburban households. We then address in turn the magnitude of racial transition of individual suburban housing units, the characteristics of those housing units, and the conditions of equity recapture

3. For a review of the literature on the characteristics of transition neighborhoods, see Karl E. Taeuber and Alma F. Taeuber, *Negroes in Cities: Residential Segregation and Neighborhood Change* (New York: Atheneum, 1969).

4. For example, Chester Rapkin and William Grigsby, *The Demand for Housing in Racially Mixed Areas*, (Los Angeles: University of California Press, 1960).

in black-owned housing in the suburbs.

BLACK SUBURBANIZATION SINCE 1970

The data on black suburbanization during the seventies reveal some slight gains in black representation in the noncentral city portions of SMSA's.[5] The characteristics of these suburban black households show them to differ from both central city blacks and suburban whites.

Growth rates

Suburban black growth rates between 1970 and 1976 have outstripped those for whites, largely as a consequence of the far smaller black population in the 1970 base year. Between 1970 and 1976, the number of black suburban households increased by 49 percent to a total of 1.4 million, compared to a 21 percent increase to 25.8 million, in white suburban households. Black owner-occupied units in the suburbs increased by 39 percent (compared to 23 percent for whites) while black renter-occupied units increased by 62 percent (compared to 16 percent for whites). Black households constituted some 5 percent of all suburban households in 1976, essentially maintaining a level that prevailed throughout the sixties and early seventies. Finally, a somewhat larger proportion of total metropolitan area black households lived in the suburbs in 1976 (23 percent)

than was the case in 1970 (19 percent). Among metropolitan area blacks in owner-occupied units, the suburban share increased marginally from 27 to 28 percent between 1970 and 1976. Among black renter households, the suburban share increased from 14 percent in 1970 to 19 percent in 1976.

Characteristics

Two sets of comparisons help clarify the nature of the black suburban niche within the current metropolitan structure. Compared to suburban white households, suburban blacks on average continue to receive short shrift. Compared to central city blacks, however, suburban residence represents a substantial improvement in both housing and neighborhood quality.[6]

Considering tenure and housing type in 1975, for example, just under half (49.4 percent) of black suburban households were owners, compared to almost three-fourths (71.2 percent) of white suburbanites, and about a third (35.4 percent) of black central city households. Conversely, some 17 percent of black suburbanites lived in structures of ten or more units, compared to only 9 percent of white suburban households and 23 percent of black city dwellers. Turning to property value, 11 percent of black suburban households, versus 2 percent of white suburbanites, and 15 percent of black city residents lived in units whose property value was less than $10,000. At the same time, 10 percent of black suburbanites lived in homes valued at $50,000 or more, in contrast to 24 percent of white suburban households, but only 3 percent of black central city residents. In terms

5. This discussion, utilizing published data sources, covers the suburban portions of *all* metropolitan areas identified in the 1970 census. See U.S. Bureau of the Census, Current Housing Reports, Series H-150-76, *General Housing Characteristics for the United States and Regions: 1976*. Annual Housing Survey: 1976, Part A, Table A-1 (Washington, DC: USGPO, 1978).

6. Data based on a limited sample of suburban housing units. See footnote 2 supra.

of overall housing satisfaction, black suburbanites were only half as likely as white suburbanites, but one and a half times more likely than black city dwellers, to rate their housing unit as excellent. Ratings of overall neighborhood quality are distributed similarly.

Two general conclusions can be drawn from this brief overview. First, compared to white households in the suburbs, black suburban households occupy less satisfactory, lower value units in less desirable neighborhood settings, and have attained lower proportions of owner occupancy. Secondly, the data indicate the extension to the suburbs of patterns previously documented for central cities: it is on average the more affluent, higher status blacks who are the first to move into previously all-white areas, thereby improving their housing and neighborhood quality.

With this brief introduction to the relative characteristics of black suburban households within the metropolitan setting, we turn now to an examination of racial transition in the existing suburban housing stock.

RACE AND TENURE CHANGE IN THE SUBURBAN HOUSING STOCK

Data from the *Annual Housing Survey* national samples provide information on 15.9 million suburban housing units for which race and tenure can be identified in both 1974 and 1975. Utilization of this data set permits identification of the magnitude of racial and tenure change within the suburban housing stock, and analysis of changes in household characteristics attendant on turnover in the housing inventory.

Total inventories

We begin by comparing the racial and tenure characteristics of the suburban inventory in 1974 with the identical units in 1975. (Table 1) As indicated above, the total suburban inventory is divided approximately 70/30 between owner and renter occupancy, and some 5 percent of total units in both years are black. The overwhelming share of units, of course, evidences no change in tenure or race from one year to the next. Relative shifts within this framework, however, provide initial evidence of differences in black and white experiences in the suburban housing market.

First, considering racial transition within the entire suburban inventory, 0.64 percent (101,000 units) of the entire 1974 supply shifted from white to black in the one year period. Disaggregating by 1974 tenure, 0.23 percent (26,000 units) of the owner-occupied stock and 1.63 percent of the renter-occupied units (75,000 units) shifted from white to black during the period. This suggests that owner-occupancy units in the white inventory become available to black buyers at a slower rate than do renter-occupancy units.

Secondly, considering tenure change within each racial category, 1.59 percent of the black-occupied inventory (11,000 units) changed from renter to owner occupancy between 1974 and 1975, but 1.88 percent (13,000 units) reverted from owner to renter occupancy. Within the white-occupied inventory, in contrast, 1.30 percent (195,000 units) changed from renter to owner while only 1.20 percent (180,000 units) reverted from owner to renter occu-

TABLE 1

TENURE AND RACIAL CHARACTERISTICS OF THE SAME-UNIT INVENTORY
U.S. SUBURBS,[a] 1975 BY 1974 (NUMBERS IN THOUSANDS)

| 1974 TENURE AND RACE (HOUSEHOLDS) | TOTAL | 1975 TENURE AND RACE (HOUSEHOLDS) | | | | | | | |
| | | OWNER OCCUPIED[b] | | | | RENTER-OCCUPIED[c] | | | |
		TOTAL	WHITE	BLACK	OTHER	TOTAL	WHITE	BLACK	OTHER
All Units	15,899	11,307	10,793	369	143	4,592	4,136	362	94
White	14,989	10,813	10,757	23	32	4,176	4,050	78	49
Black	692	363	18	345	0	329	48	278	3
Other	218	131	18	1	111	87	38	6	42
Owner-Occupied[b]	11,295	11,099	10,602	360	135	196	178	10	7
White	10,798	10,618	10,569	22	26	180	170	4	6
Black	365	352	15	337	0	13	7	6	0
Other	132	129	18	1	109	3	1	0	1
Renter-Occupied[c]	4,604	208	191	9	8	4,396	3,958	352	87
White	4,191	195	188	1	6	3,996	3,880	74	43
Black	327	11	3	8	0	316	41	272	3
Other	86	2	0	0	2	84	37	6	41

NOTES: Columns might not add to totals due to rounding.
[a] U.S. Suburbs = non-central city portions of fifty SMSA's for which intra-metropolitan location of unit is reported on AHS national survey tapes. See footnote 2.
[b] Owner Occupied = Owner occupied + condominium + cooperatives.
[c] Renter Occupied = Renter Occupied + Rented, No Cash Rent.
SOURCE: U.S. Bureau of the Census, *Annual Housing Survey*: 1974 and 1975, national sample public use tapes.

pancy. In all, focusing here on tenure changes within each racial inventory and ignoring for the present the extent of racial transition, the 1974 white inventory registered a net gain of 15,000 owner-occupied units while the black inventory registered a net loss of 2,000 owner-occupied units. A larger net share of the original 1974 stock of black units than white units, in other words, shifted out of owner occupancy from 1974 to 1975.

Housing market turnover

Of the 15.9 million suburban units described above, we have identified 2,250,000 units within the white and black suburban housing inventories that turned over between 1974 and 1975 (Table 2). This figure represents a 14.3 percent turnover rate. (We have excluded from further discussion the 218,000 units—1.4

percent of the total—occupied by "other races" in 1974.) Units occupied by a different household in 1974 and 1975 were identified as those which in the latter year survey responded to questions asked only of "recent movers," households that moved in within the twelve-month period preceding the survey. These units form the data base for our analysis of market turnover and racial transition.[7]

7. Discrepancies between totals in Tables 1 and 2 result from the procedures utilized to identify housing units occupied by different households in 1974 and 1975. Table 1 includes all suburban housing units for which race, tenure, and suburban location could be identified in both 1974 and 1975. Table 2 includes only that sub-set of Table 1 units occupied by "recent movers" at the time of the 1975 survey. As a result, some units shown as having turned over in Table 1 are not identified as "recent movers" in Table 2. "Recent movers" are defined by the Census Bureau as households which moved into the

TABLE 2

1974–1975 TENURE CHANGE BY RACIAL CHANGE, SUBURBAN HOUSING UNITS OCCUPIED
BY RECENT MOVERS IN 1975, UNITED STATES[a] (IN THOUSANDS OF UNITS)

| TENURE TRANSITION 1974–1975[b] | ALL UNITS | | RACIAL TRANSITION 1974–1975 | | | | | | | |
| | | | WHITE-WHITE | | BLACK-BLACK | | WHITE-BLACK | | BLACK-WHITE | |
	#	%	#	%	#	%	#	%	#	%
All Units	2,250	100.0	2,044	100.0	77	100.0	84	100.0	45	100.0
Own-Own	516	22.9	491	24.0	4	5.2	16	19.0	5	11.4
Rent-Rent	1,506	67.0	1,348	65.9	64	83.1	63	75.0	31	70.5
Own-Rent	133	5.9	116	5.7	6	7.8	4	4.8	7	15.9
Rent-Own	95	4.2	89	4.4	3	3.9	1	1.2	2	4.5

NOTES: Columns might not add to totals due to rounding.
[a] Suburban units are those in the non-central city portion of fifty SMSA's for which intrametropolitan location of units is specified on AHS national survey tapes. See footnote 2. Recent movers are those households which moved into the unit within the twelve month period prior to 1975 AHS enumeration.
[b] Owner-occupied units = owner + condominiums + cooperatives. Renter-occupied units = renter + rented, no cash rent.
SOURCE: U.S. Bureau of the Census, Annual Housing Survey: 1974 and 1975, national sample public use tapes.

Considering turnover by tenure, 5.8 percent of owner-occupied units in 1974 turned over during the year, while the equivalent rate for renter-occupied units was 34.8 percent. Not surprisingly, in other words, rental units in the suburbs change hands at a faster rate than owner-occupied units.

Considering turnover by race, 14.2 percent of white-occupied units and 17.6 percent of black-occupied units

unit during the twelve-month period preceding the survey. Since AHS national surveys are conducted between October and December of each year, some units may be resurveyed as much as fifteen months apart. Some households could thus move into a unit subsequent to the 1974 survey and not be counted as "recent movers" in 1975. Further discrepancies are introduced in cases where the race of the household head changes through marriage, separation, or divorce but the household continues to occupy the same dwelling unit. The effect of these accounting procedures is to decrease the within-category totals reported in Table 2 compared to Table 1. There is no evidence, however, that relationships between categories in Table 2 are skewed in any systematic way.

changed occupancy between 1974 and 1975. The higher black turnover rate is expected since blacks are more concentrated than whites in renter-occupied units.

Finally, the turnover rate in owner-occupied units is essentially identical for blacks and whites: 6.0 percent of black owner-occupied units and 5.8 percent of white. In the rental market, however, the turnover rate in white renter-occupied units (35.8 percent) exceeds that in black renter-occupied units (30.6 percent). Going somewhat beyond the data, these findings may suggest that suburban rental occupancy for whites is typically a temporary stop en route to homeownership, while it is a far more stable and permanent tenure arrangement for blacks confronted with barriers to homeownership imposed by downpayment requirements, mortgage restrictions, and discrimination.

Racial change

The final question in this section focuses on the role of racial change within the more general picture of housing turnover. Again drawing on the data in Table 2, four observations can be made.

First, white to black transition still serves as a more important source of suburban housing than does turnover within the black housing market. Of the 161,000 units with a new black occupant in 1975, 84,000 (52 percent) transferred from white to black occupancy while only 77,000 (48 percent) were already black-occupied in 1974. This finding suggests the relative recency of black arrival in the suburbs and the relatively small base of existing black settlement.

Secondly, white to black transition far outweighs black to white transition in both absolute and relative terms. As noted above, white to black change amounted to 84,000 units; in contrast, only 45,000 suburban units transferred from black to white between 1974 and 1975. Of the resulting net gain of 39,000 new black-occupied units, 10,000 came on as owner-occupied and 29,000 were renter-occupied in 1975.

The third question focuses on the probability of ownership for new black occupants. If a new occupant of a suburban housing unit is black rather than white, the likelihood is greater that the black household will rent rather than buy, regardless of the race of the initial occupant. This finding is revealed by the tenure characteristics of the units within each racial transition category (Table 2). Focusing on the race of household in the *second year*, a transfer within the rental market constitutes 83.1 percent of black-black and 75.0 percent of white-black turnover, but only 70.5 percent of black-white and 65.9 percent of white-white turnover. Combining these figures with those for trans-

fers from ownership to rental status, units rented in 1975 (rent-rent plus own-rent) constitute 86 percent of all turnovers to a new black occupant and only 72 percent of turnovers to a new white occupant.

Finally, what is the probability of a black owner-occupied unit in the initial year remaining within the owner inventory or shifting to rental status during turnover? We find that a black-owned unit is more likely than a white-owned unit to shift to renter-occupancy, again regardless of the race of the new occupant. Of white-owned transition units in 1974, 19 percent of those turned over to a white household and 20 percent of those turned over to a black household shifted to renter occupancy in 1975. Of black-owned units, in contrast, 58 percent and 60 percent of those turned over to, respectively, a white and black household shifted into the rental market. The implications for equity recapture in black- and white-owned suburban units are evident.

Summary of transition findings

The principal findings thus far can be summarized briefly. New black occupancy in the suburbs more often involves a unit shifted out of the white inventory than one transferred from a previous black occupant. Such transition, further, is predominantly a one-way street: white-black transition far outweighs transfers from black to white. Largely due to differential turnover rates, owner-occupied units in the suburbs become available to potential black occupants at a slower rate than rental units. Black units turn over faster than those occupied by whites, largely because blacks are more concentrated in rental units and these turn over faster than owner units. Black rental units, however, turn over at a slower rate than do white rental units, suggesting that black rental occupancy in the suburbs—perhaps due to fewer available options—is less temporary and more stable than white rental. While white-black transition results in a net gain in black suburban owner-occupied units, this gain is in part offset by a loss of owner units through tenure change within the black inventory.

The present data suggest, but do not allow testing, the hypothesis that black owner-occupied units, gained through racial transition, are subsequently lost by an inability to sustain adequate demand within a dual housing market context. (Further evidence on this point must await data on turnover chains over a longer time period than presently available.) In sum, black suburbanites are less likely than their white counterparts to own their own home, and those who do are more likely than white owners to transfer their unit to rental status in the event of turnover of the unit.

CHARACTERISTICS OF TRANSITION UNITS

The discussion thus far has focused on the magnitude of turnover and transition within racial segments of the suburban housing market. What of the characteristics of the housing units comprising these racial sub-markets? Are housing units transferred from white to black substantially different from those transferred within the white housing market? Do units in these categories differ in turn from those transferred within the black housing market?

To examine these questions, we compare units in each of the suburban racial transition categories in terms of four basic characteristics: age of structure, median value, median rent, and overall evaluation of housing and neighborhood quality. For this segment of the discussion, we focus on those housing units for which tenure type (own or rent) is maintained both before and after the move. Units that changed tenure type (own to rent, rent to own) are eliminated from further discussion due to small sample sizes and the resulting ambiguity of generalizations based on a relatively small number of observations.

Age of structure

Transfers within the black suburban housing market tend on average to involve substantially older units than transfers within the white market. White to black turnover appears concentrated in relatively newer units, reflecting perhaps the comparatively greater buying power of those black households who can gain access to the formerly white segment of the suburban market. In contrast, black to white transfers appear generally restricted to both the newest and the oldest suburban units, possibly suggesting that the same process of "gentrification" is at work in the suburbs as has been reported for many central cities.

Among all suburban transition units in 1975, about a third (31.3 percent) of white-white transfers, but only a fourth (26.5 percent) of black-black transfers, were built in the preceding six years (1969–1974). A higher proportion (34.2 percent) of units transferred from white to black were built in this period, as were over half (51.1 percent) of black-white units. Another third (29 percent) of black-white units were built prior to 1939.

Among owner-occupied units, fully two-thirds of the suburban units transferred between black owners were built between 1950 and 1959, making them between 16 and 25 years old. In contrast, well over half (56.7 percent) of the units transferred between white owners were fifteen years old or less— built since 1960. Within the rental market, recently-built units (1969–74) are again underrepresented among black-black transfers (28.9 percent), followed in frequency by turnover within the white market (32.9 percent), from white to black (39.4 percent), and overwhelmingly represented among black-white transfers (72.6 percent). In all, the data suggest that as gauged by age of structure, white-to-black transition results in improvement in the black-occupied suburban housing stock. Some of this improvement is offset, however, since in most cases only the newest (but also some of the oldest) units are transferred from black to white occupancy.

Median value

The median value of suburban units transferred within the white market was $40,000, compared to a median value of $36,200 for units transferred from black to black. Units transferred from white to black ownership were yet lower in value on average ($30,400). White replacement of a black household is clearly confined to the highest value units, as indicated by a median value of $55,000 for units shifting from black to white.

Transfer of a unit within the black sub-market appears to provide relatively inexpensive housing, as the median value-to-income ratio in this

market segment is only 1.8.[8] Black purchase of a previously white-owned unit results in a median value-to-income ratio of 2.4 and the figure for white-white transfers is 2.1. Clearly, black home purchase requires a significantly larger proportion of income when the previous owner is white than when the previous owner is black.

Median rent

Suburban rent levels within the all-white market ($175) are the highest among the various market segments examined; conversely, rents in black-black units are on average the lowest ($145). In contrast to the situation in owner occupancy, however, these comparatively low rents in the black rental market are coupled with the highest measure of rent as a percent of income (30.6 percent).[9] Average rent levels are identical in white-black and black-white units ($170). In the former segment, however, this rent level amounts to 27 percent of income, above the 25 percent norm, while in the latter segment the same median rental amounts to only 23 percent of income, below the norm. Indeed, suburban white renters are on average burdened with a 23 percent rent/income ratio regardless of the race of the previous renter, while black renters in the suburbs pay substantially more than a fourth of their income for housing.

Comparing rent levels with rents paid in the household's previous units, blacks renting a previously white-occupied unit experience the

8. A long-standing and well-calloused rule of thumb suggests that value should not exceed 2.5 times total family income.
9. An equally hoary rule recommends that rent should be no more than 25 percent of income.

highest increase in rent ($61) over what they were paying in their previous unit. Blacks renting previously black-occupied units experience a rent increase of $47, while whites renting previously white-occupied units increase their rent by only $20.

Housing and neighborhood quality

The distribution of responses on overall ratings of the housing unit and the neighborhood are essentially identical, and therefore can be discussed together. Fully twice the proportion of households in the white-white market (30 percent) as those in the black to black market (15 percent) rated their house and neighborhood as excellent. Black households in previously white units were more likely to offer an "excellent" rating (25 percent) than were black households in previously black units. Similarly, households in black-black units were most likely (40 percent) to evaluate house and neighborhood as only fair or poor. Only 16 percent of whites in previously white units but 26 percent of blacks in previously white units offered this low rating.

Summary

The above discussion furnishes a brief sketch of the housing available in each of the suburban racial sub-markets. Suburban units that turn over from white to white are on average recently built units, of higher value than those transferred to black occupancy, and yield a below average value-to-income ratio. Rental units in the white-white market command the highest rent but nonetheless command the low-

est proportion of their residents' income.

A direct contrast is evident in the suburban units that turn over from black to black. Such units are on average older and of lower value than white-white units. Rent levels in this market segment are the lowest but nonetheless constitute the largest percentage of income. Black suburban renters experience the biggest increase in rent over rentals paid in their previous units, regardless of whether the new rental unit was previously occupied by a black or white. Black-black units and their neighborhoods are least likely to be rated excellent by their residents and most likely to be rated fair or poor.

Units transferred from white to black occupy a position somewhere between these two extremes. These are generally newer units, contributing to an upgrading of the black-occupied suburban housing stock. However, owner-occupied units in this category have the lowest median value. Black renters of previously white-occupied units experience the largest increase in rent over their previous unit. While rental levels in white-black units are equal to those in black-white units, this amount represents a larger proportion of income for the former group than for the latter. Black occupied units formerly occupied by whites, however, are more likely than those previously occupied by blacks to receive satisfactory ratings of housing and neighborhood quality.

Finally, units transferred from black to white occupancy are in general among either the newest or the oldest portions of the suburban inventory and command the highest median value and relatively high rent levels.

BLACK HOMEOWNERSHIP
AND WEALTH

The final question posed in our analysis focuses on the efficacy of suburban homeownership as a means of equity accumulation. Numerous studies have pointed to the significance of homeownership as the principal source of savings for the lower and middle income population, and equity accumulated in the home has traditionally served as the launch vehicle for upward mobility among many immigrant ethnic groups.[10] What has been the recent experience of black suburban homeowners?

A direct response to this question would require data on the sales price of equivalent suburban homes sold by white and black owners in equivalent settings. Unfortunately, the *Annual Housing Survey* matched national samples do not contain sufficient cases of turnover of suburban black-owned units to permit adequate comparison. Even if adequate data were available, the question of "equivalence" of housing units and neighborhood settings has by no means been settled. In the absence of such direct evidence, however, substantial insight into black suburban housing market dynamics is provided through several indirect sources: (1) value change in black- and white-owned suburban units; (2) the pattern of racial and tenure change in black-owned units; and (3) the previous tenure of black suburban homebuyers.

Value change

From the standpoint of the aspiring homebuyer, the inflation of

10. See, for instance, John Kain and John Quigley, *Housing Markets and Racial Discrimination* (New York: National Bureau of Economic Research, 1975).

housing prices in recent years has caused considerable concern. From the seller's standpoint, however, such inflation simply magnifies the significance of homeownership as an investment. To what extent have black suburban homeowners shared in this equity building inflation of housing prices?

To answer this question, reported property value in owner-occupied suburban units for 1974 was compared to property value in the same units reported in 1975. According to Census Bureau definitions, these value figures represent "the respondent's estimate of how much the property (house and lot) would sell for if it were for sale." The results of this comparison are tabulated in Table 3.

At all levels of housing value, suburban units occupied by blacks in both 1974 and 1975 were less likely to increase and more likely to decrease in value than units occupied by whites. Among the lowest value properties (those valued less than $20,000 in 1974), 41 percent of white-occupied units, but only 25 percent of black-occupied units, had increased in value in 1975. Among the highest value properties (those valued $50,000 or more), 13 percent of white-occupied units but 24 percent of black-occupied units had decreased in value by 1975. At intervening value levels, black-owned units were less likely than white-owned units to increase in value and were up to twice as likely to decrease in value. For example, among suburban units valued from $20,000 to $34,999 in 1974, 20 percent of black-owned units, versus 27 percent of white-owned units, had increased in value by 1975, while 9 percent of black units, but only 5 percent of white units, decreased in value. Similarly,

TABLE 3

1975 PROPERTY VALUE BY 1974 PROPERTY VALUE, IN IDENTICAL BLACK AND WHITE
OWNER-OCCUPIED UNITS, U.S. SUBURBS (PERCENTS)

PROPERTY VALUE IN 1975	PROPERTY VALUE, 1974							
	LESS THAN $20,000		$20,000–34,999		$35,000–49,999		$50,000 OR MORE	
	WHITE-WHITE	BLACK-BLACK	WHITE-WHITE	BLACK-BLACK	WHITE-WHITE	BLACK-BLACK	WHITE-WHITE	BLACK-BLACK
Less than $20,000	59.3	75.0	4.9	8.7	0.9	6.7	0.6	12.1
$20,000–$34,999	34.5	20.9	68.4	71.6	9.0	17.1	2.3	0.0
$35,000–$49,999	4.5	4.1	24.6	17.8	67.8	58.5	10.4	11.9
$50,000 or more	1.8	0.0	2.1	1.9	22.3	17.7	86.8	76.0
Total	100.0	100.0	100.0	100.0	100.0	100.0	100.0	100.0
Number of Units (in 1,000's)	(1,123)	(98)	(3,763)	(138)	(2,499)	(47)	(1,857)	(11)

NOTE: U.S. Suburbs = non-central city portions of fifty SMSA's for which intra-metropolitan location of units is reported on AHS national survey tapes. See footnote 2.

SOURCE: U.S. Bureau of the Census, *Annual Housing Survey*: 1974 and 1975, national sample public use tapes.

increases were reported for 22 percent of white-owned, but 18 percent of black-owned units, valued between $35,000 and $49,999, while 24 percent of black units and 10 percent of white units in this value category decreased between 1974 and 1975.

In sum, when comparing reported property value of identical suburban units at two points a year apart, units owned by blacks in both years were less likely to increase and more likely to decrease in value than white owned units matched by value in the initial year. If inflation in housing prices is producing windfalls for some, the above data suggest that such beneficial effects are less likely to accrue to a suburban homeowner who is black than one who is white.

The market for black-owned units

It is an elementary economic notion that the disproportionate value increase of white-owned and black-owned units may be due to weaker demand for the latter. The data discussed above and summarized in Table 2 suggest several sources of such weakness.

First, the probability that a black-owned suburban unit will turn over to a black household is far higher than that of a white-owned unit. With black households comprising a stable 5 percent of the suburban population, roughly that proportion of housing turnovers should go to blacks in an unbiased market. Indeed, of all 649,000 owner-occupied suburban units that turned over between 1974 and 1975, 4.6 percent were black-occupied in 1975. Disaggregating this total picture by race, however, reveals a significant pattern: fully 46 percent of the suburban *black-owned units* that turned over, but only 3.2 percent of the suburban *white-owned units* that turned over, went to a black household. In short, the probability that a suburban black owner will be replaced by another black is fourteen times that of a white owner. As a result, black home sellers are more likely than their white counterparts to bear the burden of lower black purchasing power.

Secondly, suburban black home

buyers acquire white-occupied units more frequently than black-occupied units. As suggested above, this finding indicates both the recency of black arrival in suburbia and also the limited pool of desirable black-owned suburban units that potential black buyers might choose from. The data suggest further that black sellers are at a competitive disadvantage to the extent that they have to compete for buyers with the far more extensive white-owned stock available for sale.

Thirdly, the corollary to the above is that suburban black home sellers are replaced by whites more frequently than by other blacks. This may reflect in part the relative weakness of effective black demand for suburban housing units. More importantly, however, if whites constitute the largest proportion of demand for black-owned units, and white replacement is restricted to the highest value black-owned units, then it is the lower value black suburban units that are most impacted by inadequate demand.

Finally, the weakness of the market is reflected in the higher proportion of black than white owners who are replaced by renter households in the same units. Furthermore, this discrepancy is most pronounced among lower value housing units. Of units valued below $20,000 in 1974 and occupied by a different household in 1975, 9 percent of black-owned units, but only 2 percent of white-owned units, shifted to rental occupancy upon turnover.

Previous tenure

If black suburban home sellers are far more dependent on black replacements than their white suburban counterparts, then it follows that the weaker purchasing ability

of potential black buyers will impact more negatively on black sellers than on white. Previous tenure impacts on home purchase through the availability of equity to apply to the downpayment. First time homebuyers must be able to draw from personal savings, relatives, or other sources for the downpayment that second time buyers typically obtain from the equity accumulated in the previous unit. Equity accumulated through previous homeownership greatly facilitates home purchase, and racial differences in tenure of previous unit influence downpayment ability.

Fully 60 percent of black purchasers of suburban housing units in 1975, but 49 percent of white purchasers, rented their previous unit. Thus, white homebuyers were substantially more likely than black buyers of suburban units to draw on previous equity to help finance their suburban home purchase.[11]

Further, white suburban homebuyers were more likely to own than rent their previous unit regardless of whether it was located in a central city or a suburb. Among black suburban homebuyers, however, an interesting pattern emerges when location of the previous unit is considered along with tenure. Eight out of ten black suburban homebuyers whose previous residence was in a central city rented that unit; six out of ten already in the suburbs, however, were owners. Thus, while black homebuyers already in the suburbs are somewhat more likely to be previous owners when compared to their white counterparts, this former

11. U.S. Bureau of the Census, Current Housing Reports, Series H-150-75D, *Housing Characteristics of Recent Movers*, Annual Housing Survey: 1975, Part D (Washington, DC: USGPO, 1977).

group constitutes a considerably smaller share of black homebuyers than white. In sum, central city renters comprise the largest share (42 percent) of black suburban homebuyers; another 18 percent were suburban renters, and only 40 percent were owners. Among white suburban homebuyers, in contrast, only 17 percent were central city renters, and 51 percent were previous owners. The implication of these figures for our discussion is straightforward. Black suburban homeowners, more dependent than are whites on finding a black buyer to achieve a sale, are significantly confined to a segment of the market characterized by a weaker asset position as measured by equity accumulated in a previous home.

SUMMARY AND CONCLUSIONS

A growing share of the nation's metropolitan area black population is located in the suburbs. At first glance, such a shift may be thought to signal a reversal of the racial separation that has marked metropolitan patterns for decades. The evidence presented here, though partial and qualified in many ways, suggests that excessive optimism may be premature. Suburbanization per se is neither synonymous with equal housing opportunity nor will it automatically serve the wealth accumulative function it has provided for previous suburbanizing ethnic groups. Progress toward these goals requires continued monitoring of the housing market conditions governing the black suburbanization process that is underway.

Our initial look at the nature of black suburbanization has focused on three broad elements of the process: the magnitude of white to black transition as a source of suburban housing, the characteristics of the housing units involved, and the potential of homeownership thus achieved as a means of equity accumulation. As of the mid-1970's, we found that rental units become available to blacks at a faster rate than owner-occupied units, that black suburbanites are less likely than whites to own their own homes, and that those who do are more likely than whites to see their units transfer to rental occupancy with subsequent turnover. Compared to suburban units transferred within the white sub-market, units that turn over from white to black are on average older, are of lower value, and are assigned lower ratings of housing and neighborhood quality. Finally, owner-occupied units within the black suburban sub-market are less likely to increase in value and more likely to decrease in value than equivalently priced units within the white sub-market.

If these trends continue unchecked, we will have yet further evidence of the disparity between the black experience in America and that of other ethnic and immigrant groups. For the latter, dispersion into the suburbs was synonymous with assimilation, the breaking down of ethnic enclaves, and unfettered upward mobility. Initial evidence to date raises the issue of whether the equivalent process will hold for the suburbanizing black population. The spectre of "two societies" so often hailed to describe black cities and white suburbs may simply be replicated at a new metropolitan scale.

ANNALS, AAPSS, 441, Jan. 1979

Housing, Schools, and Incremental Segregative Effects

By Karl E. Taeuber

ABSTRACT: Racial segregation in housing contributes to racial segregation in schools, and racially identifiable schools contribute to the development and maintenance of segregated neighborhoods. Examination of the reciprocal interplay between housing and school segregation has been spurred by the Supreme Court's decision in the Dayton school case, which calls for determination of how much incremental segregative effect the discriminatory actions of a school board had on the racial distribution of pupils compared to what the distribution would have been if the board had never practised discrimination. In recent hearings in the Milwaukee school case, plaintiffs sought to address this specific question through the testimony of a social scientist. Discriminatory actions with respect to teacher assignment, "intact busing," student transfers, school plant utilization, and attendance zone boundary changes were identified as having pervasive and enduring effects on racial residential segregation in Milwaukee. This case study illustrates that the Supreme Court's effort to construe school cases narrowly should fail, and that policymakers, whether they are concerned with housing, schools, or other domains, should cultivate a broad perspective on the unity of the nation's racial problems.

Karl E. Taeuber received his Ph.D. in sociology from Harvard. He joined the faculty at the University of Wisconsin in 1964 and now serves as Professor of Sociology and Assistant Director of the Institute for Research on Poverty. He has published articles and monographs on migration and urbanization, with particular attention to racial differentials and segregation. Since 1970 he has testified as an "expert witness" for plaintiffs in school segregation trials in Detroit, Boston, Cleveland, Milwaukee, and a dozen other cities.

The development of these ideas benefited from the hard work and shared wisdom of attorneys Lloyd A. Barbee, Irvin B. Charne, Howard A. Pollack, and Howard B. Tolkan.

A FAMILY looking for housing is concerned with the schools that its children will attend. Within a metropolitan area the system of school districts and school attendance zones creates and sustains the identification of residential neighborhoods that vary in perceived quality. Multiple listing services identify the public and parochial elementary and secondary schools serving each house. Real estate advertisements in the daily newspapers often use school district as a neighborhood identifying characteristic. The developers of residential housing know that the location and timely opening of new schools may profoundly influence the pace and profitability of their projects. Urban planners and community organizations seeking to retain residents in older central city housing struggle to persuade school authorities to keep low-enrollment schools open.

The location and characteristics of a school exert a profound influence on the residential development of the surrounding area. The importance of the school among neighborhood amenities has increased as people have become willing to travel greater distances to jobs, shopping, and recreation. Housing and schools remain closely linked. Just as a good neighborhood tends to create or sustain a good school, a good school tends to create and sustain a good neighborhood. A residential area that is attractive in many other ways but lacks accessibility to good schooling is severely handicapped, whereas an older neighborhood that might otherwise undergo residential decay is more likely to be preserved if it is attractive to families seeking quality education.

For many families the racial composition of a school is among its most important qualities or characteristics. As a principal and visible amenity, a school may come to symbolize a neighborhood and the racial composition of the school may become a public indicator of the racial composition of the neighborhood. Any change in school racial composition may be a signal as well as cause of subsequent change in the residential area's racial composition.

SUPREME COURT DECISIONS

The Supreme Court recognized in 1971 that administrative actions by school authorities have a strong impact on residential patterns: "People gravitate toward school facilities, just as schools are located in response to the needs of people. The location of schools may thus influence the patterns of residential development of a metropolitan area and have important impacts on composition of inner city neighborhoods. In the past, choices in this respect have been used as a potent weapon for creating or maintaining a state-segregated school system."[1]

Although the language of this passage is clear, the full court may not have realized that they were undercutting the main defense of school districts, north and south, to charges of segregation—that school racial composition simply reflects neighborhood residential composition. If the decisions of school authorities are "a potent weapon" for creating and maintaining residential separation of the races, this line of defense collapses. Administrative actions that increase the segregation of races in schools foster the very residential segregation that is the purported cause.

In its recent decisions on school

1. *Swann* v. *Charlotte-Mecklenburg Board of Education*, 402 U.S. 1 (1971).

segregation, the Supreme Court has avoided giving further explicit attention to the linkage between schooling and housing, but it has, perhaps inadvertently, created the need for further examinations of these issues. In its *Dayton* decision in the summer of 1977 the Supreme Court, seeking to make more difficult the judicial task of justifying large scale desegregation remedies, set fourth three criteria to consider:

The duty of . . . the district court . . . is to first determine whether there was any action in the conduct of the business of the school board which was intended to, and did in fact, discriminate against minority pupils, teachers or staff. . . . If such violations are found, the district court . . . must determine how much incremental segregative effect these violations had on the racial distribution . . . when that distribution is compared to what it would have been in the absence of such constitutional violations. The remedy must be designed to redress that difference. . . .[2]

The three tasks assigned to district courts are not new, but their specification and the emphasis given to them in "Dayton" is shaping subsequent school segregation litigation. The first task, determination of intent, is now set in the context of doctrine enunciated by the present Court in its job discrimination and housing discrimination opinions. The third task, which may be characterized as an admonition to let the punishment fit the crime, falls within the traditional jurisprudential concern with equity. The second task has more elements of novelty, for it raises issues that are at least as amenable to social science analysis as to jurisprudence. Specification of "incremental segregative ef-

fects" and identification of what schools would be like if the specified intentional discrimination had not occurred are presented as questions for factual determination. Who other than the social scientist is presumed to be capable of developing such facts? In several school segregation cases undergoing post-Dayton litigation, both parties have enlisted social scientists to assist in identifying incremental segregative effects.

The Milwaukee school case

The Milwaukee school case provides a particularly straightforward example of a judicial effort to apply the Dayton standards and to address the issues posed by the "incremental segregative effects" language. The original lawsuit, begun in 1965, proceeded with the usual deliberate speed. The trial began in September 1973, and was concluded in January 1974. Post-trial proceedings were concluded in December 1974. In January 1976, Judge John W. Reynolds concluded that Milwaukee public "school authorities engaged in practices with the intent and for the purpose of creating and maintaining a segregated school system, and that such practices had the effect of causing current conditions of racial imbalance in the Milwaukee public schools."[3] The appeals court affirmed this decision and in the fall of 1976 the Milwaukee schools began implementation of a three-year phased desegregation plan.

In June, 1977, immediately following its Dayton decision, the Supreme Court vacated the judgment of the Court of Appeals and remanded the case for reconsidera-

2. *Dayton Board of Education et al.* v. *Brinkman*, 45 U.S.L.W. 4910, 4915 (U.S. June 28, 1977).

3. *Amos* v. *Board of School Directors of the City of Milwaukee*, 408 F. Supp. 765, 818 (E.D. Wis. 1976).

tion.[4] Judge Reynolds divided reconsideration into three parts, taking up sequentially the three components of the Dayton formula. An evidentiary hearing was held on the question of segregative intent, with 65 witnesses and almost 1,000 new exhibits. On June 1, 1978, Judge Reynolds issued a new opinion, of 132 manuscript pages, concluding: "The objective evidence . . . demonstrates that defendants' decisions, at least since 1950, with respect to teacher assignment and transfers, busing, student transfers, school siting, leasing and construction of school facilities, use of substandard classrooms, and boundary changes were undertaken with an intent to segregate students and teachers by race."[5]

Less than six weeks later, hearings resumed, this time on the issue of incremental segregative effects. I was one of the witnesses called by attorneys for the plaintiffs. The substantive portion of my testimony began with the question "Do you have an opinion as to whether the intentional segregative conduct on the part of the defendants which was found by the Court in its June 1, 1978, decision, had effects which persist at least up to 1976?"

Answer: "Yes, I do."

Question: "What is your opinion?"

Answer: "I believe the present effects are numerous and affect the entire city's demographic patterns and its entire school system."[6] I continued with a lengthy elaboration of the ways in which discriminatory actions by school officials contribute to the racial identifiability of neighborhoods as well as schools. From this elaboration, I concluded "that there was a continuing reciprocal interplay between schooling and housing, such that the highly concentrated black ghetto and the highly concentrated portions of the school system grew up together, and the reciprocal influence on the white areas produced solidly white residential and school areas."[7] This conclusion accords with the perspective quoted above from the Supreme Court's decision in *Swann*, and it has been developed in a number of other school segregation cases. The follow-on question, called for by the *Dayton* decision, has not previously received explicit attention.

Question: "Do you have an opinion as to whether in 1976 schools and housing in Milwaukee would have been segregated had the defendants not engaged in the intentionally segregative conduct found by this Court June 1, 1978?"[8]

Answer: "Yes . . . there might be . . . substantially less school segregation, substantially less housing segregation, and substantially improved race relations in all aspects of life and society in Milwaukee."[9]

To provide a basis for that opinion I reviewed each of the four main types of school discriminatory actions cited by Judge Reynolds and considered how history might have differed in the absence of those constitutional violations. It is easier to attempt such a reconstruction of history for Milwaukee than it would be for some of the cities with greater numbers of blacks. Milwaukee's period of rapid growth in black population began with the second World War, and continued during the

4. *Brennan* v. *Armstrong*, 433 U.S. 672 (1977).

5. *Armstrong* v. *O'Connell*, 451 F. Supp. at 817.

6. Hearing, *Armstrong* v. *O'Connell*, July 11, 1978, pp. 235–236.

7. Ibid., p. 255.

8. Ibid.

9. Ibid., pp. 255–256.

recent historical period that is covered in the school case. In 1940 and 1950 there were no census tracts in Milwaukee which were more than 90 percent black. In 1960 there were two such tracts and in 1970 there were seventeen. The growth of the Milwaukee black ghetto occurred simultaneously with the school board actions reviewed in the previous phase of the hearing.

Teacher assignment

The first category of discriminatory actions noted by Judge Reynolds is the policy of assigning most black teachers to the staffs of identifiably black schools. In the earlier part of the period under review, there was no affirmative recruitment policy for black teachers. In the school year 1950–51 there were nine black teachers, all of whom were assigned to the four schools that had a majority of blacks among their pupils. By 1965, there were three times as many black teachers (478) as schools in the Milwaukee system. Four-fifths of those black teachers were assigned to one-fifth of the schools—those with a majority of black pupils.

Suppose that throughout the 1950s, 1960s, and 1970s blacks had been affirmatively recruited to teaching and administrative positions in Milwaukee public schools and had been assigned in a nonracial pattern. Pupils throughout Milwaukee would have had first-hand experience with both black and white teachers. The educational system, by direct example, would have taught white pupils and white citizens generally that blacks and whites were equally capable of scholarly attainment, of handling major responsibilities, and of working together in harmony. Black pupils and black citizens generally would have been taught the same lesson and would have had the example of a major governmental agency practicing equal rights and ignoring racist prejudices. No school would have been racially identifiable on the basis of the racial composition of its staff.

Some of the black teachers assigned to schools remote from the ghetto might have chosen to live nearer their places of employment and to enroll their children in predominantly white schools. Some of the white teachers living near the original near northside areas in which black residents were concentrated might have chosen to remain if they had perceived that the school system itself was not giving in to stereotypical ideas about racial turnover. If the nonteaching staff of the school system had been integrated, and especially if the employment practices of all governmental agencies had been nondiscriminatory during this period, the likely integrative effect on housing patterns would have been even more substantial.

"Intact" busing

A second set of discriminatory actions identified by Judge Reynolds is the practice from 1959 to 1971 of "intact busing." If a school was overcrowded, or undergoing repairs, or otherwise unable to accommodate all the pupils assigned to it, children were bused to another school. If white children were involved the busing would oridinarily be mixed, that is, students would be regarded in every respect as part of the receiving school. Under intact busing "entire class groups from a sending school were picked up at the sending school and transported to a receiving school. These students were taught by teachers on the sending school's faculty and were under the primary control of the sending school's principal."

During the period in which intact busing was practiced, students from majority black schools were never bused under the mixed method. Indeed, separate treatment of a predominantly black classroom bused intact to a predominantly white school sometimes entailed separate recesses and denial of access to school lunch programs. The trial record lists 203 instances of intact busing from majority black schools to majority white schools. About half of Milwaukee's mainly black schools and nearly half of Milwaukee's white elementary schools were directly affected by the intact busing program. About 16,000 students were bused during the 12 years this policy was practiced. Additional thousands of students and parents at the receiving schools were personally affected by the program. Sixty-four different schools were involved at some time in sending or receiving intact bused pupils.

Suppose that in each of the 203 instances mixed busing had been used. The school administrators who were reportedly concerned about the difficulties of teaching in racially mixed settings could have provided appropriate in-service training and other services to take advantage of the opportunity for racial mixture in the schools. Special programs could have been devised to facilitate rather than discourage the participation of bused pupils in extracurricular activities and the participation of the parents of bused pupils in parent-teacher associations at the receiving schools.

Public controversy over intact busing became intense in the 1960s, and most Milwaukee blacks and

whites learned that the school administration was very resistant to any change in the policy. White citizens learned that the school system was going to great lengths to protect them and their children from contact with blacks. Black citizens learned that even in the highly structured situation of a public school, they were not welcome to participate on an equal basis. Many thousands of pupils of both races were deprived of a very practical civics lesson in interracial tolerance, and all of the pupils and citizens of Milwaukee were given a lesson in intolerance.

Many of the children most directly affected by the program of intact busing are now young adults. They are now renting and buying homes and deciding where to send their own children to school. If in their own schooling they had been taught tolerance rather than intolerance many more of them would now be willing and even eager to seek out racially mixed rather than racially isolated residential areas.

Open transfer policy

Throughout the period 1960 to 1976, the Milwaukee public school system operated a relatively open transfer policy. During part of the period students requesting transfer were required to state reasons, and the desire for greater racial isolation was an officially acceptable reason. Later in the period the system was made completely open, with no reasons stated, and approval subject primarily to the availability of space. Although a free transfer system is superficially nondiscriminatory, and indeed was used by black secondary students to increase their enrollment at a number of predominantly white high schools, it resembles the "freedom of choice" plans that have repeatedly been found by courts to operate in a discriminatory manner. "The abuse," Judge Reynolds noted, is the intentional "utilization of the policies to allow white students to escape those schools which they would otherwise have been required to attend with large numbers of black students." During the late 1960s and early 1970s the number of transfers granted to secondary pupils each year averaged seven percent of total secondary enrollment. Because a transfer did not have to be reviewed or renewed to be good for succeeding years, the cumulative effect was much greater.

The effect of such a transfer program on housing patterns is complex. Judge Reynolds noted that "defendants' transfer policies facilitated the flight of white students from black schools at a point in time preceeding the comparable departure of white residents from black neighborhoods." The most immediate effect, looking only at the particular students and families involved, would seem to be a slowing of the white out-movement from racially changing neighborhoods. But the perceived quality and characteristics of schools influence more generally the residential activity in the neighborhood, and hence there is a broader segregative influence on the housing market.

Every residential neighborhood has continual housing turnover. The most important housing market impact of rapidly increasing black enrollment in the local schools is to dry up the demand by white families for vacancies that do occur. The impact on white out-movement is less important because many of the white families will be changing residence within a few years anyway, and as racial transition proceeds they, like other whites, are unlikely to choose another home in the neighborhood. Thus the ultimate effect of the actions of the original white parents who transferred their children to other schools is to fuel the self-fulfilling prophecy that the neighborhood is becoming all black.

If the Milwaukee school officials had been truly concerned with eliminating the racially segregative consequences of their transfer program, and particularly if they had sought to discourage racial turnover through operation of an effective majority to minority transfer program, the cumulative effects on housing and school segregation in Milwaukee might have been substantial. The interests of white families in their local schools and neighborhoods might have been increased if their perceptions of the pace and inevitability of racial turnover had been altered by a firm school policy of combating racial identifiability. Similarly, if blacks had been made more welcome at more schools, the concentration of their residential demand on a few racially changing areas would have been reduced. The development of a solid ghetto expanding immutably might have been halted before entire areas of the city became designated for blacks only. If increased numbers of white and black pupils had spent more time together in more racially mixed schools, the entire development of race relations in the Milwaukee area might have followed a more benign path.

School construction and boundary changes

The final set of discriminatory actions identified by Judge Reynolds concerns usage of physical plant. "The steps the defendants took to deal with overcrowding . . . had the effect of increasing racial imbalance. These steps included the building and siting of new schools, building additions to existing schools, leasing or purchasing unused buildings for school purposes, utilizing substandard classrooms (and) changing district boundaries." The general pattern was described as one of boundary compression and facility expansion designed to preserve as clear a border as possible between black areas and schools and white areas and schools. The shifting boundaries used by the school administration to preserve racial identifiability in schools take on a larger purpose: they are used by public agencies and private persons as the shifting boundaries between residential areas expected and intended to be racially identifiable. No other boundary system within the city is as crucial to residential behavior as the system of attendance zones delineated by school authorities.

Taken together, the actions of Milwaukee school officials with respect to changing attendance zone boundaries, facilities utilization, the operation of transfer programs, and the manner of utilization of mixed and intact busing constitute a deliberate system-wide manipulation of school racial composition. Judge Reynolds commented that "throughout the history of this desegregation case, the defendants have time and again, with regard to nearly every specific action challenged by the plaintiffs, wielded the 'neighborhood' school policy as a shield of perceived talismanic strength in warding off liability for discrimination. . . . The neighborhood school policy did not mandate a segregated system in Milwaukee. The segregation of the system was mandated by the defendants who controlled the Milwaukee public school system

and are now seeking to take refuge for their unconstitutional conduct in that amorphous haven the 'neighborhood school policy'."

INCREMENTAL SEGREGATIVE EFFECTS IN MILWAUKEE

Deliberate segregative manipulations of the pupil assignment process, together with segregative assignment of teachers, have combined to cause, enhance, and maintain the racial identifiability of schools and neighborhoods in Milwaukee. The locations that black families would have chosen in the absence of constraints imposed by their experience with and perceptions of the school system cannot be specified with precision. Neither can precise alternatives be specified for the housing and schooling decisions of white families who were discouraged from living in "changing" or "black" areas and who were taught by a government agency that it is difficult and unwise for black and white children to go to school together.

I once wrote that "to talk about social and economic forces, attitudes and values, racial residential patterns, and white and black public school enrollments, and to exclude all mention of the suburbs is patently ridiculous."[10] Although the Milwaukee public school system serves the city of Milwaukee, the school effects clearly are felt throughout the metropolitan area. The confinement of black pupils and families to the near north side areas of Milwaukee obviously interfered with a broader residential and school dispersal. Unfortunately, from a social scientist's perspective, the jurispru-

10. Karl E. Taeuber, "Demographic Perspectives on Housing and School Segregation," *Wayne Law Review* 21 (March 1975): 845.

dential aspects of the Milwaukee school case at this stage require a focus on the city. The contribution of school discrimination to the racial character of suburbanization was not pursued in the hearings. It would be ironic if the judicial system were to ignore school segregation as an influence on the massive white suburbanization of the last 30 years, and then at the remedy stage to give great attention to desegregation as an influence on "white flight."

What would the racial distribution of the Milwaukee school population have been in the absence of the constitutional violations identified by Judge Reynolds? The conclusion of my direct testimony at the hearing follows:

Now to put all this back together, I'd like to go back to the idea that there were some specific children who experienced the Milwaukee schools thirty years ago or twenty years ago, and that many of these children still live in the area, and that these white and black people have grown up, they have families now, and they are buying homes, renting apartments, taking up responsible positions . . . these are the adults of the community today. And if they had experienced interracial education, had experienced a non-discriminatory school system, and if there had been some of these interlocking effects with the housing market to make it less segregated than it became, and to diminish the development of the ghetto as such a solid concentrated place during the period of rapid black growth, then I think that Milwaukee would be quite a different place from what it is now. From north to south and east to west, there would be much more desegregation, not only directly in the schools, but also in the housing. It would be a much more racially harmonious city today than it has become. This is what could be expected if only we could do away with the actual history of sustained intentional segregative actions specified in Judge Reynolds' order of June 1.[11]

The defendants asked for several months to prepare their rebuttal case on incremental segregative effects, and at the time this manuscript goes to press the defendants have not yet had their days in court. My purpose in not to try the Milwaukee school case out of court, but rather to use the Milwaukee case as a basis for thinking about housing segregation, school segregation, and the related legal and social policies. Experience with this case leads me to offer five tentative suggestions.

SUGGESTIONS FROM THE CASE STUDY

My first suggestion is that the jurisprudential link between school segregation and housing segregation is still in the developing stages and may have profound legal effects on both school law and housing law. In his opinion in the Detroit metropolitan case, Justice Potter Stewart referred to the "unknown and perhaps unknowable" factors accounting for city and suburban racial separation.[12] Many aggrieved citizens along with an array of attorneys and social scientists believe that the forces are largely knowable and that racially discriminatory governmental actions are prominent among them. The Dayton criteria have provided further impetus to use of the litigation process to inform courts what is known about the linkages between school segregation and housing segregation.

The second suggestion is that the use of social science evidence and

11. Hearing, *Armstrong* v. *O'Connell*, pp. 280–281.
12. *Milliken* v. *Bradley*, 418 U.S. 717 (1974).

perspectives in the establishment of proof of violation, and in the assessment of equitable remedy, will become increasingly common despite the hostility of many judges to social science. Several current members of the Supreme Court were appointed as "strict constructionists." It is ironic that in their attempts to back away from the long line of post-Brown implementation decisions they have opened the legal door even more widely to social science evidence.

My experience in the Milwaukee case suggests that the current standard of equity for remedying school segregation, as enunciated in the Dayton decision, will encourage tendentious dispute rather than simplify the heroic task laid on district judges. School cases involve hundreds of actions taken over a period of decades. The mandate to restore the situation to what it would have been in the absence of the violations requires excessive historical speculation. The "what ifs" of history can never be resolved.

My testimony for the plaintiffs in the Milwaukee case took on the tone of ascribing massive incremental effects to a single cause, much in accord with the old nursery rhyme, "for want of a nail . . . a kingdom was lost." Within the adversarial context of a trial, as well as in the arena of public policy debate, it seems to be true that for each and every Ph.D. there is an equal and opposite Ph.D. Experts for defendants will doubtless testify that many other causes suffice to account for the historical outcome, and that the vicious circle of prejudice and discrimination would spin just as fast if government had never joined in. The apparent precision of the Dayton standard is chimeric.

A fourth suggestion is that we use the present and the future as one means of assessing our perspective on the past. The role of schools and school administrative decisions on housing patterns and residential decisionmaking is a topic grossly neglected by social scientists. One aspect of the relationship is receiving virtually all the attention—the magnitude and character of so-called white flight from school desegregation actions. We should also be looking for housing integrative effects of school desegregation. Particularly in the case of county-wide and metropolitan school desegregation, where little white or black flight has occurred, we should ascertain whether there has been any reduction in the sharp differential channeling of white and black housing demands formerly stimulated by school racial attendance policies. Within Milwaukee, one predominantly white junior high school that is on a direct bus line from a black residential area has attracted approximately 20 percent black enrollment through the current open transfer system. Some black families are now moving into the residential area near that junior high school, leapfrogging over intervening white residential areas. Is there firm evidence for this example or for other examples of school actions leading to violations of the traditional ghetto expansion process?

The final suggestion stimulated by my involvement in the Milwaukee case is that coming to grips with the complexities of social life is equally hard for scholars, judges, and policymakers. All share a predilection toward narrow perspectives. Students of school segregation tend to examine the acts of school administrations. Students of housing segregation tend to examine discrimination in the housing market.

Students of racial economic differentials tend to examine the way labor markets operate. Few scholars have heeded Myrdal's plea to recognize "the unity of the Negro problem."[13] Most judges in school cases have confined their attention to school effects of school policies. To the extent they consider residential patterns, they tend to view them as an independent underlying fact. Few judges have followed the lead of the Supreme Court in *Swann* and given

close attention to the linkages between schooling and housing. Fewer still have allowed the historical basis of race relations to intrude into their jurisprudential analysis. Policymakers—executive and legislative officials and we the voters—also like neat packages, and we like to pass the buck whenever posssible. We should not, as a society, rely on district judges seeking remedies for constitutional violations to make whole our massively troubled school systems. Nor should we rely on the judiciary to play a major role in making whole our racially troubled metropolitan areas.

13. Gunnar Myrdal, *An American Dilemma: The Negro Problem and Modern Democracy* (New York: Harper, 1944), p. 73.

Race and Housing: A Review and Comments on the Content and Effects of Federal Policy

By ROBERT E. MITCHELL and RICHARD A. SMITH

ABSTRACT: Unlike school integration measures, housing and community development policies attack the causes rather than simply the symptoms of racial segregation in urban communities. Federal policies are examined with regard to two goals: protection of the individual's right to a decent home and a suitable living environment, and the social goal of achieving stable interracial residential environments. Although both supply and demand housing strategies have had some, but still unmeasured, success in realizing both goals, the public and private sector delivery systems have sustained the dual housing market. Future progress will depend on the mixture of demand and supply strategies adopted, changes in delivery systems, the success of federal enforcement efforts, the emphasis placed on broad strategy options, and socioeconomic trends not easily influenced by public policy.

Robert E. Mitchell received his Ph.D. in sociology from Columbia University. He has been coordinator of international research at Berkeley's Survey Research Center, founding director of the Social Survey Research Centre of the Chinese University of Hong Kong, Executive Director of Florida Governor Askew's Task Force on Housing and Community Development, Director of the Florida Task Force on Marriage and the Family Unit, and a housing and community development consultant to the United Nations and the Agency for International Development. Currently a Professor of Urban and Regional Planning at Florida State University. Professor Mitchell has published on housing, community development, family, and national development issues.

Richard A. Smith received his Ph.D. in planning from Cornell University. He has worked as a planner in London, England and been a consultant to public and private planning agencies in America. An Associate Professor of Urban and Regional Planning at Florida State University, and currently teaching in the University's London Program, Professor Smith has published on community decisionmaking and structures, neighborhood structure, planning theory, criminal justice planning, urbanization, and racial discrimination in housing.

THIS PAPER is concerned with an examination of federal housing and community development policies as they affect two important racial considerations: the supply and quality of housing available to minority groups, and the spatial distribution of this housing (that is, the issue of housing segregation.) While the two issues are analytically separate, the manner in which urban areas have grown has resulted in their being highly interrelated: since housing types and quality tend not to be randomly distributed across urban areas, discrimination in the allocation of housing is also likely to result in spatial segregation. Similarly, discrimination in the process whereby groups are allocated housing in space is likely to affect the supply and quality of the housing they occupy.

The extent to which disparities exist in supply and quality of housing, and in the distribution of the housing occupied by whites and blacks, has been fully documented elsewhere. Generally we recognize higher levels of overcrowding, greater density, more dilapidation, lower levels of home ownership, higher expenditures for comparable quality housing, less satisfactory housing environments, and fewer locational choices for the black population of metropolitan areas than for whites. The prospects for changing this situation without massive and dedicated interventions through public policy and programming are not good. Two trends generally believed to have ameliorating effects—the increasing income of black households relative to whites and the decreasing support for housing and other forms of discrimination within the society at large—have had only limited im-

pact. Undoubtedly, increasing the purchasing power of black households will allow for some improvement in housing quality, but as long as new housing is primarily a suburban phenomenon, and discrimination in allocating spatial locations exists, the alternative types of housing and housing environments available to blacks will be limited. We also have come to recognize that attitude changes are not sufficient. Given the complexity of home buying, locational decisions, and the operations of the housing market, neighborhoods may continue to turn from white to black under conditions of low discrimination. Even mild feelings of racial preference on the part of whites are likely to be sufficient to produce segregation patterns similar to those occurring when racial preferences are more strongly held.

Thus, government intervention, in an attempt to influence the supply and location of housing available to minorities, is a growing necessity. While the federal government has long maintained this intervention, committing the nation to the goal of a decent home and suitable living environment for every American family, it has often acted to aggravate rather than ameliorate the housing situation of minorities. Only recently have the two aspects of this goal—housing and housing environments—as they apply to black households been given official emphasis, interpreted as: 1) the rights of individuals, regardless of race, to housing; and 2) the social environment goal of racially integrated housing projects, neighborhoods, communities, and metropolitan areas.

To accomplish these goals, significant federal, state, and local civil rights legislation has been enacted, new housing and community development programs have been implemented, and older programs have been redirected with a new emphasis. Both federal administrative regulations, governing the operation and implementation of these programs, and federal court decisions, responding to legislation, and often leading to administrative reform, have occurred. Out of this array of actions, various objectives have come to be emphasized, created out of the differing perceptions of the public and private interests involved in the housing delivery system. Thus, while official federal policy is now committed to both the provision of housing and the creation of racially integrated environments, it is not entirely clear that the content and implementation of federal program activities are contributing to a unified and consistent effort to achieve these objectives. What objectives are being pursued, and to what degrees of success, become important concerns. Accordingly, in this paper we attempt to review and evaluate these policies and programs, commenting on their results and potentials for affecting both access to housing and access to integrated housing environments.

Because the body of material to be addressed is exceedingly large (a U.S. House of Representatives chronology of legislative and selected actions, between 1892 and 1974, lists 125 separate acts and 60 executive orders related to housing goals), we have endeavored to touch only on the highlights, limiting our consideration to the more significant actions within the past three decades. It should be noted that in concentrating only on federal policies and efforts, a good deal of important and interesting activity at state and local levels is omitted. The stimuli for actions at these other levels, however, frequently comes from federal policies and the administrative regulations that local communities must follow in accepting federal program funds. Thus, an exclusive focus on federal activity, while incomplete, represents a somewhat broader perspective than would at first seem to be the case.

THE CONTENT OF FEDERAL POLICY

Federal actions as they affect the housing conditions of racial minorities can be broadly classified into two types of activities: the removal of discriminatory barriers in the housing market, thereby allowing minorities to gain access to housing and neighborhoods in a nonracially discriminatory manner; and affirmative actions designed to facilitate the flow of housing on a nonsegregated basis to these same groups. Actions in the latter category may also be divided into those that primarily address the provision of housing and those that are concerned with questions of housing location, population mix, and integrated neighborhoods. While these latter divisions are somewhat artificial, they do serve to distinguish major policy foci and provide a basis for our review. As we shall see, relative success in one policy area need not be matched by positive results in another: housing programs that are administered fairly can still have negative effects on minorities and their neighborhoods because of the multiple objectives that programs are often designed to achieve. Similarly, programs aimed at increasing the supply of housing for minorities may still restrict locational choices and the achievement of integrated environments.

Individual rights

The most basic approaches aimed at reducing housing discrimination and segregation have been concerned with the protection of individuals' rights, and have focused on the elimination of a discriminatory housing market in which race has become the primary object of discrimination.

Rights and responsibilities in the Constitution are predicated on individuals, and the initial equal opportunity efforts in the housing area were to assure that individuals' rights were protected. Once assured, individual decisionmaking should result in significant changes in residential location patterns, and the success of efforts to remove discriminatory actions against racial minorities can be partially measured by the access these minorities have to credit, certain kinds of housing, and particular neighborhoods. Thus, freedom of choice is translated into proscribing particular participants in the housing process from discriminating against minorities. With the elimination of discrimination, it is assumed that the dual housing market—one for whites and the other for blacks—will also be eliminated.

Court decisions, executive orders, and civil rights legislation have addressed these individual rights and have successively diminished, on a de jure basis, the ability to discriminate on the basis of race. In 1948, the Supreme Court, in *Shelly v. Kraemer*,[1] ruled that racially restrictive covenants were unenforceable in the courts, thereby prompting the Federal Housing Administration (an agency with a long record of discriminatory practices to this date) to develop administrative procedures against insuring mortgages subject to these covenants. Significant federal action did not begin, however, until President Kennedy's executive order in 1962, directing federal departments and agencies to prevent discrimination in the sale, lease, or occupancy of federally assisted residential property. This order applied only to new FHA and VA insured units; loans made prior to 1962, as well as those made in the conventional market, were excluded.

More encompassing coverage was included in the Civil Rights Act of 1964, with Title VI prohibiting discrimination against all those eligible for federal financial assistance. The major impact of this act was on public housing; local housing authorities had to abolish the traditional practice of dual waiting lists and the maintenance of racially segregated projects. The most comprehensive legislative coverage was passed as the Civil Rights Act of 1968, including Title VIII, the "Fair Housing Law." Instead of singling out FHA for sole consideration, this new act covered all housing and related transactions, for both sale and rental, excluding only single-family units transferred without the use of an agent, and units in certain rooming houses. When it became effective on 1 January 1969, this act covered approximately 80 percent of all housing. The remaining percentage was also quickly put under control in 1968 by the Supreme Court decision in *Jones* v. *Mayer*,[2] which upheld an 1866 civil rights statute prohibiting the racially motivated refusal of a private housing developer to sell a home to a black. The statute was held to be a valid

1. *Shelly* v. *Kraemer*, 334 U.S. 1(1948).

2. *Jones* v. *Alfred H. Mayer Co.*, 392 U.S. 409 (1968).

exercise of Congress to enforce the 13th Amendment.

Other important steps have been taken to assure the rights of individuals: state governments have reformed landlord-tenant laws, state commissions on civil rights have been created, HUD and other agencies have adopted new model leases, and state and local fair housing laws have been enacted, generally patterned on federal legislation. Thus, the legal basis that permitted discrimination against racial minorities has been removed. From the initial focus on only selected discriminatory techniques and federal programs, all private and public sector housing now falls under fair housing mandates.

In spite of this comprehensive coverage, significant problems exist. The largest single deficiency of current fair housing laws remains in the weakness of enforcement mechanisms and the unwillingness of the appropriate federal agencies to utilize those mechanisms that do exist. Under the 1962 executive order, although violators could be denied FHA insurance, no evidence exists of this sanction having been imposed. Enforcement mechanisms for the 1968 Civil Rights Act are substantially weaker: complaints of alleged discrimination must be initiated by the individual, with HUD's powers limited to attempts to reach a conciliation with the parties involved. HUD has maintained a substantial backlog of these complaints, frequently referring them to state agencies in those states having comparable fair housing legislation. For the individual, discrimination may not only be difficult to prove, but the process provides little immediate relief. As the U.S. Civil Rights Commission has noted, the burden to desegregate is placed "on the person least able to accomplish this goal—i.e., the individual applicant who was to make a 'free choice' in a community in which segregated housing patterns were frequently traditional."[3]

Even with more adequate enforcement mechanisms, however, the simple removal of barriers to full participation in the housing market is not likely to be sufficient to make a significant impact on current high levels of housing segregation. Inertia, the legacy of discrimination, the traditional operation of the housing market, the ability to practice discrimination in subtle ways, and the relative disadvantages of minorities to compete with whites on the basis of the ability to pay for housing will serve to maintain these patterns. In order to effect a turnaround in the current situation, more affirmative policies and programs are necessary, aimed at increasing minority access to housing and a variety of locations.

Alternative strategies to provide a decent home

Attempts to increase the supply of housing available to the population have been a traditional focus of federal policy and program efforts, responding to the most elementary interpretations of a housing problem. While generally organized around particular income target groups, these programs have had important impacts on the availability of housing for minorities, the type and conditions of units made available, and their location. Two general strategies for providing housing can be identified: the historical, produc-

3. U.S. Commission on Civil Rights, *Twenty Years After Brown: Equal Opportunity in Housing*. (Washington, DC: USGPO, 1975), p. 68.

tion/supply approach, and the more recent demand approach.

The major historical housing strategies have been production oriented, involving varying levels of subsidies to different income groups. Shallow subsidies, aimed at stimulating housing production with a minimum of expenditure, must necessarily be directed at the nonpoor. The primary example is FHA and VA mortgage insurance and guarantee programs designed to facilitate middle-class purchase of new homes, and accounting for the dramatic growth of metropolitan suburbs since World War II. Under these programs, increased housing availability to the poor is seen as the result of the trickle-down process: new housing that is produced for the middle class creates vacancies in the housing stock for moderate and lower-income households. Supposedly, this housing trickles down with a minimum loss in quality and is appropriate to the needs of the lower-income groups. The result is then an overall increase in supply for these groups, thereby accommodating population growth, or an excess of units that allows the worst of the housing supply to be abandoned.

This process of stimulating housing production for the middle class has also been aided by federal income tax policies governing depreciation and deductions for mortgage interest and property taxes. Direct government expenditures, however, are minimal, thereby exercising a large amount of leverage. It is argued that by virtue of this leverage, more housing is produced, benefiting a greater number of families than would a deep subsidy program for the very poor. Nevertheless, because subsidies have been aimed at the middle class

and at suburban development, they have reinforced income and rent gradients within metropolitan areas. Because minorities are disproportionally concentrated in the lower-income groups, the effect has been to make housing available to them within older central city neighborhoods and within the older housing stock. Thus while supply may have been increased, quality and locational choices have not.

To further insure this result, both FHA and VA programs have been implemented so as to exclude minority participation. Early FHA underwriting standards, for example, stressed the inadvisability of 'mixing races' and introducing 'incompatible' racial and ethnic types into a neighborhood. In 1955 a Federal court, in the case of *Arthur L. Johnson v. Levitt and Sons, Inc.*,[4] held that FHA and VA had no statutory authority or other duty to assure that housing covered by their programs be sold to persons of all races. As noted, it was not until 1962 that at least the legal basis for this discrimination was eliminated. To date, however, participation in FHA and VA programs is still overwhelmingly by whites.

Moderate to deep subsidy programs also exist, the major examples being public housing and the section 235 and 236 programs. Older cities have been using the public housing program since its inception in 1937, with large fixed capital investments in central cities now existing. While originally provided on a discriminatory basis, subsequent lifting of these restrictions has resulted in a substantial turnover of units from white to black, thereby contributing significantly to the size of the hous-

4. *Arthur L. Johnson v. Levitt and Sons, Inc.*, 131 F. Supp. 144 (1955).

ing stock available to minorities within central cities. Ironically, however, this increase in the supply of units has been accompanied by increased housing segregation. Similarly, in response to the Civil Rights Act of 1964, FHA developed site selection criteria applicable only to public housing. If sites were to be selected in areas of minority concentration, the housing authority had to select alternative or additional sites outside of these areas in order to provide a more balanced distribution of the proposed housing. This rule could and was waived, however, if the authority could show that no sites with costs within HUD cost acquisition limits were available outside racially concentrated areas, or if proper rezoning was not obtained from the local government. Racial segregation was thus continued.

Recently constructed public housing outside the central city has occurred. Most, however, has been earmarked for the elderly—a group that is more acceptable to most suburbs than is a low-income minority population. Hence, locational choices and the supply of units through this program have not been substantially expanded. More recently, a federal court has ruled in *Otero vs. New York City Housing Authority*[5] that blacks displaced from housing due to urban renewal were not to be given priority in public housing built on the site, under the reasoning that the national commitment to integration took precedence over the rights of individual minority group members to secure housing on a nondiscriminatory basis. Further decisions

in this direction, compounded by the removal of units through the urban renewal process, will, in the interests of integration, further restrict the housing supply available to minorities.

The other production programs involving moderate subsidies have been the sections 235 (single family owner-occupied) and 236 (multifamily rental) authorized in 1968 and aimed predominantly at moderate income families. An advantage over traditional public housing is that these programs held the potential for increasing both housing and locational choices. Subsidies were paid directly to mortgage lenders or landlords of qualified units that could be located anywhere within the metropolitan area subject only to local government zoning approval. Analysts generally have agreed that 235/236, if continued at initial funding levels, held the potential for a significant expansion of minority housing choice; indeed, a 1971 study by the U.S. Civil Rights Commission found that minorities were participating in this program well beyond their representation in the population of the cities studied. Locational choices, however, did not appear to be expanded: the great majority of new 235 housing built in the suburbs was occupied by whites, while black participation occurred mostly in used housing located in existing ghetto areas and changing neighborhoods. Administration of the program by both public and private sector agents has failed to eliminate the traditional market.[6]

Thus, while production programs delivered through both the public and private sectors appear to have

5. *Otero* v. *New York City Housing Authority*, 344 F. Supp. 737 (S.D.N.Y. 1972), 354 F. Supp. 941 (S.D.N.Y. 1973), rev'd. 484 F.2d 1122 (2d cir. 1973).

6. U.S. Commission on Civil Rights. *Home Ownership for Lower Income Families.* (Washington, DC: USGPO, 1971).

increased the housing units available to minority families, the delivery systems involved have operated to restrict locational choices. If these delivery systems could be eliminated and families given money directly to locate their own housing, it is possible that within the context of a nondiscriminatory market, greater locational choice could be realized. This, essentially, becomes the argument for a demand strategy to housing supply. Unfortunately, present programs still fall short of this approach. The current major housing program, Section 8 of the Housing and Community Development Act of 1974 operates to subsidize approved applicants to the amount of the difference between what the family may be reasonably expected to pay in rent and the fair market value of approved housing units. Like previous programs, however, the subsidy is paid to the owner of the approved housing unit on behalf of the eligible family.

Preliminary statistics on the Section 8 program as applied to the rental of existing housing have appeared just as this paper was written. Evaluators, dividing the nation into three regions, found that in all three, black applicant households have had a lower acceptance rate into the program than have whites. In one region, blacks who moved have contributed to racially integrated neighborhoods, but white recipients were more likely to move to segregated ones.[7] Since more whites than blacks are recipients, the net effect of the program could be a greater segregation, although the data have not been analyzed in a way to confirm any such conclusion. A separate interview study of the program in Houston has concluded that it has had little success in reversing the pattern of racially segregated housing in that city. Moreover, at least one aspect of the program, the "finders incentive" (recipients are financially rewarded for locating cheaper housing) of the leased housing program, can be regarded as encouraging increased segregation since vacant, less expensive units are no doubt more common in older, lower quality, central city areas.

In general, then, it appears that increases in housing choices and locational choices have not been accomplished jointly. The continued operations of the housing market, discriminating in perhaps more subtle ways than were necessary prior to the enactment of fair housing legislation, seems to have forced an uncomfortable tradeoff: increasing the supply of housing for minorities is possible, but mostly under conditions of continued or increased segregation. Recognizing this argues for alternative interventions in an attempt to maintain an increased housing supply for minorities within the context of locational options.

Community development: strategies to achieve a suitable living environment

Historically, federal community development efforts have focused on the economic and fiscal conditions of central cities, stressing objectives that reflect the increasing loss of population, business and commercial services, and tax resources to the suburbs. In attempts to rejuvenate central cities and make them more attractive to households and continued business investment, large-scale development projects

7. U.S. Department of Housing and Urban Development, *Lower Income Housing Assistance Program (Section 8)* (Washington, DC: USGPO, 1978), p. 23.

have been undertaken, frequently with negative effects on the supply of minority group housing and the quality of minority housing environments.

During the first decade of urban renewal, for example, 60 percent of the families displaced by renewal activities are estimated to have been black. Several studies have indicated that inadequate replacement housing was provided these families, resulting in further crowding and deterioration of existing ghetto areas, and undoubtedly contributing to the pressure on adjacent neighborhoods, stimulating their transition. The construction of middle-class housing on these sites added further insult to injury. Federal, as well as state and local highway programs, have had similar black-removal effects, as well as serving to isolate some black neighborhoods from adjacent white residential areas. The subsequent development of project selection criteria in federal programming, whereby attention is focused on the most blighted and depressed areas of central cities—often black neighborhoods—rather than on neighborhoods where incipient decline could still be arrested, also has meant a disproportionate removal of black units and a consequent shift of black households to other ghetto areas.

Some corrective responses have been made to these indictments. Thus, displaced families are given priority access to public housing; new housing must be built to replace units removed; and relocation responsibilities have been expanded. Similarly, administrative requirements for communities awarded federal community development and planning funds to produce workable programs and plans, (insuring that federal monies are used in ways consistent with community goals), have required communities to address the relocation problem. While all of these changes address the national goal of a decent home, they are, however, silent on integration issues, thereby allowing federally assisted planning and capital projects to reinforce and further contribute to the presently high levels of urban racial segregation.

Partially in response to these early abuses, and partially in response to the recognition that central city redevelopment efforts that ignored growing social and physical deficiencies in decaying neighborhoods were insufficient responses to the central city problems (even with increasing segregation, the central city could not be made attractive with the potential for increases in crime, civil disorders, etc.), federal programming has also come to address particular neighborhoods and neighborhood problems. Major programs have included code enforcement, rehabilitation, and neighborhood development. Most of these have, as their primary focus, housing and physical environment conditions. More encompassing was the now defunct Model Cities program in which the attempt was made to focus different federal agency funds on single neighborhoods in ways that combined physical with socio-economic development efforts.

Public spending per capita increased in these neighborhoods; human services assumed importance along with traditional hardware expenditures; residents themselves had a role in identifying and developing programs; and many target neighborhoods had high concentrations of racial minorities. Model Cities was an enrichment program attempting to improve the quality of life of residents so that they need not move elsewhere to realize social and environmental benefits. Thus, housing and neighborhoods were improved, but integration goals had low priority; enrichment and integration were not compatible strategies in the low-income target neighborhoods selected for Model Cities.

More recent attention at the neighborhood level has been focused on the discriminatory lending policies of financial institutions. Known as "redlining," this practice denies mortgage money and funds for housing rehabilitation to entire neighborhoods on the basis of neighborhood characteristics, rather than considering the merits of individual property and loan applications. Clearly, while redlining is not the prime cause of neighborhood decay—but rather a response to it—when applied during the process of decay it serves both to hasten decline and preclude the possibility of reversal. In effect, redlining writes off entire neighborhoods as poor financial risks, thereby creating a self-fulfilling prophesy. Minorities have suffered disproportionately from this situation.

A number of federal initiatives have attempted to alleviate the redlining problem. The Home Mortgage Disclosure Act of 1975 requires disclosure of mortgage lending practices, reported by census tracts, for institutions that are federally insured or regulated. Hopefully this will allow for a better monitoring of lending patterns. Similarly, FHA standards for insuring mortgage loans in central cities have been relaxed under the Housing and Community Development Act of 1968. By switching underwriting standards from "economic soundness" to "reasonable risk," the flow

of mortgage funds to blighted central city areas may be increased. However, because these initiatives target particular areas, they can only affect housing conditions in these areas. Not only are they unable to help remedy the segregation problem, they may worsen it by hastening the racial transition of some neighborhoods adjacent to ghetto areas.

This is equally true of the attempts of some private lenders to overcome charges of discrimination by "greenlining." This technique refers to the designation of locations as appropriate for loans to blacks. Again, however, presumably well intentioned initiatives have had adverse effects by accelerating the process of racial transition in the designated areas while frustrating redevelopment and preservation interests in others.

In total, however, neighborhood-level efforts are likely to have minimal impacts on the segregation problem. While potentially addressing the questions of housing quality and perhaps decreasing the number of units that would otherwise become dilapidated and abandoned, little if anything is done to increase locational choices and impact on the levels of segregation. Often the reverse is possible: by encouraging greater investment in particular neighborhoods, the potential incentive for families to leave and find housing in integrated environments is reduced.

Throughout the period of the late 1960's pressure had been building for an entirely new approach to housing and community development. While not entirely abandoning the objectives of revitalizing the declining central cities, through redevelopments designed to reattract middle-class whites, increasing emphasis was being placed on a dispersal strategy in which low-income and minority populations would be afforded increased housing opportunities throughout the central city and particularly throughout the metropolitan area. Thus, rather than attempting to achieve integration goals through return migration strategies, integration has been increasingly seen as linked to the opening up of the suburbs. In this manner the potential conflicts between central city redevelopment and increased integration, witnessed throughout the earlier part of the 1960's, would be resolved. Indeed, both objectives may be better realized under the dispersal strategy since this would help to relieve population pressures on central cities, provide room for redevelopment projects, and diminish the racial exclusivity of suburbs.

Part of the stimulus for this new approach undoubtedly has been the civil rights and fair housing legislation of the 1960s which, in spite of its enforcement gaps, has created the basis for legal challenges to discriminatory site selection procedures for subsidized housing and has paved the way for challenges of exclusionary practices in the suburbs. Some of the more significant court decisions of this period have included: *Hills v. Gatreaux*,[8] in which the court blocked all public housing in black wards and mandated the Chicago Housing Authority and HUD to prepare a plan and begin an affirmative program of placing public housing throughout the metropolitan area; *Hicks v. Weaver*,[9] in which the courts pre-

vented a public housing project from being placed in a black section of Baton Rouge, La.; *Shannon v. HUD*,[10] in which the court barred rent supplements being provided an apartment complex pending consideration of the impact the project (which was in an urban renewal area) would have on the concentration of lower income minority residents; *United States v. City of Black Jack*,[11] in which the court of Appeals ruled against the suburb's incorporation and establishment of a zoning ordinance in an attempt to prevent a previously proposed subsidized housing project; and *Banks v. Perk*[12] and *Mahaley v. Cuyahoga Metropolitan Housing Authority*,[13] in which the court ordered the housing authority to prepare plans for scattered sites in suburban areas. Numerous other cases exist addressing various discriminatory practices and attempts, issues of standing, the distinction between the intent and effect of community actions, dispersal, housing referenda, zoning, and others, resulting in a fairly substantial body of decisions concerning constitutional guarantees and civil rights law.

The Gatreaux and Shannon cases are particularly notable since out of them have come HUD's issuance of site selection criteria intended to govern all HUD programs. Under

8. *Hills* v. *Gautreaux*, 476 l. Ed. 2d 792 (1976), *affirming* 503 F.2d 930 (7th cir. 1974).
9. *Hicks* v. *Weaver*, 302 F. Supp. 619 (E.D.La. 1969).

10. *Shannon* v. *Department of Housing and Urban Development*, 436 F.2d 809 (3d cir. 1970), vacating 305 F.Supp. 205 (E.D. Pa. 1969).
11. *United States* v. *City of Black Jack*, 508 F.2d 1179 (8th cir. 1974), *cert. den.* 422 U.S. 1042 (1975).
12. *Banks* v. *Perk*, 341 F. Supp. 1175 (N.D. Ohio 1972), *affirmed in part, rev'd. in part*, 473 F.2nd 910 (6th cir. 1973).
13. *Mahaley* v. *Cuyahogha Metropolitan Housing Authority*, 355 F.Supp. 1245 (N.D. Ohio 1973), 355 F.Supp. 1257 (N.D. Ohio 973), *rev'd*, 500 F.2d 1087 (6th cir. 1974), *cert. den.* 419 U.S. 1108 (1975).

this regulation, all proposed projects within a particular area are evaluated according to seven criteria, three of which respond directly to integration goals: sites are not to be located in areas of minority concentrations (two exceptions to this rule are allowed); they must not significantly increase the proportion of minority residents in the neighborhoods; and the sites are to promote greater choices of housing but avoid undue concentrations of subsidized families in low-income areas.

Additional administrative regulations have been promulgated by HUD, attempting to influence the private sector housing delivery system. For example, under affirmative marketing regulations, developers are required to submit for approval and subsequently practice a set of procedures designed to help insure that minority households are made aware of and have access to new developments.

Within the context of this activity has come the passage of the Housing and Community Development Act of 1974. While many observers were expecting a bill that mandated a dispersal strategy for local communities, such was not passed. The 1974 act does, however, come closest to encouraging this dispersal than any previous legislation. The major provisions of this Act as they relate to dispersal and integration include: 1) the policy of avoiding concentrations of lower-income persons in central cities and the concept of accommodating both subsidized and nonsubsidized tenants in the same building; 2) the establishment of the Section 8 housing program whereby local government powers to block subsidized housing units are sharply curtailed; 3) the requirement of producing Housing Assistance Plans

(HAPs), tied to block grant funding.

The significance of these provisions can be seen in the context of historical approaches. Prior to this act, federal housing laws gave local governments two ways to exclude publicly assisted housing from their jurisdictions. First, by refusing to create a local housing authority, no public housing was possible. Second, local governments have had to give their approval before any subsidized units could be located in them, even if recommended by the local housing authority. Thus, no means existed to either force or entice communities to accept public housing, and no ways existed to encourage minimally active authorities to seek additional units, let alone disperse them. While efforts have been made to change this situation—the Housing and Community Development Act of 1968 removed the requirement for local government approval for Section 235/236 housing—the existence of a local housing authority was required so that it was still easy for suburban jurisdiction to frustrate dispersal and integration efforts.

The provision for Section 8 housing under the new act eases this situation somewhat by opening up the sponsorship of subsidized projects to a wider range of nongovernment agencies, thereby bypassing recalcitrant local delivery systems. More effective, however, are likely to be the sets of requirements and incentives that can now be applied to local communities. First, governments must prepare a Housing Assistance Plan (HAP) as part of their application for community development funds. This plan must conform to site selection criteria and must indicate the census tracts in which subsidized housing is needed. Projections must include not just the indigenous low and moderate-income households within the community but also those 'expected to reside' within the community on the basis of current and anticipated employment activities. Second, while the local community is not under any obligation to provide this housing, it also does not have the power to reject any subsidized units proposed by other sponsors that are consistent with the needs and locations specified in the HAP. Third, persons employed in a particular jurisdiction, although not resident there, are to be considered residents for the purposes of defining housing needs and approving applications for housing subsidies. Fourth, incentives are provided metropolitan areas that adopt Areawide Housing Opportunities Plans in which participating jurisdictions agree to provide a specified number of subsidized units. This incentive amounts to an additional housing allocation beyond that which the area would normally receive.

While these requirements can still be avoided simply by a jurisdiction electing not to apply for community development block grant funds, the 1974 act allows subsidized projects to be proposed to HUD for a community without a HAP. The determination of the community's need for the project then rests with HUD. The community is permitted to submit advisory comments to HUD, but has no powers to veto a HUD decision. Thus, communities are encouraged to produce a HAP, both to receive block grant funds and to protect their interests from being mandated by HUD.

While the 1974 Act provides the most concerted effort to achieve dispersal yet, problems still remain in the design and administration of the program. Section 8 housing, for example, is the major form of subsidized housing under the Act. Recent evaluations have found, however, that funding levels are not sufficiently high and that HUD's definition of 'fair market rents' for units may be too low in many areas, thereby discouraging developers and landlords from participating in the program. Large families are not being reached effectively, and this is also attributable to HUD's rent determinations. Moreover, Section 8 has been biased toward the leasing of existing units rather than the building of new ones. Since new development is most likely to take place in the suburbs while leased units are more likely to be concentrated in central cities, the emphasis on the latter compromises the dispersal strategy. This strategy is further frustrated by the application of HUD's site selection criteria only to new or substantially rehabilitated units—not to the leasing of existing ones. Without this control, and when combined with the previously mentioned 'finder's incentive' encouraging applicants to occupy less expensive housing, it is difficult to see how this program will make a significant impact on the existing segregation pattern. This conclusion is supported by a recent study in Cuyahoga County which found that: most of the families subsidized by the program in Cleveland did not make moves that contributed to dispersal; minority families encountered discrimination in their efforts to find housing; and most families remained in their present neighborhoods.

Perhaps even more critical are the failures of HUD to carefully administer these programs and to determine whether the actions of local communities and developers comply with regulations and national policy. HUD, organized in 1966, has the major responsibility for administering equal opportunity requirements, and a special office, the Assistant Secretary for Equal Opportunity, has been created within HUD to handle these matters. While HUD's enforcement powers under Title VIII of the Civil Rights Act are limited, those granted by Title VI, HUD's own regulations, and under the 1974 Act, are more substantial. Critics have consistently faulted the Department, however, for the failure to use what powers it has. It can, for example, disapprove a community development block grant application if the housing assistance plan included in the application is "plainly inconsistent" with data available to HUD, or if a program of action is "plainly inappropriate" to meeting the community's own identified needs and objectives. HUD has also been criticized for not having sufficient data to evaluate carefully a HAP and for being lax in doing so. This has resulted in at least one court case, *City of Hartford* v. *Hills*,[14] wherein the central city has challenged HUD's approval of six HAPs from surrounding suburban communities in which the expected-to-reside numbers are alleged to be patently underestimated.

A United States Commission on Civil Rights study of HUD's enforcement activities concluded that "a principal weakness in HUD's fair housing program is its failure to divide its available resources between processing individual complaints and conducting community-wide investigations to identify patterns of housing discrimination and

to review compliance with all equal opportunity requirements in HUD programs."[15] These investigations would be "aimed at uncovering violators of Title VIII and countering discriminatory local practices and policies through the examination of state and local fair housing laws, the type and quality of activity conducted by fair housing agencies, zoning ordinances, marketing activities . . . mortgage financing practices . . . and data showing the racial composition of neighborhoods."[16]

A 1972 HUD self-analysis of its enforcement of site and neighborhood selection criteria concluded that strong top-level guidance is essential to success and that a more independent HUD Office of Equal Opportunity was needed. At the time the present paper was written, President Carter's Reorganization Task Force on Civil Rights Enforcement was considering recommendations to establish an outside impartial agency to monitor HUD and other government agency enforcement efforts. A strong national leadership role seems especially important under the Community Development Block Grant Program because it tends to shift enforcement responsibilities to state and local governments which receive entitlement funds based on a formula rather than on specific applications for categorical grants.

EVALUATION AND PROGNOSIS

Two issues are of overriding importance to the consideration of the

14. *City of Hartford* v. *Hills*, 408 F.Supp. 889 (D.Conn. 1976). Appeal pending in 2d cir.

15. U.S. Commission on Civil Rights, *The Federal Civil Rights Enforcement Effort — 1974*, vol.II, "To Provide . . . For Fair Housing." (Washington, DC: USGPO, 1974), p. 329.

16. U.S. Commission on Civil Rights, *The State of Civil Rights: 1977.* (Washington, DC: USGPO, 1978), p. 18.

past and potential future impact of federal policies on the availability and quality of housing and the quality of minority group housing environments. These issues concern the content of federal policies— their objectives and the strategies designed to pursue them—and the delivery systems involved in the implementation of these policies. As noted earlier, even the best of policies and programs are insufficient; the manner in which they are applied and the agents participating in their implementation will have substantial impacts on how well, if at all, policy objectives are realized.

The content of federal policies and the strategies employed to pursue them have, as we have noted, changed substantially over time. Abstracting from the above discussion, at least three approaches to housing and community development can be identified, each of which has had different effects on the minority housing situation. The most basic approach, that of eliminating the legal basis for discrimination is, by itself, insufficient. Housing markets, being highly decentralized and composed of a variety of public and private actors, clearly do not and have not substantially changed traditional behaviors in allocating housing in response to civil rights legislation alone. Real estate agents, lending institutions and local communities may continue discriminatory and exclusionary practices in more subtle and less obvious ways than before but with similar effects. Moreover, even if fair housing legislation alone was effective, this effect is likely to be felt only as new units are added to the housing market and by the few minority families who are able to break out of existing ghettos.

It would have little impact on the existing pattern of segregation developed over many years.

The greatest benefits of this legislation are likely to be in the influences it has over the construction and operation of more affirmative programs of housing supply and redistribution, and in the basis it provides for legal challenges to discrimination at both federal and state levels. In both these regards fair housing legislation has had some success: it has redirected the focus of federal housing and community development policies and given rise to a host of administrative regulations aimed at helping to insure integration goals. Moreover, it has stimulated a national awareness and similar legislation at the state and local levels. In a number of states, legal challenges to the exclusionary practices of suburbs have resulted in progressive and farreaching decisions (see, for example, *So. Burlington Township NAACP v. Township of Mt. Laurel*).[17]

A second approach to housing and community development that has been identified focuses on central cities and has been concerned with both physical redevelopment and socioeconomic development. As noted, this strategy may increase the supply of housing available to minorities, but has frequently resulted in a worsening of the segregation problem. At least part of the reason for this lies in the objectives this strategy aims to achieve. Integration objectives are secondary to the rejuvenation of central city fiscal resources or the rejuvenation of single neighborhoods. While, in the broadest sense, increases in integration of the central city as a whole may

17. *So. Burlington Country NAACP* v. *Township of Mt. Laurel*, 67 N.J.151, 336 A.

be achieved by both retaining and reattracting whites, this does little for integration at the micro-environment or neighborhood level. Similarly, when housing opportunities for blacks are limited only to central cities, the growth in black demand for housing will invariably result in increasing pressure on white neighborhoods with their eventual transition from white to black. Again, the segregation problem is increased.

In general, it is likely that pressures on particular neighborhoods and suburbs are relaxed only where housing opportunities for blacks exist throughout the metropolitan area. Thus, many white homeowner organizations, faced with the prospect of their neighborhood undergoing racial transition, have been the strongest advocates of a metropolitan-wide dispersal strategy. This third approach is likely to have the greatest promise of success, with the additional benefit that it facilitates central city redevelopment and the pursuit of fiscal related objectives without conflicting with integration objectives. This is the focus of the 1974 Community Development Act and recent policy statements by President Carter.

However, the dispersal strategy is not without its problems, among them being the extent to which integrated neighborhoods are desired, as opposed to the more simple objective of integrated suburbs. Current federal policy favors the micro-integration alternative, as evidenced by the use of census tracts as the basis for reporting subsidized housing needs in HAPs, the site selection criteria and affirmative marketing regulations of HUD, and by the content of the 1974 Act. Available data evaluating the efficacy of this approach, and the ability to maintain stable inter-racial neighborhoods, will probably not be forthcoming until these regulations are applied, over time, to a broad cross-section of areas. The social science literature does not give much cause for optimism in these regards. The key to success may be in the scale at which these programs are applied. As a larger number of jurisdictions within a metropolitan area come under the effective enforcement of these programs and regulations, the potential attractiveness of alternative locations for white households will diminish, increasing the prospects for stability.

While housing and community development programs have changed in the direction of more fully emphasizing integration goals, programs still must depend on the delivery system for their success. The delivery system is a diffuse one, involving a number of different participants and influences over them in the preparation, production, distribution, and service phases of the housing process. Federal actors and regulations play important roles in this process, but other levels of government, and especially the private sector—in the form of financial institutions, builders/developers and the real estate industry—play a more significant role. Each of these actors can be assessed as to the impacts they have in housing for minorities and, to date, these assesments have been disappointing. Widespread evidence exists to document continued and pervasive discriminatory practices, allowing both the private and public sectors to frustrate solutions to national fair housing and integration goals. It may be impossible to correct racial injustices within the capitalist free enterprise system as we know it today. Private enterprise cannot be expected to forego profit and to serve public purposes. The continued existence of a dual housing market suggests that there is profit in discrimination. But the public sector's track record is similarly disappointing. State and local governments have been able to frustrate solutions to national problems. Those who retain faith in governmental solutions to socioeconomic problems, however, can take some comfort in federal successes in bypassing local governments, a development that partially conflicts with decentralization efforts under various forms of a new federalism.

Because of the diffuse nature of the housing system, effective federal monitoring of the actions of the many actors, even if HUD were fully committed to this activity, would be impossible. This monitoring could conceivably be handled by local governments, but to date many have been willing parties to the discriminatory practices of the private sector. Similarly, state governments, despite their demands for an increased role in administering housing and community development programs, have not proven to be significant proponents of fair housing. This has caused some observers to argue for an increased role for minorities themselves in the monitoring process. While consistent with the emphasis on the citizen participation characteristic of other programs (such as Model Cities), this again places much of the burden for effecting desegregation on the victims of it. Moreover, citizen participation requirements, under the Housing and Community Development Act of 1974, have been reduced from levels specified in many earlier programs to that of soliciting citizen contributions only during the application process.

A potentially more effective solution would involve local governments under a system in which HUD required communities to be responsible for making good faith efforts at monitoring and regulating the private sector actors within their jurisdiction. In order to be effective, this requirement would have to be tied to community development block grant funding procedures, much in the same way that the HAP is tied to funding. Thus, as part of the application process, local communities may be required to enact fair housing ordinances and designate an appropriate community agency for overseeing local activities covered by the ordinance. Administrative funds to cover local costs may be taken from the block grant entitlement. Under this arrangement, HUD's responsibilities to monitor and evaluate these regulatory activities of local communities would be both administratively possible and in keeping with their other review responsibilities.

What of the future? The changes in design and emphasis of federal housing and racial policies has progressed markedly in the past three decades. The course is committed and is unlikely to change. Indeed, with increasing recognition of the relationship between housing and other social problems, such as school segregation, emphasis on changing housing patterns is likely to increase. What remains are many program details, each of which may have important affects on integration goals. Hopefully, as data begin to accumulate on the effects of existing thrusts, necessary changes will be made and enforcement efforts will proceed more vigorously.

Major progress in meeting national housing and community development goals relating to racial minorities may depend also on changes outside the housing system and by trends not easily influenced by public policy. Among these are: population growth rates, rates of household formation, changes in population structure (age and family size), the thinning-out of both central city and metropolitan area populations, the availability of credit, growth of the national economy and proportion of the GNP devoted to housing, trends in the cost and supply of energy, changes in levels of income and housing costs, and trends in renter-ownership ratios. All of these affect the housing market, the spatial shape of cities and the welfare of minorities.

Housing Discrimination: Policy Research, Methods and Results

By JULIET SALTMAN

ABSTRACT: Ten years ago, competent scholars thought it was impossible to measure racial discrimination directly. In 1977, HUD spent $1 million to measure the nature and extent of racial discrimination in housing. This nationwide Audit was the culmination of seven years of prior auditing conducted by local volunteer community organizations across the country. The Audit is a quasi-experimental field survey, which is used not only as a baseline for measuring changes in the extent and nature of housing discrimintion, but also as a means of implementing social change on local and national levels. Four action approaches have used Audit findings to expand equal housing opportunities for blacks: Legislation, Negotiation, Remuneration, and Litigation. These are illustrated in six local case studies. The nationwide Audit differed from prior community Audits in five ways, indicating rigorous controls and standardization. Results of the HUD Audit, though incomplete, reveal persistent massive racial discrimination in housing, with some geographical variations. Policy changes are sought to strengthen enforcement of federal fair housing laws on national and local levels.

Juliet Saltman is Professor of Sociology at Kent State University, and a consultant on urban programs for government and private agencies. Educated at the University of Chicago, Case Western Reserve University, and Rutgers University (Douglass College), she is the author of OPEN HOUSING AS A SOCIAL MOVEMENT, INTEGRATED NEIGHBORHOODS IN ACTION, OPEN HOUS-

This paper is based on preliminary analyses of the Housing Market Practices Survey, commissioned by the Department of Housing and Urban Development, and does not represent final analysis or interpretation. The HMPS revealed instances of discriminatory practices which are currently under investigation by the Department of Justice. So that such litigation will not be compromised, further release of HMPS data by HUD will be postponed, probably until some time in 1979.

ING: DYNAMICS OF A SOCIAL MOVEMENT, *and numerous articles on race relations, housing, and social change. She has been involved in the open housing movement at all levels, has served on the national boards of directors of OPEN, National Neighbors, and the National Committee Against Discrimination in Housing (NCDH).*

IN 1977, HUD spent $1 million to measure racial discrimination in housing across the country. Ten years earlier, competent race relations scholars and methodologists thought it was impossible to measure discrimination directly. Hubert Blalock, for example, wrote: "Discrimination must be measured indirectly . . . necessitating theoretical assumptions . . . which will be untestable."[1] As late as 1973, William Newman said: "The interesting thing is that sociologists rarely, if ever, actually study or measure discrimination or differential treatment. As Hubert M. Blalock observes, while these two terms are conceptually useful, sociologists actually study either segregation or various forms of inequality. Thus, while the concept of discrimination holds a central place in the literature on minority groups, it is never really operationalized in empirical research."[2]

The HUD national Audit of housing discrimination was the culmination of seven years of prior auditing conducted by volunteer community organizations in their local metropolitan areas. Such auditing became a vital growing activity of open housing and neighborhood stabilization groups throughout the nation. It began in 1969 and has continued to the present.

The Audit serves a double function: 1) it is a technique for measuring the extent and nature of racial discrimination in housing; and 2) its results can be used to implement constructive social change on both local and national levels. The Audit has thus become a mainstay of the open housing movement, because of its dual research and action potential. In more than thirty areas of the country, Audits have been used to increase awareness of the reality of racial discrimination in housing, and to expand equal housing opportunities and results for blacks. Such results have achieved significance only since the passage of federal open housing legislation in 1968, which became fully operative in 1971.[3]

In 1966, two years before this legislation was passed, Thomas Pettigrew said: "Residential segregation has proved to be the most resistant to change of all realms—perhaps, because it is so critical to racial change in general."[4] Eleven years later, in 1975, Karl Taeuber observed: "Despite court rulings and legislation clearly outlawing virtually all types of racial discrimina-

---

1. Hubert Blalock, *Toward A Theory of Minority Group Relations* (New York: John Wiley, 1967), pp. 15–18.
2. William M. Newman, *American Pluralism* (New York: Harper & Row, 1973), p. 200.

3. Title VIII of the 1968 Civil Rights Act made it illegal to discriminate in the sale or rental of property for reasons of race, religion, or national origin.
4. Thomas Pettigrew, Book Review of Karl and Alma Taeuber's *Negroes in Cities*, *American Journal of Sociology* 72 (July 1966): 112–113.

tion in housing, past patterns persist, and every investigation uncovers evidence that old impediments to free choice of residence by blacks continue."[5] Now, in 1977, such evidence is available for the first time for the nation, as a result of the HUD Audit.

LOCAL AUDITS

Four action approaches

Before describing the national Audit, I will describe some of the local Audits which paved the way for the giant one. The general method is a quasi-experimental field survey. The Audit uses trained matched pairs of black and white homeseekers, who attempt to secure identical housing at different controlled times. The results are then shared with the community, the housing industry, and other relevant agencies—including law enforcement officials.

The findings in housing Audits conducted by community organizations throughout the country show remarkable consistency. They document the continued existence of racially discriminatory practices in the real estate industry, as Karl Taeuber has noted. They reveal from seven to forty-four different techniques of denying access to housing to blacks. Each Audit typically takes from six to twelve months to plan, execute, analyze, summarize, present to the public, and pursue with relevant agencies. Since Audits were done primarily by volunteer groups, it is remarkable that so many were conducted, in view of the time, effort, and coordination needed for this action research.

Each community organization has used its findings in different ways as a strategy for change. Some have used multiple action approaches. The use of Audit findings may be categorized into four major types of action: 1) Legislation, 2) Negotiation, 3) Remuneration, 4) Litigation.[6] Each is briefly explained, followed by six local Audit examples.

The legislation approach involves the use of Audit data as a basis for obtaining new community legislation to implement open housing, such as an anti-steering law, or an anti-solicitation law. These are designed to supplement or reinforce existing federal and state open housing laws.

The negotiation approach involves direct communication with all those audited in the housing industry such as real estate company presidents, brokers, agents, rental managers, and owners. Private meetings are arranged with those audited, and the pertinent data is revealed to them in order to obtain a corrective affirmative action or voluntary compliance agreement. This, of course, is only feasible because the open housing laws exist and it is known that legal action may be taken against discriminators.

The remuneration or funding approach involves the use of Audit data to secure funding from private or public sources for the operation of a metropolitan open housing program. The Audit data establish the need for a staffed fulltime effort to deal with the problem of housing discrimination. Funding enables such an effort to implement the law through monitoring, and to secure compliance through constant staffed

5. Karl Taeuber, "Racial Segregation: The Persisting Dilemma," *Annals* 422 (November 1975): 87–96.

6. This is adapted from Juliet Saltman, "Three Strategies for Reducing Involuntary Segregation," *Journal of Sociology and Social Welfare* 4 (May 1977): 806–821.

activity involving community education and legal redress.

The litigation approach involves two options: 1) filing a lawsuit against discriminating companies and/or individuals; and 2) sending the Audit data to the U.S. Department of Justice for their investigation and possible litigation. In addition, other relevant enforcement agencies may be informed of Audit results in order to initiate additional investigation and official action to bring about compliance with the law.

All four approaches are generally preceded by a public hearing or meeting, at which the Audit data are revealed to the public for the first time, with media and area organizational representatives present. No identities are revealed at the public hearing. Letters are sent to nondiscriminators as well as discriminators after the public meeting. Discriminators are invited to meet privately with the Audit supervisors, to discuss findings and options for corrective action.

Each of the four types of action approaches is illustrated in the following accounts of specific housing Audits in six different communities. These accounts are presented chronologically, and indicate growing methodological sophistication and increasing use of litigation as a technique for constructive change.

Six examples

St. Louis—The first nationally publicized report of a fair housing Audit was the 1969 study conducted by the Greater St. Louis Committee for the Freedom of Residence. "Patterns of Discrimination" describes the group's investigation of practices in fifteen real estate companies

in St. Louis.[7] The study took eight months, involved thirteen black and white testers, and culminated in a legal suit filed in March 1970 against four of the companies audited. The case was scheduled for trial in St. Louis Federal Court on 14 June 1971, but just before then the Department of Justice entered into negotiations with the four companies for a possible consent decree.

After several months of negotiations, a fair housing agreement was negotiated and agreed to by the Justice Department and the Metropolitan St. Louis Real Estate Board, consisting of 509 firms, 740 brokers, and 3300 sales personnel. This was the first time such an agreement was reached between the Department of Justice and a metropolitan real estate board. The agreement consisted of an affirmative action program of compliance to be effected by all realtors and associates of the metropolitan board within sixty days. This was first reported in May 1970, and it roused all the other fair housing groups in the country.

Palo Alto—The second report of an Audit came from Palo Alto, California in 1971.[8] The Mid-Peninsula Citizens for Fair Housing described rental Audits they conducted in the previous year at a national fair housing conference. Using black and white teams drawn from a pool of 75 volunteer testers, MCFH audited apartment complexes in seven out of thirteen surrounding suburbs, and found discrimination in over half of them. MCFH first used their findings to communicate with the hous-

7. Hedy Epstein, "Patterns of Discrimination," Greater St. Louis Committee for Freedom of Residence (1970).

8. Mid-Peninsula Citizens for Fair Housing, "The Auditing Approach to Opening Housing," Palo Alto, California (1972).

ing industry to encourage voluntary corrective action in eliminating racial discrimination. They then utilized their findings to initiate hearings with the Palo Alto City Council, leading to the adoption of new legislation on apartment licensing in 1973. Finally, their Audit findings were sent to the U.S. Department of Justice, which filed a "pattern and practice" suit against the owner of eleven apartment complexes in the Palo Alto area.

When the suit was filed by the Justice Department, only 14 (1.2%) of a total of 1133 units were occupied by blacks, and 11 of the 14 were in buildings near the East Palo Alto ghetto. Six of the buildings had no nonwhite residents. These statistics alone, the Court emphasized, constituted a prima facie case of racial discrimination which it was up to the owner to disprove. In addition, however, substantial evidence of racial discrimination was indicated by rental agents and managers in inequitable application procedures, misrepresentation of availability of units, delaying tactics, and other devices to discourage minority occupancy.

An injunction was issued, and the owner was ordered to institute affirmative action, including: an educational program to inform all employees of their duties in compliance with Federal fair housing law; installation of uniform application procedures at all apartment complexes; maintenance and prominent posting of current and upcoming vacancy lists at the central rental office and at each apartment complex; submission of detailed reports to the Justice Department for a three year period, giving the name, address and race of each applicant, and a chronological account of each step taken in processing each application.

The court decision called the MCFH's testing activities "a reasonable means by which citizens may ascertain the compliance status of landlords with fair housing laws" and found the evidence compiled appropriate "in a proceeding of this nature."[9]

Akron—Akron was next, with its longitudinal auditing in that community resulting in successive feedback and wide area and national publicity.[10] All four action approaches were used by the Fair Housing Contact Service (FHCS), which was one of the first open housing organizations in the country to be funded under the Housing and Community Development Act of 1974. The funding was, in fact, one of the results of the four-year auditing program.

FHCS, a volunteer group founded in 1965 by the author, conducted three separate Audits from 1970 to 1974. Using 17 matched teams of trained black and white volunteer homeseekers, they surveyed over 5000 rental units and 40 major real estate companies. In all three Audits, massive evidence of racial discrimination was found, along with full awareness of the existence and implications of open housing laws. Audit III, for example, indicated that 67 percent of the apartment complexes and 85 percent of the real estate companies audited practiced some form of racial discrimination. Six forms of discrimination were categorized: availability, prices, requirements, remarks, locations, discourtesy.

Audit data were used to negotiate

9. *U.S.* v. *Youritan Construction Co.*-DC, N.D. Calif., No. C-71 1163 ACW 2/8/73.

10. Akron's Fair Housing Contact Service won the National Volunteer Award in 1973, a $5000 prize given in Washington, D.C. by the National Center for Voluntary Action.

with the real estate industry, resulting in a series of joint sales training sessions for agents. Legislation was passed by City Council banning solicitation and "For Sale" signs in an integrated area. Increased awareness of the link between segregated schools and segregated housing resulted in a school plan improving racial balance. The Department of Justice conducted investigations of the housing industry, after Audit findings were sent to them. And finally, after ten years of voluntary effort, the city and county together funded a staffed countywide open housing program to alleviate the problem of racial discrimination in housing.

Baltimore—Studies conducted in 1972 by Baltimore Neighborhoods, Inc. (BNI) found that almost two-thirds of Baltimore's black families could afford to buy homes or rent apartments in suburban areas. However, they were consistently discriminated against by real estate brokers and rental agents. The studies had two primary objectives: 1) to evaluate compliance with state and federal fair housing laws, and 2) to challenge the "common belief that the main reason few blacks live in suburbia is because they can't afford to."[11] The economic analysis was based on 1970 Census data and the Multiple Listing Sales Report for a six month period.

The discrimination study was an Audit of 93 apartment complexes by 45 biracial teams of testers, who found evidence of racial discrimination 45 percent to 55 percent of the time, even prior to making an application. The Audit used the "sandwich" method of sending a

team of a white, black, and another white to all buildings. Their written reports were then examined and compared for evidence of racial discrimination.

After the release of its findings, BNI initiated overtures to housing industry representatives. It proposed and secured an agreement for the development of an affirmative marketing program to eliminate discrimination and promote equal housing opportunities. Funds were sought from HUD to implement the program, and two years later such funds were granted. The program consisted of a demonstration and analysis of an affirmative marketing plan operated by a consortium of the real estate industry and BNI. The plan was to cover both public education as well as internal practices in the real estate companies, including employment practices. The two year project was budgeted for a total cost of $323,417.

Audits by BNI also resulted in a $200,000 lawsuit filed by tenants against the owner and manager of a 295 unit apartment complex in a suburb of Baltimore. The tenants charged the landlord with assigning blacks and whites to separate areas of the complex and failing to provide blacks with equal maintenance. They asked for an injunction against the alleged practices and actual and punitive damages. The Justice Department also filed suit against the same owner and manager for discriminatory practices in violation of federal fair housing laws.

Chicago—The Leadership Council for Metropolitan Open Communities (LCMOC) conducted a one-year auditing program in the suburbs of Chicago. They used the findings to file suit against nine real estate firms, charging racial steering

11. Baltimore Neighborhoods, Inc., "Discrimination Against Blacks," Baltimore, Md.: BNI (1972).

and other practices of racial discrimination in violation of federal law. Actual and punitive damages sought were close to one million dollars. An injunction was sought to halt the alleged discriminatory practices of the firms, and to enjoin them from any efforts to illegally influence the choices of prospective home-seekers on a racial basis.

Cleveland Heights—Three action approaches were used in the Cleveland metropolitan area: legislation, negotiation, and litigation. Eighteen months of auditing by 17 teams of black and white volunteers resulted in new legislation and a $1 million lawsuit filed by Heights Community Congress (HCC) against a real estate company owned by the president of the Cleveland Area Board of Realtors. Two major types of discriminatory practices found in the Audit were racial steering and negative neighborhood reference. Steering occurred at 70 percent of the companies audited. Whites were not shown homes in already integrated areas, and blacks were directed to such areas and not to all-white areas. Negative neighborhood references about integrated neighborhoods were made by 50 percent of the agencies to white homeseekers.

The findings were publicized at suburban city council meetings, which resulted in anti-steering legislation in 1973. The lawsuit was filed in 1975, after various cooperative educational approaches with the real estate industry proved unsuccessful.

THE NATIONAL AUDIT

Request for proposals

The wave of local Audits from 1969 to 1976 constituted a mini-movement within the open housing movement. This is not surprising to sociologists, who refer to the dissemination of new ideas as cultural diffusion—one of the principal elements of social change. But what *was* surprising was the sudden appearance, in the early summer of 1976, of a request for proposals (RFP H-2551) from HUD for a $1 million nationwide Audit, sponsored and funded by the Policy Development and Research Division. In September 1976 the contract was awarded to the National Committee Against Discrimination in Housing, a 27 year old nonprofit organization considered by many to be the unofficial "parent" of fair housing groups across the country.

Audit design

The project was called by HUD "Contract H-2551, to Evaluate the Impact of Civil Rights Enforcement Activity." NCDH named it the Housing Market Practices Survey (HMPS). Where and when the actual Audit was to take place was strictly confidential. Even the consultants who designed the Audit did not know all the areas where the Audit was to occur, though they did know the time period of the Audit.

The NCDH design was as follows: The country was divided into six regions, with six to eight metropolitan areas (SMSA's) within each region to be audited. Each region was under the direction of a Regional Coordinator, selected and trained by NCDH. A total of forty metropolitan areas were audited, selected randomly from all those having at least 100,000 people and 11 percent black population (93 percent of all black people in the country live in those areas.)

Of the forty metropolitan areas, five were designated "indepth" requiring 200 site visits, and the rest

(35) were "surface" areas ranging from 60 to 80 site visits depending on the size of the SMSA. In all, there were 3290 site visits made across the country to real estate companies and apartment complexes. The entire Audit was conducted in May-June and completed by July 1. A three day intensive training period was required for local Supervisors in each metropolitan area, and later for the auditors of each area.

Subcontractors were local fair housing groups, where these existed, and other organizations where there were no fair housing groups. Other subcontractors included Urban Leagues, civic organizations (League of Women Voters), academic research groups, etc. More than 800 persons participated. Subcontractors received stipends of $9–25,000 depending on the number of site visits made and the number of auditors and staff required.

Before the actual Audit took place, there was a Pilot Audit in one metropolitan area. And before the Pilot Audit took place, there was the writing and preparation of manuals of instruction for Regional Coordinators, Supervisors, and Auditors. In addition, forms were designed and prepared for sales and rental visits.

Methods of sampling within each SMSA were thoroughly discussed. After much deliberation, news ads randomly selected from a specified date in each SMSA were agreed on. These formed the basis of the sample of real estate offices and apartment complexes visited in each area. The news ad date preceded the Audit by no more than two weeks.

Timeline

The timeline was a very tight one, with minimal lead time for the actual

Audit. The Pilot Audit was conducted in Cincinnati in January, 1977. Cincinnati was selected logically because it was not too far from Washington (where NCDH is based), it has an active fair housing group (HOME), and was thought to be not too cold in January. (That turned out to be the winter when Cincinnati was buried under ten inches of snow during the Pilot Audit time! The only people out on the streets were the Auditors.) In February, there was an evaluation and revision of all materials, based on the Pilot Audit experience. In March, Regional Coordinators began their work in preparation for the actual Audit in late May and June.

Hypotheses

The HUD/NCDH Audit tested thirty-three hypotheses. The dependent variable was, of course, discrimination (or the absence of it). The independent variables were divided into three categories: 1) eight dealt with fair housing program variables, including the existence and effectiveness of local civil rights organizations, existence and effectiveness of private litigation, existence of Department of Justice Title VIII enforcement, and existence of a local fair housing ordinance; 2) eighteen independent variables dealt with housing market and demographic factors, such as, an excess supply of housing, socioeconomic status of homeseeker vs. neighborhood, degree of racial integration of neighborhood or complex, and 3) seven variables dealt with industry awareness and attitude, obtained through surveys conducted after the Audits were completed (by a separate research firm, under subcontract.)

Rigorous controls

The HUD/NCDH Audit differed from prior community Audits in five ways: 1) it used professionally prepared manuals of instruction and survey instruments, with all forms designed for computer analysis; 2) it required standardized intensive training of all personnel, coordinators, supervisors, and auditors; 3) it conducted scientific sampling procedures; centrally controlled; 4) it mandated rigorous daily controls; and 5) it used computerized procedures for data analysis.

The controls during the actual Audit were necessarily rigid because of the standardization required across the country. For example, mandated was a daily intensive review of the completed forms of each pair of Auditors. A rigorous call-back system from the Auditors in the field was instituted for daily use, e.g., black auditor phoned Supervisor right after visiting apartment, white partner phoned Supervisor within one hour right before going out to same apartment. This was to ensure proper timing and sequence, as well as problem-free site visits (i.e., no one there, office closed, etc.)

Early conclusions

The first examination of the completed data revealed: "Discrimination in housing still persists in the U.S. in most of the housing markets audited. It is quite overt in many cases and more subtle in others."[12] Among the early conclusions were these two: 1) none of the areas surveyed were without evidence of racial discrimination; 2) none pre-

12. *Trends in Housing*, Washington, D.C.: (Vol. 21, No. 3, Fall, 1977), p. 3.

sented a solid wall of exclusion; there were some agents who seemed to treat black and white homeseekers equally. An early preliminary analysis of the mid-central region's Audit results reinforced these conclusions. That region, coordinated by the writer, included eight SMSA's; five in Ohio—Akron, Canton, Cincinnati, Columbus, Dayton; two in Kentucky—Lexington and Louisville; one in Tennessee—Nashville (all randomly selected by computer, as noted.)

The levels of racial discrimination in that entire region ranged from 33 percent to 90 percent in rentals and from 38 percent to 96 percent in sales. These results were tabulated by local supervisors, according to instructions and training in the comparative analysis of completed paired reports.

The types of discrimination encountered varied in each metropolitan area among eight possible categories: availability, prices, requirements, locations, quality, racial remarks, "artful neglect", and courtesy. Only clear-cut differential treatment in one or more of the first five categories was considered discriminatory.

Thus, in Nashville, for example, of 68 total site visits, 30 involved rentals and 38 involved sales. Of the rentals, 10 or 33 percent indicted racial discrimination, 6 were inconclusive, and 14 showed no evidence of racial discrimination. Of the sales visits, 21 or 55 percent indicated racial discrimination, 9 were uncertain, and 8 showed no evidence of racial discrimination. Of the categories, Nashville's discrimination was highest for sales in price differentials (33 percent), and availability (20 percent). For rentals, the highest categories of discrimination were in availability (30 percent) and locations (18 percent).

Canton, Ohio's results were considerably different. Of 60 total Audit visits, 30 were rentals and 30 were sales. Of the rentals, 25 or 83 percent indicated racial discrimination; of the sales, 29 or 96 percent indicated racial discrimination. The types of discrimination encountered were highest for sales in location ("steering" blacks to black or integrated areas and whites to white areas) and prices. For rentals, the most discrimination was found in the categories of availability and requirements.

HUD DISCLOSURE AND POLICY IMPLICATIONS

The first partial release of the National Audit Data appeared in a press statement from HUD on April 17, 1978, the tenth anniversary of the passage of the federal open housing law. Secretary Harris called the results "appalling," referring to initial findings which indicated that blacks could be expected to be discriminated against 75 percent of the time when trying to rent apartments and 62 percent of the time when trying to buy homes.*

A comparison of the results geographically reveals that blacks encountered more than twice as much discrimination in homebuying in the north central states as in all other parts of the country, southern, western and northeastern states. Discrimination in rentals, however, was higher in the south, west and north-central states than in the northeastern states.

* These percentages are based on attempts to find housing, an attempt being defined as four visits to rental complexes or real estate agents.

The early results were incomplete, with additional findings to be released over the next six to eight months, as they were obtained and analyzed. No attempt had yet been made to analyze the data for locational "steering" on a national basis. It was estimated that the extent of discrimination found would be higher when the analysis was completed.

Policy changes which may result from the Audit findings appear to be of two types: legislative and remunerative. Both relate to stronger enforcement of existing laws. Secretary Harris, in her public disclosure of the preliminary Audit analysis, referred to the need for pending congressional legislation that would increase the enforcement power in HUD and the U.S. Department of Justice. At the same time, she announced a $500,000 federal project to test whether local fair housing agencies can aid in the enforcement of fair housing laws.

There are three bills before Congress, two in the House and one in the Senate, that would enlarge the Federal Fair Housing Law's (Title VIII) enforcement power.[13] There is little question that this legislation is needed, in view of the fact that massive racial discrimination still exists, ten years after the passage of federal fair housing law. Not only was that law weak from its inception, but the implementation of it was even weaker by HUD itself. Par-

13. The Edwards-Drinan (House) bill includes cease-and-desist powers for HUD and a litigation fund for plaintiffs in discrimination lawsuits. The Spellman-Holtzman (House) bill would give the HUD Secretary authority to initiate lawsuits to enforce Title VIII, if voluntary compliance has not occurred within 30 days after a complaint was filed. The Mathias (Senate) bill is similar to the Spellman-Holtzman bill.

tially, this was due to the inadequacies of the law, which did not allow HUD to enforce it effectively. Much was also due to insufficient allocation of funds to permit enough staff to conduct prompt, vigorous investigation and apply strong sanctions against law-breakers.

If racial discrimination in housing is to end in this country, the fair housing laws must be enforced by the same means used to obtain compliance with other laws. Otherwise, the fair housing law is ineffectual, the million dollar Audit will have been conducted in vain, and the nation will continue to have apartheid, American style.

CHICAGO

HOUGHTON MIFFLIN UPDATE:

Morlan

AMERICAN GOVERNMENT
Policy and Process
Third Edition
Robert L. Morlan
University of Redlands
About 840 pages / paper
Instructor's Manual
Just published

In a highly readable style, Morlan concisely yet fully describes how the contemporary American political system works. His Third Edition continues to engage student interest with its emphasis on realistic political dynamics and on the critical contemporary issues of social policy. His inclusion of numerous case studies stimulates active learning situations where students confront issues and come to understand complex decision-making processes. New or revised topics in this edition include presidential character and symbolism, congressional ethics, welfare reform proposals, national energy policy, human rights in international policy.

Ray

GLOBAL POLITICS
James Lee Ray
University of New Mexico
About 448 pages / Instructor's Manual / Just published

Ray's introduction to international relations focuses on three areas: post World War I history, scientific analysis, and the future. While turning attention to problems and crises that demand immediate concern in a global system, Ray also explains how historical, quantitative, and philosophical approaches complement each other in interpreting international affairs.

Wiarda/Kline

LATIN AMERICAN POLITICS AND DEVELOPMENT

Howard J. Wiarda and
Harvey F. Kline
Both of University of
Massachusetts, Amherst
About 560 pages / Early 1979

A comprehensive study of Latin American politics embracing each country on the continent, isthmus, and in the Caribbean, with special emphasis on Argentina, Brazil, Mexico, and Cuba. Studies of countries contributed by noted scholars offer a rich variety in contemporary interpretations of political development; yet parallel organization permits consistent topic coverage and ease of comparison.

Grieves

CONFLICT AND ORDER
An Introduction to International Relations

Forest L. Grieves
University of Montana
409 pages / Instructor's
Manual / 1977

A concise survey of major theories, emphasizing the nation-state system and supported by in-depth case studies. Grieves structures his text around the impetus toward conflict and the search for order.

Feit/Braunthal/Dittmer/King
Kline/Ryavec

GOVERNMENT AND LEADERS: An Approach to Comparative Politics

Edward Feit, University of
Massachusetts, Amherst
Gerard Braunthal, University of
Massachusetts, Amherst
Lowell Dittmer, University of
California, Berkeley
Jerome King, University of
Massachusetts, Amherst
Harvey Kline, University of
Massachusetts, Amherst
Karl Ryavec, University of
Massachusetts, Amherst
552 pages / 1978

Innovative study of leadership and the political systems of Great Britain, France, West Germany, U.S.S.R., Cuba, and China. Details each country's governmental operations, political character, and the role of its leaders.

For adoption consideration, request examination copies from your regional Houghton Mifflin office.

Houghton Mifflin

Dallas, TX 75235   Geneva, IL 60134
Hopewell, NJ 08525   Palo Alto, CA 94304
Boston, MA 02107

Book Department

INTERNATIONAL RELATIONS AND POLITICS

ALBERT FISHLOW, CARLOS F. DIAZ-ALEJANDRO, AND ROGER D. HANSEN. *Rich and Poor Nations in the World Economy*. Pp. xii, 264. New York: McGraw-Hill, 1978. $6.95.

W. HOWARD WRIGGINS AND GUNNAR ADLER-KARLSSON. *Reducing Global Inequities*. Pp. xiv, 193. New York: McGraw-Hill, 1978. $5.95.

In its 1980s Project, The Council on Foreign Relations seeks to identify for a New International Economic Order "goals . . . compatible with the perceived interests of most states, despite differences of ideology and level of economic development . . . (which) lead to the satisfaction of the most basic needs of all the people in the shortest possible time." The Council describes the Project as the largest studies-research project in its history. It includes 10 working groups, involves more than 300 participants, and nearly 100 authors from more than a dozen countries. These companion books report what the Council describes as part of a "stream of studies" planned for the 1980s.

Albert Fishlow was asked to examine, within the present world economic framework, "A New International Economic Order: What Kind?" With strong pressures in some quarters for "collective self reliance" among the countries of the South, Carlos F. Diaz-Alejandro considers alternatives in his "Delinking North and South: Unshackled or Unhinged?"

On his assumption that most southern leaders want reforms in the international economy rather than a "closed" economic system in the South, Fishlow offers a number of proposals. They include: more generous and patient lending to the South; absorption by international agencies of part of private loans; international rules to liberalize trade in labor-intensive products, with penalties for unfair competition; financial flows rather than buffer stocks to stabilize commodity markets, but with a global reserve of food to guard against shortfalls; lower cost transfer of technology, along with international monitoring of the multinationals. He also proposes at least one international tax on, for example, common ocean resources, pollution, and nonrenewable resources, to be distributed to meet "minimum needs" in poverty sectors, and to finance special programs such as family planning. Fishlow thinks the Conference on International Cooperation provides the framework to negotiate the type of proposals he offers for a New International Economic Order.

While suggesting that the time has come for southern countries to increase trade among themselves, Diaz thinks the developing countries will fare better in a competitive international market than in a system of "collective self-reliance" in the South. He advocates selective de-linkage and linkage: by commodities, and by countries—North or South—capitalist or socialist. Meanwhile, Diaz recommends going considerably further than Fishlow in reforming international rules governing the multinationals, international investment, and transfer of technology. He also proposes political mechanisms to control oceans, space, and Antarctica; and discusses the virtues of Keynesian ITO Commodity Agreements.

In "Third World Strategies for Change: The Political Context of North-South Interdependence," W. Howard Wriggins appraises trends, and the future, in international relations and southern countries' goals. He then weighs six major leverages of the "politically weak" to redress imbalances. With examples for each, he treats: building coalitions such as OPEC; regional coalitions such as the Organization of African Unity, the Association of Southeast Asian States, and the Andes Pact; universal coalitions such as The Group of 77 and the Non-Aligned, working with UN bodies; affiliations with major powers to pursue, on their own, problems as well as Northern patrons; threatening and precipitating war, involving major powers; and irregular violence such as national liberation movements and terrorism. For each category, Wriggins itemizes in considerable detail conditions, pros and cons, and future prospects.

With the one-quarter of the world population in the poverty class as a primary target in economic reform, three authors address the need for new development strategies: Roger D. Hansen in his critique of the Fishlow-Diaz-Fagen papers, in "The Political Economy of North-South Relations: An Overview and an Alternative Approach;" Richard R. Fagen in "Equity in the South;" and Gunnar Adler-Karlsson in "Eliminating Absolute Poverty."

A few touchstones in their thinking include: Hansen—The elite-poverty gap in the South is widening; Fagen—the bargaining to increase the South's equity is strengthening the elite; Adler-Karlsson—on balance, the multinationals are having an adverse effect on poverty.

In considering correctives, Fagen believes profound changes in development strategies and leadership are required at international and national levels, including eventual transformation of northern society—with minimum and maximum income and consumption levels both in the North and South—effecting transformations comparable to the Chinese and Cuban models for the South. Hansen, however, sees a growing climate of North-South responsiveness to the poverty problem, especially with approaches which call for less apparent costs to the upper and middle income groups. He further sees promise in a mix of Basic Human Needs and Human Rights which would make them more acceptable to southern leaders. Hansen offers a proposal for a northern comprehensive poverty program of about $20 billion a year.

The reviewer adds this postscript. Contrary to the neglect and opposition during the past 25 years, of a quorum of international developers and their country understudies, most country leaders (as Hansen hints) are vitally interested in pragmatic ways to productively involve their masses in building a popular base. For even the most backward poverty areas, there are demonstrated techniques of leader-people dialogue-planning to build confidence and political will, and examples of how to harness existing leadership and institutions to bring beginnings of improved administration, services, and economic programs. Every country has available the resources for the beginnings, say, in two years, with the suggested $20 billion a year for follow-up. The requisite: new international and national organizations for the poverty groups, headed and staffed by experienced, committed personnel.

DANA D. REYNOLDS
International Center for Dynamics
   of Development
Arlington
Virginia

ALISTAIR HORNE. *A Savage War of Peace: Algeria 1954–1962*. Pp. 608. New York: The Viking Press, 1978. $19.95.

A Savage War of Peace leads general readers skillfully through the complex events which culminated in Algeria's independence; it also provides specialists with important new insights, especially in its analyses of information Horne gained in interviewing surviving protagonists. Algerians, both in Algeria and abroad, and loyal Frenchmen, as well as those freed by deGaulle's 1968 amnesty, speak openly about who led the 1961 Algiers putsch.

As one might expect from the author of three major studies of post-1870 France, Horne's most convincing chapters deal with French, rather than Muslim Algerian, agonies. Several issues, like torture and deGaulle's abandonment of *Algerie francaise* (and hence a million settlers and his own army), ring somewhat false if one denies France's legitimacy in Algeria and accepts that of the FLN, as most Algerians had done by 1958. Horne's French orientation is best illustrated by his sympathetic evocation of the dilemma of General Challe, who reluctantly agreed to lead the 1961 coup attempt largely because he could not honorably abandon his Algerian troops (*harkis*) to the tender mercies of the FLN. Challe's drama is valid only if its logical resolution, *Algerie francaise*, is assumed to be morally admissible. Horne considers it valid drama.

In fact, save for a brief chapter lauding the FLN's wartime social achievements, the consistent implication here is that the Algerian people were essentially terrorized into accepting FLN leadership. How else can one consider "tragic" deGaulle's failure to outmaneuver the FLN and negotiate peace instead with Kabyle separatists, Muslim loyalists, gallicized intellectuals, and guerrilla leaders alienated from their leaders in Tunis? Still, Horne's account significantly deepens our understanding of the FLN, its internal crises, and its relations with France. Nevertheless, one regrets that this work's deservedly wide reception may popularize an essentially French (albeit humane French) view of the conflict.

In his preface, Horne thanks Anthony Nutting for "graciously withdrawing from an identical project where his wide knowledge of the Arab world might have stood him in better stead than mine." That the two did not opt to collaborate is unfortunate—a joint work might have transcended, while incorporating, Horne's approach to the events resulting from France's refusal (in deGaulle's apt phrase) "to marry her time."

Nevertheless, this is magnificent history, thorough, scholarly, and literate. No student of insurgency, the Maghreb, the twentieth century, or—and especially—contemporary France should miss it.

RICHARD SIGWALT

Radford College
Radford
Virginia

FRIEDRICH V. KRATOCHWIL. *International Order and Foreign Policy: A Theoretical Sketch of Post-War International Politics*. Pp. xix, 298. Boulder, CO: Westview Press, 1978. $20.00

This is in sketch form, a self-contained theory deriving ordered interaction among states from interaction itself, at both its "strategic" (bargaining) and "symbolic" (signaling) levels of expression (pp. 1–2, 74–76, 209–210). Pending extreme diversity, irrationality, and multipolarity, frequent interactions make common background knowledge (about decision premises or inference rules of each actor) the ordering principle—a surrogate for global coercion/consensus—to guide bargaining away from conflictual outcomes (Part I). The US/USSR (1945–72) case classifies those premises—historical analogies ("Munich," "encirclement"), metaphors ("containment," "liberation"), myths ("two camps," "Red Scare"), doctrines (defense, deterrence), and laws (SALT I)—*en route* to a bipolar order (Part II). The commentary presumes an advanced reading competence.

Order may prove a wiser focus than conflict, since it can address other problems besides conflict, and order qua political laws can complement social-scientific laws to explain behavior—conflictual and otherwise. International order is especially apt as it differs from domestic and world order, not in quality as the author argues, but in complexity: While order elsewhere may entail the presence of overarching consensus/coercion, order among nations entails its absence (between blocs) but also its presence (within blocs) and resurgence (over time). Hence, the best theory of international order may be a general theory of order.

An "interaction" approach illumines the evolutionary process toward order by replacing single (synoptic) with sequential (iterative) interactions, thus permitting a dynamic theory about the rules of the game. Alas, the very birth of those rules eludes explanation since criteria governing even the choice of historical precedents—for example, Munich 1938—to guide rule formation are obscure. Nor does the approach anticipate a need for rule formation without historical precedents, as when newly independent states lacking a history enter a disordered system—a "lord of the flies" scenario. This calls for a revised approach to explain rule creation.

The US/USSR ordering process is a strategic case—recent enough to remain manipulable via new interaction patterns guided perhaps by this very theory, yet pervasive enough to facilitate manipulation elsewhere. But other case-studies might better depict the overall process from even lower levels of order (the Mideast) to still higher thresholds (the EEC) than observed here. They might then gauge the theory's limits—indeed, gauge whether greater interaction and attendant background knowledge than observed here threaten over-order or rigidity, including intolerance toward new actors on the world stage.

CRAIG McCAUGHRIN

University of Pennsylvania
Philadelphia

ZARA S. STEINER. *Britain and the Origins of the First World War: The Making of the 20th Century.* Pp. vi, 305. New York: St. Martin's Press, 1977. $16.95.

This is an intriguing, thought-provoking volume, in an excellent series, which probes both within and beyond the traditional reservoirs of diplomatic research and balances the evidence gained therein with that drawn from selective monographs, memoirs, contemporary articles and accounts. It is well-written, heavily documented and, in some respects, most engrossing.

The author approaches the subject of British policy vis-à-vis Europe from the premise that the time-honored and realistic diplomacy of detachment, a "splendid isolation" of sorts, was abandoned somewhat hastily despite the assumption that involvement would entail sacrifice and tragedy on a scale beyond comprehension. The culprits in this departure from practicality, it seems, were for the most part dead at the time of the catastrophe of August, 1914. But the legacy of decisions made in the interests of national security, party politics, and even personal ego hovered above and haunted English statesmen of that fateful summer as effectively as if the bodies themselves were present. And not all of those in the decisionmaking councils in Britain at that time realized the degree to which they were shackled to the past.

The approach to and the decision for war, as the writer demonstrates, seemed to betray an unnatural, almost artificial manufacturing of crisis. A United Kingdom that stood supreme, with a mixture of world envy and pride as its chief name-identification, having no immediate association with either the assassins of Sarajevo or the Serbian irritation to Austria, reacted with a blend of deepening concern, or alarm, or studied hostility, patriotic fervor, righteous indignation, and resignation in such a fashion as to transform a hereditary defensive posture to one of continental commitment and intervention.

The vehicle selected by the writer in presenting the evidence and the conclusions drawn therefrom is that of case study, specifically the isolation of impulses, trends, pressure groups, ideas and anxieties, political factions and personalities, and power blocs. Consequently, the reader is led from the political - economic - imperial - military background of 1901 through the evolution of the shifting sands of alliance-making, war scares, naval and economic rivalries, quests for a type of détente, and a final polarization of powers in an attitude of confrontation. The reader is then directed through a rather complicated assessment of British internal politics for the decade preceding July, 1914, which is handled quite satisfactorily, considering the fractured and oftentimes contradictory nature of British politics at that time, or, for that matter, any time.

Next comes a long and excellent inquiry into the moods and theories driving the imperial professionals— "The Foreign Office" and "The Military and Naval Establishments" respectively. In the reviewer's opinion this chapter alone makes the book worthwhile, the other sections serving to reinforce this singular contribution. Finally, and knowing as we do the outcome of that melancholy summer, one reaches "The July Crisis" when all the vector forces came to play their specific and collective roles in the decision for war—the heritage of obligation, the strategic consideration, the public's mood, the arrogance of pride and the fear that a once-dominant position might evaporate. Thus did the war come to that generation, which was nearly exterminated, to either uphold or prevent balances from shifting or the calendar from turning.

CALVIN W. HINES

Stephen F. Austin
State University
Nacogdoches
Texas

ELLEN KAY TRIMBERGER. *Revolution from Above: Military Bureaucrats and Development in Japan, Turkey, Egypt, and Peru.* Pp. viii, 196. New Brunswick, NJ: Transaction Books, 1978. $14.95.

Revolution from Above is a significant, pioneering, and provocative study on revolution. Trimberger's purpose in writing this book is to "develop a model of revolution from above by military bureaucrats as distinct from either coup d'etat or mass—bourgeois or socialist— revolution from below." Her original model of revolution from above later was revised in light of recent "attempts at development through military initiative in Nasser's Egypt and Velasco's Peru."

In five well-written and coherent chapters and a lucid conclusion, the author, in the reviewer's judgment, has fairly attained her main objective. Trimberger defines a revolution from above on the basis of five characteristics: the extralegal takeover of political power and the initiation of change is organized; there is little or no mass participation in the revolutionary takeover; extralegal takeover of power is accompanied by very little violence; initiation of change is . . . with little appeal to radical ideology; and military bureaucrats destroy the economic and political foundation of the aristocracy or upper class. The author then proceeds to document and analyze the case of the Meiji Restoration of 1868 in Japan, and of the Ataturk takeover of 1923 in Turkey. She further discusses Nasser's revolution in Egypt and Velasco's takeover in Peru.

This volume challenges the conventional wisdom that revolutions originate mainly from below, from the disgruntled and impoverished masses of peasants and workers in the third world. Through a comparative historical and structural approach to military bureaucrats and development, in Japan, Turkey, Egypt, and Peru, Trimberger argues that revolutions from above are the rule and not the exceptions. In addition to the theoretical significance of Trimberger's study, her research also offers clues on the nature and consequences of revolutions in selected societies of Asia, Africa, and Latin America.

On the other hand, the reviewer is constrained to ask the following fundamental questions: How valid and reliable are the author's conclusions on revolution from above, based solely on four case studies? Are her units of analysis comparable? To what extent is the role of context, values, meaning, and symbolism crucial in her analysis of the four cases? How useful is her style of analysis for theory construction? How relevant is this volume to events in Southeast and East Asia—Marcos' Philippines or Park's Korea?

The questions posed do not in any way detract from Trimberger's imaginative, interesting, and challenging publication. The author and her publisher are to be congratulated for this volume of high quality and readability.

MARIO D. ZAMORA

The College of William and Mary
Virginia

PAUL WILKINSON. *Terrorism and the Liberal State*. Pp. xiv, 257. New York: John Wiley, 1977. $14.95.

It is possible that no single word provokes stronger emotions and reactions in the modern world than the word terrorism. Terrorists and their activities often dominate the day's headlines. And the controversies between terrorists' supporters and their opponents linger on, causing more problems even as the headlines from each succeeding terrorist act fades. Nowhere is this controversy more heated and troublesome than in western governments and societies. Yet very little serious scholarly study or writing has been done in this problem area. It almost seems that academicians have been reluctant to write or do research in this important area of study, but that era of reluctance may be ending with the publication of what is sure to be a controversial study by Paul Wilkinson.

Wilkinson is a Senior Lecturer in Politics at University College, Cardiff, United Kingdom. His book, *Terrorism and the Liberal State*, represents an extremely ambitious undertaking. The author takes terrorism, which he defines as the use of violence to achieve political goals, as a given in our modern world. He suggests that the problem of terrorism will not simply fade away, and it is important that we study it carefully to ascertain its effect on society in general and the so-called western governments and societies in particular. This is an extremely ambitious undertaking. Wilkinson is not modest in his goals. As he himself describes it in the preface "a main concern of the present work is to try to improve our understanding of the problem of terrorism against the whole background of contemporary international relations and continuing ideological conflict."

This study is interesting primarily because it is so ambitious. The author does not deal in minutiae. He asks the big questions. For example, are there any circumstances when terrorism can be morally justifiable in a liberal democratic society. He poses a number of such pointed questions; in the heart of the book he concentrates on the peculiar problems which revolutionary political terrorism raises in liberal democracies. In this section he also discusses and evaluates the means which a liberal democratic state can use to prevent and deter acts of terrorism both external and internal.

One can quarrel with some of Wilkinson's conclusions, but his major point is well taken. Liberal democracies are particularly vulnerable to acts of international terrorism; this area of study has been long neglected. Wilkinson's book is an interesting step in the right direction of further study.

PHILIP J. HANNON

Texas Tech University
Lubbock

AFRICA, ASIA AND LATIN AMERICA

JOHN CHANCE. *Race and Class in Colonial Oaxaca*. Pp. xiv, 250. Stanford: Stanford University Press, 1978. $14.00.

John Chance's case history of the city of Oaxaca during the colonial period is a superb study, combining the methods and insights of history, sociology, and anthropology. By applying the theoretical framework developed by Max Weber to well documented data, obtained through archival research, Chance has provided new insights into the evolving socioeconomic structure of this city—then known as Antéquera—from the time of the conquest to the early nineteenth century. His work also draws on the contributions of several leading contemporary social scientists who have written on the subjects of social stratification, and race and ethnic relations, including Gerhard Lenski, Oliver Cox, Frederick Barth, Marvin Harris, and Charles Wagley. The main thesis of this book is that the elaborate system of legal categories, known as the *sistema de castas*, did not correspond to the static, estate-like system of social stratification portrayed by numerous historians. Rather, such ranked ethno-racial categories as peninsulars, creoles, castizos, pardos, free mulattos, mulatto slaves, Negro slaves, and Indians reflected the viewpoint of a light-skinned Spanish elite who elaborated increasingly finer distinctions among racially-defined groups, to defend their eroding power as a dominant minority in the Spanish-American empire. Paradoxically, as the author points out, the *sistema de castas*, in its legal form, became more rigid precisely during a period of increasing social mobility associated with a local boom in commerce and manufacturing, thus creating a growing discrepancy between the feudally-derived *sistema de castas* and a capitalist-oriented class system.

Chance shows how racial mixture, associated with high rates of social mobility (both upwards and downwards), meant that class and race were no longer strongly correlated, except at the top and bottom of colonial society, in Oaxaca after the middle of the seventeenth century. For the growing middle sector of artisans, small merchants, and skilled laborers, who were predominantly found in urban centers, racial identity became ambiguous as the boundaries between colonizers and colonized, or among whites, blacks, and Indians became increasingly blurred. In fact,

Chance argues in a convincing fashion that race relations in colonial Oaxaca, especially relations between 'white Spaniards' and people with Negroid phenotypic features, were probably very similar to those found in contemporary Brazil. In short, wealth enabled a person who might otherwise be classified as colored to attain 'white' (Spanish) status through strategic marriage alliances or by manipulating the complex and confusing system used to register one's status at birth, marriage or on other occasions. While not denying the existence of more subtle forms of discrimination, the author clearly debunks the notion that colonial Mexico was characterized by a rigid hierarchy of racially defined strata. The author also invalidates several other ideas, such as Gideon Sjoberg's position that all preindustrial cities had a rigid caste-like social system.

Although this book is theoretically sophisticated, this reader was somewhat disappointed that Chance did not draw on the insights or even mention the works of other social anthropologists or sociologists who have written on social stratification and ethnicity, such as Rodolfo Stavenhagen or Theotonio Dos Santos. Both of these authors, for example, make a distinction between the concepts of class structure and social stratification in the context of Latin America, within a more sophisticated Marxist perspective, a perspective which would have been useful for analyzing the data presented by Chance. It was also surprising that in dealing with the early transition from pre-Hispanic society to colonial Mexico, he did not at least refer to the concept of the tributary, or so-called Asiatic mode of production, as developed by Maurice Godelier, the French anthropologist, which has been the object of so much controversy among anthropologists and historians alike. Nevertheless, the book is, on the whole, well written, well documented, and refreshingly innovative on the topic of class and race in colonial Mexico.

FRANS J. SCHRYER

University of Guelph
Ontario

ALVIN D. COOX and HILARY CONROY, eds. *China and Japan: A Search for Balance Since World War I.* Pp. xxii, 468. Santa Barbara, CA: American Bibliographical Center, 1978. $19.75.

WOLF MENDL. *Issues in Japan's China Policy.* Pp. xii, 178. New York: Oxford University Press, 1978. $18.50.

These two works on Sino-Japanese relations provide a solid and useful background to August's Treaty of Peace and Friendship between Tokyo and Peking. As their titles indicate, the author/editors have viewed those relations from different perspectives. Wolf Mendl has concentrated almost entirely on Japan and the evolution of her post World War II China policy. More than three quarters of his text is devoted to a chronological analysis of the period since Prime Minister Tanaka's visit to Peking in 1972.

Alvin D. Coox and Hilary Conroy broaden the view by pushing back to World War I and by encompassing both nations in their focus, although limitations on evidence necessitate much closer attention to Japanese than Chinese motivations during the recent period. In a series of seventeen articles, their work moves slowly from the Shantung Problem and the Twenty-One Demands up to the present, converging with Mendl's material only in the last quarter of the book. The one, a tightly-focused monographic analysis, the other, a somewhat sprawling series of disparate essays, the goals of both are the same—to explore the hows, whys, and where-do-we-go-from here's of this summer's treaty.

As they converge, both works stress the present and past heterodoxy of Japanese views of China, and both give considerable attention to the policy making process in Japan—specifically the process that led to detente with China. There are minor points of disagreement. Yung H. Park, in an excellent article on the Tanaka period, holds that public opinion, the press, and opposition parties had virtually no part in Japan's China policy decisions; Mendl finds it difficult to gauge the importance of those

elements, but sees them as definite factors in the process. Both cite the business community as the prime advocate of improved relations with China, and businessmen as much quicker to act than the politicians. Business, however, was divided, too, with articulate sectors tied by interest to Taiwan. Both cast careful glances into the future of Sino-Japanese relations, and as Tang Tsou, Tetsuo Najita, and Hideo Otake put it, see a relationship "not of alliance but not of confrontation either." There is no consensus as to the relative importance of factors which might destroy detente. Mendl gives special prominence to Korea as such a factor, while Tsou and others see Taiwan as the major potential irritant, at least in this decade.

Although both books make valuable contributions to an understanding of the Sino-Japanese relationship, neither is perhaps the ideal. Mendl's chief contributions are his chronological coverage of policy developments in Japan and the useful data in his appendices. He tends to make his points at rather inordinate length, obscuring some of the basic excitement of his material, and his conclusions are somewhat timid, which may, of course, extend the shelf life of his work in a world of continuous change.

Coox and Conroy note that few guidelines were set for the contributors to their volume, and thus the search for the balance of their sub-title is carried to a number of rather obscure corners. While all the essays are of a very high order of scholarship and discrete interest, not all contribute a great deal to the main theme. After an excellent introduction by Robert A. Scalapino and an "overview" by Chalmers Johnson, there follow a long series of articles, some of which revise some rather minor misconceptions or illuminate rather minor episodes in past Sino-Japanese relations. As the chronological coverage of the collection moves into the post World War II period, the focus broadens from the forgotten corner to the general theme. The shift is one in genre and is abrupt; the two sections of the book do not hold together. The earlier essays contribute to chronological advance, but not really to chronological development and they therefore seem minor, and unfortunately sò. The volume is a very fine showpiece of the varieties of perspective, technique, and style that a group of scholars can train on a single field of enquiry—a useful pedagogical tool if not the perfect collection of essays.

Two works on a single theme—the monograph, published by a prestigious press in a dignified and lasting form, or the collection of essays, uneven and disparate, in its rather flimsy and slick trade edition? The essays have it, for despite a lack of continuity or unity, they are an interesting and thought-provoking group of papers. Their editors have demonstrated, too, that with little loss and a good deal more verve, Mendl's subject can be condensed into a couple of relatively brief articles.

R. KENT LANCASTER
Goucher College
Baltimore

MICHAEL C. HUDSON. *Arab Politics: The Search for Legitimacy.* Pp. xi, 434. New Haven, CT: Yale University Press, 1977. $22.50.

There are now many works dealing with various aspects of the processes of change and modernization in the Arab world. Professor Hudson's weighty volume literally covers the Arab sea, air, and sand front from beyond "the shores of Tripoli" to the Tigris-Euphrates, the Arab Peninsula and the Persian Gulf. This is the first systematic, basic, comparative study of political behavior. The author draws on all the social sciences—history, political science, anthropology, religion—to illustrate and deepen his analysis. Part I discusses political and social change in the Arab world and deals with the elements of Arab identity, cultural pluralism, the crisis of authority, the legacy of imperialism, and modernization and its consequences. Part II provides a series of eighteen case studies of the politics of legitimation in the various Arab States—Tunisia, Libya, Egypt, Syria, Lebanon, and Saudi Arabia.

Professor Hudson considers the current malaise in Arab politics the consequence of insufficient legitimacy accorded by the people to their ruling structures, ideologies, and leaders. In his view, the basic requirement for legitimacy, or meaningful political participation, has not been met anywhere in the Arab world and is not likely to be so in the near future. He expects continued turbulence in Arab politics before the threshold of genuine structural legitimacy is reached. But the solution is clear enough—the development of meaningful broad-based participation in the political process in accordance with accepted procedures "so that government will be more responsive and responsible to public opinion." That is a very large order, indeed.

Beyond their volatility, Professor Hudson found two aspects of Arab politics both fascinating and puzzling, and he therefore concentrated his attention on them. These were "the lack of congruence between all-Arab identifications and aspirations and the political realities of discrete political systems; and the multiple effects of rapid, uneven modernization on Arab political culture and subcultures" (p. ix).

All students of the Middle East will welcome publication of this volume, which should be read and pondered by those who deal with the problems of the Arab world. It is well-organized, clearly presented and should help the reader to understand Arab politics and come to grips with the grave problems of the Middle East.

HARRY N. HOWARD
Middle East Institute
Washington D.C.

OSCAR J. MARTÍNEZ. *Border Boom Town: Ciudad Juárez Since 1848.* Pp. xvi, 231. Austin, TX: University of Texas Press, 1978. $12.95.

Border Boom Town is more than a tale of two cities, Ciudad Juárez and El Paso; it is a story of two societies, Mexico and the United States, and of the 1900-mile border between them. Nowhere else in the world, Oscar Martínez notes, is there a frontier so long with an income differential so wide. Born of the 1846–48 war between the two countries, the border has found its historic problems made more acute by rapid urbanization and by massive migration of Mexican labor to the United States. Ciudad Juárez, originally known as Paso del Norte, has become Mexico's largest border city, mushrooming from 50,000 inhabitants in 1940 to over 500,000 today. Half of that growth has come since 1960 alone. External factors stemming from the city's location have, in the view of Martínez, shaped its history in a way illustrative of the dilemmas faced by generations of Mexican border residents.

Situated far from the densely populated heartland of central Mexico, amid an arid region with limited natural resources, Ciudad Juárez has had to rely heavily upon trade and other outside factors for its sustenance. During the last half of the nineteenth century, the city sought to avoid dependency upon the rapidly expanding southwestern United States through the establishment of a free trade zone along the Mexican side of the border. Mexico's national government vetoed such a zone. Mexican nationalism and the maintenance of sovereignty required, in the opinion of the government, a policy of firm control from central Mexico, combined with protection for domestic industrialization. With the restoration of stability after the Mexican Revolution of 1910–16, "dependence on the U.S. side has become a way of life" for the border cities.

As the two cities of El Paso and Ciudad Juárez became one urban area, the international frontier separated the stronger and weaker parts of a dynamic interrelationship. Inhabitants of Ciudad Juárez travelled across the river to gain access to work, cheap staples, and affordable consumer goods. Residents of the U.S. side, whether Anglos or Mexicans, journeyed to Juárez to see the sights, visit relatives, or find entertainment. During Prohibition, Ciudad Juárez became a center for liquor manufacture and consumption, as well as for gambling, and prostitution. Juárez found its relationship to El Paso necessary for survival, but inadequate to the creation of a stable way of life. Mexicans constantly feared that the city would lose its national character. Government regulations from the interior or from across the border could undermine prosperity from one day to the next. Major external changes, like the legalization of liquor in the U.S. or the advent of the depression, suddenly thrust the city into economic ruin.

Mexico's efforts to improve frontier life over recent decades have centered on building modern industry and infrastructure in border cities like Juárez. Ironically, as Martínez emphasizes, the National Frontier Program and other Mexican government policies have ultimately increased border dependency upon the United States. In-bond manufacture in Mexican communities by U.S. capital exploits cheap labor and develops a taste for consumer goods better supplied across the river. Mexico's rapid population growth provides masses of migrants to Ciudad Juárez seeking work and a better life. Their numbers exceed available jobs, undermine border stability, and generate further illegal labor in the United States.

Martínez, himself the son of migrants to Ciudad Juárez, articulates the seriousness of the border's historic plight, but does not create a good work of either urban or regional history. He switches focus too quickly back and forth between Ciudad Juárez and the entire border. His explanations of community life, economic trends, and the role of political leaders are particularly shallow. He frequently uses sources uncritically. The value of *Border Boom Town*, however, outweighs these deficiencies. It is a timely historical introduction to a range of critical issues that will vex Mexico and the United States for decades.

ARTHUR SCHMIDT

Temple University
Philadelphia

LAURISTON SHARP and LUCIEN M. HANKS. *Bang Chan: Social History of a Rural Community in Thailand.* Ithaca, NY: Cornell University Press, 1978. $17.50.

In 1948 Sharp selected the farming village of Bang Chan, some forty kilometers from Bangkok, as a site for intensive study by the nascent Cornell-Thailand Project; he was joined by Hanks in 1952. Bang Chan has subsequently been studied by numerous Thai and Western researchers representing many disciplines. This book is a distillation of the accumulated experience of the two authors and the colleagues who worked with them. It is a social history of Bang Chan based on the memories of informants, contemporary observations, and whatever local or national history that could be brought to bear.

The authors acknowledge the limitations and pitfalls of this approach, but note that the documentary evidence favored by conventional historians is lacking or of doubtful utility for such villages. The book is then a perspective and sympathetic reconstruction of Bang Chan's past and a characterization of its present seen largely through the lives of its people.

The foundation of Bangkok as the Thai capital in the late eighteenth century sets the stage. The area then surrounding Bangkok was a vast plain inhabited by roaming herds of elephants and containing a few villages located on accessible streams. Bang Chan's first settlers came as pioneers from the Chinese quarter of Bangkok in the 1840's, though settlements of Lao and Muslim prisoners of war already existed nearby. The ebb and flow of people into and out of the village and their waxing and waning fortunes are traced from this beginning, affected by natural disasters and by various changes emanating most directly from Bangkok.

More than a chronology of Bang Chan's transformation from an isolated farming village to its contemporary situation as a "suburb" of Bangkok, each chapter illustrates how Thai values, customs, and institutions merge in the lives of the villagers, influencing their choices and decisions and affecting their day to day activities. Change is not something that happens *to* the people of Bang Chan, they are a part of it.

This is a book about people, not statistics or sociological abstractions. Written engagingly, it is not marred by the intrusion of heavy doses of social science jargon. For those who wish documentation, this is conveyed in appendices, a glossary and extensive notes. The book successfully conveys the multiple dimensions of Thai life. It is a remarkable achievement, a fitting monument to the authors and the people of Bang Chan which it celebrates.

A. THOMAS KIRSCH
Cornell University
Ithaca

ROBERT G. SUTTER. *Chinese Foreign Policy after the Cultural Revolution, 1966–1977.* Pp. x, 176. Boulder, CO: Westview Press, 1978. $15.00.

This is a handy little book: the first eighty page section consists of a concise overview of Chinese foreign policy during the past decade, while the second half is divided into capsule summaries of China's policy on ten specific issues. These small sections (on the Soviet Union, the United States, Taiwan, Southeast Asia, Japan and Korea, South Asia, Europe, the Middle East and Africa, Disarmament, and Foreign Trade) are organized in the manner of intelligence reports, with a summary followed by a more detailed narrative of several pages. Another innovation for easier reading is achieved by incorporating source documentation (primarily translations provided by the Foreign Broadcast Information Service (FBIS)) within the course of the narrative. The style is a familiar one to the author who served as a Chinese foreign policy analyst with the Central Intelligence Agency for ten years.

Sutter identifies domestic and international sources for a foreign policy "designed on the one hand to guarantee the development and advancement of China's vital interests in world affairs, and on the other hand to spread Maoist ideology and world revolution." While the foreign policy of the Cultural Revolution was based upon domestic sources and promoted the "idealism" of world revolution, the foreign policy of the period after 1969 had a different focus and source. During the latter period, a more "realistic" policy of moderation resulted from the primacy which international events took over domestic considerations.

The change in policy was a result of the Soviet invasion of Czechoslovakia and the border clashes of the following year. Since then, Peking's relations with every country has been colored by the overriding concern that the USSR is the main antagonist in the world arena. The United States, the enemy during the Cultural Revolution, was now seen as a valuable counterweight to Soviet attempts at world hegemony.

This altered perception of the international scene was paralleled by changes in the Chinese domestic scene as well. With Chou En-lai firmly in control of foreign policy in the early 1970s, China was more able to pursue the "conventional" diplomacy of power politics. Even challenges by the Gang of Four during the 1974 campaign to criticize Lin Piao and Confucius, for example, failed to elicit a change in policy as the primacy of external concerns remained intact. The author hazards the prediction that the pragmatic foreign policy will continue because of the elevation of Chou's protegés following his death.

There is a six-page chronology and an index of equal length. A thirty-item bibliography is provided which might be more appropriately labelled "suggested reading." In sum, this is a fine book which can be used in part or in its entirety with great profit, although the inflated price may prevent some from investing in this slender volume.

WAYNE PATTERSON

Saint Norbert College
De Pere
Wisconsin

EUROPE

MORRIS BERMAN. *Social Change and Scientific Organization: The Royal Institution, 1799–1844*. Pp. xxv, 224. Ithaca: Cornell University Press, 1978. $17.50.

Berman's thoroughly documented work argues that by the middle of the nineteenth century the British government had accepted the notion that science could solve most social problems, and that the Royal Institution contributed importantly to this acceptance.

The author discusses the foundation of the Institution, dominated in its early days by the "improving" agriculturalist, and its growth and change as the industrial revolution advanced. By the 1840's, indeed, the professional middle classes ran it. In the process, the tradition of the gentleman amateur gave way to the "scientific" approach, although science was not yet considered a separate occupation by mid-century. One still was a scientist in order to use one's skills for practical purposes. Thus the Institution constantly employed its leading scientists and its facilities in public service, such as building a telescope for the navy.

Berman stresses that the Institution's scientists, through their work on various public projects, were most active in prodding the British governing classes to favor science as an answer to social problems. Even Farraday, who yearned to engage in pure research rather than applied sciences, spent much of his time on practical work, often little more than drudgery.

If one accepts the fact that the British ruling classes believed the use of science could promote the common welfare, or at least keep the lower classes from rebelling against their lot (which notion Berman favors), this book shows clearly how the upper classes arrived at such a belief. One might question, however, whether the deeply religious Gladstone or the consummate politician Disraeli really arrived at their policies because of advice by scientific experts. Nonetheless, Berman makes a good case.

One might more readily quarrel

with his prejudices. He points out, for example, that Farraday investigated the Haswell mine disaster at the home secretary's request, and concluded that it was an unavoidable accident, thus converting a "highly charged political issue" into a "technical difficulty." But Farraday had missed the essential problem. According to the author, "the cause of mine disasters was not simply a dysfunction in the Davy lamp, but an industrial economy based on profit and production" (p. 175). Unfortunately, Berman gives little documentation for this thesis, which seems either unprovable or in historical terms not very meaningful. For what industrial economy, whether promoted by private capital or state capital, has not been based on profit and production?

For the most part, Berman sticks to his major thesis and does not allow such biases to intrude. The result is a sound, scholarly, and very interesting work.

FRANKLIN B. WICKWIRE
University of Massachusetts
Amherst

JOHN CANNON, ed. *The Letters of Junius*. Pp. xxxiii, 643. Oxford: Clarendon Press, 1978. $49.50.

"Junius" was a pseudonym for the writer of a series of letters opposing King George III and the policies of the ministries of the Duke of Grafton and Lord North. The first Junius letter appeared on January 21, 1769 in the *Public Advertiser*, a London daily newspaper published by Henry Sampson Woodfall. Although the "acme of audacity" was reached in the famous letter to King George III of December 19, 1769, the series did not come to an end until January 21, 1772. The *Letters of Junius* have survived as an English classic and owe their influence to three factors: (1) the high Whig philosophy espoused in the *Letters*—the freedom of the press— and their attacks on Tory policies and politicians of the times; (2) the literary power of the *Letters*, possibly the most effective use of slanderous polemic ever employed in English political controversy; and (3) the mystery surrounding their authorship.

Cannon (University of Newcastle-Upon-Tyne) has produced a sumptuous edition of the *Letters*: it is meticulously edited, the most complete edition as yet to appear, and the first new edition of the *Letters* since C. W. Everett's edition of 1927. It is an auspicious event in the huge literature (*cf.*, F. Cordasco, *A Junius Bibliography*, rev. ed., 1974) which surrounds Junius and his celebrated *Letters* since it affirms the continuing importance of the *Letters* for the study of the political, social, and intellectual history of 18th century England. No expense has been spared by the publisher, and the volume is an excellent example of the superb typography of the distinguished Oxford imprint which in 1978 celebrates the quincentenary of its founding.

Cannon has based his edition on the collected edition of the *Letters* authorized and prepared for the press by Junius, which Woodfall published in 1772; he has not chosen to use the text of the *Letters* as originally printed in the *Public Advertiser* "since the author added many important explanatory footnotes, expanded obscure references, and corrected certain misprints and faults of style." Yet, it should be noted that a set of the *Public Advertiser* letters exists and is deposited in the London Library (14 St. James Square, S. W. 1), and is complete for the critical years (1769–1772) of the Junius corpus. Also, Cannon has included necessary and valuable appendices: private Letters between Junius and Henry Sampson Woodfall; private Letters between Junius and John Wilkes; private Letters to Lord Chatham and George Grenville; additional and false Junius Letters; miscellaneous Letters; comparison of the 1772 Collected Edition with the Letters as First Printed in the Public Advertiser; a List of Signals to Junius in the *Public Advertiser*; a Note on Authorship.

Cannon's "A Note on Authorship" must be read with caution; he is not incorrect in observing that "I do not doubt that my conclusions will appear to some readers woefully wrong-headed." The note is not without value in providing guidance through a landscape strewn with the *disjecta membra* which surround the controversy over the authorship of the *Letters*. Cannon offers no new evidence; he is, moreover, not an advocate for Sir Philip Francis: he acquits himself by observing that "I do not propose to say how decisive the case for Francis is, since the object of this appendix is to place the reader in a position to form his own conclusion" (571). The case for Francis was completely destroyed by Charles Wentworth Dilke in the last century; no student of Junius has argued Francis' case since. And Cannon is felicitously wise in his concluding observation on the authorship: "If a cautious conclusion is unacceptable to some readers, they are at liberty to be as dogmatic as they wish: it would certainly have pleased the author himself, who wrote 'the mystery of Junius increases his importance.'"

FRANCESCO CORDASCO
Montclair State College
New Jersey

RAYMOND PEARSON. *The Russian Moderates and the Crisis of Tsarism 1911–1917*. Pp. x, 208. New York: Barnes & Noble, 1977. $22.50.

The author, a lecturer in history at the University of Ulster, spent several months in the USSR where he carried out his research. In a clear, readable style, he presents an account of the closing days of the Russian Monarchy, and offers condensed though significant accounts of political groupings such as the early formed Octobrists, the Kadets, the later Union Sacre, known for its blend of patriotism and expediency, and the Progressive Bloc of the last years of the Monarchy. All these seem to have come to life as emergency organizations to forestall the oncoming cataclysm.

Placed between reaction and revolution, the vast middle classes hoped and schemed to find a peaceful solution or at least a means of survival if the looming crisis should culminate in violence. The moderates, the Kadets or the Octobrists, desperately sought means to avoid violent encounter. Not even the

Mensheviks accepted violence for fear they might be crushed in the emerging clash. Organizations of the Right, in common with the middle classes, tried to stem the oncoming storm by setting up peaceful negotiations. However, frequent military adversities at the front, creeping demonstrations throughout the Empire, and the decline of loyalties throughout the country all served to multiply and perpetuate fears of looming events.

Despite all efforts, events did not move into anticipated channels. One of the major reasons for this was the gigantic military force present in the country. In the end, all parties shifted from the conference rooms to the battlefields, adding a totally different dimension to forthcoming events.

Very well presented, this volume offers a clear picture that is far superior to numerous other documented accounts. It is an intriguing chapter in modern history. Once the reader begins, he will find it extremely difficult to put the narrative down until the account comes to an end; assuming, of course, there is an end to the account!

ANATOLE G. MAZOUR
Stanford University
California

MAX E. RIEDLSPERGER. *The Lingering Shadow of Nazism: The Austrian Independent Party Movement Since 1945*. Pp. xi, 214. New York: Columbia University Press, 1978. $14.00.

In the decade after the end of the second World War, the dominant themes in Austrian political life were the occupation and a system of coalition government with its unique proportional arrangements between the Social Democratic Party of Austria and the Austrian Peoples Party. The subject of this book is the effort by many inheritors of the German national tradition to operate politically outside of the postwar coalition and to develop a third force, aspiring even to a balance of power within the Austrian political life. Through newspaper accounts, journal articles, personal interviews, and official statistics the author has sought to reconstruct the struggles of this third force in the early years of the Second Austrian Republic, and to analyze the initial limited success and the eventual failure of the movement. It was this third force, according to the author, that attracted the former Nazis and never fully escaped from the lingering shadow of Nazism.

The best parts of the book are those sections which describe the efforts by Kraus and Reiman, two men who bore no trace of Nazism in their past, to transform the Club of Independents into an effective third force in Austrian politics. Appeals, for example, to end the persecution of former Nazis and to call for their reintegration into society, when made by men who had been imprisoned during the Nazi era, won a large personal following among the disenfranchised but also received a permanent taint from the Nazi shadow. The author is also very effective in dealing with the problems centering on the German national heritage. Admittedly, most Austrians did not want to reunite with Germany, but at the same time many Austrians did not want to develop too distinctive a heritage. Moreover, the omnipresent economic ties reminded everyone of the close relationship between Germany and Austria.

The sections on voting analysis are weaker than the descriptive narrative. In particular, the author emphasized the elections of 1949 and those of 1953 to 1956, the latter years marking the end of the occupation and the formulation of the Austrian State Treaty. Often the inferences drawn from aggregate voting tables appear too farreaching for the voting statistics on which they are based. While his research is primarily from the fifties and the sixties, the author's conclusion provides a sensitive discussion of Austrian politics in the last decade.

This work is a solid introduction to a fascinating problem. Students of Austrian politics will obviously profit from it.

CHARLES J. HERBER

George Washington University
Washington
D.C.

REBA N. SOFFER. *Ethics and Society in England: The Revolution in the Social Sciences 1870–1914.* Pp. 366. Berkeley: University of California Press, 1978.

As the subtitle suggests this is a book with a thesis. The author attempts to rescue English social thought during the decades before World War I from undue neglect and from those who deny that the English made any "distinctive contribution to the rethinking of the fundamental concepts" of social theory. Ms. Soffer argues, in brief, that the work of Alfred Marshall in economics, William James in psychology, and Graham Wallas in political science, constituted a "revolution." In place of the positivistic outlook and deductive methods which dominated these areas of inquiry in the nineteenth century, the new social scientists were empirical in approach and practical in their purposes. And in opposition to the deterministic bent of earlier social theory the new thinkers affirmed human agency. Alongside the "revolutionaries," Ms. Soffer also delineates a new school of social psychologists, particularly William McDougall and Wilfred Trotter, whom she designates "revisionists." Occupied mainly with collective or "crowd" behavior, fearful of the irrational tendencies of modern democracy, McDougall and Trotter reinstated the older conservative emphasis on the role of elites in solving social problems.

Ms. Soffer commands a large and complex body of material, not only the writing produced by her protagonists, but that of a number of transitional figures including Spencer, Jevons, Sidgwick, and Pearson. She also relates her themes quite successfully to the late Victorian cultural crisis, conveying both a sense of the growing uncertainty about values and the continuing reformist commitments of the new generation of social thinkers. She is less successful in showing how the deepening economic and political conflicts of the period influenced the new theories.

The study is marred by dubious assertions. Does it make sense, for example, to say that "Weber, Freud, Durkheim, and Croce succumbed to a psychological malaise" because they acknowledged "irrational forces underlying even the most rational behaviour and institutions?" And there are errors of fact. The "Economic Circle" did not lead to "the founding of the Fabian Society" though it had some influence on Fabianism. Moreover, Ms. Soffer's treatment of social thought is, like so much of her subject matter, rather insular. The absence of any reference to Parson's classic study, in which Marshall is treated along with Pareto, Durkheim and Weber, is indicative. So too is the absence of any reference to Marx. Indeed, from a broader framework one might question the usefulness of her distinction between "revolutionaries" and "revisionists." Marshall, James, and Wallas after all remained firmly wedded to the essentially individualistic commitments of their liberal predecessors. McDougall and Trotter, in contrast, made the fundamental methodological shift which Durkheim had made earlier— to the "social fact" or society as a reality *sui generis* as the main object of investigation. From a European perspective who, then, were the revolutionaries in England?

STANLEY PIERSON
University of Oregon
Eugene

GEOFFREY WILLIAMS. *The Permanent Alliance: The European-American Partnership, 1945–1984.* Pp. xii, 407. Leyden: Sijthoff, 1977. $37.00.

This extended essay about relationships between the United States and Western Europe in the period since World War II concentrates primarily on security and military strategy issues, and especially on the problem of security of Western Europe vis-à-vis the Soviet Union. The North Atlantic Treaty figures prominently in the analysis. Although the broad outline of the book follows a chronological sequence, it is not a history and within chapters events are treated topically rather than chronologically. At least half of the book deals

with the 1960s. Great attention is given to the disagreements, controversies, and conflicts among the NATO members. The final chapter of the book calls for a new institutional relationship between the United States and the members of the European Economic Community, and it expresses the hope that Japan could be brought into this arrangement. The author adjures that the "super-super power" thus created could "ensure peace for a generation or more" (p. 365).

Unfortunately the prescription for the new institutional relationship between the United States and Western Europe is not very detailed. It is asserted that Europe must be an equal partner to the United States, and that European leadership is vitally needed. Both points are persuasive, but the real issues concern the details of implementing these suggestions, not the broad goals. The real issues involve bringing several key European polities together for the pursuit of coordinated or joint policies. One cannot recommend how to do this without examining issues that have traditionally been considered domestic rather than international.

There is little analysis of such issues in this book, and what analysis there is is confined largely to the United States and the United Kingdom. There is even little analysis of such matters as the successes and failures of the Eurogroup within NATO, and of the difficulties that have arisen in connection with the coordinated or joint production of armaments for NATO forces. A detailed analysis of these matters might have resulted in a better understanding of the difficulties that stand in the way of crafting a new relationship between Western Europe and the United States, and offered new insights concerning ways in which these difficulties might be overcome.

The book is more an account of major controversies than a detailed study of any particular aspect of the Atlantic partnership. These controversies are presented clearly and fairly, although the author's disdain for certain positions taken by various British and French officials is evident. It is regretable and annoying that the account is marred by several minor inaccuracies and errors.

HAROLD K. JACOBSON

The University of Michigan
Ann Arbor

UNITED STATES

HOWARD BALL. *Judicial Craftsmanship or Fiat? Direct Overturn by the United States Supreme Court.* Pp. xiv, 160. Westport, CT: Greenwood Press, 1978. $18.95.

In 1959 Herbert Wechsler rekindled the long-standing debate regarding the need for principled decisions in constitutional interpretation. To Wechsler—and to many others before, such as James Bradley Thayer in the nineteenth century—the limits of the judicial function are prescribed by the logic and language of law itself. For judges to go beyond such externally imposed limits leads to an adulteration of the judicial process. But can the outcomes of difficult constitutional cases rest solely upon the logic, consistency, and general principles of law? Of course not. To try to understand—and then to cast into intelligible language—the nature of the judicial function has been the mission of many. Few have succeeded. Benjamin Cardozo, Felix Frankfurter, and Glendon Schubert (each in his own diverse way) have. Howard Ball has not.

Ball has attempted to create an operational definition of judicial craftsmanship using Wechsler's notion of a principled decision. In order to exhibit such craftsmanship, the United States Supreme Court, in reversing itself, must decide "in a principled manner." Ball goes on: the "thesis posited is that when the Court overturns, it must base its stance on one of three justifications: rightness, factual correctness, and constitutional principles" (p. xiii). The absence of craftsmanship is decision by fiat.

Undaunted by the overwhelming problems (which eventually ensnare the author himself) of trying to operationalize rightness, factual correctness, and extant general principles, Ball produces a chapter each on three Supreme Court reversals of the twentieth century. He examines: *United States* v. *Darby Lumber Co.* (1941) (overturning *Hammer* v. *Dagenhart*); *West Virginia Board of Education* v. *Barnette* (1943) (overturning *Minersville* v. *Gobitis*; and *Hudgens* v. *National Labor Relations Board* (1976) (overturning *Amalgamated Food Employees Union* v. *Logan Valley Plaza*).

His conclusions are that both *Darby* and *Barnette* (the *Second Flag Salute Case*) are good examples of judicial craftsmanship because they right the errors of anachronistic precedents. That *Minersville* was an anachronism is not so clear cut, Ball seems to tell us, because of the complicating factors of external political conditions (the coming of World War II) and Mr. Justice Frankfurter's call for judicial restraint. *Hudgens* is a decision by "judicial fiat" in large measure because Ball regards *Logan Valley Plaza* as correctly decided, for the latter "took cognizance of changing economic and social conditions and began to develop the law in light of these realities" (p. 133).

By the conclusion of the three "case studies," one can only agree with the implicit thesis embedded in the analysis: it is indeed necessary to go beyond the general principles woven into constitutional law in order adequately to understand the judicial process. That Ball so steadfastly refuses to recognize (as contemporary political scientists almost universally do) the importance of such factors as changed Court personnel, justices' ideologies and role definitions, and collegial or group decisionmaking, in explaining the judicial process will, if nothing else, surprise his readers.

There are other surprises. Noted constitutional scholars Alpheus T. Mason and Walter F. Murphy became Arthur T. Mason and William Murphy in bibliographic citations.

ROBERT G. SEDDIG

The University of Minnesota
Twin Cities

MARTIN K. DOUDNA. *Concerned about the Planet: The Reporter Magazine and American Liberalism, 1949–1968.* Pp. xi, 197. Westport, CT: Greenwood Press, 1978. $14.95.

The *Reporter* announced itself as "a magazine of facts and ideas, not of news and opinions." It was founded, and throughout its brief existence was directed, by Max Ascoli, voluntary exile from Mussolini's Italy; and this book shows, with considerable quotation, his concern for freedom as a moral value, his distrust of large-scale organization, his opposition to Fascism and Communism alike. Doudna describes how Ascoli separated himself from groups whose views on foreign policy he thought unsound, what staff and contributors he assembled, and how many people of importance subscribed. Even more information on the human relations involved would have been welcome; how did an editor of powerful intellect and intense convictions handle men and women of exceptional ability, most of them in the middle of successful careers? One would have welcomed, too, more detail on the magazine's finances; all we are told is that Ascoli and his rich wife were willing to make up the regular losses.

The *Reporter's* editorial policy is shown to have been: hostile to the China Lobby and Senator McCarthy; favorable to civil rights though sensitive to the human problems involved for southern whites; cool in appraising successive presidents; and skeptical toward the United Nations. Ascoli supported Truman's foreign policy, but as early as 1950 urged the recognition of Red China. He was critical of John Foster Dulles and admired Konrad Adenauer and Charles de Gaulle. He dreaded a revival of American isolationism; and, although he saw the difficulties, he supported the intervention in Vietnam. "Our normal relations with the Communists," he wrote in November 1962, "should never be of war and can never be of peace."

Such attitudes fully justify Doudna in pointing to the contradictions and dilemmas of American liberalism. How far does the promotion of a righteous cause justify intervention in the affairs of others? What kinds of force may be employed? How much government control is permissible in the interests of social justice? What kinds of ally should a liberal be willing to accept?

This is not, however, the only context in which the magazine can be placed. Doudna himself notes that, despite Ascoli's own emphasis on international relations, most of the *Reporter's* many awards were gained for articles on American issues; and since, like Doudna, I was a subscriber during the 1950s, I can recall what my own attitude was in those days. To put it simply, I seldom read the editorials—though I was aware of and respected their general tone—and it never occurred to me to discover just who Ascoli was. Rather, I read articles individually, precisely as a source of "facts and ideas"; and I still have some of them, especially those bearing upon Congress, regulatory agencies, and interest groups. To record this is to change the emphasis from editor to contributors, though of course it was Ascoli and his editorial associates who gave them their chance.

So I can readily agree with Doudna's analysis. But I lived through that period too—remembering how I joined American academic colleagues in nocturnal mourning as Adlai Stevenson conceded the 1952 election, I can almost feel myself an honorary American liberal—and it is the great American tradition of investigative journalism that I prefer to stress.

P. A. M. TAYLOR
University of Hull
England

JOHN N. INGHAM. *The Iron Barons: A Social Analysis of an American Urban Elite 1874-1965.* Pp. xix, 242. Westport, CT: Greenwood Press, 1978. $19.95.

This is a scholarly examination of the social background of some nineteenth century American iron and steel manufacturers. Professor Ingham selected six iron and steel producing cities—Bethlehem, Pittsburgh, Philadelphia, Cleveland, Youngstown and Wheeling—for an in depth study of this wealthy and prestigious elite. He found many similarities in the backgrounds of the members of these upper class groups.

Most of them came from successful business and professional families, rather than from the laboring class. They did not follow the Horatio Alger pattern from rags to riches. Religiously, they were Episcopalians and Presbyterians, with some Quakers in Philadelphia, but practically no Catholics and no Jews. They belonged to the same restricted social clubs; their names were usually found on the social register. Their children attended private grade schools or academies and private universities. They customarily lived in the same residential areas of the cities or in the same suburbs. Their repetitious endogamous marriages were taken for granted.

Unfortunately this book is not easy to read; it is too weighted with technical data. There are 52 tables of information which the text largely repeats and explains. The book's use probably will be confined mainly to specialists in the field of social analysis and they may find it tedious.

GEORGE OSBORN

Gainesville
Florida

ARTHUR S. LINK et al., eds. *The Papers of Woodrow Wilson*, Vols. XXII, 1910–1911, Pp. xxii, 630; XXIII, 1911–1912, Pp. xiv, 687; XXIV, 1912, Pp. xii, 672. Princeton: Princeton University Press, 1976. $25.00 each.

The distance between these volumes and those preceding is phenomenal, though inadvertently deceptive to a degree. These are, after all, Wilson's papers; Theodore Roosevelt and Republicanism are little represented. Indeed, Wilson pointedly ignored them as none of his business. More significantly, there is close to no insight in these 2600 pages into the changing pattern of American life involving youth, labor, women, and the world, which war would raise to the surface, inundating Wilson himself.

But there is here, in addition, the distance between the emergent 1910 Wilson and the earlier Wilson: a Wilson of uncertain academic status and political potential who consorted with deans, trustees, businessmen, philanthropists, and civic groups. The New Jersey politics undoubtedly saw him as malleable. They missed the combination of general pieties and personal realism which, for example, enabled Wilson to philosophize that city machines served voters, in effect accepting boss rule while condemning it.

Politics in earlier volumes are dim becauses Wilson is negotiating with his sponsors. His private letters now become fewer and shorter. He is sometimes almost daily on public platforms, mixing humor with earnestness, a belief in "state vitality" with the inevitability of Federal power, an attack on trusts with praise for individual initiative. The chrysalis of a statesman becomes a statesman and is immediately so recognized across the country almost before he has assumed the New Jersey governorship.

Wilson's break with the "machine" is almost wholly symbolic in retrospect. "Why congratulate me?" he asks reporters. "It is the people who are to be congratulated. All you have to do is tell them what is going on and they will respond" (XXII, 367). In fact, they were not told the details of the break, but Wilson's rhetoric was far superior to that of the politicos.

Later, following the liberal successes of the 1911 Legislative Session, he remarks how easily they were achieved. Considering the times, it is hard to fault such unawareness that government was being streamlined rather than transformed. Wilson fought for commission government, "people's government," for example. As a result, Jersey City assumed it, electing as mayor, Frank Hague, the city boss.

Although Wilson put out continuous feelers regarding the presidency, hundreds of responsible civic leaders came to him without solicitation. His emergence tallied with theirs. Wilson makes a triumphal cross-country tour, is proudly received in his own South, and more and more comments publicly on national and related affairs: Alaska, Czarist policy toward the Jews, a bitter strike in the bituminous coal fields of Pennsylvania. He is wary of entrapments. As a Democrat he is friendly to liquor, but, he tells a Texan, what might be right in one place might not be in another. "I hope you will feel at liberty to absolutely deny the statement that I have made a declaration against State-wide prohibition" (XXIII, 176).

Wilson had many more difficult chasms to cross. It is impressive how many helped him to cross them. The Hearst newspapers play up his cavalier statements in books about immigrants. He is somewhat embarrassed by publication of his attempts to get early retirement money as educator, before reaching 65. He is adroit in his own defense, and is aided by suggestions and endorsements. As he says calmly: "Scores of [politicians] . . . are engaged in electing me President of the United States" (XXIII, 256).

Wilson now makes full claim to the Progressive label, and the Progressives proper split their loyalty between him and Roosevelt. In April of 1912 national democratic leaders confer with him in Washington: a high moment among a forest of warmly received speeches in numerous cities under varied auspices. But the national Democratic machine is not wholly persuaded. Wilson loses esteemed primaries, and by May is a bit downcast: "[I/t begins to look as if I must merely sit on the sidelines and talk" (XXIV, 402). He continues to talk, however, and to be sustained by determined managers. The Baltimore convention is thick with excitement. Champ Clark is favored on the first ballot. Wilson is soon ready to concede defeat, but a turmoil of conflicting strategies among his managers keeps his candidacy alive until victory.

Volume XXV is almost an anticlimax. The historic split in the Republican party all but ensures the Democratic candidate the election. Wilson's "New Freedom" speeches sum up 25 years of literary and political comment and persuasion. They are still impressive in their successful reaching out to auditors, and even in some of their principles. Wilson will not, for example, deal with women suffrage, though it is thundering across the land, believing it "is not a question that is dealt with by the national government at all, and I am here only as the representative of a national party" (XXV, 438). As his first administration looms, the task is to assess his role as leader of the national government.

LOUIS FILLER

Antioch University
Yellow Springs
Ohio

DONALD SPIVEY. *Schooling For The New Slavery: Black Industrial Education, 1865–1915.* Pp. xiii, 162. Westport, CT: Greenwood Press, 1978. $14.95.

This book begins with an account of conditions in Hampton, Virginia, where, says the author, some thousands of blacks were treated so badly by Union troops that they feared reenslavement should the North win the war. For a brief period, however, the Bureau of Negro Affairs gave lands to freedmen, a policy which changed drastically with the establishment of the Freedmen's Bureau at the war's close. Indeed, says the author, the Bureau was more intent upon reconciling Northern and Southern whites than upon helping former slaves.

The author is severe on General Samuel Chapman Armstrong, local Bureau superintendent, who believed blacks were inferior, lazy, and irresponsible. In 1868, Armstrong founded Hampton Normal Institute with the help of the Bureau and the American Missionary Association. Hampton provided a program of industrial education compounded of work, discipline, and religion to prepare blacks for the hard work in the New South's industry and agriculture. Hampton graduates carried the Armstrong gospel throughout the South.

But if the author found Armstrong an unsatisfactory educational leader for freedmen, he was even more critical of Booker Taliaferro Washington, Armstrong's star pupil, who founded Tuskegee Institute in Alabama in 1881. Although Washington did not admit white superiority, he saw his fellow blacks mainly as a reservoir of reliable and compliant labor, and the author likens him to the earlier black overseer "who worked diligently to keep intact the very system under which they both were enslaved" (p. 66).

The author moves on from Hampton and Tuskegee to the General Education Board and other agencies which he says sponsored industrial education to assure a supply of menial black labor for northern-financed railroads and other enterprises in the South. Captains of finance and industry, such as Rockefeller, Morgan, and Carnegie pass in unfavorable review, as do many educational leaders, North and South, not excluding Dr. G. W. Carver. The book closes with a chapter on the popularity of industrial education among imperialistic powers, notably Britain, and of efforts to introduce it widely in African colonies and in the Republic of Liberia.

The author makes it abundantly clear that many persons who promoted industrial education were motivated by exploitative and selfish interests. Even so, it is difficult to avoid the conclusion that he has overdone this thesis and that his well-researched monograph is weakened by its almost totally negative appraisals of persons, institutions and agencies connected with the industrial education movement.

JENNINGS B. SANDERS
Kensington
Maryland

THEODORE H. WHITE. In Search of History: A Personal Adventure. Pp. 561. New York: Harper & Row, 1978. $12.95.

In 1976 Theodore White began working on what was to have been the fifth of his Making of the President books. During the campaign, however, White began to doubt his own assumptions about America and American politics, and more particularly his own conception of history. He laid aside his chronicle of the election and wrote instead this book, to be not "mere storytelling," but an attempt at history, which "organizes and analyzes facts to tell 'what it is really all about.'" The result is a combination of autobiography, an episodic account of fifty years of American history, and an essay on White's concept of the meaning of America's existence.

The Prologue, Epilogue and three of the chapters are told in third person, while the balance of the volume provides a first person account of White's life from his birth in a Boston Jewish ghetto in 1915 to his interview with Jacqueline Kennedy just one week after her husband's assassination. The author traces his career at the Boston Latin School and Harvard (where he was a "meatball"—a poor kid), to China (where he reported for Time from 1939 until his break with Henry Luce in 1946), to Europe (where he covered the Marshall Plan and the rebuilding of postwar Europe), and back to the United States (to become "the storyteller of elections"). Throughout his tales are well told and interesting, exhibiting the author's superb skill as a journalist. For this alone the volume is well worth reading.

The author has long been enamored of the place of the hero in history, and heroes abound in this volume, the paramount one being John F. Kennedy. White wonders to what extent even heroes control their own destiny, and struggles with the concept of accident. Interlaced with this concern is the uniqueness of the hero in America, the land of opportunity. This American hero is remembered not for his conquests, as he would be elsewhere, but "for the degree by which he enlarged Opportunity." There is interesting argument here, which will engage both layman and scholar alike.

White finds the assassination of Kennedy a "great divide" in American history, ignoring a host of political, social, and economic factors which resulted in the changes in America between the 1950's and 1970's. Elsewhere he hypothesizes that the American involvement in Vietnam would not have occurred had Kennedy remained President. While the book has flaws of this sort, it has much more to commend it.

We are told that a second and possibly a third memoir will follow this, but asking "whether the old ideas that had made America a nation could stretch far enough to keep it one." *In Search of History* is well worth reading, as its successor(s) will be if they maintain the excellence of this volume.

DONALD B. SCHEWE
Franklin D. Roosevelt Library
Hyde Park
New York

SOCIOLOGY

AUGUST BEQUAI. White-Collar Crime. Pp. xvi, 186. Lexington, MA: Lexington Books, 1978. $14.95.

The costs of business crime are pervasive and exorbitant. As one judge said, "In our complex society the accountant's certificate and the lawyer's opinion can be instruments for inflicting pecuniary loss more potent than the chisel or the crowbar."

During the last few years there has been increased attention given to the problem of crime in the "White Collar" world. Except for a few radical critiques of capitalism, though, there has been little effort by legal scholars to examine the problem. This book tries to fill that gap by examining the existing patterns of violations of the law by businessmen and corporations, and by developing a framework within which to investigate business crime. Although no original data are presented in this book, it is this reviewers' hope that this synthesis of existing material might find a place among the readings of those

charged with the administration of justice.

The author relies on crisp short chapters written as individual box cars that, when hooked together, clearly answer the question "What is White Collar Crime?" "What Can Be Done to Halt It?" "What is Law Enforcement Doing About It?" "What does The Future Hold For a Modern Society which tolerates a $40 billion annual financial loss, either by criminal actions or from noncompetitive market financial conspiracy situations, in a society based upon a free market place allowing the consumer to have freedom of choice?

Chapter 1 seeks to define the problem of white-collar crime, while Chapters 2 and 3 attempt to explain why both jurists and academics have long neglected its study and classification, and Chapter 4 deals with frauds in the securities industry. The next four chapters address themselves to various other categories of frauds: for example, in the area of bankruptcy, bribes to both corporate and public officials; consumer frauds; and frauds in government contracts and programs.

Chapters 9 and 10 deal with insurance swindles and insider-related frauds, such as embezzlement and pilferage by employees. The next four chapters deal with monopolies and price fixing (antitrust), computer-related crimes, offenses against our physical environment, and tax frauds. Chapter 15 deals with the influx of organized crime into the white-collar crime area and the need to adopt a new strategy and policy in combating it. Chapters 16 and 17 deal with problems investigators and prosecutors face in white-collar crime cases, and the need to modernize these two key law enforcement mechanisms. Chapter 18 deals with problems related to litigating white-collar crime cases, such as hearsay and best-evidence rule roadblocks. Finally, Chapter 19 deals with crimes of the future, those made possible by our growing automation and technology, and the failure of our present laws to adequately deal with them.

The author, using vibrant examples and supportive data, clearly illustrates that local investigation and prosecutional apparatus is too fragmented, illtrained and lacking in resources to be effective in the complex field of "White-Collar" crime. Further, he shows that the federal apparatus is too antiquated and bureaucratically bound to effectively pursue violators of law, leading internal governmental agency prosecutions to be resolved by consent decrees to avoid further violations of law in 90 percent of determinations.

He further suggests that our entire penal code, designed to deal with traditional criminals, correlated with poverty or with the psychopathic and sociopathic conditions associated with poverty, is meaningless when applied to the white-collar criminal and needs to be reviewed. This is a valuable book which deserves to become a force in the galvanization of efforts to turn back the tide of crime in the American and international marketplace.

Perhaps the author says it best when he concludes:

"White-collar crime is on the increase; the cost to society is also increasing, not only in terms of money and property stolen yearly by these felons, but also in terms of the loss of confidence and respect by the public at large in our institutions of government. With the growth in federal spending in both defense and social programs, white-collar crime has found fertile ground. It is a "growth industry." Unless we study it and develop tools to deal with it effectively, we may be witnessing only the tip of the iceberg."

GERALD L. SBARBORO

Chicago
Illinois

JACK GREENBERG. *Judicial Process and Social Change: Constitutional Litigation Cases and Materials.* Pp. xxxiv, 666. St. Paul, MN: West Publishing Company, 1976. $15.95.

This is not really a book about the "judicial process and social change" as the title indicates, but merely a collection of materials relevant to only one part of the judicial process—social change interface, namely, the *adjudication of social issues.* Contemporary

policy analysts commonly distinguish between "outputs" (the formal policy statements of governing institutions like courts) and "outcomes" (the impact of those policy statements on social change, the final policy results in society). This book clearly deals only with the former. And even there it largely accepts judicial decisions and opinions at their face value, not really examining the politics of producing outputs. In other words, law is both effect *and* cause. It is the response of lawmakers to prior stimuli (effect), *and* it is stimuli to the subsequent responses of law appliers and law recipients (cause). Law as effect is dealt with here. As a result, we are told something about how *some* courts have responded to *some* policy issues brought before them but nothing about how the judicial process functions as a policymaking instrument.

Of course, the book reviewer's job is not to criticize an author because he failed to study what the reviewer thinks is important but to assess the author's efforts to achieve his own objectives. Proceeding accordingly, I would say that Professor Greenberg is somewhat successful. He carefully treats four areas of legal subject matter: the desegregation of public schools and public accommodations, welfare rights, women's rights, and the attempts to abolish capital punishment. In each of the four areas, the order of presentation is chronological (that is, from *Plessy* to *Sweat* to *Brown*) and the style of presentation is traditional (that is, literary—descriptive). It is superior to most other West-published collections of edited legal materials because of the unusually generous insertion of such materials as briefs of counsel, amicus briefs, legislative materials, and jurisprudential observations.

Still, the book has several shortcomings. First, its canvass is surprisingly narrow: substantial legal change has occurred in recent years in many areas that go entirely untreated—environmental defense, consumer protection, inmates' rights, rights of Indians, of aliens, voting rights, and debtors' rights. Second, its chronology stops short of significant recent developments: school desegregation is covered in 119 pages ending with *Brown* but there is only a one and a half page epilogue devoted to such cases as *Swann* and *Milliken v. Bradley*. Third, conceptualizations are often dubious if not simply wrong: for example, activists are treated as the opposites of conservatives, when historically some of our leading activists have been ultra-conservatives. Fourth, there is a sixty-page collection of analysis and commentary on law and social change in the last chapter, but even here the works presented, though classic, are not current—Cardozo and Bickel. The editor's concluding contribution is sound history but devoid of explanation and theoretical value. In short, this volume tells us nothing new about the law as a social policy instrument. And as a classroom text it is too narrow in canvass, too dated in content, and too uncertain in concept.

WILLIAM C. LOUTHAN
Ohio Wesleyan University
Delaware
Ohio

ALLEN GUTTMANN. *From Ritual to Record: The Nature of Modern Sports.* Pp. 198. New York: Columbia University Press, 1978. $12.95.

All Americans talk about sports (endlessly), but nobody does anything about analyzing them except for Allen Guttmann, head of American Studies at Amherst. Disillusioned by the galloping trivialism of the Popular Culture Association (their Big Deal of Summer 1978 was a Rollercoaster Symposium in Sandusky's amusement park!), I am genuinely heartened by the intelligence of this 161 page essay, and impressed by the (largely unglossed) 22 pages of footnotes which display cross-cultural and multi-disciplinary research of Teutonic thoroughness (a happy spinoff of the author's Fulbright stints in Europe). In short, here is a study of popular culture as imaginatively serious as the best humanistic studies in literature and philosophy. And, special blessing, its style is graceful, demotic, witty. One doesn't talk about not being able to put

down a scholarly book, but except for a few rough miles of track between New York and Trenton, I didn't. It's that compelling.

Six chapters and a conclusion deal credibly with the following agenda: the distinctions among play, games, contests, and sports in which typology never becomes a Procrustean bed; the transformation of the play instinct from roots in the ritual of primitive cultures to commercialized industries characterized by secularism, equality of access, specialization of roles, rationalization, bureaucratization, quantification, and the quest for records; speculations centering on Marxist, Neo-Marxist, and Weberian models about the connections between capitalism, protestantism, and modern sport; an essay published elsewhere on why baseball *was* our national game; an attempt to explain the fascination of football; an intriguing series of reflections on why loner America prefers team sports to individual ones; and a short (and perhaps too modest) conclusion discussing the tradeoffs between "freedom from" and "freedom to" opportunities in modern societies. His concluding sentence is worth quoting, suggesting as it does the easy mix of learning and liveliness which Guttmann achieves in this book: "When we are surfeited with rules and regulations [of contemporary sport culture], when we are tired—like Robert Frost's applepicker—of the harvest we ourselves desired, we can always put away our stopwatch, abandon the cinder track, kick off our spiked shoes, and run as Roger Bannister did, barefoot, on firm dry sand, by the sea." This is the best of both worlds in many ways: the deft use of fiction to deepen understanding of the place of baseball and football in America, the firm but unpushy display of statistics to reveal differences in the way sports are experienced in diverse non-American cultures, the patient but noncondescending way idées fixes (such as Marcusean notions that sports are safetyvalves that capitalism devises to fend off its own deserved Armageddons with the working classes; or the facile *post hoc, ergo propter hoc* equating of football's new favor with Vietnam induced fascism) are defused intellectually.

I have only one quibble with this book. It's almost a tour de force to talk in such detail about sports in America while barely mentioning media. Neither radio nor television makes the index although Mr. Monday Night Football does by virtue of his place in Guttmann's opening line in the football chapter: "Is there an American sportswriter or broadcaster, some mute, inglorious Howard Cosell or George Plimpton, who has failed to comment upon the football boom of the 1960s?" (p. 117). No, surely. But there is at least one reader ready to brandish Occam's Razor: Instead of fertility rituals hyped up by the need to discharge aggression in routinized societies, television is not a necessary but certainly a sufficient condition to explain football's eclipse of baseball. Football watches better, is more amenable to commercial insertions, and it's over more or less on time. (Think of how extra inning ball games muck up the advertising schedules of the Johnny Carson Show.) Besides, summer is ebb time viewing. Even Guttmann's ingenious use of *Sports Illustrated* covers is TV-tainted evidence. For it is a truism in magazine promotion and newsstand sales circles that the cover of almost every general audience magazine below the middlebrow level has become telecentric. Empirical evidence in the form of returned, unsold magazines has led most mass magazines into a lemming-like line up of TV-related covers.

The logic Guttmann uses in explaining the diffusion of "national" sports like rugby and baseball to foreign cultures is sufficiently explained as a geo-political spinoff (Japan and Cuba admired America at the turn of the century—so they imported baseball) rather than through national character symmetries. I would explain baseball's hegemony as *the* national pastime between 1920 and 1960 as a result of the media boom of the 1920's. Tabloid journalism and radio played hard ball in competing for the newly enfranchised (culturally speaking) blue and dirty white colors. Babe Ruth is as much a media invention as the Tin Lizzie. The point is that just as Detroit has an interlocking half-Nelson on the nation's economy *and culture*, so the Madison Avenue/Radio City axis (and its Freddie Silverman lengthening fields of force) sets the frame of attention for the mass, non-Thoreau public—which is to say all of us at least some of the time.

It's exhilarating and sometimes convincing to trace baseball and football back to mythic roots, but the bottom line so to speak is the attendance at next week's game, the circulation of this month's magazine, and the complex symbiosis that we now see develops in all modernized societies, where the media are, quite simply, the metabolism. "Freedom to" change these conditions quickly or radically is, in my opinion, "freedom from" reality.

But these are nit picks engendered by a splendid essay. It is immensely satisfying to know that so perversive, yet paradoxically so neglected a topic, as sports now has a solid foundation for further research and speculation. A prime theme I'd propose to Guttmann's followers: What is there about the ecology of imagination in America that sports talk can be as pervasive as the weather while sports analysis is as rare as snow in July. Perhaps a foundation ought to give *Newsweek*'s Pete Axthelm a sabbatical to look into the issue. (But even he, having done so brilliantly as a sports writer, appears to be aspiring to general punditry rather than to staying a mere prattler about punting.)

PATRICK D. HAZARD

Beaver College
Glenside
Pennsylvania

MARK POSTER. *Critical Theory of the Family.* Pp. xx, 233. New York: Seabury Press, 1978. $14.95.

This book offers a critical analysis of current theories of the family, supplemented by the author's own eclectic synthesis of interpretation. It is Poster's thesis that family structure must be redefined away from issues of family size and toward issues concerned with emotional patterns.

As a historian, the author contends that the history of the family has been discontinuous, containing more than one distinct form, each of which has its own emotional pattern; and that these different forms are not capable of correlation in their growth with any one variable such as industrialization, patriarchy, economic system, or urbanism. His thesis is that the basic issues of the family exist on the psychological level, where varieties of emotional structure produce changes in deep individual needs. Freud is criticized as being ahistorical, unable to place his contribution within a wider framework of historical and social theory.

In a chapter entitled "The Radicalization of Eros," Poster deals with the Marxist view of the family, with reference to the writings of Engels; the synthesis of Marx and Freud as attempted by Wilhelm Reich; Reich's analysis of fascism; the Frankfurt School as represented by Max Horkheimer; and Herbert Marcuse. The following chapter, "Ego Psychology, Modernization and the Family," sees striking comparisons between Erikson and Parsons in their denial of Freudian instinct theory. For Parsons, social order rather than anatomy, is presented as destiny. Poster is also critical of Parsons for seeing the patriarchal middle class family as the norm. Jacques Lacan's rebuilding of Freudian theory in terms of linguistic and anthropological structuralism is viewed as significant, as is Gregory Bateson's new approach in communication theory as a foundation for psychotherapy.

The author's own theory of the family is posited on the need for flexibility and coherence of categories on a psychological level that recognizes hierarchies of age and sex. Biological reductionism is seen as inadequate. A critical theory of the family would seek to answer such questions as when the modern family emerged, its historical significance, and what family structures predominated in society before the modern family. Four European models are succinctly de-

scribed, and the author concludes by presenting a fifth synthetic model drawn from several disciplines.

This is a scholarly and stimulating book that should be of value to all students interested in theoretical approaches to the family.

JOHN E. OWEN
Arizona State University
Tempe

RONALD F. PRICE. *Marx and Education in Russia and China*. Pp. 376. Totowa, NJ: Rowman and Littlefield, 1977. $18.50.

As the title implies, the author, Senior Lecturer in Comparative Education at La Trobe University, Melbourne, Australia, sets out diligently to present official educational theory and practice in both the Soviet Union and Communist China.

The study unfolds to familiarize the presumably ignorant reader with the views of Marx and Engels on the subject of education, the ultimate aim of which, according to Mr. Price, is to mold a revolutionized, well-rounded individual within a harmoniously organized cooperative society. This individual is what the author later refers to as "the new, socialist man." Copious quotations from the socialist fathers and also such followers as Bukharin, Stalin, and Mao Tse-tung (the last always spelled Mao Ze-dong by Mr. Price) plus commentary, again from various pundits, manage to fill up a sizable portion of the book. Lenin and Sun Yat-sen are certainly downgraded and neither is even listed in the far from adequate index. And whoever transliterated from the Russian has made many grievous errors.

The author moves on to deal with schooling in the two countries and education in the wider sense; that is, education and the economy, labor and education, and the collective as educator. Text is accompanied by an imposing battery of tables and charts, usually of planned systems and taken from other specialists. The whole is rounded off with a long bibliography of titles, mostly in English, but including some in Russian and Chinese. The presentation, however, is, finally, bewildering and misleading in terms of historical reality and actuality. This is especially true for China where, for example, the social convulsions and violence of the "Cultural Revolution" of the late 1960's, with their baleful effects upon education, are almost completely ignored.

The author's admiration for Chairman Mao is plain. Indeed, the late Mao Tse-tung could evidently say or do no wrong in Mr. Price's view—incidentally to read this book one would not even realize that Mao is dead! In conclusion, let the author speak for himself: "Marxism in the USSR has in the main degenerated into official apologetics, or a technicism of economic growth and bureaucratic planning. The goal of free, classless man has been embraced only to empty it of real content. In China the Marxist vision reappears in Mao who both understands the distant future of its possible realization and the need to struggle for it now."

Such a book needs to be read with the greatest caution.

DAVID HECHT

Pace University
New York City

PAUL A. STRASBURG. *Violent Delinquents: A Report to the Ford Foundation from the Vera Institute of Justice.* Pp. xvi, 272. New York: Monarch Publications, 1978. $8.95.

Human violence is one of the greatest threats to modern civilized society. One can take comfort in the apparent reality that violence and rumors of violence are always with us. The spiritual, economic, moral, psychological, and social components of the problem of violence are extremely complex. The causes and consequences of violence are welded into a complex dynamic social system that will not stand still for the analysis of the social behavior.

In an advanced technological society with finite resources, most of the resources spent on violence are spent on dealing with the legal, social, and economic consequences of violent acts, and attempting to protect society from them.

Comparatively little is committed to understanding the nature and the causes of violence. It should not surprise anyone, therefore, to find our knowledge of violence and the efficacy of interventions to prevent or deter crime very thin.

In *Violent Delinquents: A Report to the Ford Foundation from the Vera Institute of Justice*, Paul Strasburg has, in my opinion, made an important contribution to the literature on violence. Its importance rests not only in the data he presents but also in his thoughtful analysis and discussion of his findings.

Strasburg was primarily interested in the frequency and seriousness of juvenile violence, and the patterns of behavior of the juvenile justice system in dealing with that violence. Strasburg's study, on which his book is based, was an effort to bring some understanding to what is behind or beneath the problem of juvenile violence. He conducted an extensive review of the literature on the causes, treatment and official responses to juvenile violence. When he found the literature contained little reliable information on the size of the problem, Strasburg decided to study juvenile court records in three counties in the metropolitan New York area in an effort to obtain descriptive data on the number and nature of violent criminal acts committed by youth. He was interested in the number of violent crimes, the number of delinquents committing them, and the seriousness of the consequences of crimes committed by juveniles brought before the courts in these three counties. In addition to analyzing five hundred (500) court records, Strasburg interviewed many individuals whose work directly or indirectly interacts with the problem of juvenile violence. He also visited many programs for juvenile offenders.

Strasburg is very careful not to overstate the reliability or the validity of his study. It is a descriptive study and does not claim to present data on the causes of juvenile violence. There are important substantial methodological constraints on his study which he is careful to point out. Noting the philosophical and legal problems involved in defining violence, he focuses primarily on acts of physical force directed against people, excluding crimes of acts against property.

In addition to the philosophical and legal problems involved in defining violence, there is the very serious problem of sampling. Strasburg does not claim to have a comprehensive study of juvenile violence. His study is limited to violent acts committed by juveniles who have ben arrested and brought to court. Even this data on court cases, which represents only a portion of the larger problem of juvenile violence, is not always clear or complete.

The author collected an enormous amount of data. One of the positive features of the book is the way in which he has organized the material and the extent to which he has been successful in distilling and presenting the salient features of his data and his findings.

Data collected in the Vera study on the common characteristics of violent delinquents were consistent with the findings of other descriptive studies. Violent delinquents are most likely to be minority group males who live in lower class or slum neighborhoods in the inner city. They tend to come from broken homes, have poor relationships with their parents, and they are usually school failures.

The Vera data raised some very important questions, as have other studies, about the juvenile justice system. Strasburg reported ineffective interventions to end juvenile violence after the juvenile had been adjudicated of a violent crime. The most common correctional responses, probation or training school, appeared to have "little or no constructive impact on subsequent criminal behavior" (p. 183). Strasburg goes on to point out that treatment-oriented programs have generally been closed to violent juvenile offenders.

Strasburg notes that "on the whole the evidence gathered in the course of this study supports a conclusion that juvenile violence is a serious and growing problem" (p. 179). His insightful analysis of the Vera data is useful for our understanding of the problem of juvenile violence and especially helpful, in my opinion, in suggesting some priorities in the research that is needed on this problem.

Perhaps the greatest value of this study is in the potential it provides for suggesting important changes in the correctional system. Senator Birch Bayh, Chairman of the Subcommittee on the Constitution, in his foreword to *Violent Delinquents*, states that "much of the information presented in Mr. Strasburg's report to the Ford Foundation reflects the need for a long awaited reform of the juvenile justice system (p. x).

JAMES L. PAUL
University of North Carolina
Chapel Hill

GÖRAN THERBORN. *What Does the Ruling Class Do When it Rules?* Pp. x, 290. London: New Left Books, 1978. $14.95.

Intent on searching out the alleged "contradictions" of capitalism, Marxists have long overlooked contradictions within their own world view. Prominent among these has been the contradiction between a concern with political power as a revolutionary goal and the virtual absence of a serious Marxian literature on politics. Responsibility for this puzzling incongruity partly lies with Marx himself: often brilliantly provocative, Marx's own political writings are nonetheless scattered and fragmentary, thereby encouraging a "vulgar" predisposition towards economic reductionism among his followers. Ignoring the dialectical character of politics, Marxist intellectuals have tended to adopt a Leninist perspective: the complexities of bourgeois political institutions being consistently undervalued in favor of a tactical emphasis on revolutionary mobilization.

Fortunately, this narrow focus is now being repudiated by younger radical scholars, including the author of the book under review. Freely admitting errors and omissions, Therborn sets out to specify significant research areas and to provide a theoretical framework adequate to accommodate future empirical studies. These ambitious goals help bind together the book's three essays, but are not carried through with complete success.

In his first essay, Therborn offers a comparative typology of state organization in feudal, capitalist, and socialist settings. Primarily valuable as a heuristic exercise, the essay employs a systems approach to denote each epoch's organizational features: inputs, outputs, tasks, and personnel recruitment all receive extensive and methodical coverage. On the other hand, however, the stylistic mixture of systems and Marxist jargon often proves rather irritating, while the treatment of socialist state organization leaves much to be desired. Assigning undue significance to mass organizations, such as trade unions, and to the alleged "political supremacy" of the working class, Therborn glosses over important, if unattractive, features of socialist state organization. Thus, he ignores the possibility that state/party elites now constitute a ruling class and dismisses their privileged status as a "relic of capitalism." Ideological rather than scientific, this nonexplanation conflicts with his call for a reassessment of socialist realities.

Therborn's title question provides the theme for his second essay in which the author surveys and largely discounts various pluralist and elitist theories. Both perspectives, he argues, skirt the fundamental issue of how ruling classes are able to perpetuate their dominance. The reproduction of dominant-subordinate relations is thus made the focus of analysis, with particular attention beng paid to "formats of representation," various forms of bourgeois political organization. Too little attention is devoted to the role of ideology and the discussion of social democratic parties needs refinement, but overall the treatment is sophisticated and persuasive.

In the final essay, Therborn turns from theory to the politics of Eurocommunism. Following a brief but useful summary of the movement's development, Therborn identifies various problems confronting Western communist parties: notably, their still ambiguous

relationships with allied socialist groups, and failure to specify the nature of post-capitalist society. Surprisingly, he looks to Japan, rather than France or Italy, as the likeliest locale of a socialist breakthrough, perhaps underestimating the profound psychological and political consequences of a left victory in Europe.

In summary, then, these essays are uneven in quality but sufficiently stimulating to inspire confidence in a revitalized Marxian scholarship.

DAVID H. KATZ
Michigan State University
East Lansing

ECONOMICS

JOHN ELLIOTT. *Conflict or Cooperation? The Growth of Industrial Democracy.* Pp. xiv, 306. Totowa, NJ: Rowman and Littlefield, 1978. $21.50.

Throughout Europe there has been interest in such social innovations as co-determintion, workers' councils, and workers self-management, all of which are designed to increase worker and union input into managerial decisions affecting worker interests. In Britain this concept has come to be known as "industrial democracy;" in practice it has meant adding union representatives to company boards of directors.

This book, written by the Industrial Editor of the London *Financial Times*, describes how industrial democracy came to be a key political issue, leading to the Labour government's appointment, in 1975, of the Bullock Committee charged with considering the details of *how* (not whether) worker directors might be introduced. The committee's majority report called for a law requiring companies with more than 2000 employees to institute single-tiered boards (not two-tiered, as in Germany), which would have equal stockholder and union representation (but no representation for nonunion workers), and a smaller neutral third group to be selected by the two parties, or, failing agreement, by the government. These recommendations closely followed the original union position; the management representatives dissented; and the report ran into a hornet's nest of opposition which led, in May 1978, to a government White Paper (but no immediate legislation) calling for worker directors to be introduced gradually, and primarily through the process of bargaining. Postponed for the moment, the issue is far from dead.

Besides describing the committee's background and work, Elliott presents a reasoned but (to an American reader) unconvincing case for worker directors. First, they represent a logical extension of the British union-management-government "social contract." Second, since unions already make substantial inputs at other levels, through shop-steward representation, industry-wide bargaining, and the national social contract, the company level is the only one at which union-management collaboration does not occur. Third, although unions can bargain over wages and working conditions, they now have no direct influence over the key decisions made by boards of directors regarding investments, plant shut downs, and so forth; such decisions are critical for job security. Fourth, once given responsibility for running the company, unions would adopt "more positive and innovative outlooks," the "energies and loyalties of shop stewards" could be enlisted for organizational purposes, with the net result being better labor relations and higher productivity and satisfaction all around. Fifth and finally, since British management is so inefficient and British industry in such a bad way, worker directors are unlikely to make things worse; at least there would be a new start.

On the other hand, industrial democracy might kill the patient. Elliott argues that since codetermination works well in Germany, it should also do well in Britain. But aside from differences in the two plans, German unions lack the British tradition of "bloodyminded" hostility to management. Elliott seems to concede that the worker director system won't work unless there is good will on both sides, yet it is hard to see how a structural change, introduced over management's objections, is likely to transform years of antagonism into peace. Some unions object to industrial democracy altogether, on the grounds that it would blur the union's essential adversary role. Even among those which support the scheme, many perceive it as a means of extending power rather than calling a truce in the class war. In any case, few union leaders give the issue high priority and there is other evidence (not presented in this book) suggesting that workers themselves are more interested in participation at the shop floor level.

To conclude, regardless of industrial democracy's merits as a solution to the "British disease" (now spreading to the U.S.), it remains a viable alternative in Britain. For those wishing to view this issue through British eyes, this is a useful, though incomplete book. And for close students of contemporary British industrial relations it represents an almost essential source of data. For others, it may tell them more than they want to know.

GEORGE STRAUSS
University of California
Berkeley

DANIEL A. NOVAK. *The Wheel of Servitude: Black Forced Labor After Slavery.* Pp. 126. Lexington: University of Kentucky Press, 1978. $9.50.

The author, assistant professor of political science at the State University of New York at Buffalo, condemns the interpretation of Reconstruction by Professor William A. Dunning which "defended the Black Codes, grossly exaggerated black political influence and corruption, and excused or discounted the use of violence by whites" (p. 117). Revisionists have generally limited their writings to contradictions of this view, and, like other historians, have therefore failed to give adequate attention to peonage, especially its legal aspects. In this scholarly work, Professor Novak used as his major sources the collected statutes and cases of the various states involved to portray the pervasive and lingering patterns of involuntary servitude of Negroes after Emancipation. But it was white peonage that, at the turn of the century, spurred enforcement of the Anti-Peonage Act of 1867.

The plaintiff in the supposedly landmark case, *Bailey* v. *Alabama*, 1911, was a Negro. Justice Hughes, who spoke for a majority of seven, dismissed the fact that the plaintiff was a black man—because the statute made no racial discrimination—but did find it in violation of the Thirteenth Amendment's prohibition against involuntary servitude. Justice Holmes dissented, arguing that the statute was no more than a punishment for fraud and did not produce peonage. The effectiveness of the decision was lessened by two findings. One, it declared unconstitutional only one sort of peonage—"the sort containing the presumptive clause" of evidence. Two, "the only sort of evidence which had been attacked was that which involved debt, 'the basal fact of peonage' " (p. 63). But there were other kinds of forced labor including involuntary contracts, labor enticement and private convict-labor.

In 1939 the Civil Liberties Unit (later called the Civil Rights Section) was established in the Criminal Division of the Department of Justice to "direct, supervise and conduct prosecutions of violations of the provisions of the Constitution or Acts of Congress guaranteeing civil rights of individuals."

One of the first issues listed for review was peonage. But the definition in the Anti-Peonage Act was unclear, and peonage had to contain an element of debt. Since it was found difficult to prove this "basal fact," Attorney General Francis Biddle in 1941 sought prosecutions because of involuntary servitude. Not until 1944 did the U.S. Supreme Court rule in *Pollock* v. *Williams* that the Anti-Peonage Act covered *all* contract-labor statutes (p. 81).

Pollock was the last peonage case to come before the Supreme Court which has been so inadequate in dealing with the problem that "one is led to doubt its good faith" (p. 83). The "continued occurrence" of peonage, "however sporadic and illegal, to the present time,

reflects shamefully on the American system of justice" (p. 91).

RAYFORD W. LOGAN

Howard University
Washington, DC

PETER PASSELL and LEONARD ROSS. *State Policies and Federal Programs: Priorities and Constraints*. Pp. xvii, 168. New York: Praeger, 1978.

American federalism was invented by the men-who-gathered-in-Philadelphia-in-the-hot-summer-of-1787 as a pragmatic response to political necessity—the states could be expected to countenance no greater centralization of government. At the same time, however, federalism was upheld as a good—a shield against tyranny. Our ideals and our necessities color state/federal relations yet. In the latter part of the 20th century do we want a central government truly empowered to uphold a national norm? If we desire states to be able to practice diversity is that an option open to them?

The study under review states at the outset that it is concerned with "state power" as well as "state intentions and skill" in social policy. Passell and Ross, economists writing for the 20th Century Fund, try to find out what is *possible* for a state, California being the case in point. In order to examine choices they look at fiscal policy, school finance reform, higher education, and health care. In so doing they cover concisely an impressive amount of material: the problems with present policies, proposed alternatives, and possible complications of reforms. Although there is the suggestion of impatience with the untidiness of the real world ("School finance 'reform' is not a coherent program, but a series of dissatisfactions with present financing systems . . . "; "federal programs for aid to higher education have been designed (as) . . . political compromises rather than as fulfillment of any master plan"), the authors are not unattuned to the impact of political vibrations. "After case loads stabilized and reform efforts failed in the early 1970s, the welfare system receded somewhat from its former political prominence. Although the system has changed little, reform seems less urgent to all concerned" (p. 156).

Although the writers believe that the states have considerable leeway, in fact if not in theory, to moderate their income support and their health care programs, the conclusion is reached that "national systems . . . although not compelled by the nature of federalism . . . are . . . the only likely means of extending and nationalizing coverage." Educational policy issues appear too diffuse to allow of present recommendation.

The professionalism of the writing is not matched, unfortunately, by the production of the publisher. Typographical errors abound. For example, during a discussion of disincentives to work in AFDC we are told that the program "provides a family of four with an income of $4,560 a year while taxing them at a rate of 66.67 percent on monthly earnings about $30" (p. 133). Even the most meager of proof reading efforts should have caught "about" instead of "above."

Passell and Ross deserve better. This is a carefully constructed and very helpful study which will be meaty enough for specialists and pointed enough for generalists. If it doesn't resolve our national ambivalence about our governmental form, it supplies a balanced and sophisticated view of the terrain.

JANET HANNIGAN
Lafayette College
Easton
Pennsylvania

BENEDICT STAVIS. *The Politics of Agricultural Mechanism in China*. Pp. 288. Ithaca: Cornell University Press, 1978. $17.50.

Chinese attempts at revolutionary modernization involve putting technology in the service of ideological means and ends rather than allowing it to dictate the human condition. The policy struggle between Mao and Liu Shao-ch'i in the 1950's over whether collectivization should precede mechanization reflected this effort to conscript technology in the modernization process rather than submit to its demands. But, having won the battle of first firmly establishing collective agriculture, Mao still had to win the war of effectively mechanizing China's countryside in socialist ways, the threat of technology dictating economic and social relations being perennial.

The Politics of Agricultural Mechanization in China is an account of the passage of agricultural mechanization policy and practice over the rocky road of modernization driven by China's leaders. The Chinese struggle with mechanization is traced: from 1949 on, dealing first with the problem of agricultural mechanization analytically, and then with policy and practice during the land reform period; while collectivization was being achieved; during the Great Leap Forward and its aftermath; and while the Cultural Revolution was unfolding and being consolidated. The chronological discourse focuses on key issues: mechanization and collectivization; machines and their management, ownership and control; mechanization and training of laborpower; tool-reform and intermediate technology; trustification and decentralization.

After carefully ploughing through the varied data, policies, programs, sharp political conflicts, zig-zagging agricultural practices, and other related political and economic materials, Professor Stavis not only presents a coherent and insightful review of China's agricultural mechanization process, but also throws light on the political mechanism and how it operates in propounding, implementing, reinforcing, getting feedback, and modifying or intensifying agricultural policy and practice. Stavis' assessment is that policies on agricultural mechanization have been consistently made in spite of widespread periodic political disruption, that ideology and politics have been critical factors in the mounting of "sensible policies," and that the Chinese seem to have enlisted technological development in the service of a modernizing socialist society. This accomplishment is distinctive from other nations' modernization processes, not in technical (engineering and agroeconomic) terms but in the sociopolitical context which shapes mechanization policies as a function of raising peasants' living levels to urban conditions, relieving grueling farm work, containing bureaucratic power, transforming rural communities, and other collectivist goals.

Professor Stavis' essay offers rich analytic and empirical material with which to understand more fully China's commitment to a collective agriculture and its decentralized political base. If he has been more successful in recounting past political conflict over agriculture than in identifying current and future problem areas, this does not detract greatly from his fine grasp of a principal aspect of China's revolutionary modernization.

CHARLES HOFFMANN

State University of New York
Stony Brook

OTHER BOOKS

ADAMS, JAN S. *Citizen Inspectors In The Soviet Union: The People's Control Committee*. Pp. xv, 232. New York: Praeger, 1977. No price.

BALL, ROBERT M. *Social Security: Today and Tomorrow*. Pp. xv, 528. New York: Columbia University Press, 1978. $14.95.

BEDLINGTON, STANLEY S. *Malaysia And Singapore: The Building of New States*. Pp. 285. Ithaca, NY: Cornell University Press, 1978. No price.

BERGSTROM, A. R. et al. eds. *Stability and Inflation*. Pp. xvii, 323. New York: John Wiley, 1978. $40.00.

BERKLEY, GEORGE E. *Cancer: How to Prevent It and How to Help Your Doctor Fight It*. Englewood Cliffs, NJ: Prentice-Hall, 1978. $8.95. Paperbound, $3.95.

DE MENIL, LOIS PATTISON. *Who Speaks For Europe? The Vision of Charles de Gaulle*. Pp. viii, 232. New York: St. Martin's Press, 1978. $12.50.

DE ST. JORRE, JOHN. *A House Divided: South Africa's Uncertain Future*. Pp. ix,

136. New York: Carnegie Endowment for International Peace, 1977. $4.00. Paperbound.

DOOB, LEONARD W. *Panorama of Evil: Insights from the Behavioral Sciences*. Pp. 188. Westport, CT: Greenwood Press, 1978. $14.95.

DUBOFSKY, MELVYN, ATHAN THEOHARIS, and DANIEL M. SMITH. *The United States In The Twentieth Century*. Pp. xiv, 545. Englewood Cliffs, NJ: Prentice-Hall, 1978. $13.95. Paperbound.

DUGARD, JOHN. *Human Rights and the South African Legal Order*. Pp. xix, 470. Princeton: Princeton University Press, 1978. $27.50. Paperbound, $12.50.

GALLOWAY, L. THOMAS. *Recognizing Foreign Governments: The Practice of the United States*. Pp. xiv. 191. Washington, DC: American Enterprise Institute for Public Policy Research, 1978. $4.75. Paperbound.

GORDON, GEORGE J. *Public Administration In America*. Pp. xii, 470. New York: St. Martin's Press, 1978. No price.

GREENBERG, MARTIN HARRY and JOSEPH D. OLANDER, eds. *International Relations Through Science Fiction*. Pp. ix, 236. New York: New Viewpoints, 1978. $12.50. Paperbound, $6.95.

GRIFFITH, LIDDON R. *Mugging: You Can Protect Yourself*. Pp. xi, 212. Englewood Cliffs, NJ: Prentice-Hall, 1978. $11.95. Paperbound, $4.95.

HARRIGAN, JOHN J. and WILLIAM C. JOHNSON. *Governing the Twin Cities Region: The Metropolitan Council in Comparative Perspective*. Pp. xii, 167. Minneapolis, MN: University of Minnesota Press, 1978. $14.95. Paperbound, $4.95.

HAUGE, RAGNAR, ed. *Drinking And Driving In Scandinavia*. Vol. VI. Pp. 143. New York: Columbia University Press, 1978. $14.00.

HAYWARD, JACK, and OLGA A. NARKIEWICZ, eds. *Planning in Europe*. Pp. 199. New York: St. Martin's Press, 1978. $18.95.

HERBERT, D. I. and R. J. JOHNSON, eds. *Geography And The Urban Environment: Progress in Research And Applications*. Vol. 1. Pp. xiii, 363. New York: John Wiley, 1978. No price.

HIRSCH, FRED, MICHAEL DOYLE, and EDWARD L. MORSE. *Alternatives To Monetary Disorder*. Pp. xiv, 153. New York: McGraw-Hill, 1977. $3.95. Paperbound.

HULL, Roger H. *The Irish Triangle: Conflict in Northern Ireland*. Pp. xi, 312. Princeton: Princeton University Press, 1978. $4.95. Paperbound.

JO, YUNG-HWAN, ed. *U.S. Foreign Policy In Asia: An Appraisal of America's Role in Asia.* Pp. vii, 488. Santa Barbara, CA: Clio Press, 1978. $19.75.

JOHNSON, ALLEN W. *Quantification in Cultural Anthropology: An Introduction to Research Design.* Pp. x, 231. Stanford, CA: Stanford University Press, 1978. $12.50.

KEETON, GEORGE W. and GEORGE SCHWARZENBERGER, eds. *The Yearbook Of World Affairs, 1978.* Pp. vii, 353. Boulder, CO: Westview Press, 1978. $28.50.

LANDAU, ELLIOTT D., SHERRIE L. EPSTEIN, and ANN P. STONE, eds. *The Exceptional Child Through Literature.* Pp. xvi, 286. Englewood Cliffs, NJ: Prentice-Hall, 1978. $7.95. Paperbound.

LANE, FREDERICK S. ed. *Current Issues in Public Administration.* Pp. xiii, 572. New York: St. Martin's Press, 1978. No price.

LUNDESTAD, GEIR. *The American Non-Policy Towards Eastern Europe 1943–1947.* Pp. 653. New York: Columbia University Press, 1978. $18.00. Paperbound.

MAFFEI, PAOLO. *Beyond the Moon.* Pp. vi, 377. Cambridge, MA: MIT Press, 1978. $12.50.

MAYO, SAMUEL H. *A History Of Mexico.* Pp. ix, 454. Englewood Cliffs, NJ: Prentice-Hall, 1978. $9.95. Paperbound.

MCMAINS, HARVEY and LYLE WILCOX, eds. *Alternatives for Growth: The Engineering and Economics of Natural Resources Development.* Pp. xiii, 256. Cambridge, MA: Ballinger, 1978. No price.

MECHANIC, DAVID. *Students Under Stress: A Study in the Social Psychology of Adaptation.* Pp. xxxv, 231. Madison, WI: University of Wisconsin Press, 1978. $15.00. Paperbound, $5.95.

MEYER, MILTON W. *China: An Introduction.* Pp. 251. Totowa, NJ: Littlefield, Adams, 1978. $4.95. Paperbound.

MILLER, EMMETT E. and DEBORAH LUETH. *Feeling Good: How To Stay Healthy.* Pp. xvi, 269. Englewood Cliffs, NJ: Prentice-Hall, 1978. $12.95. Paperbound, $4.95.

MOLNAR, MIKLOS. *A Short History Of The Hungarian Communist Party.* Pp. 168. Boulder, CO: Westview Press, 1978. $16.50.

MOORE, JONATHAN and JANET FRASER, eds. *Campaign for President: The Managers Look at '76.* Pp. viii, 194. Cambridge, MA: Ballinger, 1977. $12.95.

NELSON, DANIEL J. *Wartime Origins Of The Berlin Dilemma.* Pp. ix-219. University, AL: University of Alabama Press, 1978. $11.95.

NORTHRUP, HERBERT, R., et al. *The Impact Of OSHA.* Pp. xxii, 565. Philadelphia: University of Pennsylvania Press, 1978. No price.

OLSEN, EDWARD A. *Japan: Economic Growth, Resource Scarcity, and Environmental Constraints.* Pp. xi, 139. Boulder, CO: Westview Press, 1978. $15.00.

PAUKER, GUY J., FRANK H. GOLAY, and CYNTHIA H. ENLOE. *Diversity And Development In Southeast Asia: The Coming Decade,* Pp. xiv, 191. New York: McGraw-Hill, 1978. $5.95. Paperbound.

PECHMAN, JOSEPH A., et al. eds. *Setting National Priorities: The 1979 Budget.* Pp. xiv, 319. Washington, DC: Brookings Institution, 1978. $12.95. Paperbound, $5.95.

PETERS, B. GUY. *The Politics of Bureaucracy: A Comparative Perspective.* Pp. v, 246. New York: Longman, 1978. $12.50. Paperbound, $6.95.

PETERS, RONALD M., JR. *The Massachusetts Constitution of 1780: A Social Compact.* Pp. 240. Amherst: University of Massachusetts Press, 1978. $15.00.

RACKHAM, OLIVER. *Trees And Woodland In The British Landscape.* Pp. 204. Totowa, NJ: J. M. Dent, 1978. $11.95.

REVEL, JEAN-FRANCOIS. *The Totalitarian Temptation.* Pp. 332. New York: Penguin Books, 1978. $2.95. Paperbound.

RHODES, WILLIAM C. and JAMES L. PAUL. *Emotionally Disturbed And Deviant Children: New Views And Approaches.* Pp. vi, 282. Englewood Cliffs, NJ: Prentice-Hall, 1978. $12.95.

RITCHIE, OSCAR W. and MARVIN R. KOLLER. *Sociology of Children.* 2nd ed. Pp. vii, 312. Englewood Cliffs, NJ: Prentice-Hall, 1978. $12.95.

ROBERTSON, JAMES and CAROLYN ROBERTSON. *The Small Towns Book: Show Me the Way to Go Home.* Pp. 208. New York: Anchor Press, 1978. $5.95. Paperbound.

ROHMUS, CHARLES M., DORIS B. MCLAUGHLIN, and FREDERICK H. NESBITT, eds. *Labor And American Politics: A Book of Readings, Revised.* Pp. ix, 445. Ann Arbor: University of Michigan Press, 1978. $15.00. Paperbound, $7.95.

ROTHMAN, ROBERT A. *Inequality And Stratification In The United States.* Pp. ix, 243. Englewood Cliffs, NJ: Prentice-Hall, 1978. $8.50. Paperbound.

SAUL, JOHN RALSTON. *The Birds of Prey.* Pp. 247. New York: McGraw-Hill, 1978. $9.95. Paperbound.

SILVERMAN, ROBERT E. *Psychology.* 3d ed. Pp. xvi, 602. Englewood Cliffs, NJ: Prentice-Hall, 1978. $14.50.

SOLDON NORBERT C. *Women In British Trade Unions 1874–1976.* Pp. xiii, 226. Totowa, NJ: Rowman and Littlefield, 1978. $23.50.

STERNLIEB, GEORGE, and JAMES W. HUGHES, ed. *Revitalizing The Northeast*. Pp. 443. New Brunswick, NJ: Rutgers University Press, 1978. No price.

TAYLOR, TREVOR, ed. *Approaches and Theory In International Relations*. Pp. 314. New York: Longman, 1978. $4.95. Paperbound.

THANE, PAT, ed. *The Origins of British Social Policy*, Pp. 209. Totowa, NJ: Rowman and Littlefield, 1978. $17.75.

WACHER, JOHN. *Roman Britain*. Pp. 286. Totowa, NJ: Biblio, 1978. $15.00.

WATTS, WILLIAM, and LLOYD A. FREE. *State of the Nation III*. Pp. xiii, 238. Lexington: MA: Lexington Books, 1978. $13.50.

WERTSCH, JAMES V. ed. *Recent Trends In Soviet Psycholinguistics*. Pp. xxiii, 207. White Plains, NY: M. E. Sharpe, 1978. $17.50.

WHITE JOSEPH L. *The Limits of Trade Union Militancy: The Lancashire Textile Workers, 1910–1914*, Pp. x, 258. Westport, CT: Greenwood Press, 1978. $16.95.

WRIGHT, DEIL S. *Understanding Intergovernmental Relations*. Pp. xv, 410. North Scituate, MA: Duxbury Press, 1978. No price.

YELLOWITZ, IRWIN, ed. *Essays in the History of New York City: A Memorial to Sidney Pomerantz*. Pp. 152. Port Washington, NY: Kennikat Press, 1978. $9.95.

INDEX

236

MAIN TRENDS OF RESEARCH IN THE SOCIAL AND HUMAN SCIENCES

Published by the United Nations Educational, Scientific and Cultural Organization (UNESCO)

Available from UNIPUB, exclusive United States distributor of UNESCO publications

Just published, this two-volume study completes a major undertaking by UNESCO, designed to explore the entire range of research into the social and human sciences.

The object is not to describe contemporary research and its results, but to locate the direction

also available:

Part 1: Social Sciences
819 Pages / ISBN:
92-3-100828-5 / $55.00

of scientific activity at the level of actual practice and in the dynamic process of change.

A specialist of world renown was entrusted with the work of author-rapporteur for each subdivision of the book. To support and enrich the author's effort, contributions were made by international organizations, national research institutions, and scholars representing a broad spectrum of thought.

To order your copy, or to receive more information, write:

unipub

345 Park Avenue South
New York, NY 10010

Part 2:

Anthropological and Historical Sciences; Aesthetics and the Sciences of Art; Legal Science; Philosophy

An Unprecedented Survey of the Human Sciences...
1,591 pages / ISBN: 92-3-101013-1 / two-volume set, $125.00

General Table of Contents

The American Academy of Political and Social Science

3937 Chestnut Street　　　　　　　　　　　　Philadelphia, Pennsylvania 19104

Origin and Purpose. The Academy was organized December 14, 1889, to promote the progress of political and social science, especially through publications and meetings. The Academy does not take sides in controverted questions, but seeks to gather and present reliable information to assist the public in forming an intelligent and accurate judgment.

Meetings. The Academy holds an annual meeting in the spring extending over two days.

Publications. THE ANNALS is the bimonthly publication of The Academy. Each issue contains articles on some prominent social or political problem, written at the invitation of the editors. Also, monographs are published from time to time, numbers of which are distributed to pertinent professional organizations. These volumes constitute important reference works on the topics with which they deal, and they are extensively cited by authorities throughout the United States and abroad. The papers presented at the meetings of The Academy are included in THE ANNALS.

Membership. Each member of The Academy receives THE ANNALS and may attend the meetings of The Academy. Annual dues: Regular Membership—$18.00 (clothbound,

$23.00). Special Membership—contributing, $40.00; sustaining, $60.00; patron, $100. A life membership is $500. Add $2.00 to above rates for membership outside the U.S.A. Dues are payable in U.S. dollars in advance. Special members receive a certificate suitable for framing and may choose either paper or clothbound copies of THE ANNALS.

Single copies of THE ANNALS may be obtained by nonmembers of The Academy for $4.50 ($5.50 clothbound) and by members for $4.00 ($5.00 clothbound). A discount of 5 percent is allowed on orders for 10 to 24 copies of any one issue, and of 10 percent on orders for 25 or more copies. These discounts apply only when orders are placed directly with The Academy and not through agencies. The price to all bookstores and to all dealers is $4.50 per copy ($5.00, clothbound) less 20 percent, with no quantity discount. Orders for 5 books or less must be prepaid (add $1.00 for postage and handling). Orders for 6 books or more must be invoiced.

All correspondence concerning The Academy or THE ANNALS should be addressed to the Academy offices, 3937 Chestnut Street, Philadelphia, Pa. 19104.